SHARON TYLER HERBST

Sharon Tyler Herbst, my wife and my coauthor, passed away in January 2007, five months after the manuscript for this book was finished.

Sharon established herself as the bestselling author of user-friendly reference books with the publication of *The Food Lover's Companion* in 1990. It was an immediate success, with four editions and millions of copies in print. For Sharon, however, most of the joy from writing her books came from the journey. Her tireless research and love of writing resulted in tightly written descriptions of thousands of food and drink entries. It gives me comfort to know that *The Food Lover's Companion* as well as Sharon's other books can be found in professional kitchens, on the desks of food writers and editors, and in the homes of those with culinary curiosity.

Sharon wrote many other culinary reference books, including *The Wine Lover's Companion,* which was the first book I coauthored. While writing the wine book I became aware of what a perfectionist Sharon was, both with reference to the information contained and how it was written. *The Cheese Lover's Companion* represents another full-out effort by Sharon.

. . .

On a personal note, Sharon's death is devastating, yet I also realize how very lucky I am. I was married to Sharon for thirty-eight fantastic years. For the last three and a half years of her life, we lived in a small town in a beautiful location on the northern California coast working and playing together. I spent every day and night of those last years with my best friend and the love of my life. We worked many twelve-hour days on this book, sharing the same office, yet we never tired of each other's company. I loved watching her light up a room with her positive attitude and marvelous energy. I got to hear her marvelous laugh and see that radiant smile every day while everyone else could only enjoy them occasionally. You should all be jealous—I am the lucky one. And I miss her immensely.

—*Ron Herbst*

THE
CHEESE
LOVER'S
COMPANION

THE
ULTIMATE
A-to-Z
CHEESE
GUIDE

With More Than
1,000 Listings for
Cheeses & Cheese-
Related Terms

THE
CHEESE
LOVER'S
COMPANION

SHARON TYLER HERBST
AND RON HERBST

WILLIAM MORROW
An Imprint of HarperCollins*Publishers*

HarperCollins books may be purchased for educational, business, or sales promotional use. For information please write: Special Markets Department, HarperCollins Publishers, 10 East 53rd Street, New York, NY 10022.

FIRST EDITION

Designed by William Ruoto

Library of Congress Cataloging-in-Publication Data

Herbst, Sharon Tyler.
   The cheese lover's companion : the ultimate A-to-Z cheese guide with more than 1,000 listings for cheeses and cheese-related terms / Sharon Tyler Herbst and Ron Herbst.
        p.   cm.
   Includes bibliographical references.
   ISBN: 978-0-06-053704-3
   ISBN-10: 0-06-053704-3
   1. Cheese—Dictionaries. 2. Cookery (Cheese) I. Herbst, Ron. II. Title.

   SF270.2.H47 2007
   641.3'73—dc22   2006046866

07 08 09 10 11 WBC/RRD 10 9 8 7 6 5 4 3 2 1

Dedicated to

Our good friend Bethan Powell, without whom
there would simply be no *Cheese Lover's Companion,*
and
the dear Bonnie Castello, whose strength and
determination to see things through enabled
us to do the same.

We are forever in your debt.

CONTENTS

ACKNOWLEDGMENTS

Myriad people are involved in a tome of this scope—some trying to make sure the book is as error free as possible, many happily providing information when needed, others simply there because they love and support us. So here's a warm and affectionate hug of gratitude to all those special people, with apologies to anyone we may have inadvertently omitted.

Harriet Bell, dear friend, confidant, and a woman of many titles, the most recent of which was vice president and editorial director at William Morrow. She's been the guiding light behind seven of our books, always with brilliance, sage advice, and sassy humor—few can make us laugh out loud like Harriet. Among her many talents is matching one of her inspired book ideas (her brain never stops) with the right author. We've been the beneficiaries of that match game several times, most recently with *The Cheese Lover's Companion*. Thank you, thank you, dear Harriet . . . you always make it enlightening and fun.

A special and heartfelt thanks to Sara and Ron Ryba, friends who opened their home and their hearts when it was most needed.

And a toast to close friends and family, who lovingly

and enthusiastically support us no matter what we do. It seems like the list gets longer with every book, but that's just because the number of wonderful people in our life keeps multiplying. We consider ourselves lucky indeed.

Family members who love and care for us and fret that we're working too hard: Catherine Tyler (Sharon's mom), Tia and Jim McCurdy (Sharon's sister and her husband), Lew and Joyce Herbst (Ron's brother and his wife), Tyler and Andrew Leslie, Kathy and Barry Herbst, Julie and Ron Goodlin, and Gabe and Brian Herbst.

Loving friends who grin ruefully whenever we declare that we can't go somewhere because of a book deadline, but with whom we've managed to spend plenty of great times over copious amounts of good food and wine: Sue Bain and her dear Gene, who left us too early; Ginny Bassi and Cathy Tennant; Leslie and David Bloom; Carol and Walt Boice; Leslie and Dickie Brennan; Beth Casey; Constance Clover and Duncan King; Illene and Nick Colby; Laura and Ed Dangers; Lisa Ekus; Floranne Fanti and Gary Musco; Jan and Bob Fisher; Linda Gomez and Greg Rockwell; Arlene and Bob Harchut; Holly Hartley and Oscar Anderson; Ruth and Phil Hicks; Susan and Lee Janvrin; Wes Jones and Emma Swain (thanks for all the goodies!); Suzann and Gary Mathers; Daniel Maye and Philip Cooke; Ellen and Paul Meuse; Mary O'Hara-Devereaux and Hughes Andrus; Cindy Pawlcyn; Pat Pettibone; Alice and Shay

Pickton; Tania and Kevin Scheer; Jackie and Jim Smith; Lissa Vecchio; and last, but far from least, dear Susan and George Williamson.

Special thanks go to Marco Gallazo for his wit, humor, and help with the Italian pronunciations. And to two other language experts—Scott Givot for helping us with the impossibly complex Norwegian language and Paula Lambert for her input on Spanish.

And to Anne Lovi, cheesemonger extraordinaire at the Fiesta Market in Sebastopol, California, and Robert Deakins, her counterpart at Whole Foods in the same city. Their knowledge and enthusiasm are contagious.

And, of course, the William Morrow family, without whom you would not be holding this book in your hands: Henry Ferris, vice president and executive editor, who guided this book through its final stages; editorial assistants Stephanie Fraser and Peter Hubbard, who always have a smile in their voices and an answer for everything; copy editor Chris Benton, for her talent and expertise and her special aptitude for the French language; proofreader Leda Scheintaub, whose eagle eye spotted the tiniest flaw; production editors Christine Tanigawa and Ann Cahn, who shepherded this book into its final form; creative director William Ruoto, whose genius created the book's "look"; design manager Leah Carlson-Stanisic, who makes things look as good as they do; art director Will Staehle and Roberto de Vicq de Cumptich, who cre-

ACKNOWLEDGMENTS

..d one of our favorite book jackets ever—so much fun; publicity wizard Milena Perez, who gets the word out; and the dozens of behind-the-scenes people who labor tirelessly and without fanfare or credit to make William Morrow books the best they can be.

Finally, we lift a glass to the creative, talented, and innovative cheesemakers, *affineurs,* and cheesemongers around the world. We're grateful to be the recipients of your genius and hard work.

Thank you, one and all!

INTRODUCTION

Cheese is a mysterious, passion-inspiring, mind-boggling force of nature that leaves in its wake a sensual afterglow and longings for more. Arguably the world's most popular food, cheese nourishes the body, energizes the spirit, and satisfies hunger on all levels. It waits quietly in the wings to be noticed yet demands attention once on stage. It sustains, it teases, it begs an encore. As well it should. For cheese is one of humankind's greatest treasures.

> Cheese is probably the friendliest of foods. It endears itself to everything and never tires of showing off to great advantage.
> —James Beard

We've long been passionate about cheese, but it wasn't until we undertook the odyssey that was to become *The Cheese Lover's Companion* that we could truly comprehend the complex nature of the cheese-making craft. Understanding the patience and skill and artistry that goes into producing cheese makes our respect for cheesemakers that much more profound. The art of cheesemaking is a delicate balance—an intricate, seductive dance—between the worlds of nature, science, and art. A craft meticulously mastered by the world's cheesemakers.

We could write pages about the countless theories

of how cheese came to be, but that would leave less room for the fact-based nuggets that follow in the A-to-Z section. And the truth is that the origins of cheese will undoubtedly forever remain a mystery. Archeologists have discovered cheese-related hieroglyphics in both Egypt and Mesopotamia (circa 3,500 to 2,800 B.C.), but historians believe cheese may date back to prehistoric times—though one would be hard-pressed to find complete agreement on the subject.

One popular premise is that the ancient art of cheese-making originated in the Middle East during Neolithic times. The most exotic legend tells of a nomad who poured milk into his saddlebag (theoretically made from the dried stomach of a ruminant, probably a sheep) and set out across the desert, riding for hours in the hot sun, both he and his saddlebag rhythmically rocking on his camel or horse. When the parched traveler stopped to slake his thirst, he discovered (undoubtedly much to his chagrin) that the milk had separated into a strange mixture of white solids and a thin, milky liquid—curds and whey. At first, one might imagine, the traveler was not amused. But craving moisture, he drank the liquid and tentatively tasted the curd. Mmmm, not bad!

And that, as they say, was the start of something big, for in this mysterious and fortuitous tale we see the combination of the four primary cheesemaking essentials— milk, stirring, heat, and rennet from the sheep's stomach. A hot and weary wanderer gets the credit in this telling, but what's undoubtedly true is that, as with countless other foods and potables, cheese was discovered simultaneously by different cultures. And so the saga began as humankind discovered a simple yet brilliant way to preserve surplus milk, which has evolved today into the production of thousands of cheeses around the world.

Choosing which of those myriad cheeses to include in this book was certainly no easy task. Including even a third of them would have produced a high-priced, unwieldy tome that simply wouldn't fit within our reader-friendly parameters. What you'll find in the following pages is a selection of over 500 of the world's cheeses—some of them well known, others relative newcomers bound for glory. We approached the selection challenge by starting with traditional favorites, then added most of the world's name-protected cheeses because the quality standards of such classics guarantees consistency. The United States doesn't have an equivalent system, so our American choices focused on award-winning farmstead or artisanal cheeses (our angst in having to rule out so many was eased only by the fact that there are books entirely devoted to American artisanal cheeses). And then there are those cheeses that are so immensely popular that they could not be excluded. Lastly, we included our favorites—some cheeses simply too wonderful to be left out.

That said, as with our *Food Lover's Companion* and *Wine Lover's Companion*, we tried very hard not to editorialize. Cheese is an intensely subjective experience and *our* personal opinions are not what count. The goal of *The Cheese Lover's Companion* is to deliver the facts and provide the information you need in order to choose *your* favorites.

We've organized the listings in a user-friendly A-to-Z format, rather than by country. This makes it easy to flip to a term (cheese or otherwise) without having to check an index. In the *otherwise* category are definitions for everything from cheesemaking terms (such as BANDAGING, CHEDDARING, and RIPENING), to foreign terms (like AFFINATORE, L'ÂME, and PECORA), to traditional cheese dishes (such as CHILE CON QUESO, FONDUE, and FRICO), to various cheese classifications (such as ARTISAN, BLUE-VEINED, and BLOOMY RIND), and so on. Naturally, phonetic pronunciations are included for all but the most obvious listings.

Of course we couldn't write a book on cheese without including sections on how it's made, how to buy and store it, tips on cooking with cheese, serving cheese, and how to pair cheese with wine, beer, and ale. There's also a Glossary of Cheese Descriptors for those who want to learn "cheesespeak." Lastly, there are three sections for those who are looking for a cheese by specifics, be it country of origin, milk type, or type.

In the end we were indelibly enriched by our *Cheese Lover's Companion* adventure and came away with a new respect and even awe for the wondrous and complex world we'd been exploring. Cheese can be simple or complicated, assertive or gentle, luxurious or everyday, and stinky or not. It can revive a bored appetite, nourish body as well as spirit, and invite invigorating conversation. It's one of nature's more prized miracles, and one bite is rarely enough. In the culinary universe, the impressive diversity of cheeses must, we think, be matched only by that of wines.

What's true is that the world of cheese is never boring, which is why it took us almost three years to research and write this book, and which is why we didn't want to quit. Ancient Greeks declared that cheese was a gift from the Gods, and you know what? They just may have been right.

HOW to USE this BOOK

ENTRIES are arranged alphabetically, and alphabetization is by letter, rather than by word, so that multiple-word entries are treated as single words. For instance, **acid curd** is handled as though it were spelled without spacing (*acidcurd*) and therefore follows **achiote** and precedes **acidic**. Acronyms and abbreviations appear in their natural alphabetical order. For example, **PDO** follows **Pavé du Plessis** and precedes **pecora**. Unless capitals are required for the proper form of the word, entries are in lowercase. There are some instances where both the capitalized form and the lowercase form may be used, as in **Cheddar** and **cheddar**. A term with more than one definition will list all its meanings in numerical order within the main listing.

PRONUNCIATIONS are included for all but the most basic words (see Pronunciation Guide, page xxvii).

CROSS-REFERENCES are indicated by SMALL CAPITALS and may appear in the body of a definition, at the end of a definition, or in lieu of a definition. Cross-references are used within the body of a definition primarily when the term may not be readily familiar to most readers. For instance, "The monks produce their own FARMSTEAD cheese . . ." or "This cheese is RIPENED for 4 months and has a FAT CONTENT of 45 percent." A word that is cross-referenced will be set in small capitals only the first time it's used within the entry. Cross-references at the end of a definition refer to other entries related to the word being defined. When a word is fully defined elsewhere, a cross-reference rather than a definition is listed. Many cheeses have more than one name, which often depends on the region in which they're used. For example, **Piticelle** is cross-referenced to its more common name, **Burrino.** Different spellings of a term are also cross-referenced. **Ackawi,** for instance, refers the reader to the more common spelling of **Akawi.**

INDIVIDUAL CHEESE DESCRIPTIONS are preceded by a list of pertinent points designed to give the reader a quick reference to the following information: **origin** (where the cheese is made); the kind of **milk** from which it's made; the **types** of cheese it is (such as soft, pressed and uncooked, natural rind, and farmstead); the **appearance** of the cheese (including size and shape and exterior and interior colors, plus any distinguishing characteristics, such as mold); the **texture** of the cheese; and the **flavor** attributes. Within the body of the listing will be other information, such as historical and production notes. Where possible, the FAT CONTENT (the fat in the total DRY MATTER of the finished cheese) is listed. However, some producers don't have such fat content tested, so the information is unavailable.

ITALICS are used in this book for several reasons, one of which is to point out that the term being defined also goes by another name. **Rind,** for example, is also called *crust*. Additionally, italics are used to indicate foreign words and publication titles and to highlight cross-references at the end of a listing (the end of the **flavored cheeses** entry states: *See also* PICKLED CHEESES; SMOKED CHEESES).

BOLDFACE PRINT is used not only for main entry headings but also for subentries within a definition. For example, the definition for **milk** uses boldface to highlight the headings of its various types (**whole milk, fat-free milk,** and so on), which are defined within the body of that entry. Additionally, boldface print is used to emphasize items within an entry that have been cross-referenced to it, such as **Montgomery's Cheddar** within the **Cheddar** listing, so you can easily spot the information you're seeking within an entry.

BRACKETS surround an entry's pronunciation, which immediately follows the listing and precedes the definition. See the Pronunciation Guide for complete information.

PRONUNCIATION GUIDE

All but the most basic words are accompanied by pronunciations, which are enclosed in brackets [————]. We find that the standard phonetic alphabet and diacritical marks such as a tilde (~), diaeresis (¨), breve (˘), and circumflex (^) slow readers down by forcing them to look up the symbol often to see how it affects a word's pronunciation. So, as with *Food Lover's Companion* and *Wine Lover's Companion*, we've used the phonetic method, with the accented syllable(s) indicated by capital letters.

On a word like **acidification,** for example, the common dictionary-style phonetic is *ə-sĭd´ə-fĭ-kā´shən*, which would force most readers to look up the sounds represented by the diacritics. In this book, however, the word is simply sounded out as *uh-sid-ih-fih-KAY-shuhn*.

Following is a list of the basic sounds (based on common American usage) employed in this book's pronunciations.

a	as in **can** or **add**	**j**	as in **gin** or **juicy**
ah	as in **father** or **balm**	**k**	as in **cool** or **crisp**
aw	as in **down** or **awning**	**o**	as in **odd** or **bottle**
ay	as in **date** or **face**	**oh**	as in **open** or **boat**
ch	as in **church** or **beach**	**oo**	as in **food** or **boo**
ee	as in **steam** or **beer**	**ow**	as in **cow** or **flour**
eh	as in **set** or **check**	**uh**	as in **love** or **cup**
g	as in **game** or **green**	**y**	as in **yellow** or **yes**
i	as in **ice** or **pie**	**zh**	as in **beige** or **vision**
ih	as in **if** or **strip**		

NOTE A single *i* is used for the long *i* sound, as in *pie*. The exception to the single *i* rule is when an *i* is followed by a consonant, in which case an *e* is appended.

Foreign Sounds

e u   A sound made with the lips rounded as if to say *oo* (as in *food*) while trying to say *a* (as in *able*).

e u h   An *e* in French (not é or è) is often pronounced with an *oo* sound, as in book or wood.

n   An italicized *n* is used to indicate that the *n* itself is not pronounced and that the preceding vowel has a nasal sound.

r   An italicized *r* indicates that the *r* sound should be diminished, with a sound more like *w*.

rr   The appearance of *rr* indicates the sound of a rolling *r*.

HOW CHEESE
IS MADE

Cheesemaking is a blend of art and science that's intriguingly simple yet remarkably intricate. This process differs with each cheese, and there are myriad variations at every juncture, including temperature, cutting of the curd, draining, molding, and ripening. Of course each step requires perfect timing, which is just as pivotal to making good cheese as it is to all of life.

The soul of every cheese is the MILK used to make it, and cheesemakers know that success relies not only on the animal (and its breed) from which the milk comes, but on the TERROIR and the time of year that produced the plant life on which the animal grazed, not to mention the time of day it was milked. The complex formula for success continues with numerous other factors, including whether the milk is pasteurized or raw, starter cultures and molds, the production techniques, and the aging process. All are aspects masterfully manipulated by the cheesemaker.

Following are the basic steps for making most cheeses. For broader descriptions of individual cheesemaking-related terms (such as BANDAGING and MILLING) or techniques for special cheese styles (such as BLUE-VEINED

CHEESES and PASTA FILATA CHEESES), see the cross-reference list at the end of this section.

COAGULATION: This initial step transforms the milk into curd (solids) and WHEY (liquid). The milk may be allowed to sour and curdle naturally, a process that, for most cheesemakers, requires too much time. To speed the natural process, cheesemakers typically begin by adding a STARTER to slightly warm milk to ripen it. This starter (also known as a *bacterial culture*) converts the milk sugar (LACTOSE) into lactic acid and balances the acidity (pH level) so the milk protein (CASEIN) will continue to coagulate with the addition of RENNET. Finally, the rennet is added and the milk completes its coagulation, forming one huge curd. It should be noted that the rennet and starter are symbiotic and the starter remains alive and active during the ripening process, contributing characteristics such as flavor, texture, and complexity.

CUTTING THE CURD: The curd is cut when it reaches the appropriate texture for the cheese being made. CUTTING, which may be done manually or by machine, separates the curd into uniform pieces and helps expel the whey. The cut curd is stirred and the whey drained off. The smaller the curds, the more liquid is released, the result of which will be a denser, drier cheese. For example, CHEDDAR is typically made from rice-size bits. On the other hand, softer cheeses are made from larger curds, which contain more whey. For many cheeses—such as CAMEMBERT and some CHÈVRES—the curd isn't cut at all but simply scooped directly into perforated molds from which the whey drains.

COOKING (OR HEATING) AND STIRRING THE CURDS:

Depending on the type of cheese being made, the curds may or may not undergo COOKING or heating, the latter a less heat-intensive process. Heating the curds tightens the protein network, firms the texture, and expels more whey. As a rule, cooking the curds at higher temperatures and for longer times produces firm cheeses; lower heat for shorter periods creates softer cheeses. Curds for some cheeses, BLUE-VEINED CHEESES, for example, must remain uncooked for the texture to be porous enough to allow in air to feed the bacteria that creates the bluing. During cooking, the curds are stirred (either by hand or mechanically), which keeps them from forming a skin. Generally speaking, the curds for soft cheeses are agitated gently, while those for firmer cheeses are stirred more vigorously. Once the curds reach the desired consistency, the resulting whey is drained or pumped off.

DRAINING:

The process of draining the whey from the curds is continuous in the previous two steps. In fact, drainage continues, little by little, throughout much of the cheesemaking process. Besides during the steps of cutting and cooking the curds, drainage takes place during processes like CHEDDARING (stacking large blocks of curd to expel the whey), MOLDING (where the liquid drains naturally through perforated molds), and PRESSING.

SALTING: The SALTING procedure may either be done now, with salt added directly to the curds, or after the cheese is molded, in which case the cheese may be dry-salted or soaked in BRINE. Salting seasons and preserves the cheese, reduces its moisture content, and helps impede bacterial growth, which slows the aging process so the cheese can acquire the desired flavor and texture for its type.

MOLDING AND PRESSING: This is the step where the curds may be turned into a MOLD, which will give them their final shape. That mold may be a simple muslin bag, a perforated mold, or simply a hoop (with open top and bottom) to support the sides. During molding the whey continues to drain off. Depending on the cheese being made, this process may occur naturally through gravity, or the cheese may undergo PRESSING, either mechanically, by hand, or by stacking the molds so the weight presses the cheese. The more a cheese is pressed, the harder the final texture.

RIPENING: This is the final and, most would say, most important stage of cheesemaking. Of course, not all cheeses are ripened (or aged), specifically fresh cheeses such as COTTAGE CHEESE, CREAM CHEESE, and RICOTTA. But for most cheese, RIPENING is a critical component contributing to its final and distinctive flavor, texture, aroma, and character. It's also during this aging period that the rind of the cheese is developed, either naturally or with assistance, as with WASHED-RIND CHEESES. Cheesemakers carefully monitor the ripening environment (be it a natural cave or specially designed room) to keep the temperature (around 50°F) and humidity constant. How long a cheese is allowed to ripen is also an art. Soft cheeses ripen quickly and therefore require relatively low temperatures and high humidity (around 95 percent). On the other hand, hard cheeses typically require less humidity, usually no more than 80 percent. Bottom line: moisture accelerates ripening. Many cheeses need frequent turning during aging for even distribution of BUTTERFAT. Throughout the ripening period, cheese goes through numerous processes, all of which contribute to its final character. It's during this time that the bluing occurs in BLUE-VEINED CHEESES, that the EYES appear in Swiss-style cheeses such as EMMENTAL, and that the RINDS develop, either naturally or with cheesemaker assistance, such as with WASHED-RIND CHEESES. How long a cheese is allowed to ripen depends on its style and can take from a few days to several weeks to up to 3 or more years. Long ripening periods produce a higher moisture loss, which intensifies the flavor.

The following terms relate to the process of cheesemaking and cheeses that require special techniques for production: ACIDIFICATION; ARTISAN CHEESES; BACTE-RIA; BANDAGING; BLOOMY RIND; BLUE-VEINED CHEESES; CHEESE, CHEESEMAKING; CHEESEMAKER; COAGULATION; COOKING; CURD; CUTTING; DOUBLE-CREAM AND TRIPLE-CREAM CHEESES; DRAINING; EYES; FARMSTEAD CHEESE; FAT; FRESH CHEESES; GRANA CHEESES; KOSHER CHEESES; MILK; MILLING; MOLDED UNCOOKED CHEESES; MOLDING; NATURAL RIND; NEEDLING; ORGANIC CHEESES; PASTA FILATA CHEESES; *PENICILLIUM;* PRESSED COOKED CHEESES; PRESSED UNCOOKED CHEESES; PRESSING; PROCESS(ED) CHEESES; RENNET; RIND; RIPENING; SALTING; SOFT-RIPENED CHEESES; STARTER; TOP STIRRING; TYPES, CHEESE; WASHED RIND; WHEY; WHEY CHEESES.

BUYING AND STORING CHEESE

BUYING CHEESE

First of all, shop for cheese where there's a large assortment and speedy turnover. Naturally, either a specialty cheese shop or a gourmet market with an expansive cheese selection is best. There you'll typically be offered tastes of the cheeses in which you're interested. If not, don't hesitate to ask. Good cheese is expensive (as is some mediocre cheese), and a tiny taste will tell you whether it's worth your investment. But know that taking advantage of sampling is tacky—they're tastes, not lunch.

Retailers may organize their cheeses by country, by milk type, or by texture (soft, semisoft, and so on). Make your shopping easier by asking how the cheeses are arranged. If you're unsure of what you want, discuss your tastes with the salesperson and ask for suggestions.

Any retailer interested in cheese will have someone knowledgeable on hand to help you. If you're lucky, your retailer will offer cheeses cut to order. Home storage is typically less than ideal, and your best bet is to buy only what you'll consume in a few days. If you live in an area without a good cheese market, farmers' markets are often a good resource. And you can always let your fingers do the shopping on Web sites—those of individual cheesemakers as well as specialty online cheese stores. Following are a few basics for how to choose cheese in a market.

General Guidelines for Buying Cheese

READ THE LABEL—Here you'll find the country of origin, the name of the producer, the type of MILK used (cow's, sheep's, goat's), whether the milk was pasteurized or unpasteurized (raw), whether it has ORGANIC or KOSHER certification, whether it's made by FARMSTEAD or ARTISAN methods (FACTORY-made cheeses won't say anything), weight, price, and, on some labels, nutritional information. If you have dietary, religious, or animal rights concerns, you might want to know what type of RENNET was used—animal, microbial, or vegetable. The cheesemonger should be able to give you any information that's not on the label.

CHECK THE PACKAGING—The wrapping on prepackaged cheeses should be clean and intact—a breach in the packaging allows in air, which will dry the cheese. The inside of the wrapping shouldn't show any signs of moisture.

Foreign Words for Milk Type

Cow: French *(vache)*, Italian *(vacca)*, Spanish and Portuguese *(vaca)*

Goat: French *(chèvre)*, Italian *(capra)*, Spanish and Portuguese *(cabra)*

Sheep: French *(brebis)*, Italian *(pecora)*, Spanish *(oveja)*, Portuguese *(ovelha)*

EXAMINE THE CHEESE—It should fully adhere to the rind and show no signs of drying, cracking, or uneven texture. If you can, smell the cheese—it should not have any strong off odors, such as rancidity, ammonia, sour milk, or barnyard (though washed-rind cheeses are supposed to be stinky). Naturally, if you can taste the cheese, do so. Where appearance is concerned, know that artisanal and farmstead cheeses often look more rustic than those that are mass-produced because they're handmade, which is certainly an attribute. Unintentional molds, particularly black ones, are suspect—choose another cheese. The PASTE should show no sign of off colors, particularly reddening. If there's a grayish brown powdery substance on the cheese, it may be infested with CHEESE MITES, not a good thing.

Tips for Buying Specific Cheese Types

HARD CHEESES—(such as aged ASIAGO and PARMIGIANO-REGGIANO) can be tricky from the standpoint that they are, after all, older and drier than their counterparts. In general, there should be no discoloration and the color should be fairly even from the outer edge to the center. There may be slight darkening toward the rind, but you don't want radical color change, a sign that the cheese is beginning to dry out. Likewise, avoid cheeses that show marked cracking (a little is okay) and mold on the PASTE—both signs of mishandling or poor storage.

SEMIHARD CHEESES—(such as EMMENTAL and JACK) and **Semisoft Cheeses** (such as EDAM and MUNSTER) should be firm, smooth, solid, and uniform in texture. There should be no sign of cracking or dried edges. The rind should be intact and mold-free. There should be no off odors, such as strong ammonia.

SOFT-RIPENED CHEESES—(such as BRIE and CAMEMBERT) should smell fresh, not ammoniated, and have a pure white rind—any signs of pink means the cheese is heading south. Lightly press the center of the cheese with the ball of your thumb—if it gives slightly, it's ready. It should be as soft in the middle as on the edges and not hardened or dried-looking in any way. If the bottom is slightly wet, flip it over when you get home so the moisture can redistribute.

WASHED-RIND CHEESES—(such as ÉPOISSES DE BOURGOGNE and TALEGGIO) naturally have rinds that have a wide range of colors including pinkish to orangey red and burnt umber. Many but not all rinds have a moist quality that would be a detriment in other cheeses but is normal with washed-rinds. These cheeses will be aromatic in a pleasantly pronounced and pungent way but shouldn't reek of ammonia or smell putrid. The strong aroma is part of the charm and in no way impairs the rich and complex flavors. Wedges that have been wrapped will look quite oozy, but that's good. Many washed-rind cheeses come in their own boxes. Turn out the cheese when you get home—if the bottom's wet, flip it over so the moisture can redistribute.

BLUE CHEESES—(such as GORGONZOLA and ROQUEFORT) should have distinctive veining, a clean-looking PASTE, and never smell of ammonia. The interior should be moist but not wet and free of slime or pinkish mold.

FRESH CHEESES—(such as COTTAGE CHEESE, CREAM CHEESE, and fresh MOZZARELLA and CHÈVRE) are highly perishable, so a market with rapid turnover is important. Most fresh cheeses will be sealed, so you won't be able to factor smell into your decision. But the cheese should appear fresh, sans discoloration or, of course, mold. Most fresh-cheese packaging will have an expiration date by which you can make your selection.

How Much Cheese to Buy

Assuming you're purchasing cheeses at their optimum ripeness, buy only as much as you plan on using within a few days. Of course, the amount of cheese you need will depend on how hungry your guests are, factoring in time of day and how much wine is flowing. For a general rule of thumb, multiply the number of people by the number of ounces per person to find how much you should buy.

Cheese tastings: 6 to 8 cheeses are about all one palate can manage. Count on about ½ ounce each cheese per person.

Cheese as an hors d'oeuvre with other snacks: 3 cheeses, 1 to 1½ ounces each per person

Cheese as the only hors d'oeuvre: 3 to 4 cheeses, 1 to 2 ounces each per person

Cheese plates to begin or end a meal: 3 to 4 cheeses, ¾ to 1 ounce each per person

Cheese preceding dessert: 3 cheeses, ¾ ounce each per person

STORING CHEESE

- A rule of thumb: the harder the cheese, the longer it will last.

- Cheeses like the same environment in which they were nurtured into existence—a cool temperature somewhere between 42°F and 52°F, high humidity (around 80 percent), and darkness. Excessive conditions invite deterioration—too much warmth will cause cheese to seep butterfat and become smelly, too cold and it'll dry out, and too much air will not only dry out cheese but also expose it to uninvited mold-causing bacteria. Without a critter-free cellar, the only place for most of us to store cheese is in the refrigerator. Though its exceedingly dry, frigid atmosphere is far from ideal, it's the best those of us who are not cheesemongers can do. And the ideal place in the fridge for cheese is the warmest part, which is typically a vegetable drawer (check the manufacturer's booklet for guidance). Remember that refrigerated cheese doesn't go into a state of stasis—it continues to ripen.

- Knowing that this book will be read by the every-day cheese lover, we're not going to declare that the only proper wrap for cheese is hard-to-find specialty paper. But there is such a thing, available at cheesemaking-supply stores and online from cheese making.com. Some specialty gourmet and cheese shops also carry permeable cheese-wrapping paper. Essentially, such paper is typically comprised of two layers—a greaseproof "inside" sheet (to pull moisture away from the cheese's surface) bonded to a microperforated polypropylene layer (which allows gases to be exchanged while controlling moisture loss). Other specialty papers include butcher paper and pastry paper, available at restaurant supply stores. However, what most of us have at home is aluminum foil, plastic wrap, and wax or parchment paper, and they will all work just fine.

- Each time a cheese has been opened, rewrap it in fresh wrapping.

- Cheese wrapped in plastic wrap should be opened every few days to allow it to breathe. Cover with fresh wrapping.

- Smelly cheeses should be double-wrapped and placed in an airtight container so the entire refrigerator doesn't reek.

- Heighten the humidity for those cheeses that need it (like soft-ripened and washed-rind cheeses) by placing a small, clean dampened towel on the bottom of the container in which they're being stored. Change the towel every 2 days.

- Freezing cheese: Yes, it *can* be frozen, a thought that gives purists the vapors. But *should* you freeze cheese? Absolutely not—it's an assault on a living thing. If, however, you have so much on hand that it'll go bad before you use it, it's better to freeze it than to throw it out. *(Personally, we'd rather invite a few friends over to help us enjoy the excess . . . or be excessive ourselves and polish off a meal consisting entirely of cheese. But that's us.)* Know that freezing causes cheese to undergo a textural change, and the flavor will be seriously affected. In general, cheeses made from goat's or sheep's milk freeze better than those made from cow's milk. Hard and semihard cheeses will freeze better than softer cheeses but will often turn crumbly. Softer cheeses might separate slightly; soft-ripened cheeses become watery. Such changes won't be as noticeable if you use the cheese in cooked dishes. Grating the cheese before freezing will make it easier to use. To freeze cheese, double-wrap it airtight and freeze for up to 2 months. Thaw slowly in the refrigerator and use within a few days.

Tips for Storing Specific Cheese Types

HARD AND SEMIHARD CHEESES—If they come from the store sealed tightly in plastic, remove it and rewrap the cheese loosely in wax or parchment paper, then in plastic wrap or foil. If storing for only a day or two, simply cover the paste with plastic wrap, leaving the rind uncovered.

SEMISOFT AND SOFT CHEESES—Loosely wrap in wax or parchment paper, then in plastic wrap or foil. Soft cheeses may also be placed in a like-size plastic container with an airtight cover (or seal with plastic wrap or foil).

SOFT-RIPENED CHEESES—Lightly wrap in wax or parchment paper, then plastic wrap, and, if it came in a box, return it there. Or place on a small plate and cover with plastic wrap or in a plastic storage container with a lid.

WASHED-RIND CHEESES—These need a higher humidity level than others, so you might want to wrap them in a damp, good-quality paper towel, then return the cheese to the box in which it came. If it wasn't sold in a box, lightly wrap it in wax or parchment paper, then in plastic wrap or foil. Or put it in a plastic storage container with a lid.

BLUE CHEESES—Wrap snugly in foil or plastic wrap.

FRESH CHEESES—Most of these cheeses come in a plastic or wax-coated paper tub—leave them there, sealing tightly after each use. Store such cheeses in the coldest part of the refrigerator. Any sign of mold means the cheese should be thrown out; there's no way to salvage it.

TIPS FOR COOKING WITH CHEESE

American author Clifton Fadiman wrote that cheese is "milk's leap toward immortality." True, so true. But cheese, in all its glory, can also be the careless cook's curse. It has a reputation for being quite temperamental, particularly when confronted with too much heat, which can transform it from a smooth, creamy mass into a stringy, rubbery mess. Here are some ideas for working with cheese in the kitchen—everything from how to make grating it easier to tips for creating a smooth and creamy hot cheese mélange.

WORKING WITH CHEESE IN THE KITCHEN

Grating cheese (either by hand or in the food processor) like Cheddar, Swiss, and Jack is easier if the cheese is cold. Hard cheeses like Parmesan and Romano grate more easily when at room temperature. Be sure to cut off any tough rind before grating the cheese.

- When grating by hand, do so over a piece of wax paper, which you can easily lift and use to funnel the cheese into the bowl or pan to which it's being added.

- Food-processor grating: Use the steel blade for hard cheeses like Parmesan. Cut cheese into 1-inch chunks—larger pieces can jam the blade. Use the shredding disk for cheeses like Cheddar and Jack. Spray the metal blade or grating disk with cooking spray and cleanup will be a breeze. When working with softer cheeses like Munster, also spray the inside of the workbowl and cover.

- A box grater with large holes does a good job of grating semisoft cheeses. Spray the grater with cooking spray to keep the cheese from sticking and facilitate cleanup.

- Refrigerate grated cheese in an airtight container for up to a week to have on hand when needed.

- A citrus zester or a rasp is good for shredding small amounts of hard to semihard cheeses.

- Use two forks to crumble blue cheeses like Roquefort. It'll be easier going if the cheese is chilled.

- Use a vegetable peeler to carve off thin shavings or slivers of hard to semihard cheese for salads and garnishes.

- To remove the white rind of a soft-ripened cheese like Camembert for use in a recipe, chill the cheese and use a sharp knife to cut away the rind. Or soften the cheese at room temperature, remove the top, then use a spoon to scoop the paste out of the rind.

- Cream cheese can be softened quickly in the microwave oven. Remove it from the foil package and place uncovered on a microwave-safe plate. For 8 ounces, heat at medium (50 percent power) for about a minute, 3 ounces for about 20 to 30 seconds. Let stand for 1 minute before using.

- A chunk of cheese can be brought to room temperature by heating it in the microwave at medium (50 percent power) for 30 to 60 seconds. Watch it *carefully*—overheat the cheese and the butterfat can begin to seep. Next time, remember to remove the cheese from the refrigerator an hour before you want to use it.

- Use the wax rind of cheeses like Edam as a decorative container for dips or spreads. Bring the cheese to room temperature (important for easy removal of the cheese), cut off the top inch, then use a spoon to scoop out most of the cheese, leaving a ¼-inch shell.

- Use cubed or grated leftover cheese in myriad ways, including in salads, pasta dishes, scrambles, and omelets and as a garnish for vegetables.

Equivalents
- Cottage or ricotta cheese: 16 ounces (1 pound) = 2 cups
- Cream cheese: 8 ounces = 1 cup; 3 ounces = 6 tablespoons
- Semihard or semisoft cheese: 4 ounces (¼ pound) = about 1 cup grated
- Hard cheeses: 4 ounces (¼ pound) = about 1¼ cups
- Blue cheese: 4 ounces = about 1 cup crumbled

- Leftover Heaven: Make a spread by combining leftover pieces of room-temperature cheese in a food processor fitted with the metal blade, processing until smooth. A tablespoon at a time, add enough milk, cream, or wine to create a smooth, soft mixture, scraping down the sides of the workbowl as necessary. Season with freshly ground pepper, chopped herbs such as tarragon or basil, and minced garlic if you like. Serve with bread or crackers.

Heating Cheese

- High-fat and soft, moist cheeses are typically good candidates for melting. Low-fat (light) cheeses contain less fat and therefore don't melt well.

- Hard and semihard cheeses should be grated before being used in cooking; soft and semisoft cheeses should be cut or crumbled into very small pieces.

- Bring cheese to room temperature before adding it to a hot mixture.

- Stronger-tasting cheeses add more flavor to a sauce or baked dish, which means you can use less.

- Blue cheese should be used in moderation for hot dishes—heat intensifies their flavor, which can easily overpower a dish.

- Though decried by cheese lovers, PROCESS(ED) CHEESES melt more easily and with fewer problems because they contain emulsifiers. That's why they're often used in warm cheese dips such as CHILE CON QUESO and QUESO FUNDIDO. Of course such dips have flavorful additions, so one might not notice that the mediocre cheese has no flavor.

- Cheese can turn stringy, rubbery, or grainy when exposed to high heat, which causes the protein (CASEIN) to separate from the fat and liquid. Circumvent this problem by shredding the cheese or cutting it into small pieces. Bring it to room temperature and add it to a sauce or other mixture toward the end of the cooking process. Cook slowly over low heat, stirring slowly but constantly, only until the cheese is melted and incorporated.

- Cooking a cheese sauce in the top of a double boiler over simmering water is a good way to keep the mixture from overheating and turning grainy. Make sure the bottom of the top pan doesn't touch the water. Add the grated cheese a little at a time, stirring constantly until it melts.

- Or remove the hot mixture from the burner and add the room-temperature grated cheese. Stir slowly and constantly and let the residual heat melt the cheese. If necessary, gently reheat the sauce to melt the cheese fully.

- Long-cooking cheese dishes like casseroles and FON-DUES won't separate if you toss a little flour or cornstarch with the grated cheese. Count on a rounded tablespoon of starch per pound of cheese. Put the grated cheese and flour or cornstarch in a bowl and toss with your fingers.

- The classic use of wine in fondue not only flavors the mixture but contributes acid, which helps prevent the mixture from becoming stringy because it combines with and binds the calcium in the cheese. Adding a little wine, vinegar, or lemon or lime juice to a mixture in which you plan to melt cheese will help emulsify the mixture.

- Don't add cheese to the top of a casserole or other baked dish until the final 10 minutes of baking. That way the cheese will be soft and creamy, not tough and dried out.

- Broiling a cheese topping creates an appealing browned and bubbling effect. Position the dish so the top is 3 to 4 inches from the broiling unit and watch carefully until the cheese is broiled to your taste.

- Baked Brie or Camembert makes a quick and easy appetizer. Remove the cheese from the wooden box and unwrap. Cut away the top of the rind, leaving the bottom and sides intact (do this when the cheese is cold). Return the cheese to the box, rind side down. Place on a baking sheet and bake at 350°F for about 30 minutes, or just until the cheese melts. Serve with baguette slices.

- Toss chunks of room-temperature Brie or Camembert (rind removed) with hot pasta. The cheese melts quickly and deliciously coats the pasta.

> ### There's Nothing New in the Food World
> A Greek writer named Athenaeus (A.D. 170–230) recorded what was undoubtedly one of the first recipes for cheesecake: "Take some cheese, pound it, and then put it in a brazen sieve. After straining it, add honey and flour made from spring wheat. Heat it all together in one mass, and when it is cooled, you have a cheese food that is sweet and worthy of the gods."

SERVING CHEESE

Cheeses can be served to begin or end a meal, as the course just before dessert, or with cocktails. They can even comprise the main course, accompanied by lightly dressed salad greens and seasonal fruit. Let's face it, for some of us, any occasion deserves cheese.

A cheese plate (also called a *cheese board*) can be a large platter with the cheeses displayed uncut for all to serve themselves. Or it can be a selection meant for one person for a pre- or postprandial course, in which case the cheeses are cut in advance. Whatever your pleasure, the following general guidelines should help make your cheese-tasting experience eminently enjoyable.

- Choosing a theme for your cheese course makes the tasting more fun, not to mention enlightening. The premise could be cheeses from only one country or different cheeses from a single cheesemaker or those from one milk type, such as only sheep's-milk cheeses. Or it could be a comparison of a similar style of cheese made with different milks, of only American farmstead cheeses, of several different versions of a cheese (such as CHEDDAR) made by different producers, or of three or four BLUE CHEESES. The possibilities are myriad—let your imagination take wing.

- Next, think about visual diversity in shape, size, and color. Shapes can include rounds, balls, wedges, squares, truncated pyramids, or logs; sizes can range from a petite round of chèvre to a large chunk of Cheddar. Most cheeses are light in hue, though the colors of the rinds will be different. Color can be added to the selection with a lively veined blue cheese or a cheese such as SHROPSHIRE BLUE with its blue-mottled orangey paste or with one like LIVAROT with its golden interior and reddish orange rind.

- Flavor and texture also should be a factor, and a well-rounded cheese plate could include a sharp farmstead cheddar, a semisoft but heady ÉPOISSES, a fruity well-aged EMMENTAL, a tangy fresh CHÈVRE, and a rich, full-flavored blue cheese, such as POINT REYES ORIGINAL BLUE.

- It's best not to include cheeses that are smoked or spiced in the selection. They have a tendency to overpower other cheeses and can ruin your palate for milder flavors. Save such cheeses for another time and let them stand on their own.

- Remember that it's better to serve one or two exquisite cheeses than five mediocre examples.

- For the utmost in flavor, aroma, and texture, cheeses should always be served at room temperature (65°F to 70°F), so take them out of the refrigerator about an hour before serving. Larger pieces and harder cheeses require more time than do softer cheeses, which may need only 30 to 40 minutes. Of course the timing will depend on how warm the room is.

- Don't remove more cheese from the refrigerator than you plan to use. If you're serving only a portion of a large wedge, don't bring it all to room temperature. Cut off what you need while the cheese is cold and immediately rewrap the remainder, returning it to the fridge. Every time a cheese is allowed to come to room temperature it begins to dry out and deteriorate.

- If a spot or two of mold has formed on the paste of a hard, semihard, or semisoft cheese, trim away beneath the mold by ½ inch. If a large patch is involved, cut the entire section out. Small pieces of cheese that have turned quite moldy should be discarded. And if mold forms on soft cheese, throw it out—it can't be salvaged safely.

- Keep hard, semihard, and semisoft cheeses wrapped while bringing them to room temperature. Softer cheeses that may become runny can be put on the serving plate and covered lightly with plastic wrap. Or position all the cheeses on the tray and cover with plastic wrap until they're ready to be served. In that case make sure there are no cheeses so pungent that their odor would permeate the others on the plate. Bottom line: don't unwrap a cheese or uncover a cheese plate until it's ready to be served.

- The plate or tray on which you present the cheeses can be any of several forms. A marble cheese round is classic, but other choices include a wooden plate or tray, a granite tile, a footed cake plate, or just about any flat surface on which the cheeses will fit. Some people use straw or wicker trays, but such surfaces are uneven, which makes cutting the cheese difficult.

- When choosing the palette for cheese, think contrast. Because most cheeses are light colored, a dark background displays them more dramatically. We have a large black square plate that makes the cheeses "pop" visually. But you can create a dark background by lining the platter with large pesticide-free green leaves. And cheese shops often have large wax-coated paper leaves for such a purpose.

- The size of the plate needed depends on how many cheeses are to be served. There should be enough room for the cheeses to be spaced well apart so people can easily take a portion of one cheese without running into another.

- For a large cheese plate that will be passed, don't precut the cheese—let the guests help themselves to what they want. Precut cheese dries out more quickly, and slices of cheese aren't nearly as appealing as larger chunks of cheese.

- For individual cheese plates served as an appetizer or at the meal's end, a small portion of each cheese is typically cut and arranged on the plate. For such courses, salad plates are fine for about three cheeses; a dinner plate will probably work better for more than that. Any fruit or other accoutrement may be either placed on the plate or passed.

- It's easier to cut hard to semihard cheese at room temperature, semisoft cheese when cold. To cleanly cut soft, fresh cheeses such as chèvre into slices, wrap a long piece of strong thread or unflavored dental floss around it from bottom to top and slowly pull the ends together. An egg slicer makes cutting tiny soft cheeses like BOCCONCINI a breeze. Place the cheese in the slicer, then slowly bring the cutting wires down and through the cheese.

- Whether preparing a large or individual cheese plate, leave the rind on cheeses, including the downy-white rind of soft-ripened cheese, which is completely edible.

- How the cheese is presented on the serving piece generally depends on its size and shape. Wedges or large chunks of cheese should be served that way. Small rounds of goat cheese and the like should remain whole. And never put strong cheeses next to milder ones.

- When tasting cheeses, do so from mildest to strongest, which is also how cheese should be arranged on the plate. Otherwise your palate will be overwhelmed and won't be able to taste the more delicate cheeses.

- Each cheese should have its own serving utensil placed alongside it. Using a single knife for all cheeses will mingle and adulterate the flavors. Serving and cutting tools can range from a spreader for soft cheeses to a sharp knife for hard ones. In fact, that's all one really needs—knives (which can be as simple as a butter knife for cheeses that are semisoft or a paring knife for those that are semihard) and spreaders for soft cheeses. But many cheese tools are available at gourmet and cheese markets. A special "cheese knife" has a sharp edge and is tipped with two prongs that are used to spear the cheese that's just been cut. The skeleton knife is a cheese knife with openings in the middle of the blade, making it good for cutting soft cheeses because there's less knife surface to which the cheese can stick. There's also a flat, stubby, oval-shaped knife with a pointed tip, used to gouge pieces out of very hard cheeses like PAR-MESAN. A cheese plane can be used for hard cheeses, though it creates hollows in the cheese. And wire slicers can cut slices of various thicknesses off semisoft to semihard cheeses.

- Bread or crackers are the classic complement for cheese. We prefer bread, as the texture doesn't interfere with that of the cheese. But many people like the cracker crunch factor—it's all a matter of personal taste. One choice is to serve simple baguette slices or unflavored crackers, letting the taste of the cheese shine sans competing flavors. Of course some cheeses pair beautifully with flavored breads—triple-cream cheeses with nut bread, goat's milk or sheep's milk cheeses with olive bread, blue cheeses with fruit-and-nut bread, and hearty aged cheeses like cheddar with whole-grain bread. Bottom line, don't choose a bread so strongly flavored that it will overpower the taste of the cheese. And never serve cheese-flavored breads or crackers, for obvious reasons.

- Accompaniments for cheese can be either arranged on the plate with the cheese or served on the side. Foods with a natural affinity for cheese include fresh, seasonal fruit (including apples, figs, grapes, pears, and melon), dried fruit (like dates, figs, raisins, and prunes), raw or toasted nuts (think almonds, cashews, hazelnuts, pecans, or walnuts), green or black olives as long as they're not too salty (rinse off any brine with cool water), cured meats (such as prosciutto or jamón serrano), chutneys or mostardas (the latter is fruit preserved in syrup and flavored with powdered mustard

CHEESE TALK

Big cheese:	An influential or important person
Cheesy:	Someone or something that's cheap or chintzy
Cheesed; cheesed off:	Upset or disgusted
Cheese eater:	A rat (informer)
Cheese head:	Green Bay Packers' fan
Cheese it!:	A warning to look out, usually because the cops are coming
Cheese paring:	Miserly or stingy
Hard cheese:	Tough luck; an unpleasant situation

seed), honey, which is heavenly drizzled over blue cheese, and specialty adjuncts like Spanish membrillo (quince paste), available at gourmet markets and cheese stores.

- Leftover cheese should be wrapped and refrigerated as soon as possible. Leaving a cheese at room temperature for more than 4 hours invites deterioration, from mold growth to drying out. For ideas on using cheese scraps, see the last two tips under "Working with Cheese in the Kitchen," page 18.

PAIRING WINE
AND CHEESE

Among the treasures discovered in the tomb
of Egyptian King Aha (also known as King
Menes), circa 2950 B.C., were desiccated remnants of cheese and nearby earthenware jugs that later
were proven irrefutably to have
contained wine. That means that
wine and cheese have been part
of humankind's culinary history
for almost 5,000 years and undoubtedly longer!

That said, and given the fact
that we've had eons to perfect the
art, one would think that pairing
these two soul mates would by
now be easy. After all, they have a lot in common—the
genesis of both of these natural creations involves fermentation, both reflect the TERROIR of their source,
both are alive and continually changing, and both have
an end result that can be delectable whether young and
uncomplicated or older and more complex. So, with all
these commonalities, pairing wine and cheese should
be simple, right?

Not in the least. In fact it can be downright tricky,

> Wine and cheese
> are ageless
> companions, like
> aspirin and aches, or
> June and moon, or
> good people and noble
> ventures.
>
> —M.F.K. Fisher

and for most of us it's not at all intuitive. Take for example the time-honored maxim of serving only red wine with cheese. Well, that theory may be an oldie, but it's no longer a goodie. Many experts have denounced the red-wine-with-cheese dictum, declaring that white wines are better partners for cheese because they lack the astringency contributed by the tannins in red wine. Then there are those who've declared that wine and cheese shouldn't ever be paired. Spoilsports!

The truth is that wines and cheeses vary significantly, and there's simply no way a single rule will work. Bottom line? Matching cheese with wine is intensely subjective and always a bit of a gamble.

As with all foods, cheese will affect how a wine will taste. And the world of cheese is vastly complex with myriad combinations of flavors and textures. As is the wine universe. The issue is further complicated by the fact that individual taste is exceedingly subjective. The truth is that a wine or cheese that someone's wild about may be viewed by some as simply passable and by others as detestable. So how *could* one rule ever apply to pairing all wines and cheeses? It can't, which is why there can never be any ironclad imperatives on the subject.

We could all make life simpler, of course, by pairing one great cheese with one fabulous wine. But often multiple cheeses are served together, as with a cheese plate. One approach is to serve small amounts of several wines with each cheese as some restaurants do. However, it simply may not be practical to open three or four bottles for a few guests, meaning one bottle might have to match up with three or four cheeses.

Should you decide to serve only one wine with several cheeses, first decide if you're showcasing the wine or the cheese. If a special bottle of wine from your cellar is to take center stage, determine its characteristics and choose cheeses that will complement it. In this case, you'll have more success if you choose a group of cheeses that are similar in flavor. If, on the other hand, you want to highlight a group of cheeses with a range of flavors, then choose a wine that will be compatible with a broad flavor palate, such as a white wine with a trace of residual sugar. In the end, one should always choose a better wine that may not be an exact fit for the cheese, rather than a mediocre potable that's purportedly a perfect match.

Pairing these classic partners can be both challenging and exceedingly enjoyable, and the right choice is ultimately a matter of personal taste. The goal is for the cheese to enhance the wine's flavor rather than affect it negatively. And vice versa. Naturally, a cheese that makes the wine taste sour or bitter or intensifies the tannins is a bad match. However, you know you've hit the mark if the pairing seems to make a wine's flavor richer, mellower, and somehow better—and the cheese makes magic in your mouth.

SOME BASIC FLAVOR CHARACTERISTICS

Unlike most prepared dishes, the flavor of cheese can't be adjusted with a dash of salt, a splash of vinegar, or a little lemon juice. So it's important to taste the cheese and determine its flavor aspects before trying to pair it with wine. Following are some basic guidelines for how different flavor aspects of cheese can affect the wine with which it's paired:

- **Sweetness**—Cheese with a sweet characteristic will increase sensitivity to any tartness, bitterness, or sharpness in wine.

- **Acidity**—Cheese with a tangy or acidic (sour) quality makes wine taste fuller, fruitier, and more mellow. And acidic wines stand up well to acidic cheeses. As a cheese matures and loses moisture, the perception of acidity intensifies.

- **Saltiness**—A salty aspect in cheese tends to counteract any bitter or acidic quality in wine. As with acidity, saltiness also makes the wine seem fruitier. For many cheeses, the salty quality intensifies with age.

- **Bitterness**—A bitter quality in cheese is a fault and can actually increase the sense of bitterness in wine.

- **Spiciness**—Foods that are spicy (hot) intensify the astringent impression created by wines that are tannic, such as many young reds. Therefore, cheeses flavored with hot paprika or pepper will clash with a tannic wine.

- **Umami**—Known more as an overall palate sensation rather than a taste, UMAMI is a distinctively savory characteristic that will also increase the sense of bitterness in wine. Long-ripened cheese will have a higher level of umami than the same cheese at a younger age. However, the fact that an aged cheese typically tastes saltier helps balance any impression of bitterness in wine.

Following are some cheese types and the wine styles with which they are most likely to pair.

- **Fresh cheeses** such as CREAM CHEESE, RICOTTA, fresh MOZZARELLA, and fresh MURAZZANO are moist, mild, and sometimes slightly tart. They go best with light to medium-bodied white wines such as Orvieto, Soave, and Trebbiano d'Abruzzo from Italy, as well as Pinot Gris (also called *Pinot Grigio*), Riesling, Pinot Blanc, Sauvignon Blanc, and lighter unoaked Chardonnays. Other good pairings include rosés, light-bodied red wines such as Bardolino, Lambrusco, Beaujolais, Valpolicella, Dolcetto, and lighter Burgundy, Pinot Noir, and Merlot.

- **Soft Cheeses** like BRIE, CAMEMBERT, and CRESCENZA match nicely with a wide variety of wines depending on their flavor characteristics. Such cheeses can range from mild, tangy, and salty to rich, buttery, and more strongly flavored. A single type of cheese like Brie, depending on its producer and where it's produced, can have a dramatic range of flavors. Champagne and sparkling wine generally match well with soft cheeses. Choose lighter-style sparkling wines to go with simpler cheeses like Crescenza and more complex sparkling wines to match more complex cheeses like many American farmstead and most imported Bries and Camemberts. Champagne and sparkling wine producers have different house styles, but generally Blanc de Blancs (made from Chardonnay) are lighter in style than Blanc de Noirs (which are primarily Pinot Noir) or rosé sparkling wines. Slightly sweet wines like some Rieslings or sherries match well with the tangier cheeses like a young CHAOURCE. Creamier cheeses such as BOURSAULT and TELEME go with wines with more acidity such as New Zealand and some American Sauvignon Blancs or French Sancerre. Creamy cheeses also go well with amontillado and oloroso sherries. Some of the more flavorful cheeses like Camembert and ÉPOISSES DE BOURGOGNE

work with a big Chardonnay or a red wine like Pinot
Noir, Sangiovese, or Chianti or even Cabernet Sauvignon, Bordeaux, or Burgundy. But a spicy Gewürztraminer or Alsatian Riesling would also work.

- **Semisoft to Semihard Cheeses** such as BEL
  PAESE, relatively young CHEDDAR, DOUBLE GLOUCES-
  TER, young GOUDA, and MORBIER, vary widely in firmness and flavor complexity. In general, they are more
  flavorful than soft cheeses (but not always), which
  means many of them are compatible with bigger
  wines. Lighter-style cheeses like Bel Paese or young
  Gouda match up best with lighter-style wines. Consider (from lightest to heaviest) Italian whites such as
  Frascati, Orvieto, and Soave, as well as Pinot Gris,
  Riesling, Pinot Blanc, Chenin Blanc, Sauvignon Blanc,
  Gewürztraminer, and Chardonnay. Oaked versions
  will be fuller flavored than those that are unoaked.
  White wine from Burgundy and the northern Rhône
  can be some of the fullest flavored. Bigger, bolder
  cheeses such as MUNSTER or SAINT-NECTAIRE can be
  paired with bigger, bolder wines such as the following reds (from lightest to heaviest): Bardolino,
  Beaujolais, lighter Burgundy, Chianti, Pinot Noir,
  lighter Bordeaux, Burgundy, Merlot, Syrah, Zinfandel, Bordeaux, and Cabernet Sauvignon.

- **Semihard to Hard Cheeses** include ASIAGO,
  aged CHEDDAR, DRY JACK, aged GOUDA, GRUYÈRE,

PARMIGIANO-REGGIANO, harder PECORINO, and ZAMOR-ANO. As a group, such cheeses are usually the easiest to match with wine because they're more similar to one another than cheeses in other categories. They don't have the buttery consistency of softer cheeses because aging gives them a firmer texture and flavors that are mellow yet complex. They're also generally saltier, which, as previously noted, makes wines taste fruitier. These factors allow such cheeses to match well with full-bodied, complex red wines, particularly if the wines have some age themselves. Good matches with such cheeses include Brunello di Montalcino, Barbaresco, Barolo, Cabernet Sauvignon, Merlot, Syrah, Zinfandel, better vintages of Bordeaux and Burgundy, and wines from the Rhône (especially northern Rhône). Cheeses with a "nutty" essence also pair well with tawny port and sherry. White wine fanciers should look to rich Chardonnay and French white Burgundy as well as vintage Champagne.

• **Blue Cheeses** vary widely in flavor intensity. Milder blue cheeses like Gorgonzola Dolce and MAYTAG BLUE go with fruity white wines like Chenin Blanc, Gewürztraminer, and Riesling and fruity reds like Beaujolais, lighter Zinfandel, and Pinot Noir. As blue cheeses age they generally become saltier and more pungent, which means the wines they partner with should be sweeter. Again, Chenin Blanc, Gewürztraminer, and Riesling work, but even better are those with some residual sugar such as Muscat- (or *Moscato-*) based wines. Mature red wines with resolved tannins also pair well. Of course the classic pairings for semihard blues are ROQUEFORT with Sauternes and STILTON with vintage port. Both of the wines are quite sweet and match well with the slightly salty, complex flavors of these classics.

PAIRING BEER AND ALE WITH CHEESE

Many beer aficionados are adamant that beer goes even better with cheese than wine. They could be right. After all, the flavors of many beers and cheeses are naturally compatible because the two have more elements in common than wine and cheese. Beer lovers point to the fact that over the ages many monasteries have produced both products, long staples in the diets of monks. Modern-day examples include the renowned Chimay cheeses and beers made by Belgium's Cistercian Trappist monks, who've been producing both since 1862.

In general, complex beers with full flavors work very well with cheeses with round, multifaceted profiles, although if both are powerful contenders they're likely to clash. Likewise, beers that are light in body most often do nicely with lighter-style cheeses. And then there are contrasting beer and cheese combos that work particularly well, such as when a beer's carbonation plays off a rich, creamy cheese.

> Drink a pot of ale and eat a scoop of Stilton every day and you will make "old bones."
> —Nineteenth-century British saying

ELEMENTS THAT INFLUENCE THE TASTE OF BEER

Water comprises about 90 percent of beer, so the character of the water greatly affects the taste of the brew. This is particularly true in lighter styles that aren't heavily influenced by other ingredients.

Malt is a germinated grain (usually barley) that adds a slightly sweet trait to beer. It can be processed in different ways, including drying, stewing, smoking, or roasting to varying degrees from light to very heavy. Each process affects the flavor and color of the resulting brew. Darker malts impart deeper colors and flavors, like chocolate, coffee, and espresso.

Hops are conelike flowers that are used to give beer its bitter, dry character and help balance the sweetness conveyed by the malt. Different varieties of hops produce various results, and the way the hops are processed will also make a declaration in the final flavor and aroma of the beer.

Yeasts of varying types are used in brewing, and each brewer picks a particular cultivated yeast for the style of beer being produced. In the case of lambic beer, wild yeasts are used for spontaneous fermentation.

Additional flavorings are sometimes used to introduce a characteristic taste to certain beers. These include herbs (such as coriander leaf or clover), spices (like cinnamon, coriander, or cloves), fruit (such as cherries, raspberries, or peaches), and even chocolate or coffee beans.

PAIRING PRIMER

Following is a short guide to various styles of beer and ale. **Beer** is bottom-fermented—that is, the yeast sinks to the bottom of the tank during fermentation. Such brews ferment at colder temperatures for longer periods of time, which produces a lighter, crisper-tasting beverage. **Ale** is a generic category for top-fermented beers where the yeast rises to the top of the tank. The result is a higher level of alcohol and a stronger flavor. By the way, so as not to confuse, the word *beer* is commonly used in the brewing world to cover both categories. The following listings should give you a head start on your next pairing of beer and cheese.

Amber Ale, sometimes referred to as *Irish ale,* has a rich golden color and tends toward the malty side.

- Pair it with sheep's milk cheeses like ABBAYE DE BEL-LOC, ARDI-GASNA, or LAMB CHOPPER. Also try amber ale with WASHED-RIND cheeses like BRICK, MUNSTER, or PONT L'ÉVÊQUE. Last but not least, these ales pair beautifully with cheeses characterized by butterscotch, caramel, or toffee flavors, such as CARMODY RESERVE, aged COOLEA, ETORKI, or GOUDA.

Bock beer is creamy and somewhat sweet with malty and hoppy traits. It's generally dark colored, although American versions are lighter in color and flavor and less bitter than German styles.

- Bock beer goes well with cheeses that are slightly sweet, salty, and nutty or full flavored, such as aged BRA, FARMSTEAD CHEDDAR, FARMSTEAD CHESHIRE, EMMENTAL, GRUYÈRE, and PECORINO TOSCANO. A smoked or aged GOUDA would be a good fit, as would WASHED-RIND cheeses like CHIMAY Trappiste with Beer, HOOLIGAN, or LIVAROT.

Brown Ale is usually very full bodied and slightly sweet. As the name implies, the color is dark brown.

- Brown ales pair well with cheeses that have butterscotch, caramel, or toffee traits, such as CARMODY RESERVE, COMTÉ, or aged COOLEA or GOUDA. Also consider cheeses with a complex flavor profile like

FARMSTEAD CHEDDAR and aged GRUYÈRE. WASHED-RIND cheeses like CHIMAY, HOOLIGAN, LIVAROT, or PONT L'ÉVÊQUE will match well; for contrast, try BRIE or CAMEMBERT.

Lager is generally light flavored, effervescent, and pale golden in color, though some styles are stronger and slightly darker.

• Cheeses that go with lighter lagers include young, fresh, tangy styles like CHÈVRE, CRESCENZA, and MOZ-ZARELLA or fresh soft cheeses like POT CHEESE or RICOTTA. Slightly bolder lagers do well with BRIE or young, mild GOUDA. If the lager is very full flavored, it will match up well with EMMENTAL, GRUYÈRE, or TOMME DE SAVOIE. Blue cheeses like BAYLEY HAZEN BLUE and ROQUEFORT will also pair nicely.

Lambic Beer is a wheat beer fermented with wild yeast and produced in Belgium. Unlike the majority of beers and ales, lambics are aged. Young lambics can be on the sour side but become much mellower with aging. Sometimes these brews are infused with the essence of cherries, raspberries, or peaches, which lends a light fruity quality.

• Tangy goat cheeses like EVANGELINE, GARROTXA, HOJA SANTA, HUMBOLDT FOG, or MONTE ENEBRO go well with lambic beer. Also try MASCARPONE with lambics with a fruit quality.

Pale Ale has a light to amber color with flavors that are typically stronger than most lagers. Such potables typically have a good balance between the influence of malted barley and hops. **India Pale Ale (IPA)** is generally a bit more substantial than regular pale ale and also slightly more bitter.

- For both pale ale and India pale ale, choose WASHED-RIND cheeses like BRICK, PONT L'ÉVÊQUE, or TALEGGIO as well as complex, full-flavored cheeses like FARMSTEAD CHEDDAR, COMTÉ, aged GOUDA, GRUYÈRE, and PARMIGIANO-REGGIANO. If an IPA has a slightly sour note, try it with a mildly tangy aged goat cheese like CHABICHOU DU POITOU, HUMBOLDT FOG, or BONNE BOUCHE. Those with a bitter edge pair well with one of the rich farmstead cheddars.

Pilsner is essentially a pale, light-colored lager with a very mild flavor, though some can be somewhat hoppy.

- Compatible cheeses for hoppy Pilsners include white CHEDDAR, HAVARTI, young MUNSTER, and Monterey JACK. For Pilsners with a somewhat tart finish, try goat cheeses like HUMBOLDT FOG, SELLES-SUR-CHER, or a young CHABICHOU DU POITOU.

Porter is a high-alcohol, strong-flavored ale dark in color with a rich malty taste. Depending on style, some porters are bitter and others are slightly sweet.

- Porters pair nicely with cheeses that have butterscotch, caramel, or toffee traits, such as CARMODY RESERVE, COMTÉ, or aged COOLEA or GOUDA. Also consider complex cheeses like FARMSTEAD CHEDDAR and aged GRUYÈRE, spicy blue cheeses like BLEU D'AUVERGNE, BLEU DES CAUSSES, ROGUE RIVER BLUE, or ROARING FORTIES BLUE, or WASHED-RIND cheeses like CHIMAY, HOOLIGAN, LIVAROT, or PONT L'ÉVÊQUE. A compatible contrast would be MASCARPONE.

Stout is a very dark ale that comes in several variations. **Irish stout** (also called *dry stout*), of which Guinness is the most famous, is light on the malt and heavier on the hops. **Sweet stout**—also called *milk stout* because of a somewhat milky flavor—is often lower in alcohol and less bitter than Irish stouts. **Russian stout,** also known as *Imperial stout,* is a high-alcohol, robustly flavored ale.

- Try all the cheeses listed under the previous listing for porter. Stronger stouts can stand up to some of the more powerful blues like longer-aged GORGONZOLA and ROQUEFORT.

Trappist Beer is a strong-flavored, high-alcohol ale with a color that can range from dark amber to brown. Trappist beers are produced by six brewing abbeys: Chimay, Orval, Rochefot, Saint Sixtus, Schaapskooi, and Westmalle. Many of these brews have a distinct spicy character.

- The classic pairing, of course, is CHIMAY cheeses with Chimay ales. But other WASHED-RIND cheeses like HOOLIGAN, LIVAROT, MAROILLES, or PONT L'ÉVÊQUE will also do nicely. Try blue cheeses with a spicy character like BEENLEIGH BLUE, BLEU D'AUVERGNE, CASHEL BLUE, ROQUEFORT, and STILTON.

Vienna beer has a fuller flavor than many lager-style beers—it's malty with a hint of hops and an amber-red color.

- Pair it with EMMENTAL, GRUYÈRE, PROVOLONE, or TOMME DE SAVOIE. Vienna beer is also good with blue cheeses like BEENLEIGH BLUE and ROQUEFORT.

Wheat Beer is made from malted wheat and, though technically an ale, has a lighter color and flavor that resembles a lager.

- Wheat beer goes well with young, fresh, tangy cheeses like CHÈVRE, CRESCENZA, and MOZZARELLA, or fresh soft cheeses like POT CHEESE or RICOTTA. Some wheat beers with a slightly bolder flavor do well with BRIE or young, mild GOUDA.

A-TO-Z
DEFINITIONS OF CHEESES AND CHEESE-RELATED TERMS

A

A

Abbaye de Belloc (Bellocq) (AOC) [ah-bay-EE deuh behl-LAWK]

Origin	France (Pays Basque)
Milk	Unpasteurized sheep's
Type	SEMIHARD; PRESSED UNCOOKED; NATURAL RIND; FARMSTEAD
Appearance	Rounded 8- to 11-pound wheels; rind is hard and pitted, the color brownish with orange and yellow splotches; interior is pale ivory-yellow
Texture	Firm, dense, yet creamy
Flavor	Rich, buttery, nutty, and fruity, with caramelized notes

> A cheese may disappoint. It may be dull, it may be naive, it may be over sophisticated. Yet it remains cheese, milk's leap toward immortality.
> —Clifton Fadiman

For centuries this cheese has been made by Benedictine monks at the Abbey de Belloc in Pays Basque. Its APPELLATION D'ORIGINE CONTRÔLÉE (AOC) classification comes under the OSSAU-IRATY umbrella. This cheese is traditionally made with milk from Manech sheep, though milk from other breeds may be used. Abbaye de Belloc undergoes RIPENING for 6 months and must have a minimum FAT CONTENT of 60 percent.

abomasum [ab-oh-MAY-suhm] *see* RENNET

A

Abondance; Tomme d'Abondance (AOC; PDO) [ah-bohn-DAHNS; tom dah-bohn-DAHNC]

Origin	France (Savoie)
Milk	Unpasteurized cow's
Type	SEMIHARD; PRESSED COOKED; WASHED RIND; ARTISAN, COOPERATIVE, and FACTORY
Appearance	15- to 20-pound wheels; rind is thin, dark yellow (sometimes with brownish splotches), and has cloth markings; interior is pale golden
Texture	Supple, smooth, and firm
Flavor	Aromatic, fruity, nutty, and complex

This cheese dates back to the fifth-century monks of l'Abbaye de Saint d'Abondance. The name has two origins—Abondance cattle, one of the breeds from which the milk comes, and the Abondance Valley in the Haute-Savoie. This cheese became renowned in 1381, when the abbey was named the official supplier of Savoyard cheeses for the pope's election at the conclave of Avignon. APPELLATION D'ORIGINE CONTRÔLÉE (AOC) regulations state that Abondance can be made only from milk from the Abondance, Montbéliard, and Tarine breeds. It must undergo RIPENING for a minimum of 90 days, during which time the cheese is alternately rubbed with salt and wiped with a MORGE-soaked cloth. Its FAT CONTENT ranges from 40 to 49 percent. Abondance is also called *Tomme d'Abondance*.

Acapella [ah-kah-PEHL-lah] *see* NOCTURNE

Achadinha Cheese Company [ah-shah-DEE-nah] *see* CAPRICIOUS

achiote [ah-chee-OH-tay] *see* ANNATTO

acid curd; acid curd cheeses When milk sours naturally,
it forms a custardlike solid (CURD) in which liquid (WHEY) is
trapped. At this point, the solid portions are referred to as
acid curd. In cheesemaking, this state is achieved through
ACIDIFICATION—increasing milk's acidity (typically by adding
a STARTER), which rapidly transforms milk protein into solids.
Fresh **acid curd cheeses,** such as COTTAGE CHEESE and CREAM
CHEESE, are produced by acidification (sometimes by combining heat and acid) and are ready for consumption once production is completed.

acidic; acid [uh-SIH-dik] *see* Glossary of Cheese Descriptors,
page 493

acidification [uh-sid-ih-fih-KAY-shuhn] The process of increasing
a milk's ACIDITY by lowering the pH, typically through the
addition of a STARTER.

acidity [uh-SIH-dih-tee] The term *acidity* can be used to describe
flavor (*see* Glossary of Cheese Descriptors, page 493), but in
cheesemaking it refers to the percentage of LACTIC ACID in
milk, WHEY, or CURD. Raw (unpasteurized) milk has natural
acidity, which may be increased with the addition of a
STARTER. A suitable level of acidity (established by a pH
reading) is a major determinant in the formation and
firmness of the curd and crucial in the production of good
cheese.

Ackawi [ah-COW-ee] *see* AKAWI

acrid [AK-rid] *see* Glossary of Cheese Descriptors, page 493

Adagio [ah-DAH-joh; ah-DAH-jee-oh] *see* NOCTURNE

A

aerobic bacteria [a-ROH-bik] *see* BACTERIA

Affidélice [ah-fee-day-LEESS] *see* ÉPOISSES DE BOURGOGNE

affinage [ah-fee-NAHZH] The French term for the process of RIPENING (or finishing) cheese to its optimal maturity. *See also* AFFINÉ.

affinatore [ah-fee-nah-TOH-ray] Italian for a specialist in RIPENING cheese. *See* AFFINÉ.

affiné; affineur; affinatore [ah-fee-NAY; ah-fee-NYOUR; ah-fee-nah-TOH-ray] In the cheese world *affiné* can refer to either (1) the process of RIPENING cheese or (2) a WASHED-RIND CHEESE, which can be finished (washed) with anything from saltwater to wine. *Affineur* (French) or *affinatore* (Italian) means an expert in finishing (aging) cheese. Some cheesemakers sell their unripe cheese to an *affineur,* who uses traditional methods to bring cheese to its peak maturity. An *affineur*'s duties may also include everything from packaging the cheese to marketing it. Both words are from the French *affiner* ("to finish"). *See also* AFFINAGE.

Afuega'l Pitu [ah-FWAY-gahl pee-TOO]

Origin	Spain (Asturias)
Milk	Pasteurized or unpasteurized cow's
Type	SOFT TO SEMISOFT; MOLDED UNCOOKED; NATURAL RIND; ARTISAN
Appearance	Depending on where it's made, this 10- to 16-ounce cheese can come in pumpkin-shape bundles (with marks at the top where the cloth was twisted and tied) or be conical, with a

flat bottom and top; rind is very thin, with a
color that can range from beige to deep orange
(the latter is the paprika version); interior is
white to ivory—the paprika style is pale orange

Texture   Ranges from creamy and delicate to almost
granular, depending on age

Flavor   When young it's piquant and nutty with a
grassy aroma; aged versions are boldly astringent and slightly musty; paprika style can be
assertively spicy, depending on whether mild or
hot paprika was used

In bable (the regional Asturian dialect) the name *Afuega'l Pitu* is
variously translated as "to choke the chicken," "to choke the
throat," "fire in the gullet," and "fire in the throat"—all purportedly referring to the fact that in ancient times the test to see if the
CURDS had been drained enough was to give some to a chicken,
and if it had trouble swallowing, the curds were ready. Another
interpretation to the choking and fire references is that the paprika version is so hot and spicy that it makes one choke. Of
course, that's true only if it's made with hot, rather than mild,
paprika. This cheese is exceedingly popular in Asturias and comes
in two styles—plain and *rojo* (or *roxo*) *del Aramo,* the latter flavored
with salt and paprika. The milk that produces Afuega'l Pitu
comes primarily from Friesian cows, though milk from Ratina,
Roxa, or Carreñas cows may also be used. The cut CURDS are
drained, then scooped into small cloth bags (*fardelas*) that are
gathered at the top, tied off, and hung in a dark cellar. Alternatively, the curds may be placed in perforated cone-shape molds.
RIPENING continues for a minimum of 15 and up to 50 days.

aged; aged cheese Aged cheese has undergone a RIPENING period
to produce a characteristic texture, flavor, and aroma. This

time is typically a minimum of 2 months, although there are myriad exceptions.

A

aging *see* RIPENING

Ahumado de Áliva [ah-hyoo-MAH-doh day ah-LEE-vah] *see* QUESU-COS DE LIÉBANA

Airedale [EHR-dayl] *see* WINDSOR BLUE

Aisy Cendré [ay-ZEE sahn-DRAY]

Origin	France (Burgundy)
Milk	Unpasteurized cow's
Type	SEMISOFT; MOLDED UNCOOKED; WASHED RIND; ARTISAN
Appearance	7- to 9-ounce wheels; rind is brownish and covered with a thick layer of gray ash; interior is ivory
Texture	Smooth, creamy outer layer with a chalky center
Flavor	Creamy, savory, tangy, and nutty

This Burgundian cheese was created by Robert and Simone Berthaut, the same couple who revived ÉPOISSES DE BOUR-GOGNE in the mid-1950s. Like its older sister, Aisy Cendré is a washed-rind cheese that undergoes frequent brushings with a mixture of water and MARC, which helps spread desirable bacteria evenly over the cheese's surface. It's then covered with ASH (*cendre*) for about a month. The ash slows down RIP-ENING by reducing the cheese's oxygen exposure, thereby af-fecting both flavor and texture. Aisy Cendré, also called *Cendré d'Aisy,* has a minimum FAT CONTENT of 50 percent.

Before serving, gently brush off the ash, which can be quite gritty on the palate.

Akawi; Ackawi [ah-COW-ee]

Origin	Various Middle Eastern countries, primarily Lebanon and Syria
Milk	Unpasteurized cow's
Type	SOFT TO SEMISOFT; rindless; primarily FACTORY
Appearance	Variously sized cakes or chunks packed in brine, typically in a jar; the color is stark white
Texture	Smooth
Flavor	Mild, very salty, and slightly tangy

Native to Lebanon and Syria, Akawi is a favorite table cheese in the Middle East and a best-seller among Arab Americans. This 40-percent-fat cheese is brined (*see* SALTING) for up to 16 hours, which makes it intensely salty and gives it a very long shelf life—at least 6 months. If the texture is firm enough, the cheese may be rinsed with cold water to reduce the saltiness. Akawi that isn't brined is used for desserts. The Czech Republic uses almost 25 percent of its milk production to make Akawi, primarily for export to Arab countries. **Naboulsi** (also spelled *nabulsi, nabulsieh,* and *nabulsiyye*), which means "boiled cheese," is fresh Akawi that's been boiled in brine, flavored with spices and seeds, then packed in more brine.

Alderbrook *see* VERMONT BREBIS

Áliva [ah-LEE-vah] *see* QUESUCOS DE LIÉBANA

A

Allgäuer Bergkäse (PDO) [AHL-gow-er BEHRK-ki-zer (-kah-zeh)]

Origin	Germany (Allgäu)
Milk	Unpasteurized cow's
Type	HARD; PRESSED COOKED; NATURAL RIND; ARTISAN, FARMSTEAD, COOPERATIVE, and some MOUNTAIN
Appearance	33- to 110-pound wheels; rind is thin, hard, and dark yellow to brown in color; interior is ivory to medium yellow with a random scattering of small EYES
Texture	Supple and smooth
Flavor	Mellow, slightly sweet, earthy, fruity and nutty when young, becoming more piquant with age

Allgäuer Bergkäse dates back to at least the early nineteenth century. It's made in Allgäu, an area that straddles the southern German states of Bavaria and Baden-Württemberg, bordering on Austria. *Bergkäse* means "mountain cheese" and refers to the Bavarian Alps that dominate this area. The best Allgäuer Bergkäse is made from the milk of cows that graze in mountain pastures (at altitudes of between 3,000 and 6,000 feet) during the late spring and summer. The cheese is produced in the alpine huts scattered throughout the Alps. As winter approaches, the cows are herded down into the valley, where the cheese is made in dairies. Allgäuer Bergkäse is often viewed as a smaller version of Allgäuer Emmentaler (*see* EMMENTAL), which also has PROTECTED DESIGNATION OF ORIGIN (PDO) status. It's made from evening milk (which is skimmed), combined with whole milk from the following morning. Allgäuer Bergkäse is brined (*see* SALTING) for at least 24 hours, then RIPENED for at least 4 months

and sometimes for up to a year. It has a minimum FAT CONTENT
of 45 percent.

Allgäuer Emmentaler [AHL-gow-er EM-men-tah-ler] *see* EMMENTAL

Almkäse [AHLM-ki-zer (-kah-zeh)] German term for cheeses made
in mountain pastures from herds that have grazed there. Often
used synonymously with *Alpenkäse* and *Alpkäse. See also* ALPAGE;
MOUNTAIN CHEESES.

alpage; alpage cheeses [ahl-PAHZH] Synonymous with TRANSHU-
MANCE, alpage is the gradual summer migration of herds from
the valleys to lush mountain pastures. The herders (known as
bergers or *alpagistes*) not only accompany and tend the animals
but also milk them twice a day and produce **alpage cheeses** in
small chalets scattered throughout the mountainsides. These
wonderful handmade cheeses are the product of contented
animals that have consumed fresh mountain water, lush grasses,
and flowers.

Alpage Prättigau [ahl-PAHZH PRAH-tee-gow] *see* PRÄTTIGAUER

Alpenkäse; Alpkäse [AHL-pen-ki-zer (-kah-zeh)] *see* ALMKÄSE

Altenburger Ziegenkäse (PDO) [AHL-ten-ber-ger TSEE-gern-ki-zer
(-kah-zeh)]

Origin	Germany (Thuringia)
Milk	Pasteurized cow's and goat's
Type	SOFT; MOLDED UNCOOKED; BLOOMY RIND; ARTISAN, FARMSTEAD, and COOPERATIVE
Appearance	5½-ounce cylinders; rind is thin with a velvety coating of white mold that shows patches of

	beige, orange, and red as it ripens; interior is pale to medium yellow
Texture	Soft, smooth, and creamy
Flavor	Mild, delicate, nutty, milky, and slightly tangy

This cheese hails from Altenburger Land, a district on the far eastern edge of Thuringia, a small state in central Germany. Although Ziegenkäse means "goat cheese," the PROTECTED DESIGNATION OF ORIGIN (PDO) regulations for this cheese say that a minimum of 15 percent goat's milk must be used—the remainder is cow's milk. During the first week of RIPENING the surface begins to develop a CAMEMBERT-like mold, which continues to grow as the cheese ripens from the outside in. Altenburger Ziegenkäse is ripened a minimum of 2 weeks before being wrapped in foil and placed in small boxes for protection. Its relatively short ripening time (Camembert ages a minimum of 3 weeks) and the minimal use of goat's milk give Altenburger Ziegenkäse a uniquely mild flavor. Labels that indicate *mit Kümmelzusatz* signify the cheese is flavored with caraway seed. The FAT CONTENT for this cheese ranges from 30 to 45 percent.

Alt Urgell, l' *see* QUESO DE L'ALT URGELL Y LA CERDANYA

Amarelo (da Beira Baixa) [er-mah-REH-loo] *see* QUEIJO AMARELO DA BEIRA BAIXA

âme, l' [LAAHM] *Âme* is French for "soul," and in the cheese world *l'âme* describes the characteristic chalky center of soft-ripened cheeses like CHAOURCE and COULOMMIERS.

American cheese *see* PROCESS(ED) CHEESES

American cheeses *see* Cheeses by Country of Origin, page 516

ammoniated; ammoniacal [uh-MOH-nee-ay-ted; uh-MOH-nee-uh-kal] *see* Glossary of Cheese Descriptors, page 493

anaerobic bacteria *see* BACTERIA

analog cheese Another name used for both IMITATION CHEESE and SUBSTITUTE CHEESE.

Andante Dairy [ahn-DAHN-tay] *see* NOCTURNE

añejo enchilado [ah-NYAY-hoh en-chee-LAH-doh] *see* ENCHILADO

annatto [uh-NAH-toh] A flavorless coloring agent used in cheesemaking to tint cheeses like CHEDDAR an orangey color. It comes from the flavorless red-orange pulp that covers the seeds of the achiote (or annatto) tree, widely grown in South America.

Anthotiro; Anthotyro [ahn-THOH-tee-roh] *see* MIZITHRA

Antigo Cheese Company *see* PARMESAN

AOC Abbreviation for APPELLATION D'ORIGINE CONTRÔLÉE (AOC), France's system of standards for various products such as cheese and wine.

AOP *see* PROTECTED DESIGNATION OF ORIGIN

à point [ah PWAN] *see* Glossary of Cheese Descriptors, page 494

Appellation d'Origine Contrôlée (AOC; A.O.C.) [ah-pehl-lah-SYAW*N* daw-ree-ZHEEN kaw*n*-troh-LAY] French for "controlled designation of origin," Appellation d'Origine Contrôlée is France's legal system of standards for cheeses, dairy and farmstead products, *eaux de vie,* and wines. Cheeses weren't AOC classified until 1979, and to date there are only forty French cheeses (out of perhaps six hundred; no one knows for sure) that have met the stringent standards. The four main criteria for AOC cheeses are (1) The cheese's origin (including milk, production, and at least partial RIPENING) must be from a geographically precise region (municipality, district, etc.); (2) Cheese production must adhere to strictly defined, high-quality methods that have been handed down over the centuries; (3) The characteristics of each cheese type (size, rind, texture, minimum fat content, and so on) are specifically defined and must be precisely adhered to; and (4) Manufacturers must submit to inspections by a control commission (government representatives) to guarantee product authenticity and quality. AOC cheeses are easily recognizable by a distinct trademark on the rind or on the cheese label. Switzerland has also adopted an AOC system for its name-controlled cheeses. In 1992, the European Union approved protected name standards for cheeses produced by member countries. Such cheeses can be classified as either PROTECTED DESIGNATION OF ORIGIN (PDO) or PROTECTED GEOGRAPHICAL INDICATION (PGI). Countries may use these new designations with cheeses (and other products) that qualify.

Appellation d'Origine Protégé [ah-pehl-lah-SYAW*N* daw-ree-ZHEEN proh-tayzh-AY] *see* PROTECTED DESIGNATION OF ORIGIN

Appenzeller [AP-pent-tsehl-ler]

Origin	Switzerland (Appenzell, Saint Gallen)
Milk	Unpasteurized and pasteurized cow's
Type	SEMIHARD to HARD; PRESSED COOKED; NATURAL RIND; FARMSTEAD and COOPERATIVE
Appearance	11- to 26-pound wheels; rind is hard and pale yellow to orange-brown; interior is ivory to pale yellow with a scattering of irregularly sized EYES
Texture	Smooth, dense, firm, and supple
Flavor	Spicy, flowery, smoky, fruity, and tangy, becoming spicier and more piquant with age

It's believed that Appenzeller dates back to Charlemagne's time and was considered so valuable during the eighth and ninth centuries that it was used as currency. The first written mention of Appenzeller dates back to 1282. The name goes back to the eleventh century, when the monastery at St. Gallen established the parish of Abbacella ("abbot's cell"), the area encompassing today's Appenzell cantons. Appenzeller is produced in eastern Switzerland throughout the cantons of Appenzell Innerrhoden and Appenzell Ausserrhoden and in parts of Thurgau and Saint Gallen. Out of over 70 dairies, only 3 make this cheese with raw milk—the rest use pasteurized. Appenzeller's distinctive aroma and flavor are in great part the result of being initially soaked in *sulz*, a mixture that can include wine, cider, yeast, herbs, spices, and salt—every cheesemaker has a different recipe, some of which can include as many as 20 ingredients. During RIPENING each Appenzeller wheel receives regular brushings with this mixture. This cheese is marketed at 3 different ripening levels: **Classic** (silver label) is ripened for 3 to 4 months, **Surchoix** (gold label) for 4 to 6 months, and **Extra** (black and

A

gold label) for at least 6 months. Appenzeller's FAT CONTENT is at least 48 percent. Reduced-fat versions have a minimum fat content of about 18 percent. They're called *Appenzeller ¼-Fat Mild* (silver and green label) and *Appenzeller ¼-Fat Mature* (silver and brown label), the latter being ripened for 6 to 8 months. At this writing, Swiss producers are still arguing over regulations for protecting the name *Appenzeller,* with some wanting to allow pasteurized-milk cheeses to use the name and traditionalists revolting against that sacrilege.

Arab cheeses *see* Cheeses by Country of Origin, page 508

Ardi-Gasna [ahr-dee GAHZ-nah]

Origin	France (Aquitaine)
Milk	Unpasteurized sheep's
Type	SEMIHARD to HARD; PRESSED UNCOOKED; NATURAL RIND; FARMSTEAD
Appearance	Rounded 6½- to 11-pound wheels; rind is hard and pitted, the color brownish yellow with white and gray mold; interior is pale ivory-yellow
Texture	Ranges from smooth and supple when young to hard and grainy for older cheeses
Flavor	Rich, nutty, and slightly caramelized, becoming tangier with age

Ardi-Gasna has been made for centuries in southwestern France's Basque country. It's similar to the APPELLATION D'ORIGINE CONTRÔLÉE (AOC) cheeses ABBAYE DE BELLOC and OSSAU-IRATY, which are made with sheep's milk in this same area. Ardi-Gasna is classically produced with unpasteurized milk in a farmstead tradition. It's RIPENED from 2 to 3 months to as long as 2 years.

This cheese has a FAT CONTENT of about 50 percent. Spring and summer cheeses are considered best. This cheese is sometimes called *Iraty,* which can be confusing as Ossau-Iraty is also shortened to that name.

A

Ardrahan [AHR-dran]

Origin	Ireland (Cork)
Milk	Pasteurized cow's
Type	SEMISOFT; PRESSED UNCOOKED; WASHED RIND; FARMSTEAD
Appearance	11-ounce and 2¼-pound wheels; rind is moist and beige to orangey gold in color; interior is ivory to light gold with a small scattering of EYES
Texture	Smooth, creamy, and supple
Flavor	Buttery, savory, mushroomy, and nutty

A highly esteemed cheese made by Mary Burns and her son Gerald on their family farm in Duhallow in northwestern county Cork. Although Ardrahan was not produced until 1983, its beginnings date back to 1925, when Mary's future father-in-law, Eugene Burns, Sr., established the superior Ardrahan farm herd by buying the best pedigreed Friesian cattle he could find in the United Kingdom. Today's herd is comprised of descendants of that noble beginning. Ardrahan is produced with pasteurized milk and uses vegetarian RENNET. It's washed with BRINE and turned frequently during its 4- to 8-week RIPENING period. The end result is a pungent, flavorful cheese similar to LIVAROT or MUNSTER.

Argentinean cheeses *see* Cheeses by Country of Origin, page 508

Armada *see* COLOSTURM

A

Armenian string cheese *see* STRING CHEESE

aroma *see* Glossary of Cheese Descriptors, page 494

aromatic *see* Glossary of Cheese Descriptors, page 494

artificial rinds Any rind that isn't intrinsic to the cheese itself. Such
rinds might include WAX, such as is commonly found on EDAM.
Some goat cheeses are coated with a layer of ASH (in which case
they're called *CENDRE*) or herbs; some cheeses are wrapped in
leaves or bark. *See also* RIND.

artisan (artisanal) cheeses [AR-tih-zen] This term implies that a
cheese is primarily handmade and produced in small batches by
traditional, nonmechanical methods. High-quality ingredients
and attention to detail and excellence limit the quantities of
artisan cheese and, naturally, increase the price. Unlike
FARMSTEAD CHEESES, artisan cheeses can be made with milk
from other farms, although many artisan cheesemakers use
only their own animals for milk. Any type of milk may be
used, and artisan cheeses may also include flavorings.

Arzúa Ulloa (DO) [ar-THU-ah OOL-lyoh-ah]

Origin	Spain (Galicia)
Milk	Pasteurized cow's
Type	SEMISOFT TO SEMIHARD; PRESSED UNCOOKED; NATURAL RIND; FARMSTEAD and FACTORY
Appearance	1- to 5-pound wheels, though the 2-pound size is the most common; rind is pale golden, smooth, and waxy; interior is ivory colored with a scattering of EYES

| Texture | Creamy and smooth, firming as it ages |
| Flavor | Mild, tangy, and slightly salty |

One of the traditional and most popular of the Galician cheeses, Arzúa Ulloa is DENOMINACIÓN DE ORIGEN PROTEGIDA (DO) regulated and can be made only in the Coruña and Lugo provinces. The milk must come from specific breeds—Alpine, Blond Galician, Friesian, and Spanish Brown. Arzúa Ulloa is brined (*see* SALTING) and RIPENED for a minimum of 15 days and up to 4 months for "cured" versions. This cheese is also called *Queso de Ulla, Queso de Ulloa,* and *Queso Gallego.* It has a FAT CONTENT of 45 percent.

asadero [ah-sah-DEH-roh]

Origin	Mexico
Milk	Pasteurized cow's
Type	SEMISOFT; PRESSED UNCOOKED; PASTA FILATA; NATURAL RIND; FACTORY
Appearance	This cheese can weigh from 8 ounces to 11 pounds and comes in various sizes and shapes including that of braids, balls, and loaves; rind is thin, smooth, glossy, and pale yellow; interior is off-white with a scattering of EYES
Texture	Firm and smooth
Flavor	Delicate, buttery, and mildly tangy

Asadero is made by the PASTA FILATA process, whereby the CURD is immersed in hot WHEY or water and continually stretched until it reaches the pliability necessary to form it into the desired shape. It has good melting properties and more flavor than many of the blander Mexican cheeses, which makes it popular for baked dishes and quesadillas. Asadero is also sometimes referred to as *Oaxaca,* after the Mexican state where it originated.

ash One of the many coatings used for cheeses (*see* RIND). Traditionally, ash comes from burned grapevines and roots. Today, however, ash is commonly a powdered mix of charcoal and salt. Vegetable ash is simply comprised of dried vegetables that have been reduced to ash. Ash coatings have long been used by cheesemakers to protect and dry a cheese's exterior, as well as promote RIPENING. Today ash is used in some cheeses as a stylish accent, such as the thin layer in the center of HUMBOLDT FOG.

Asiago (DOC; PDO) [ah-SYAH-goh]

Origin	Italy (Veneto)
Milk	Unpasteurized or pasteurized cow's
Type	SEMISOFT to HARD; PRESSED COOKED; NATURAL RIND; ARTISAN, COOPERATIVE and FACTORY
Appearance	18- to 33-pound wheels; rinds range from straw colored and elastic to brownish gray and hard, contingent on age; interiors range from white to dark yellow (depending on age) with small to medium EYES
Texture	Ranges from smooth and supple for young examples to hard and grainy for older cheeses
Flavor	Younger versions have a blander, slightly sweet, milky flavor, whereas aged versions are full flavored, sharp, and pungent

This cheese takes its name from *l'Altopiano di Asiago* ("the Asiago Plateau"), which is located in the foothills of Italy's Veneto region. Cheese has been made in this area for over a thousand years, originally from sheep's milk (when it was called *Pecorino*

di Asiago), but now from cow's milk. Asiago's PROTECTED DES-
IGNATION OF ORIGIN (PDO)—approved area of production encompasses areas around many towns and villages in the provinces
of Padua, Treviso, and Vicenza in the Veneto region and the
Trento province in the Trentino Alto Adige region. Two types
of PDO cheese are made—Asiago d'Allevo and Asiago Pressato.
Asiago d'Allevo is made from unpasteurized, partially skimmed
milk and may be either dipped into a brine solution or dry salted
(*see* SALTING). It's matured to create different styles—*mezzano*
(aged for at least 3 months), *vecchio* (aged for roughly 9 months),
and *stravecchio* (aged for up to 2 years). Less mature cheeses are
semisoft in texture, whereas aged versions can be very hard. As
the cheese matures, the color turns from white to straw to dark
yellow and amber. The fat content of Asiago d'Allevo is at least
34 percent. **Asiago Pressato** is made from pasteurized whole
milk and has a higher fat content (minimum 44 percent). It's
aged for only about a month, which produces a softer, blander
cheese. **American Asiago** is made in three types—fresh, medium, and aged (also called *old*). All three are produced similarly except for milk type and aging. Fresh, a soft cheese, is
made from whole milk, is aged for 2 to 4 months, and has a fat
content of not less than 50 percent. **Medium** uses slightly
skimmed milk, is aged for at least 6 months, and has a fat
content of not less than 45 percent. **Aged** uses more heavily
skimmed milk, is ripened for at least 1 year, and has a fat content of not less than 42 percent. The latter is a hard cheese used
for grating.

Aspenhurst *see* LEICESTER

assertive *see* Glossary of Cheese Descriptors, page 494

astringent *see* Glossary of Cheese Descriptors, page 494

au lait cru [oh lay KROO] French for "with raw milk," specifying cheeses made with unpasteurized (raw) MILK. *See also* PASTEUR-IZATION.

Australian cheeses *see* Cheeses by Country of Origin, page 508

Austrian cheeses *see* Cheeses by Country of Origin, page 508

Autumn Oak *see* VERMONT BREBIS

Azeitão [ah-zhey-TAWN (TER*N*)] *see* QUEIJO DE AZEITÃO

B

baby A general term for cheese formed into small WHEELS or cylinders.

Baby Swiss *see* SWISS CHEESE

> **A**ge is not important unless you are a cheese.
> —Helen Hayes, actress, in the play *NEW WOMAN*

bacteria In general, bacteria are freely circulating microscopic organisms that can produce positive or negative consequences. Among the friendly bacteria are those that produce LACTIC ACID, either naturally or through the addition of a STARTER. Such bacteria contribute to a cheese's aging and flavor. **Aerobic bacteria** are microorganisms that live in the presence of oxygen; **anaerobic bacteria** live in the absence of it. Some of the bacteria used in cheese-making are *Propionibacterium shermanii* (which contributes to flavor and EYE formation in SWISS CHEESES; *Lactobacillus bugaricus, Lactobacillus lactis, Lactobacillus helveticus, Streptococcus durans,* and *Streptococcus faecalis,* which supply acid and flavor; and *Streptococcus thermophilus, Streptococcus lactis,* and *Streptococcus cremoris,* all of which contribute acid. *See also* MOLD.

bacterial culture *see* STARTER

bacterial-ripened cheeses *see* SOFT-RIPENED CHEESES

bakers' cheese *see* COTTAGE CHEESE

bandaging; bandaged In the cheese world, bandaging refers to lining cheese molds or hoops with CHEESECLOTH or MUSLIN. After the CURDS are added to the mold, the fabric is folded over the top of the cheese. Bandaging, also called CLOTH-WRAPPED, protects the cheese from drying out and helps it retain its shape. It is not typically removed until the cheese has ripened fully (*see* RIPENING). *See also* MOLDING.

Banon; Banon (AOC) [bah-NAW*N*]

Origin	France (Provence)
Milk	Unpasteurized and pasteurized cow's, goat's, and/or sheep's
Type	SOFT TO SEMISOFT; MOLDED UNCOOKED; NATURAL RIND; ARTISAN and FARMSTEAD
Appearance	3½- to 4¾-ounce rounds wrapped in chestnut leaves; thin rind is wrinkled, off-white, and

B

develops light blue and gray molds as it ripens;
interior is white

Texture   Firm and crumbly, becoming soft and creamy
with ripening

Flavor   Milky, lightly tangy, and savory with nutty traits;
becomes more complex with age

Named after a town in northern Provence, Banon has been made in this area since the Romans occupied it. In fact, Roman emperor Antoninus Pius is said to have died from eating so much Banon cheese. APPELLATION D'ORIGINE CONTRÔLÉE (AOC) regulations require that Banon be made with unpasteurized goat's milk and wrapped in chestnut leaves that have been soaked in MARC, white wine, or vinegar water. The leaves are tied around the cheese with raffia. This chestnut-leaf style is also called *Banon à la Feuille.* Other versions are **Banon Herbes de Provence** (also called *Tomme à l'Ancienne*), which is seasoned with local herbs, and **Banon Poivre,** which is sprinkled with black pepper. Banon cheeses are typically ripened for 2 to 3 weeks but sometimes for up to 2 months. The FAT CONTENT is about 45 percent. Because AOC versions of Banon are made with unpasteurized milk and are RIPENED for less than 60 days, they cannot be imported into the United States at this writing (*see* UNPASTEURIZED MILK/IMPORTED CHEESE DILEMMA). Non-AOC versions— made from pasteurized cow's, goat's, or sheep's milk or blends of these milks—continue to be exported to the United States.

barnyardy; barny *see* Glossary of Cheese Descriptors, page 494

barrel A 500-pound barrel of cheese (usually COLBY or CHEDDAR) produced for wholesale distribution, typically for the purpose of being processed further, as for shredded cheese. To make barrel cheese, the CURDS are poured into a film-lined barrel and the WHEY is removed by suction before the barrel is sealed. *See also* CHEESE SIZES AND SHAPES.

B

basket cheese A general term for any of various white, mild cheeses that are formed in a basket. Such cheeses are typically SOFT to SEMISOFT (depending on how much WHEY is drained off) and are distinctively marked with the imprint of the basket weave.

Batzos (PDO) [BAHD-sohss]

Origin	Greece
Milk	Unpasteurized sheep's and/or goat's
Type	SEMIHARD to HARD; MOLDED UNCOOKED; FARMSTEAD and FACTORY
Appearance	Chunks or squares packed in brine; exterior is rindless and off-white in color; interior is off-white and replete with small EYES
Texture	Firm, compact, and dense
Flavor	Salty, piquant, and slightly sour

This PROTECTED DESIGNATION OF ORIGIN (PDO) cheese may be produced only in the areas of Thessaly and western and central Macedonia from sheep and goat breeds in those regions. Batzos was once the by-product of MANOURI, but the latter is now primarily a WHEY-based cheese, so the manufacture of Batzos is no longer dependent on it. In fact, some Manouri is produced from the high-fat goat's milk whey obtained during the production of Batzos. The cut CURD for Batzos is drained in cheesecloth bags in cool rooms (about 60°F) for up to 2 days. The cheese is then sliced into slabs and dry-salted (*see* SALTING) several times over 4 to 5 days. It's placed in metal containers filled with brine where it RIPENS for 2 to 3 months in a cold room.

B

Bayley Hazen Blue

Origin	United States (Vermont)
Milk	Unpasteurized cow's
Type	SEMIHARD; MOLDED UNCOOKED; BLUE-VEINED; NATURAL RIND; FARMSTEAD
Appearance	6- to 7-pound and 12- to 14-pound wheels; rind is beige to golden tan with a thin layer of white mold; interior is ivory with bluish green veins and crevices—older versions are pale yellow
Texture	Firm, somewhat dry, and crumbly
Flavor	Complex array of rich, creamy, and savory flavors nuanced with anise, nuts, and grasses

This blue cheese is named after the 54-mile-long Bayley-Hazen Road, built in the 1770s in northern Vermont to assist with the American Revolution against the British. The road was never used militarily, but it did allow the area to be developed by settlers. Bayley Hazen Blue is produced by the Kehler families at their **Jasper Hill Farm**, located in Greensboro in northeastern Vermont. Mateo and Andy Keyler and their wives, Victoria and Angela, raise a small herd of registered Ayrshire cows that produce the milk for their farmstead cheeses. Bayley Hazen Blue is made from the morning milking, which has a lower FAT CONTENT, and CONSTANT BLISS is produced from the evening milk. Both cheeses have won awards at the annual American Cheese Society competition. Bayley Hazen Blue has *Penicillium roqueforti* (the same mold used for GORGONZOLA, ROQUEFORT, and STILTON) added to the milk during production. It's RIPENED for 4 to 6 months.

Beacon Fell Traditional Lancashire (PDO) *see* LANCASHIRE

Beaufort (AOC; PDO) [boh-FOR]

Origin	France (Savoie)
Milk	Unpasteurized cow's
Type	HARD; PRESSED COOKED; NATURAL RIND; FARMSTEAD, ARTISAN, COOPERATIVE, and some MOUNTAIN
Appearance	Round 40- to 150-pound wheels with concave sides; rind is thin, hard, slightly sticky, and golden brown in color; interior is off-white to pale yellow, developing small holes and cracks with age
Texture	Firm and supple
Flavor	Mild, buttery, fruity, and nutty, becoming more complex as it ages

Hailing from Beaufort, a small town in the *département* of Savoie in France's alpine region, this cheese was famous in ancient Roman times and has remained popular over the centuries. Many think Beaufort is the best of the GRUYÈRE-style cheeses. According to APPELLATION D'ORIGINE CONTRÔLÉE (AOC) rules, it can be made only in the Savoie and Haute-Savoie *départements* in the Rhône-Alpes region of eastern France. In addition to the regular Beaufort there is a **Beaufort d'Été** ("from summer"), which is made from June to October. There's also the highly popular **Beaufort d'Alpage** ("of mountain pasture"), which is made only in the summer in mountain chalets. The milk comes from the Tarentaise cows that graze at altitudes of 6,000 feet or more. Beaufort cheeses are brined (*see* SALTING) for about a day and aged for a minimum of 4 months, during which time

B

they are frequently brushed with brine. They have a FAT CONTENT of approximately 48 percent.

Beemster [BEEM-ster] *see* GOUDA

Beenleigh Blue [BEEN-lay; BEEN-lee]

Origin	England (Devon)
Milk	Pasteurized sheep's
Type	SEMISOFT; MOLDED UNCOOKED; BLUE–VEINED; NATURAL RIND; ARTISAN
Appearance	6- to 8-pound wheels; rind is rough, moist, slightly sticky, and ivory colored with splotches of blue, gray, and green molds; interior is ivory with blue-gray-green veining and a scattering of irregular EYES
Texture	Soft, moist, and creamy, yet crumbly
Flavor	Rich, savory, spicy, and slightly tangy with a hint of butterscotch

Robin Congdon and Sarie Cooper, partners at Ticklemore Cheese, produce this award-winning sheep's milk blue, which is only one of three made in England. Although created in a fashion similar to ROQUEFORT, Beenleigh Blue isn't as salty or powerful as that cheese, and its mellower flavor profile has become extremely popular. Beenleigh Blue is available seasonally because the sheep are milked only from March through July. It's RIPENED for 4 to 8 months and has a FAT CONTENT of 45 to 50 percent.

beer cheese *see* BIERKÄSE

Beer Käse; Beer Kaese [BEER-ki-zer (-kah-zeh)] *see* BIERKÄSE

B

beestings *see* COLOSTRUM

Belgian Cheeses *see* Cheeses by Country of Origin, page 508

Bella Sorella [BEH-lah soh-REHL-lah] *see* SERENA

Bellelay [behl-leh-LAY] *see* TÊTE DE MOINE

Bellwether Farms *see* CARMODY; CRESCENZA; RICOTTA; SAN ANDREAS

Bel Paese [BELL pah-AY-zeh]

Origin	Italy (Lombardy)
Milk	Pasteurized cow's
Type	SEMISOFT to SEMIHARD; PRESSED UNCOOKED; NATURAL RIND; FACTORY
Appearance	Thick, 4½- to 6-pound wheels; rind is thin, pale yellow, and covered with wax; interior is pale yellow with small irregular EYES
Texture	Supple, smooth, and firm
Flavor	Mild, delicate, buttery, and slightly tangy

Bel Paese ("beautiful country") is a mild Italian cheese created in 1906 by cheesemaker and entrepreneur Egidio Galbani, founder of The Galbani Group of dairies. Galbani took the name from the book *Bel Paese,* written by his friend Abbot Stopani, who undoubtedly was inspired by the originator of the phrase, fourteenth-century master poet Dante. Originally made in Melzo, a small town outside of Milan, Bel Paese's wildly popular success enabled the company to establish many other cheese factories in Italy as well as one in the United States. The wrappers on U.S. versions show a map of the Americas, whereas the Italian-produced cheeses show a map of Italy. Bel Paese is usually RIPENED for 4 to

B

8 weeks and has a FAT CONTENT of 45 to 50 percent. In addition to the plain version, there's one flavored with sun-dried tomatoes and basil.

Bergkäse [BEHRK-ki-zer (-kah-zeh)] German and Austrian for "mountain cheese," referring to cheeses made throughout the Alps. *See also* ALLGÄUER BERGKÄSE; TIROLER BERGKÄSE; VORARL-BERGER BERGKÄSE.

Berkswell [BERKS-well]

Origin	England (Warwickshire)
Milk	Unpasteurized sheep's
Type	HARD; PRESSED COOKED; NATURAL RIND; FARMSTEAD
Appearance	5- to 9-pound wheels; rind is reddish gold to reddish brown with markings from basket mold; interior is light to deep gold, depending on age
Texture	Very dense and compact yet supple when young, becoming harder and granular in older versions
Flavor	Rich, sweet, nutty, and savory with hints of caramel and pineapple

Berkswell is made on Stephen Fletcher's farm close to the village of Berkswell near Coventry in Warwickshire. Since the late 1980s, when the Fletchers shifted from raising cows to raising sheep and began making Berkswell, they've won numerous awards for their cheese. Today, they have over 400 Friesian sheep and continue to expand the flock. Berkswell, which is made with vegetarian REN-NET, is RIPENED for 6 to 9 months prior to release for sale. It has a FAT CONTENT of about 45 percent.

Bermuda Triangle

Origin	United States (California)
Milk	Pasteurized goat's
Type	SEMISOFT; MOLDED UNCOOKED; BLOOMY RIND; ARTISAN
Appearance	1-pound triangular log; rind is ash–coated and topped with a velvety thick layer of white mold; interior is cream colored
Texture	Firm yet smooth, creamy, and sometimes crumbly near the center, becoming slightly runny near the rind
Flavor	Mild, earthy, and slightly tangy, becoming stronger and more complex with age

Yet another winner from **Cypress Grove Chèvre**, located in the lush Humboldt County town of Arcata amid the striking California redwoods. Bermuda Triangle has taken multiple gold medals over the years at the annual American Cheese Society competition. It's RIPENED for 2 weeks and has a flavor that's slightly more meaty than Cypress Grove's flagship cheese, HUMBOLDT FOG. Cypress Grove Chèvre produces a wide variety of cheeses, including fresh CHÈVRE, FROMAGE BLANC, and a goat's milk CHEDDAR. *See also* LAMB CHOPPER and MIDNIGHT MOON.

besace [beh-SAHC] French for "beggar's purse" and one of the many shapes into which CHÈVRE is formed.

bicorne [bee-KORN] French for "two horns" and one of the many shapes into which CHÈVRE is formed.

Bierkäse; Bierkaese [BEER–ki–zer (–kah–zeh)]

B

Origin	Germany; United States (Wisconsin)
Milk	Pasteurized cow's
Type	SEMISOFT to SEMIHARD; MOLDED UNCOOKED; WASHED RIND; FACTORY
Appearance	2½- to 9-pound loaves; rind is sticky, wrinkled, and pinkish orange to reddish brown in color; interior is off-white to pale yellow with numerous irregular slit-shaped EYES
Texture	Firm, elastic, and supple
Flavor	Savory, tangy, and piquant, becoming quite pungent with long ripening

Bierkäse originated in Germany and is exceedingly popular in surrounding countries such as Austria and the Czech Republic. It's also produced in Wisconsin, where it's a local favorite. There is no beer in Bierkäse; rather the name is said to derive from the German practice of dipping the cheese into beer as it's eaten. Though there are regional variations, all Bierkäses are generally similar in style and comparable to LIMBURGER. They can be made from whole, partially skimmed, or fat-free milk. Bierkäse can be RIPENED for from 6 weeks to 3 to 4 months and has a FAT CONTENT of from 15 to 50 percent, depending on the type of milk used. This cheese is known by many names, including *Bierkaese, Beer Käse, Beer Kaese, Weisslacker* (short for *Weisslacker Bierkäse*), and simply *beer cheese*.

Big Holmes

Origin	United States (Wisconsin)
Milk	Pasteurized sheep's

B

Type	SEMISOFT tO SEMIHARD; MOLDED UNCOOKED; NATURAL RIND; FARMSTEAD
Appearance	1½-pound misshapen wheels topped with cedar boughs, sumac, and juniper berries; very thin rind is off-white to beige spotted with multicolored mold intermixed with pieces of its rosemary, mint, and cedar coat; interior is off-white to ivory
Texture	Creamy, smooth, and velvety, becoming firmer with age
Flavor	Sweet, mild, creamy, herbal, and "woodsy," becoming nutty and tangy as it RIPENS

Big Holmes is produced by David and Mary Falk on their 200-acre sheep farm called **LoveTree Farmstead**, located in northern Wisconsin near Grantsburg (60 miles northeast of Minneapolis). Big Holmes is the eponym of one of the eight small lakes on the farm. The farmstead itself is named after a pair of trees that twisted together, essentially becoming one, and this "lovetree" is the symbol on LoveTree Farmstead's packaging. To protect the sheep from local predators, the Falks use guard dogs, including some Spanish ranch mastiffs, brought in from Spain because of their mellow yet protective demeanor. Big Holmes has won numerous awards over the years, including the Best Young Sheep Milk Cheese Award at the annual American Cheese Society competition. The cheese is RIPENED for 4 to 6 weeks in a fresh-air cave, which allows the north woods–scented morning fog to creep in and influence the flavor. **Little Holmes,** named after another lake on the property, is also an award winner. It's similar, but coated with peppermint flakes, ripened for about 4 weeks, and wrapped in wild nettle that's been soaked in vodka. LoveTree Farmstead also makes **Gabrielson Lake,** a natural-rind, raw cow's milk cheese that's aged a minimum of 3 months and has a nutty, fruity flavor.

Bijou [bee-ZHOO] *see* BONNE BOUCHE

Bishop Kennedy

Origin	Scotland (Perthshire)
Milk	Unpasteurized cow's
Type	SEMISOFT; MOLDED UNCOOKED; WASHED RIND; ARTISAN
Appearance	Flattened cylinders weighing about 3 pounds; rind is wrinkled, moist, and yellowish orange; interior is off-white to pale yellow
Texture	Creamy and supple, becoming thickly fluid as it RIPENS
Flavor	Complex blend of creamy, savory, spicy, and smoky

Bishop Kennedy is named after the fifteenth-century bishop who founded the United Colleges at the University of Saint Andrews. However, it's a modern cheese—created in 1992 by a French cheesemaker who assisted Howgate Cheese in developing a WASHED-RIND cheese on the order of ÉPOISSES DE BOURGOGNE or LANGRES but with a Scottish influence. And what better way to suggest Scotland than to add Scotch whisky to the wash for the rind. Bishop Kennedy is a past winner at the British Cheese Awards for the Best Scottish Cheese. It's RIPENED for 7 to 8 weeks and has a FAT CONTENT of about 45 percent.

bitter *see* Glossary of Cheese Descriptors, page 494

Bittersweet Plantation Dairy *see* CREOLE CREAM CHEESE; EVANGELINE; FLEUR-DE-LIS; FLEUR-DE-TECHE

Bitto (DOC; PDO) [BEE-toh]

Origin	Italy (Lombardy)
Milk	Unpasteurized cow's, plus 10 percent or less goat's
Type	SEMISOFT to SEMIHARD; PRESSED COOKED; NATURAL RIND; MOUNTAIN; ARTISAN
Appearance	18- to 55-pound wheels; rinds are thin and range from straw colored when young to brownish gray as they age; interiors are compact with tiny EYES and range from off-white to golden yellow, deepening in color with age
Texture	Ranges from smooth and supple to almost granular, depending on age
Flavor	Younger cheeses are mild, delicate, and slightly sweet, and aged cheeses are stronger, savory, tangy, and more aromatic

The name of this cheese comes from the Bitto River in the Sondrio province in northern Italy's Lombardy region. The word *Bitto* is derived from a Celtic word meaning "perennial." The PROTECTED DESIGNATION OF ORIGIN (PDO)–approved production area is in the Lombardy region and includes the Sondrio province (particularly an area called the *Valtellina*) and certain towns and villages in the Bergamo province, including Averara, Carona, Cusio, Foppolo, Mezzoldo, Piazzatore, Santa Brigida, and Valleve. Bitto is produced only from June through September, when cows can graze in alpine pastures. The cheese must be made at an altitude of at least 4,900 feet. A small amount of goat's milk is used for additional flavor. The cheese is handmade in copper kettles and formed in wooden molds. It's then dry-salted (*see* SALTING) for about 3 weeks. Initial aging

B

takes place in mountain huts (*caseras*). The cheeses are then taken to the factories farther down in the valley for their final aging. Although the minimum aging requirement is 70 days, top-quality Bitto is aged for at least 1 to 2 years, some as long as 10 years. This cheese has a FAT CONTENT of approximately 45 percent.

Bla Castello *see* BLUE CASTELLO

Black Label Black Waxed Cheddar; Black Label Cloth-Matured Cheddar
see CHEDDAR

Blanca Bianca [BLAHN-kah bee-AHN-kah]

Origin	United States (Texas)
Milk	Unpasteurized cow's
Type	SOFT to SEMISOFT; MOLDED UNCOOKED; WASHED RIND; ARTISAN
Appearance	1½-pound wheel; rind is very thin and golden with a pinkish tinge; interior is cream colored
Texture	Soft, supple, and moist
Flavor	Elegant, yeasty, and earthy, with notes of wine and nuts; aged cheeses become more pungent but not strong

This cheese was created in 2003 by Paula Lambert, master cheesemaker and founder of the famous **Mozzarella Company**. Lambert has a broad line of cheeses that includes everything from classics like fresh MOZZARELLA, RICOTTA, and QUESO BLANCO to originals such as DEEP ELLUM BLUE, HOJA SANTA, and MONTASIO FESTIVO. Blanca Bianca is Lambert's only raw-milk offering and only washed-rind cheese. This handmade gem is made with milk from nearby dairies and RIPENED for a minimum of 2 months, during which time the cheeses are bathed daily with white wine. Blanca Bianca's slightly pungent aroma belies its elegant flavor. The name references the fact that this white cheese is washed with white wine—white on white, with the Spanish *blanca* ("white") playing off the Italian *bianca,* which also means "white."

bleu [BLEUH] French for "blue," used in the cheese world to refer to the many varieties of BLUE-VEINED CHEESE.

Bleu d'Auvergne (AOC; PDO) [bleuh doh-VEHRN]

Origin	France (Auvergne)
Milk	Unpasteurized or pasteurized cow's
Type	SEMIHARD; MOLDED UNCOOKED; BLUE-VEINED; NATURAL RIND; COOPERATIVE and FACTORY
Appearance	Either 12-ounce to 2-pound or 4½- to 6½-pound foil-wrapped wheels; rind is thin, moist, and pale yellow to gold with splotches of blue-green mold, which turns reddish orange with age; interior is white to ivory with plentiful blue-green veins scattered throughout
Texture	Moist, creamy, and slightly crumbly
Flavor	Mild and buttery with a light spiciness that intensifies as it ages

This cheese was discovered by accident in the mid-1800s in Laqueuille, a small town in the mountainous region of Auvergne in south-central France. Once the technique for creating it was replicated, cheesemakers around the region began producing what is now known as *Bleu d'Auvergne.* APPELLATION D'ORIGINE CONTRÔLÉE (AOC) regulations state that this cheese can be made only in certain *départements* in the following regions: Auvergne,

B

Midi-Pyrénées, Limousin, and Languedoc-Roussillon. Today's production methods include inoculating the milk with *Penicillium roqueforti,* the same mold used for producing ROQUEFORT, GORGONZOLA, and STILTON. Once the cheese has formed, thick needles are used to pierce it, first on one side, then, several days later, on the other. This allows air to access the interior, which encourages mold growth. Small wheels of Bleu d'Auvergne are aged for at least 2 weeks, larger wheels for a minimum of 4 weeks. It has a FAT CONTENT of about 50 percent.

Bleu d'Aveyron [bleuh dah-vay-RAWN) *see* BLEU DES CAUSSES

Bleu de Bresse [bleuh deuh BRESS]

Origin	France (Rhône-Alpes, Burgundy)
Milk	Pasteurized cow's
Type	SOFT; BLUE-VEINED; MOLDED UNCOOKED; BLOOMY RIND; FACTORY
Appearance	5-ounce to 4-pound wheels; rind is thin and beige in color with a velvety coating of white mold—perfectly aged versions will have patches of beige to gray mold; interior is pale yellow with patches of blue-green mold
Texture	Soft, smooth, and creamy
Flavor	Mild, buttery, slightly tangy

The name of this cheese comes from Bresse, a former French province that encompassed areas that are now part of the *départements* of Saône-et-Loire, in the Burgundy region, and Ain, in the Rhône-Alpes region. Bleu de Bresse was created in the 1950s to contend with the popularity of Italy's GORGONZOLA, though it's a milder version of the full-flavored Italian blue cheese. Bleu de Bresse is made like a pasteurized-milk

BRIE, only the CURDS are injected with *PENICILLIUM* spores, which results in a mild and creamy Brie-style cheese with a blue-cheese tang. It's RIPENED for from 2 to 4 weeks and has a FAT CONTENT of about 55 percent. This cheese has been a popular choice in the United States (where it's named *Bresse Bleu*) since the French established a production plant in southeastern Wisconsin. The U.S. version is blander than the original.

B

Bleu de Gex [bleuh deuh ZHEH; ZHEX] *see* BLEU DU HAUT-JURA

Bleu des Causses (AOC; PDO) [bleuh day KOHS]

Origin	France (Midi-Pyrénées)
Milk	Unpasteurized cow's
Type	SEMISOFT; MOLDED UNCOOKED; BLUE-VEINED; NATURAL RIND; COOPERATIVE
Appearance	5- to 6½-pound foil-wrapped wheels; rind is thin, moist, and light reddish gold with splotches of blue-green MOLD; interior is ivory with blue-gray EYES generously distributed throughout
Texture	Creamy, moist, and firm
Flavor	Creamy with a zesty spiciness that intensifies as it ages

Bleu des Causses dates back to ancient Roman times—about the same time frame as ROQUEFORT, which is made in the same area. Roquefort is made from sheep's milk, while Bleu des Causses is made from cow's milk. The cheese gets its name from the area in which it's made—the Causses, rocky limestone plateaus in south-central France's Midi-Pyrénées region. This area is full of natural caves where cool, moist air

B

circulates—the perfect breeding ground for the beneficial molds that make Bleu des Causses what it is. Though this cheese was originally called **Bleu d'Aveyron,** after one of the region's *départements,* the name was changed in the 1930s to cover its larger area of production. According to APPELLATION D'ORIGINE CONTRÔLÉE (AOC) rules, Bleu des Causses can be made only in specific *départements* in the Midi-Pyrénées and Languedoc-Roussillon regions. Once the CURDS have been inoculated with *Penicillium roqueforti,* they're MOLDED and allowed to drain without PRESSING. The cheese is then salted and pierced with thick needles to help the mold indigenous to the region's limestone caves grow. Bleu des Causses is aged for a minimum of 70 days and generally for 3 to 6 months. It has a FAT CONTENT of about 45 percent.

Bleu de Septmoncel [bleuh deuh sept-moan-SELL] *see* BLEU DU HAUT-JURA

Bleu du Haut-Jura (AOC; PDO) [bleuh doo oh-zhew-RAH]; **Bleu de Gex** [bleuh deu ZHEH]; **Bleu de Septmoncel** [bleuh deu sept-moan-SELL]

Origin	France (Rhône-Alpes and France-Comté)
Milk	Unpasteurized cow's
Type	SEMISOFT; MOLDED UNCOOKED; BLUE-VEINED; NATURAL RIND; FARMSTEAD and COOPERATIVE
Appearance	16½-pound relatively flat wheels; rind is thin and coated with dry, powdery beige and gray molds with occasional red splotches; interior is ivory, marbled with blue-green veins
Texture	Moist and creamy
Flavor	Mild and slightly pungent with nuances of nuts and fruit

These cheeses date back to the fourteenth century. Bleu du Haut-Jura is the official APPELLATION D'ORIGINE CONTRÔLÉE (AOC) name, but cheeses made in this area are also called *Bleu de Septmoncel* or *Bleu de Gex,* after two neighboring towns in the region. The milk comes from Montbéliard cows that graze in the high mountain pastures of the Haut-Jura. Although Bleu de Septmoncel and Bleu de Gex were once slightly different, today they are essentially the same as Bleu du Haut-Jura. No longer do the cheeses rely on mold derived from wildflowers to inoculate the milk. Today the milk is inoculated with *Penicillium glaucum,* which starts the beneficial mold growth. The CURDS are poured into molds and drained without pressing. Once the cheese begins to form, it's frequently rubbed with salt for several days. During RIPENING, needles are inserted into the cheese to create air passages to help interior mold growth. Bleu du Haut-Jura is aged for a minimum of 3 weeks, but 2 to 4 months is more common. It has a FAT CONTENT of about 50 percent.

Bleu du Vercors-Sassenage (AOC; PDO) [bleuh doo vehr-kor sah-seuh-NAZH]

Origin	France (Rhône-Alpes)
Milk	Unpasteurized cow's
Type	SEMISOFT; MOLDED UNCOOKED; BLUE-VEINED; NATURAL RIND; MOUNTAIN FARMSTEAD, and COOPERATIVE
Appearance	9- to 10-pound wheels; rind is thin and coated with dry, powdery white mold with occasional orange splotches; interior is ivory marbled with blue-green veins
Texture	Moist and creamy
Flavor	Mild with nuances of nuts and fruit

B

Although this cheese dates back to at least the fourteenth century, it was not granted APPELLATION D'ORIGINE CONTRÔLÉE (AOC) status until 1998. It takes its name from the Vercors Massif, a mountainous area featuring limestone plateaus lying east of the Rhône Valley in eastern France. Sassenage, a town near Grenoble, is historically linked to this cheese, although most of the production takes place higher in the mountains. The only cattle breeds that can be used for milk are Abondance, Montbéliard, and Villard. The cows must feed on fodder grown in the AOC-defined area. The milk, which can be whole or partially skimmed, is inoculated with *Penicillium roqueforti* to establish the beneficial mold that creates blue cheese. When the cheese begins to set, it's frequently rubbed with salt for several days. It must be AGED for a minimum of 3 weeks, but 2 to 3 months is more common. During aging, needles are inserted into the cheese to create air passages to help the mold grow in the interior. This cheese has a FAT CONTENT of about 45 percent.

blind *see* Glossary of Cheese Descriptors, page 495

block A size descriptor for blocks of cheese (most commonly weighing 40 pounds) produced for wholesale distribution. Block cheese is a natural cheese that's produced in a variety of styles, such as CHEDDAR, JACK, and so on. *See also* CHEESE SIZES AND SHAPES.

Block's Landing *see* DUTCH FARMSTEAD

bloomy rind; bloomy-rind cheeses An edible downy coating found on SOFT-RIPENED CHEESES such as BRIE and CAMEMBERT. This rind is a result of the cheese having been either coated with a bacterial spray (typically *Penicillium candidum*) or exposed to molds naturally. The color of bloomy rind (also called *flowery rind*) can range from white to off-white with patches ranging in color from beige to golden to red; the coloration typically occurs on cheeses with more RIPENING.

Blü [BLOO] *see* COLOROUGE

Blue Castello [Kas-TEHL-loh]

Origin	Denmark
Milk	Pasteurized cow's
Type	SEMISOFT; MOLDED UNCOOKED; BLUE-VEINED; NATURAL RIND; FACTORY
Appearance	2-pound wheel, sometimes half wheels, wrapped in foil; rind is moist with blue and white molds when the cheese is young, developing reddish brown mold as it ages; interior is white to ivory with blue streaks and splotching
Texture	Moist and creamy (spreadable)
Flavor	Mild, creamy, spicy, and tangy

Blue Castello, also known as *Bla Castello,* is a popular Scandinavian blue cheese produced by Tholstrup (now owned by Arla Foods). It's patterned after GORGONZOLA but has blander flavors, and added cream boosts its FAT CONTENT to about 70 percent, taking it into the DOUBLE-CREAM category. Blue Castello is unusual in that it's inoculated with both blue and white PENICILLIUM spores, which produce a mellow blue cheese flavor but a BRIE-like texture.

Blue Cheshire *see* CHESHIRE

Blue Fade *see* CHESHIRE

B

blue mold *see* MOLD (2)

Blue Ridge Dairy Company *see* MASCARPONE

Blue Stilton *see* STILTON

blue-veined cheeses; blue cheeses; blue-mold cheeses; bleu cheeses
A family of cheeses that have interior veins and small pockets
that can range in color from dark blue to blue-green to blue-
black and everything in between. Such colorful markings are
the result of the presence of PENICILLIUM spores—either
P. glaucum, P. gorgonzola, or *P. roqueforti.* In certain circum-
stances the spores may be naturally airborne. For consistency,
however, most cheesemakers add the blue-mold strain (either
in a powder or in a liquid) to the milk or to the curds, as in
the case of some soft BRIE-style blues. In some instances, the
formed cheese is sprayed or inoculated with the mold
organisms. In general, blue-veined cheeses are made by
pouring or scooping the cut curd into cylindrical molds and
allowing them to drain naturally (without PRESSING) for a
period that can range up to 2 weeks, during which time the
molds are turned frequently. Of course there are always exceptions, and some blues, such as Blue Cheshire (see CHESHIRE),
are pressed. Once the cheese is set, the forms are removed and
the cheeses are rubbed with salt and returned to caves, cellars,
or rooms with exacting temperature and humidity controls.
The bluing in the cheese's interior doesn't happen just because
the cultures are in place—it won't occur without air to feed
the bacteria. So the cheeses are now pierced with metal
skewers (known as *NEEDLING*) so that oxygen can reach the
interior, thereby feeding the bacteria and producing the
veining. *See also* Cheeses by Type, Blue, page 535.

Blue Wensleydale *see* WENSLEYDALE

bocconcini [bohk-kohn-CHEE-nee] Small nuggets of fresh MOZZARELLA about 1 inch in diameter. Bocconcini are sold packed in water, BRINE, and sometime WHEY. They can also be found marinated in olive oil and flavorings such as herbs or red chile pepper flakes. Bocconcini are great as an hors d'oeuvre or as an addition to salads.

body *see* Glossary of Cheese Descriptors, page 495

Boerenkaas [BOH-ren-kahss] *see* GOUDA

Boeren-Leidse met Sleutels (PDO) [BOOR-en LAY-dzuh (LI-dzuh) meht SLUR-terls]

Origin	Netherlands (Zuid-Holland)
Milk	Unpasteurized cow's
Type	SEMIHARD to HARD; PRESSED COOKED; NATURAL RIND; FARMSTEAD
Appearance	6½- to 22-pound wheels; rind is reddish orange to reddish brown, sometimes covered with red plastic; interior is pale yellow to golden with seeds distributed throughout
Texture	Firm and somewhat elastic, becoming stiff and granular with age
Flavor	Nutty, creamy, and spicy flavors, dominated by cumin seeds; flavors intensify with age

Although the cheesemaking history of Boeren-Leidse met Sleutels dates back to at least the twelfth century, today this cheese is made in the traditional farmstead way by fewer than

B

two dozen member farmers around the town of Leiden in the Zuid-Holland province. Cheese from this area is also sometimes called as *Leyden cheese, Leiden cheese,* or *Leidenkaas.* However, the official PROTECTED DESIGNATION OF ORIGIN (PDO) name is Boeren Leidse met Sleutels, which translates to "Farmers' Leiden cheese with keys," the last word referring to the imprint on the rind of crossed keys, which represents Leiden's coat of arms. Only union members of the Vereniging van Boeren-Leidse Kaasmakers, founded in 1927, can use this imprint on their cheese. Boeren Leidse met Sleutels is made with the partially skimmed milk of one or two milkings (if two, they must be successive). A small amount of the CURD, called *witte bodems* ("white bottoms"), is set aside, and cumin seeds are blended with the rest. When the curd is placed in molds, the *witte bodems* are used to prevent the seeds from collecting in the rind. The cheese goes through 2 pressings—during the second the crossed keys are imprinted on the surface. The cheese is then soaked in BRINE for 5 or 6 days. The rind is usually colored orangish red with ANNATTO or coated with red plastic. Boeren Leidse met Sleutels is RIPENED anywhere from 3 months to 2 years and has a FAT CONTENT of between 30 and 40 percent.

Boilie [BOY-lee]

Origin	Ireland (Cavan)
Milk	Pasteurized cow's and goat's
Type	SOFT; FRESH; rindless; ARTISAN and FARMSTEAD
Appearance	Small rindless white balls packed in 7- to 8-ounce glass jars with sunflower oil and herbs and garlic
Texture	Delicate, soft, creamy, and spreadable
Flavor	Fresh, milky, and tangy

These cheeses are made at Ryfield Farm, which is nestled in the rolling hills above the shores of Lough Ramour, about 50 miles northwest of Dublin in county Cavan, Ireland. John and Anne Brodie began making the delicate Boilies to help improve cash flow while their CHEDDAR was aging. But the cheeses became so popular that the Brodies had to expand production. This cheese comes in two styles—the cow's milk version is made from the milk of Ryfield Farm's herd of cows; the goat's milk Boilie is produced with milk from local goat farms. These cheeses, which are hand-made in very small batches, are akin to fresh FETA but not nearly as salty. Boilie is packed in herb- and garlic-flavored sunflower oil, which allows it to retain its fresh character for 4 to 5 months. The Brodies think the flavored oil makes a great salad dressing.

bondon [baw*n*-DAWN] French for "bung" (a wine cask stopper) and one of the many shapes into which CHÈVRE is formed.

Bonne Bouche [buhn BOOSH]

Origin	United States (Vermont)
Milk	Pasteurized goat's
Type	SEMISOFT; MOLDED UNCOOKED; NATURAL RIND; ARTISAN
Appearance	4-ounce wheels; rind is thin and coated with ash and white mold, becoming wrinkled and mottled with age; interior is white to ivory
Texture	Soft, becoming creamier with age
Flavor	Delicate, floral, nutty, and tangy when young, developing stronger and more savory and complex flavors as it ages

Made by the **Vermont Butter & Cheese Company,** Bonne Bouche (French for "delicious mouthful") is patterned after

B

the Loire Valley's SELLES-SUR-CHER. Co-owner Allison Hooper spent two summers in Europe learning traditional cheesemaking methods. She and partner Bob Reese connected in 1985 when Bob was looking for someone who could make goat cheese for a chef in Stowe, Vermont. Their collaboration produced the Vermont Butter & Cheese Company, and after 20 years and several expansions their company is still going strong. Bonne Bouche—the flagship of their artisanal line—won first place for aged goat cheese at an American Cheese Society competition. This handmade cheese is RIPENED for anywhere from 7 to 45 days. Bonne Bouche is part of a triumvirate of aged pasteurized goat's milk cheeses that includes **Bijou** (French for "jewel"), a smooth, creamy cheese patterned after CROTTIN DE CHAVIGNOL, and **Coupole**—a meld of the Bijou and Bonne Bouche but milder than both. Vermont Butter & Cheese Company also makes award-winning chèvre, FROMAGE BLANC, MASCARPONE, and QUARK.

bouchon [boo-SHAWN] French for "cork" and one of the many shapes into which CHÈVRE is formed.

boule; boulette [BOOL; boo-leht] French for "ball," a popular shape for CHÈVRE, as in Boule de Lille (see MIMOLETTE).

Boule de Lille [bool deuh LEEL] *see* MIMOLETTE

Boursault [boor-SOH]

Origin	France (Île-de-France)
Milk	Unpasteurized and pasteurized cow's
Type	SEMISOFT; TRIPLE-CREAM; MOLDED UNCOOKED; BLOOMY RIND; FACTORY
Appearance	7- to 8-ounce paper-wrapped wheels; soft

	white rind that develops a downy mold as it ripens; interior is off-white to pale yellow
Texture	Soft, creamy, and moist
Flavor	Rich, creamy, sweet, and nutty

Created in the 1950s by Henri Boursault, this triple-cream cheese is made much like BRIE, with cream added to increase its FAT CONTENT to slightly over 72 percent. Boursaults are RIPENED for 2 to 8 weeks. Those with a gold label are made with raw milk and cannot be imported to the United States at this writing (*see* UNPASTEURIZED MILK/IMPORTED CHEESE DILEMMA). A silver label signifies the cheese has been made with pasteurized milk, the version that is available in the United States. Avoid Boursaults wrapped with paper that's damp and moldy.

Boursin [boor-SAN]

Origin	France (Normandy)
Milk	Pasteurized cow's
Type	SOFT; TRIPLE-CREAM; FACTORY
Appearance	3½- to 5-ounce cylinders wrapped in foil; rindless and white; interior is white flecked with bits of flavoring including herbs and pepper
Texture	Soft, smooth, moist, and creamy
Flavor	Mild, delicate, and creamy with the flavor of specific herbs that have been added

Frank Boursin created this cheese in 1957 in Normandy. Added cream places it in the triple-cream category (minimum FAT CONTENT of 72 percent), and each type of Boursin is variously flavored. The original Boursin, "Garlic & Fine Herbs," is flavored with garlic, salt, pepper, parsley, and chives. This was

B

followed by a black pepper version, one with shallots and chives, and one with figs, raisins, and nuts. The fifth and most recent addition to this cheese family is "Boursin Light Garlic & Fine Herbs," based on the original but with 78 percent less fat and 64 percent fewer calories. Needless to say, the "light" version isn't a triple-cream cheese. Although not considered a serious cheese by most aficionados, Boursin became very popular in France through the first French TV promotions ever produced for a cheese.

bouton [boo-TAWN] French for "button" and one of the many shapes into which CHÈVRE is formed.

Bra (DOC; PDO) [BRAH]

Origin	Italy (Piedmont)
Milk	Mainly unpasteurized or pasteurized cow's, but the addition of small amounts of sheep's or goat's milk is allowed
Type	SEMISOFT TO HARD; PRESSED UNCOOKED; NATURAL RIND; some MOUNTAIN, some FARMSTEAD
Appearance	13- to 18-pound wheels; rinds range from off-white in color, thin and elastic to brownish beige and hard, depending on age; interiors range from off-white to a dark yellow-orange (depending on age) and are compact with small EYES
Texture	Ranges from smooth and supple to firm, contingent on age
Flavor	Younger versions have a mild, slightly spicy, milky flavor, whereas aged versions are full flavored and pungent

This cheese takes its name from Bra, a town south of Turin in the Cuneo province in northwestern Italy's Piedmont region. Bra is made from fat-free milk and comes in three varieties, all with DENOMINAZIONE DI ORIGINE CONTROLLATA (DOC) and PROTECTED DESIGNATION OF ORIGIN (PDO) status. **Bra Tenero,** the "tender" or soft version, is aged for up to about 6 months. **Bra Duro,** the "hard" version, is aged for 1 to 2 years or longer. **Bra d'Alpeggio** is made only from the milk of cows that graze in mountain pastures during the months of June to October and is more of a handmade cheese than the others. Use of *d'Alpeggio* in the name differentiates it from the other Bra cheeses made in lower-lying areas. Bra Tenero and Bra Duro can be made in Piedmont, in the entire Cuneo province, and in the village of Villafranc Piemonte in the province of Turin. Bra d'Alpeggio can be produced in essentially the same area except that it's further restricted to towns and villages defined by Italian law as "mountain." The fat content for Bra cheeses ranges from 39 to 49 percent.

Braukäse *see* GRANQUESO

brebis [breuh-BEE] French for "ewe" (female sheep). *La brebis* is the sheep itself; the cheese is called *le brebis, fromage de brebis,* or simply *brebis.*

Bresse Bleu [bress BLEUH] *see* BLEU DE BRESSE

Brevibacterium linens [breh-vee-bak-TEER-ee-uhm] Highly desirable, friendly BACTERIA that thrive in moist settings, such as those encouraged with WASHED-RIND cheeses. Such bacteria give cheeses like BRICK and LIMBURGER their pungent aroma and flavor. Also called *red bacterium.*

brick; brick cheese

B

Origin	United States (Wisconsin)
Milk	Pasteurized cow's
Type	SEMIHARD; PRESSED UNCOOKED; WASHED RIND; FACTORY
Appearance	5- to 5½-pound loaves; rind is sticky, wrinkled, and pinkish orange to reddish brown in color; interior is off-white to pale yellow with numerous irregular EYES
Texture	Firm, elastic, and supple
Flavor	Sweet, spicy, savory, and tangy, becoming quite strong and pungent with longer aging

Brick, one of the relatively few American-created cheeses, was developed in Wisconsin by cheesemaker John Jossi in the late 1800s. It resembles other washed-rind cheeses (like LIMBURGER), but has a firmer texture that's dense enough to be sliced. This characteristic consistency is achieved by scooping the CURDS into special rectangular forms, placing the molds on a draining table, and turning the cheese to drain the WHEY before the cheese is PRESSED, which was originally done with a 5-pound brick. Whether or not the name of the cheese comes from this practice or because it's brick shaped is still debated. Brick cheeses are frequently washed with BRINE during the early stages of RIPENING and aged a total of 2 to 3 months. Young brick can be very mild, aged versions more pungent, and some renditions are flavored with caraway seeds. Brick has a FAT CONTENT of about 50 percent.

B

Brie; brie [BREE]

Origin	France (Île-de-France)
Milk	Unpasteurized and pasteurized cow's
Type	SOFT; MOLDED UNCOOKED; BLOOMY RIND; ARTISAN, COOPERATIVE, and FACTORY
Appearance	Flattened 1- to 6½-pound wheels; rind is thin with a velvety coating of white MOLD that shows patches of beige and red as it ages; interior is pale yellow to gold
Texture	Soft, smooth, and creamy to somewhat firmer, depending on style
Flavor	Artisan versions range from rich, sweet, and nutty with flavors of smoke and wild mushroom to more pungent and savory; factory versions are milder—not as rich and complex

Brie is the historic name of the region that lies about 30 miles east of Paris and that now generally corresponds to the modern *département* of Seine-et-Marne in the Île-de-France region. This is where Brie cheeses originated and have been made since at least the eighth century. These soft French cheeses are known around the world for their velvety, bloomy rinds and luscious, buttery-soft interiors, which can be thickly fluid when perfectly ripe. Naturally, the growth of desirable molds to create such rinds is essential, and some producers add the beneficial microorganisms to ensure that end. There are numerous Bries made within the region, most appended with the name of the originating town or commune. BRIE DE MEAUX and BRIE DE MELUN have APPELLATION D'ORIGINE CONTRÔLÉE (AOC) status and are considered the standard bearers. Several other ARTISAN Bries are considered excellent, including **Brie de Coulommiers** (*see* COULOMMIERS), **Brie de Montereau, Brie de Nangis,** and **Brie de Provins**. Bries can

B

be made from either whole, fat-free, or partially skimmed cow's milk. The CURDS are scooped into round metal hoops and allowed to drain for at least 24 hours. Once the cheese is set up, it's dry-salted (*see* SALTING) and turned daily for 2 to 3 days. The cheeses are then placed in a well-ventilated room at a cool (55 to 60°F) temperature for about 8 days, during which the bloomy white mold grows rapidly. Total RIPENING time can range from 3 to 10 weeks. Brie-style cheeses are made in other parts of France as well as many other countries including the United States, and some artisan cheesemakers produce very good products. **Marin French Cheese Company** made cheese-world history at the 2005 World Cheese Competition when it bested Bries from around the world (including France) by taking the gold medal for its Triple Cream Brie. This cheese also won an American Cheese Society award for best soft-ripened cheese in North America. But many of the Bries found at supermarkets are factory-produced from pasteurized milk, most with a bland flavor and many with a texture that remains firm at room temperature. Of course Bries made with unpasteurized milk cannot be imported into the United States at this writing (*see* UNPASTEURIZED MILK/IMPORTED CHEESE DILEMMA). The FAT CONTENT of Brie ranges from 45 to 60 percent.

Brie de Coulommiers [BREE deuh koo-luhm-MYAY] *see* COULOMMIERS

Brie de Meaux (AOC; PDO) [bree deuh MOH]

Origin	France (Île-de-France)
Milk	Unpasteurized cow's
Type	SOFT; MOLDED UNCOOKED; BLOOMY RIND; ARTISAN, COOPERATIVE, and FACTORY
Appearance	Flattened 5½- to 6½-pound wheels; rind is thin with a velvety coating of white MOLD that

	shows patches of beige and red as it ages; interior is pale yellow to gold
Texture	Soft, smooth, and creamy; the best are almost but not quite oozy
Flavor	Artisan versions are rich, sweet, and nutty with flavors of smoke and wild mushroom; factory versions are milder—not as rich and complex

Brie de Meaux has a long history dating back to at least the eighth century, when Charlemagne became an ardent fan. In 1815 the title "king of cheeses" was bestowed on it by French statesman Talleyrand and others at the Congress of Vienna. Brie is the historical name of the region in which this cheese is made; Meaux, a commune in the region, is now part of the urban sprawl of Paris. Some of the APPELLATION D'ORIGINE CONTRÔLÉE (AOC) regulations for making Brie de Meaux include heating the milk to a maximum of 99°F only once, when rennet is added; using a special *pelle à Brie* (a Brie shovel) to scoop the curd into the molds; and limiting SALTING to dry-salting. Brie de Meaux is inoculated with *Penicillium candidum* and aged a minimum of 4 weeks but usually 6 to 8 weeks. FAT CONTENT is generally around 45 percent. **Fromage de Meaux** is a pasteurized-milk version of Brie de Meaux, produced to meet U.S. standards, though it does not meet AOC requirements. At this writing, cheese made with unpasteurized milk and aged under 60 days may not be imported to the United States (*see* UNPASTEURIZED MILK/IMPORTED CHEESE DILEMMA). *See also* BRIE.

Brie de Melun (AOC; PDO) [BREE deuh meh-LOON (mel-UHN)]

Origin	France (Île-de-France, Champagne-Ardenne, Burgundy)

B

Milk	Unpasteurized cow's
Type	SOFT; MOLDED UNCOOKED; BLOOMY RIND; ARTISAN, COOPERATIVE, and FACTORY
Appearance	Flattened 3½- to 4-pound wheels; rind is thin with a velvety coating of white MOLD that shows patches and lines of brown and red as it ages; interior is pale yellow
Texture	Soft and creamy
Flavor	Strong, full-bodied, savory, slightly salty

Although Brie de Melun isn't as well known as BRIE DE MEAUX, it's actually thought to be the original Brie. Brie de Melun had its share of praise from the rich and powerful, but it was Brie de Meaux that landed the title "king of cheeses." Still, many feel Brie de Melun reigns as the best of the Bries. Brie is the historical name of the region where these cheeses are made; Melun is a commune that lies in the region's southern section, southeast of Paris. APPELLATION D'ORIGINE CONTRÔLÉE (AOC) regulations for Brie de Melun state that, though rennet can be used, COAGULATION must be due primarily to lactic fermentation and must occur over a period of at least 18 hours. This standard is quite different from that for Brie de Meaux, which relies on rennet to achieve coagulation in 30 minutes or less. Curds must manually be poured into molds, SALTING is limited to dry-salting, and *Penicillium candidum* is used to encourage the bloomy rind. Brie de Melun is aged a minimum of 4 weeks but usually for 7 to 10 weeks. Compared to Brie de Meaux, Brie de Melun has a stronger and more robust flavor and firmer texture. It has a FAT CONTENT of about 45 percent. Currently Brie de Melun cannot legally be imported into the United States, though fans hope that law will soon change (*see* UNPASTEURIZED MILK/IMPORTED CHEESE DILEMMA). *See also* BRIE.

Brie de Montereau [BREE deuh mawn-teuh-ROH] *see* BRIE

Brie de Nangis [BREE deuh nahn-JHEE] *see* BRIE

Brie de Provins [BREE deuh pro-VAN] *see* BRIE

Brillat-Savarin [BREE-YAH sah-vah-RAN]

Origin	France (Normandy; Burgundy)
Milk	Unpasteurized and pasteurized cow's
Type	SEMISOFT; TRIPLE-CREAM; MOLDED UNCOOKED; BLOOMY RIND; ARTISAN and FACTORY
Appearance	1-pound wheels; rind is soft and white, developing a downy mold as it ripens; interior is off-white to pale yellow
Texture	Soft and moist
Flavor	Rich, buttery, sweet, and mild with a slight tang

A cheese named after the renowned eighteenth-century French epicure and gastronome Jean Anthelme Brillat-Savarin, author of the famous *The Physiology of Taste*. It was created by French cheesemaker Henri Androuët in the 1930s, a little over 100 years after Brillat-Savarin's death. Cream is added to this uncooked, unpressed cheese to increase its FAT CONTENT to about 75 percent, placing it in the triple-cream category. Brillat-Savarin is RIPENED for 1 to 2 weeks. Only pasteurized-milk versions may be imported to the United States at this writing (*see* UNPASTEURIZED MILK/IMPORTED CHEESE DILEMMA).

B

Brin d'Amour; Brindamour [bra*n* dah-MOOR]

Origin	France (Corsica)
Milk	Unpasteurized and pasteurized goat's and sheep's
Type	SEMISOFT TO HARD, depending on type and aging; MOLDED UNCOOKED; NATURAL RIND; ARTISAN
Appearance	1¼- to 1¾-pound squares or rounds; rind is thin and coated with Mediterranean herbs; interior ranges from white to grayish white
Texture	Soft and moist when young (can be runny), becoming very firm with longer ripening
Flavor	Sweet, mild, creamy, and herbal, becoming nutty and tangy with age

Produced on Corsica, generally with sheep's milk and sometimes goat's milk, Brin d'Amour (also spelled *Brindamour*) means "bit of love." The outside of this cheese is covered with herbs such as rosemary, savory, thyme, and coriander seeds and sometimes decorated with other savories such as juniper berries and small red chile peppers. Brin d'Amour is typically RIPENED for about 1 month but sometimes for up to 10 weeks. As it ages, the cheese first becomes runny, then turns quite firm—the flavors intensify, and the herbal influence becomes more powerful. An almost identical artisanal Corsican cheese is **Fleur du Maquis,** which means "flower of the marquis"—*marquis* being the French name for the rough, underbrush-covered Corsican countryside.

brine; brine bath A solution of water and a great amount of salt. *See also* SALTING.

brining *see* SALTING

Brinza [BRIN-zah] *see* BRYNDZA

brique [BREEK] French for "brick," referring in the cheese world to a rectangular, brick-shaped cheese.

Broccio [BROH-chee-oh] *see* BROCCIU CORSE

Brocciu Corse; Brocciu; Broccio; Brucciu (AOC; PDO) [brod-SHU]

Origin	France (Corsica)
Milk	Unpasteurized sheep's and/or goat's
Type	SOFT (FRESH versions) to SEMISOFT; fresh are rindless, and RIPENED versions can have thin NATURAL RINDS; ARTISAN, FARMSTEAD, and FACTORY
Appearance	Variously shaped 1- to 3-pound rounds; fresh versions have a milky white exterior, and ripened versions have a beige exterior and white interior
Texture	Fresh Brocciu is moist to semimoist, loose, and slightly granular; other versions range from compact and malleable to dense
Flavor	Fresh versions are delicate, sweet, creamy, and slightly tangy; ripened versions more pungent

Although not much was written about Brocciu until the nineteenth century, locals say this cheese has been made in the area for centuries, probably since Corsicans began herding goats and sheep. The official name of this cheese is *Brocciu Corse,* but in France it's called *Broccio.* In fact it's thought that the Corsican *Brocciu* comes from the French *brousse,* for cream cheese made from raw goat's or sheep's milk. And that's exactly what makes this cheese unusual—as with Italian RICOTTA, it's made from

B

sheep's and/or goat's WHEY leftover from cheesemaking. Whole milk is added to whey and reheated to about 195°F, at which point tiny clumps of protein particles rise to the surface. The solids are skimmed off, strained, and placed in perforated molds or baskets to drain further. The end result is a white, creamy, firm but moist ready-to-eat mound of "cheese." Of course, technically Brocciu is a dairy product, not a cheese, because there's no STARTER or RENNET added. Even so, it has attained APPELLA-TION D'ORIGINE CONTRÔLÉE (AOC) and PROTECTED DESIGNATION OF ORIGIN (PDO) status as a cheese. About 85 percent of Brocciu is eaten within 48 hours of production. The remaining percentage, known as **Brocciu Passu,** is drained, salted, and ripened for at least 3 weeks. Fresh goat's whey Brocciu is available only from spring through autumn; fresh sheep's whey versions are generally available from the winter months to early summer. The FAT CONTENT of Brocciu ranges from 40 to 50 percent.

brochette [broh-SHEHT] French for "skewer," describing one of the many shapes used for CHÈVRE, where the cheese is shaped around a wooden stick (as SAINTE-MAURE DE TOURAINE).

Bruder Basil [BROO-der BAH-zeel]

Origin	Germany (Bavaria)
Milk	Pasteurized cow's
Type	SEMISOFT; PRESSED UNCOOKED; SMOKED; NATURAL RIND; ARTISAN
Appearance	2- or 4-pound rectangles; rind is golden reddish brown with mold ridges; interior is pale yellow with a scattering of small EYES
Texture	Smooth, firm, creamy, and supple
Flavor	Mild, buttery, and smoky

B

A traditional smoked cheese **(Rauchkäse)** produced in Bavaria and thought to have been originated by Trappist monks at the Abbey of Rotthalmunster. In the early 1900s Basil Weixler started the Bergader Private Cheese Dairy **(Bergader Privatkäserei),** which still makes this smoked cheese using artisanal methods. Bruder Basil's unique flavor comes from being cold-smoked (*see* SMOKED CHEESES) over beech wood. It's RIPENED for 4 to 6 weeks and has a FAT CONTENT of about 45 percent. There are two other versions of this cheese—one flavored with bits of ham, the other with paprika and chili powder.

brunost [BROO-nohst] *see* GJETOST

brushed-rind cheese During RIPENING, many NATURAL-RIND cheeses are frequently brushed with liquid, typically BRINE, which helps form the rind, keeps the interior moist, and adds flavor to the finished product. An example of a brushed-rind cheese is BEAUFORT. *See also* WASHED-RIND CHEESE.

Bryndza [BRIND-zah]

Origin	Slovakia
Milk	Unpasteurized sheep's, sometimes cow's or goat's or a mixture
Type	SOFT; MOLDED UNCOOKED; FARMSTEAD and COOPERATIVE
Appearance	Various sizes, from small tubs to molded blocks; rindless; stark white in color
Texture	Soft, smooth, and spreadable to firm and slightly moist and crumbly
Flavor	Fresh, rich, tangy, and salty

Also called *Brinza,* this popular cheese is made throughout Eastern Europe, including in eastern Austria, Hungary, Poland, Romania, Slovakia, and the Ukraine. The name *Bryndza* appears to be a derivative of *brânză,* Romanian for "cheese." Though traditionally made from sheep's milk, Bryndza may also be made from cow's and goat's milk; sometimes the milks are mixed. Every day the shepherds RENNET the milk, breaking up and pressing the CURDS before hanging them to drain in cloth sacks. Usually about once a week the shepherds journey to the dairies, where the curds undergo salting and MILLING before being turned into tubs or molded into blocks. Some Bryndza is cut into chunks and preserved in BRINE, which give it a flavor and texture similar to that of FETA. This cheese may be RIPENED for 2 to 4 weeks and has a fat content of about 45 percent.

bST The commonly used acronym for bovine somatotropin, a naturally occurring protein hormone secreted by the pituitary glands of cattle, human beings, dogs, and so on. It's also referred to as a *growth hormone* because it influences the metabolism of proteins, carbohydrates, and lipids. *See also* RBGH.

bûche [BEUSH] French for "log." In cheese parlance, it describes a log-shaped cheese.

Bucheret [BOO-sher-ay] *see* CAMELLIA

bulk cheese Any cheese in its original manufactured form, such as a 40-pound FLAT or BLOCK of CHEDDAR.

burielli [boo-RYEHL-lee] *see* BURRINO

burrata [boor-RAH-tah]

Origin	Italy (Apulia)
Milk	Pasteurized cow's or water buffalo's
Type	SOFT; PASTA FILATA; ARTISAN, FARMSTEAD, and FACTORY
Appearance	$\frac{1}{2}$- to $2\frac{1}{4}$-pound globes, bag shaped with knobs; rindless exterior is white and glossy; interior is pure white
Texture	Outside is elastic, soft, and spongy; interior is creamy and soft
Flavor	Rich and buttery with a fresh milky character

In Italian cheesemaking history, burrata is a recent creation—it didn't arrive on the scene until the 1920s. It was first made in southern Italy on a small farm in the town of Andria in the region of Apulia (Puglia). Its name is derived from *burro,* Italian for "butter," and refers to its creamy interior. Some say this cheese was created as a means of using up scraps of MOZZARELLA, although only large operations would have scraps; small producers don't have such leftovers. As with mozzarella, burrata was originally produced from water buffalo's milk but today is produced primarily from cow's milk. Burrata is made by the PASTA FILATA process, which means the CURD is immersed in hot WHEY or water and continually stretched until it reaches the desired pliability. At this point the cheesemaker forms a bag (about $\frac{1}{3}$ inch thick) from the stretched curd and fills it with bits of unspun mozzarella CURDS mixed with cream. The bag is then twisted, sometimes leaving a little knob at the top, and salted with a brief dip in BRINE. The cream thickens inside the bag so that when the cheese is cut, a soft rich center oozes out. Burrata is sometimes wrapped in asphodel leaves (similar to those of a

B

leek), which can be a good freshness indicator—the greener the leaves, the fresher the cheese. Burrata is very short-lived and should be eaten within about 3 days. It should be noted that, although this cheese is imported from Italy, a California-based producer—Gioia Cheese Company—employs an Italian cheesemaker who produces an excellent burrata.

burri [BOO-ree] *see* BURRINO

burrino; pl. burrini [boo-REE-noh; boo-REE-nee]

Origin	Italy (Apulia, Basilicata, Calabria, Campania, and Sicily)
Milk	Unpasteurized or pasteurized cow's
Type	SOFT; PASTA FILATA; NATURAL RIND; ARTISAN, FARMSTEAD, and FACTORY
Appearance	1 to 3 pounds and pear shaped with a topknot; rindless exterior is ivory to pale yellow and glossy; interior is ivory with a butter center
Texture	Outside is elastic, soft, and spongy; interior is creamy
Flavor	Mild and sweetly tangy

A specialty of southern Italy, burrino is made by hand-shaping a PASTA FILATA–style CURD (such as MOZZARELLA or PROVOLONE) around a pat of very cold butter. The cheese is then tied at the top before being submerged in hot water to set it. Such cheeses are also sometimes stuffed with other edibles, such as a chunk of salami. They may also be smoked. Burrini may be either FRESH or RIPENED for a few weeks. Some are WAXED for export. Other names for this cheese include *burri, burielli, butirro, manteca, piticelle,* and *provole,* depending on where the cheese is made.

B

butirro [boo-TEE-roh] *see* BURRINO

butter cheese *see* GRÄDDOST

butterfat The fat content of milk, also called *milkfat*. *See* FAT for information on fat relating to cheese.

Butterkäse [BOOT-ter-ki-zer; BUT-ter-ki-zer (-kah-zeh)]

Origin	Germany
Milk	Pasteurized cow's
Type	SEMISOFT; PRESSED UNCOOKED; NATURAL RIND; SOME SMOKED; FACTORY
Appearance	2¼- to 9-pound loaves; rind is thin and pale yellow to reddish gold in color; interior is pale yellow with a scattering of small EYES
Texture	Smooth, creamy, and supple
Flavor	Delicate, mild, and buttery

Although Butterkäse means "butter cheese," the name refers to the color and texture, rather than the fact that it's made with butter, which it isn't. This cheese is also called *Damenkäse* ("ladies' cheese") because of its delicate flavor. Butterkäse RIP-ENS in about 30 days and has a FAT CONTENT of approximately 50 percent. It's made throughout Germany and Austria, as well as in Wisconsin by several cheese producers including **Cedar Grove Cheese,** Edelweiss Town Hall Cheese, and **Roth Käse USA, Ltd.**

butterscotch *see* Glossary of Cheese Descriptors, page 495

buttery *see* Glossary of Cheese Descriptors, page 495

C

C² [C-squared]

Origin	Australia (Tasmania–Bruny Island)
Milk	Pasteurized cow's
Type	HARD; PRESSED COOKED; NATURAL; FARMSTEAD
Appearance	13-pound wheels; rind is thin, hard, and rough with small pits; its color golden brown with some gray spotches; interior is ivory to medium yellow
Texture	Very dense and compact yet supple when young, becoming harder and flakier in older versions
Flavor	Mild, sweet, nutty, and savory

The great Norman cheeses were served as well: Camembert, Pont l'Évêque, and the stinky Livarot. But my father warned: "Not for Mademoiselle Simone, the strong cheeses." He thought young girls shouldn't be allowed to pollute their mouths with smelly odors.
—Simone Beck

A handmade cheese produced by Bruny Island Cheese Company. Bruny Island is actually two islands connected by "The Neck," a narrow stretch of land between the two. Bruny Island is part of the Australian state of Tasmania and lies just off the Tasmanian mainland, south of Hobart. Nick Haddow and Leonie Struthers are partners in this concern, with Haddow gaining skills during a decade of traveling the world, gathering recipes and studying traditional cheesemaking techniques. C^2, which is patterned after French and Italian MOUN-TAIN CHEESES, is pressed in wooden hoops before being RIPENED for 6 to 12 months.

cabécou [cab-bay-KOO] Languedoc dialect for "little goat," typically referring to tiny (1- to 1½-ounce) disks of goat's milk cheese made by small producers throughout western and southwestern France. Cabécou is typically ripened for 10 to 15 days but sometimes for up to 6 weeks. Depending on age, it can range from soft, white, and mild to extremely hard, brown, and pungently goaty. In the United States, **Laura Chenel Chèvre** produces a 1-ounce FARMSTEAD cabécou that's marinated in herbs, spices, and extra virgin olive oil from California.

Cabécou de Rocamadour [cab-bay-KOO deuh ROH-kah-ma-dohr]
see ROCAMADOUR

cabra [Sp. KAH-bhrah; Port. KAH-brehr] Spanish and Portu-guese for "goat," *cabra* is seen on some goat's milk cheese labels from those countries.

Cabrales (DO; PDO) [kah-BRAH-lays]

Origin	Spain (Asturias)
Milk	Traditionally a mixture of cow's, sheep's, and goat's—pasteurized and unpasteurized; today most Cabrales is made of 100 percent cow's milk
Type	SEMISOFT; MOLDED UNCOOKED; BLUE-VEINED; NATURAL RIND; FARMSTEAD
Appearance	4- to 8-pound wheels wrapped in dark foil with the DO logo; rind is rough, buff-colored,

C

	and can be somewhat sticky; interior is ivory colored with prevalent cobalt-colored veining and plentiful EYES
Texture	Soft, moist, and creamy yet crumbly
Flavor	Powerfully pungent and salty, very complex, spicy finish

Considered one of the world's great blue cheeses, Cabrales can be produced only in its namesake village and three villages of the Peñamellera Alta township, located on the northern side of the Picos de Europa mountains. Although today's Cabrales is produced primarily of cow's milk, traditional mixed-milk (cow, sheep, and goat) versions are still made in the summertime, though rarely available outside of Spain. Cabrales is made in small quantities at family dairies. It undergoes SALTING for 3 days before being transferred to a RIPENING room for 2 to 3 weeks. After that it's taken to natural caves and pierced with needles to allow air access to the interior to create the bluing from the natural bacteria present in the caves. There it ripens for at least 2 more months. Although Cabrales was once traditionally wrapped in leaves, today's versions are foil wrapped. It has a FAT CONTENT of 45 percent.

cabreiro *see* QUEISO DE CASTELO BRANCO

cacio [KAH-choh] From the Latin *caseus* ("cheese"), this Italian word is used as a prefix for cheeses such as CACIOCAVALLO.

Caciocavallo; Caciocavallo Silano (DOC; PDO) [kah-choh-kuh-VAH-loh; see-LAH-noh]

Origin	Italy (southern Italian regions of Calabria, Campania, Molise, Apulia, Basilicata, and Sicily)

C

Milk	Unpasteurized or pasteurized cow's
Type	SEMISOFT to SEMIHARD; PRESSED UNCOOKED; PASTA FILATA; NATURAL RIND; ARTISAN, FARMSTEAD, COOPERATIVE, and FACTORY; some SMOKED
Appearance	Depending on where it's made, this cheese weighs from 2½ to 22 pounds and comes in various shapes, mostly gourdlike and often with a knob at the top where the cheese has been tied, but also—as with Caciocavallo del Monaco—with small grooves in the body left from cords tied around the cheese and, atypically, a rectangular block of Caciocavallo Palermitano; rind is thin and hard and varies in color from off-white to gold to yellowish brown, depending on age; the interior ranges from off-white to a darker straw white to gold
Texture	Elastic and stringlike—smoother when young and more granular as it ages
Flavor	Mild and slightly salty when young, becoming tangier as it ages

Caciocavallo comes from various areas in southern Italy and can be found with different names, including Caciocavallo del Monaco, Caciocavallo di Agnone, Caciocavallo Palermitano, Caciocavallo Podolico Alburni, and Caciocavallo Podolico Pientino. Caciocavallo Silano is the only one currently with DENOMINAZIONE DI ORIGINE CONTROLLATA (DOC) status. It can be produced in southern Italy in a number of village areas in the regions of Calabria, Campania, Molise, and Basilicata and in the provinces of Foggia, Bari, Brindisi, and Taranto in the Apulia region. The milk can come from various breeds of cows, but the best cheeses come from the Podolian breed, which live in a

C

semiwild state. They don't produce as much milk as other cows, but it's very high quality and excellent for cheesemaking. Caciocavallos are PASTA FILATA CHEESES and are RIPENED from 2 months to 2 years. The name means "cheese on horseback," referring to the traditional aging process of tying two cheeses together and dangling them side by side over a horizontal rod (as when riding horseback). Caciocavallos labeled *affumicato* have been smoked (*see* SMOKED CHEESES).

caciotta [kah-CHOHT-tah] A generic name for cow's or sheep's milk cheeses made throughout Italy. Such cheeses are simple, soft, and mild. *See also* CASCIOTTA D'URBINO.

Cadenza [kuh-DEN-zah] *see* NOCTURNE

Caerphilly [kar-FILL-ee]

Origin	Wales
Milk	Unpasteurized and pasteurized cow's
Type	SEMISOFT to SEMIHARD; PRESSED COOKED; NATURAL RIND; FARMSTEAD and FACTORY
Appearance	1- to 9-pound flat wheels; rind is dry, thin, and gold to gray-brown in color—aged versions have a velvety coating of mold; interior is white to ivory
Texture	Moist, loose, and crumbly when young; aged versions will be creamier near the rind, while still chalky and crumbly in the center
Flavor	Mild, salty, and buttery with a lemony tang, becoming richer and more piquant with age

Wales's best-known cheese, Caerphilly takes its name from a small town near Cardiff at the southern end of the country. This cheese, which is soaked in BRINE to help form the rind, became extremely popular during the 1800s. Welsh miners took to its fresh saline character as a means of replacing salt lost working in the mines. As Caerphilly's popularity grew, the Welsh couldn't keep up with demand and convinced English farmers across the Bristol Channel in Somerset to make it. Somerset cheesemakers, who typically made long-aging CHEDDAR, liked the fact that Caerphilly's shorter RIPENING time greatly improved their cash flow. Today a few farmstead versions are being made in Wales as well as in the Somerset region of England. Factory versions are also available but are not as well regarded. Although Caerphilly is ready to eat within a few weeks of being made, some are ripened for up to 6 months. This cheese has a FAT CONTENT of about 48 percent.

Cambozola [kam-boh-ZOH-lah]

Origin	Germany
Milk	Pasteurized cow's
Type	SEMISOFT; MOLDED UNCOOKED; BLUE-VEINED; TRIPLE-CREAM; FACTORY
Appearance	5-pound wheels; rind is thin and beige in color with a velvety coating of white mold; interior is pale yellow with patches of blue-green mold
Texture	Soft, smooth, and creamy
Flavor	Mild, buttery, slightly tangy

Germany is the home to Cambozola, which was created in the 1970s by the well-known Champignon Company. This cheese is like a blend of CAMEMBERT and GORGONZOLA, its name an amalgam of the two. Cream is added to Cambozola to boost the FAT CONTENT to 70 percent, moving this cheese into the TRIPLE-CREAM stratosphere. It's made like a pasteurized-milk BRIE, then

C

injected with blue MOLD *PENICILLIUM* spores and RIPENED for about 3 weeks. The result is a mild and exceedingly creamy Brie-style cheese with a blue-cheese whisper. Although Cambozola is very popular, it's not greatly admired by true cheese aficionados.

Camellia

Origin	United States (California)
Milk	Pasteurized goat's
Type	SEMISOFT; MOLDED UNCOOKED; BLOOMY RIND; FARMSTEAD
Appearance	4-ounce rounds and 2¼-pound wheels; rind is thin, snowy white, and downy; interior is ivory colored
Texture	Moistly soft and oozy
Flavor	Creamy, rich, and concentrated, increasing in pungency with age

Redwood Hill Farm is nestled among the picturesque redwoods of western Sonoma County, about 60 miles north of San Francisco. The goat dairy dates back to 1968, and Jennifer Lynn Bice with partner Steven Schack took it over from her parents a decade later. Though raw goat's milk was the original product, Bice and Schack—wanting to extend the milk's shelf life—began producing yogurt and, subsequently, cheese. Today the Bice family (Jennifer works alongside sister Sharon and brother Scott) has a mixed herd of 350 Nubian, Alpine, Saanen, and LaMancha goats, each of which has a name. Their hormone-free goat's milk cheeses are certified kosher and made with organic practices, nonbioengineered vegetable rennet, and French cheese cultures. Camellia, a CAMEMBERT-style goat cheese, was named after one of the dairy's favorite does. As with BRIE and Camembert, the milk for Camellia is inoculated with *Penicillium*

C

candidum. This SOFT-RIPENED cheese is aged for 6 to 8 weeks and perfectly ripe when it feels soft to the touch—if the rind is yellow or rust colored, the cheese is past its prime. The Redwood Hill cheeses are consistent award winners at the annual American Cheese Society competition and include FETA, CHÈVRE, CROTTIN, and **Bucheret,** a bloomy-rind handmade cheese.

Camembert de Normandie (AOC; PDO); Camembert [KAM-uhm-behr deuh nor-mahn-DEE]

Origin	France (Normandy)
Milk	Unpasteurized cow's
Type	SOFT; MOLDED UNCOOKED; BLOOMY RIND; ARTISAN, COOPERATIVE, and FACTORY
Appearance	5- to 10-ounce wheels; rind is thin with a velvety coating of white mold that shows patches of beige, orange, and red as it ripens; interior is pale yellow to gold
Texture	Soft, smooth, and creamy; the best are almost (but not quite) oozy
Flavor	ARTISAN versions are rich, sweet, and nutty with flavors of smoke and wild mushrooms; non–APPELLATION D'ORIGINE CONTRÔLÉE pasteurized versions are milder—not as rich and complex

Named for Normandy's small village of Camembert, this cheese was first made in 1790. Legend has it that a villager, Marie Hariel, learned the techniques from a priest from Brie who used her farm as a shelter from political persecution. But there are references to cheeses from Camembert dating back to the mid-1500s, as well as French dictionaries dating back to 1708 that mention this cheese. Such is the way of legends.

C

Many believe the cheeses predating the 1700s were not at all like today's Camembert and that Hariel did indeed change the way local cheeses were made. What's known for sure is that in 1890 a French engineer named Ridel created the thin, round wooden boxes that allowed this delicate cheese to be transported damage-free. Without such packaging, Camembert may not have become one of the world's most popular cheeses. The official name for this cheese is Camembert de Normandie, though it's typically simply called *Camembert*. To make this cheese, the CURD is cut into layers, placed in perforated molds, and turned frequently to drain the WHEY. The cheese is then unmolded, salted, and allowed to dry for a couple of days. Then it's sprayed with *Penicillium candidum*, which encourages the mold growth that gives this cheese its character. Camemberts must be aged a minimum of 21 days, but 30 to 35 days is more customary. Camembert de Normandie has a FAT CONTENT of about 45 percent. Unpasteurized versions are labeled *au lait cru* ("with raw milk"). Only pasteurized-milk versions may be imported to the United States at this writing (*see* UNPASTEURIZED MILK/IMPORTED CHEESE DILEMMA). The labels of pasteurized versions cannot refer to APPELLATION D'ORIGINE CONTRÔLÉE (AOC) accreditation but will say *fabriqué en Normandie* ("made in Normandy"). In addition to Camembert de Normandie, numerous Camembert cheeses are produced in France, Italy, Switzerland, South America, and the United States. Much of this production is from cheese factories using pasteurized milk. Such cheeses may look like Camembert de Normandie but typically do not have the full flavor or soft, creamy texture of the original. Two exceptions are California's **Marin French Cheese Company**'s Rouge et Noir Camembert (a first-place American Cheese Society award) and New York's **Old Chatham Sheepherding Company**'s **Hudson Valley Camembert,** made with a combination of cow's milk and sheep's milk (Best Cheese in America, United States Championship Cheese Contest, and Best of Class, World Championship Cheese Contest).

Canadian cheeses *see* Cheeses by Country of Origin, page 509

Canestrato Pugliese (DOC; PDO); Canestrato [kah-neh-STRAH-toh poo-LYAY-zay]

Origin	Italy (Calabria, Apulia, and Sicily)
Milk	Unpasteurized sheep's for DOC cheeses; pasteurized and unpasteurized cow's and goat's may be used in others
Type	SEMIHARD to HARD; PRESSED UNCOOKED; NATURAL RIND; some FARMSTEAD
Appearance	4- to 44-pound wheels marked by indentations caused by the rush baskets in which they are formed and aged; rinds are hard, embossed with a basket pattern, and vary in color from yellow to yellow-brown to gray-brown; interiors range from pale yellow to darker yellow and sometimes contain tiny EYES
Texture	Firm, sometimes crumbly
Flavor	Fresh versions are mild and sweet, but aging lends savory, tangy flavors and aromas; those with peppercorns or chile pepper flakes can be spicy

Taking its name from the hand-woven rush baskets (*canestre*) in which it's formed, Canestrato cheese is made in Calabria, Apulia, and Sicily. The only Canestrato cheese with DENOMINAZIONE DI ORIGINE CONTROLLATA (DOC) status is Canestrato Pugliese, made in Apulia. The approved production area includes the

C

complete province of Foggia and adjacent towns and villages in the Bari province. The cheese must be made from unpasteurized milk taken only from Apulian Gentile or Merino sheep that graze on grasses or other plant material—no hay or feed is allowed unless weather conditions are severe. The CURD (which may be flavored with peppercorns or chile pepper flakes) is scooped into reed baskets, pressed (*see* PRESSING), then typically dipped in very hot water or WHEY to help form the rind. The cheese is then either brined or dry-salted (*see* SALTING). Olive oil is usually rubbed over the rind during aging. Fresh Canestrato is only RIPENED for 10 to 15 days, whereas aged versions can take over a year. The FAT CONTENT of this cheese ranges from 40 to 45 percent. Non–DOC/PDO Canestrato cheeses may also be made with either pasteurized or raw goat's or cow's milk. Sometimes PECORINO cheeses are referred to as *Canestrato,* presumably because they're formed in rush baskets. For example, Pecorino Siciliano is sometimes called *Canestrato Siciliano,* and Pecorino di Moliterno is sometimes dubbed *Canestrato di Moliterno.*

Cantabria *see* QUESO DE CANTABRIA

Cantal; Fourme de Cantal (AOC; PDO) [kahn-TAHL; FORM deuh kahn-TAHL]

Origin	France (Auvergne, Midi-Pyrénées)
Milk	Unpasteurized and pasteurized cow's
Type	SEMIHARD; PRESSED UNCOOKED; NATURAL RIND; FARMSTEAD, COOPERATIVE, and FACTORY
Appearance	Tall wheels that come in three sizes, the largest weighing up to 100 pounds, medium size (**Petit Cantal**) about 44 pounds, and the smallest (**Cantalet**) about 22 pounds; rind is

	thick and dark yellow with splotches of gray, red, and orange; interior is ivory to gold, depending on age
Texture	Firm and elastic when young, becoming denser and harder with age
Flavor	Young versions are mild, milky, and buttery with a slight tanginess; older versions are more complex with piquant and nutty characteristics

Cantal is one of France's oldest cheeses, dating back at least 2,000 years. It's named after the Cantal mountain range that runs through central France's Auvergne region. Traditionally, Cantal has been produced from unpasteurized milk. Today, however, most of it is factory-made with pasteurized milk—such renditions are not as highly regarded as the raw-milk FARMSTEAD versions. Fortunately, SALERS (AOC; PDO)—a raw-milk MOUNTAIN cheese known as an "elite" Cantal—is made in the same area and in a similar fashion with unpasteurized milk. APPELLATION D'ORIGINE CONTRÔLÉE (AOC) regulations require that Cantal undergo a double PRESSING, unique for French cheeses. The CURD is first cut into ½-inch cubes, wrapped in cloth and pressed, then allowed to rest for about 8 hours. It's then put through a grinder to break it into small pieces, salted (*see* SALTING), molded, and pressed a second time. For the next month the cheese is frequently turned and rubbed with salt. There are three categories of RIPENING for Cantal cheeses: *jeune* ("young"), ripened for 30 days; *entre-deux* ("between the two"), which has 2 to 6 months of aging; and *vieux* ("old") for cheeses matured for 6 months or more. Cantal's minimum FAT CONTENT is 45 percent.

Cantalet [kahn-TAH-lay] *see* CANTAL

Cantaré Foods [kan-TAH-ray] *see* MASCARPONE

capra [KAH-prah] Italian for "goat," *capra* is seen on some labels for cow's-milk cheeses.

Capricious [kah-PREE-shuhs]

Origin	United States (California)
Milk	Pasteurized goat's
Type	SEMIHARD TO HARD; PRESSED COOKED; NATURAL RIND; ARTISAN
Appearance	7-pound wheels; rind is thin and golden; interior is ivory, turning pale golden with age
Texture	Firm and supple, becoming harder and slightly flaky with age
Flavor	Fresh, nutty, creamy, slightly salty, and mild

This cheese is the progeny of the Achadinha Cheese Company in Petaluma, California, run by the Pacheco family, third-generation cheesemakers and dairymen. Jim and Donna Pacheco named their company Achadinha after a town in Portugal from which Jim's father hailed. They also own and operate the Pacheco Family Dairy, which currently is home to a mixed-breed herd of twelve hundred goats that roam freely on 230 of their 350-plus acres. Much of the milk is sent to the neighboring **Marin French Cheese Company** and **Redwood Hill Farm,** which use it for their goat's milk cheeses, but the Pachecos save enough rich product to make their cheeses. This WASHED-CURD aged goat cheese is completely handmade and aged for at least 3 months and up to 7 months. Capricious walked away with the coveted "Best in Show" honor at the annual American Cheese Society competition and continually gets high marks from TUROPHILES.

Donna Pacheco also makes a pasteurized goat's milk FETA that she soaks in sea-salt brine before delivering it to market at 4 weeks. It has a creamy flavor and texture and a fresh briny finish.

Capriella [kap-ree-EHL-lah] *see* MOZZARELLA

Capriole Goat Cheese *see* CROCODILE TEAR; MONT ST. FRANCIS; O'BANON; WABASH CANNONBALL

Carmody; Carmody Reserve [KAR-muh-dee]

Origin	United States (California)
Milk	Pasteurized and unpasteurized cow's
Type	SEMIHARD; MOLDED UNCOOKED; NATURAL RIND; ARTISAN
Appearance	3½-pound wheels; rind is thin, smooth, and golden—the Carmody Reserve's rind has a dusting of white mold; interior ranges from ivory to straw colored with a scattering of small EYES
Texture	Smooth and supple
Flavor	Carmody is mild and buttery; Carmody Reserve is nutty, tangy, and caramellike

Hailing from California's **Bellwether Farms,** Carmody is an award-winning Italian-style cheese based on techniques that founder Cindy Callahan learned from studying with Italian master cheesemakers. Son Liam Callahan, who also studied in Italy, is now the cheesemaker and produces Carmody from the pasteurized high-fat milk of Jersey cows that graze on a neighboring farm. Carmody is RIPENED for at least 6 weeks. Callahan employs exactly the same recipe for **Carmody Reserve** but uses raw milk and ripens the cheese for about 4 months. The lengthened aging gives the reserve a deep, rich flavor profile akin to a blend of CHEDDAR and aged GOUDA. Both cheeses have a FAT CONTENT that ranges between 28 and 35 percent. Bell-wether Farms also makes SAN ANDREAS, FROMAGE BLANC, RICOTTA, CRESCENZA in traditional Italian squares, and **Pepato,** a semisoft peppercorn-studded raw sheep's milk cheese that's aged for 2 to 3 months and that won first-place honors at the annual American Cheese Society competition.

carré [kah-RAY] French for "square" and one of the many shapes into which CHÈVRE is formed.

Carr Valley Cheese *see* CHEDDAR; COLBY

Casciotta d'Urbino (DOC; PDO) [kah-SHOH-tah d'oor-BEE-noh]

Origin	Italy (Marche region)
Milk	Pasteurized and unpasteurized sheep's and cow's
Type	SEMISOFT; PRESSED COOKED; NATURAL RIND; FARMSTEAD
Appearance	Small 1¾- to 2¾-pound wheels; rind is thin and straw yellow; interior is pale yellow with a few small eyes
Texture	Semisoft and crumbly
Flavor	Sweet, milky, and pleasantly acidic

The Marche region, located in east-central Italy, has been producing this style of cheese since the thirteenth century. It's said that Casciotta was a favorite of Michelangelo and that he eventually bought farmland in the region to ensure his sup-ply. The DENOMINAZIONE DI ORIGINE CONTROLLATA (DOC) regulations state that Casciotta d'Urbino can be produced only in the Pesaro-Urbino province. It's made with 70 to 80 percent sheep's milk and the balance cow's milk. Casciotta d'Urbino is either brined or dry-salted (*see* SALTING). It's aged for 30 days or less, which gives it a sweet, fresh flavor. Fat content is 45 percent or more. *See also* CACIOTTA.

casein [KAY-seen; KAY-see-ihn] White, odorless, and tasteless, casein is the primary protein in milk. In the initial stage of cheesemaking, the milk's acidity is balanced by a STARTER, causing the milk protein to begin to bond and clump. The addition of RENNET completes the COAGULATION process, producing formation of the CURD.

Cashel Blue; Cashel Irish Blue [KASH-uhl bloo]

Origin	Ireland (Tipperary)
Milk	Pasteurized cow's
Type	SEMISOFT; MOLDED UNCOOKED; BLUE-VEINED; NATURAL RIND; ARTISAN and FARMSTEAD
Appearance	3- to 3½-pound, gold-foil-wrapped wheels; rind is thin, moist, crusty, and beige with splotches of gray, blue, and green MOLDS; interior is ivory with blue-gray-green veins
Texture	Firm and crumbly when young, becoming creamier with age
Flavor	Lightly salty and tangy when young; older versions are richer, mellower, and have a zesty spiciness

Louis and Jane Grubb developed Cashel Blue in the mid-1980s as a means of diversifying their family farm business and to fill a void in Ireland's cheesemaking—the lack of an Irish blue cheese. Their farm is in Beechmount near the Rock of Cashel,

C

a dramatic limestone outcrop in south-central Ireland's County Tipperary. Cashel Blue is made primarily with milk from the Grubbs' herd of 110 Friesian cows. Recently, however, they've begun purchasing limited amounts of high-quality milk from neighboring farms. Production includes using vegetarian RENNET and inoculating the CURD with *Penicillium roqueforti*, the same mold used to produce ROQUEFORT, GORGONZOLA, and STILTON. Cashel Blue is aged for a minimum of 3 to 4 weeks, but more often for 6 to 12 weeks and sometimes longer for aficionados of stronger blue cheese. It has a FAT CONTENT of about 51 percent. In 1999, the Grubbs and their nephews began producing **Crozier Blue,** which is made from sheep's milk (as with Roquefort) in a similar fashion to that of Cashel Blue.

cassata [kah-SAH-tah] A classic Italian dessert, the most common form of which is a rich filling of RICOTTA mixed with chopped chocolate and candied fruit, then completely encased by slices of sponge cake (or halved ladyfingers) that have been soaked in rum, liqueur, coffee, or a combination of like liquids. The word *cassata* means "in a case (or chest)." This dessert is covered, weighted, and refrigerated overnight, then either dusted with confectioners' sugar or coated with whipped cream before serving.

Castelmagno (DOC; PDO) [kah-stehl-MAH-nyoh]

Origin	Italy (Piedmont)
Milk	Unpasteurized cow's, goat's, and/or sheep's
Type	SEMIHARD; PRESSED UNCOOKED; sometimes BLUE-VEINED; NATURAL RIND; FARMSTEAD; ARTISAN

C

Appearance	$4\frac{1}{2}$- to 15-pound wheels; rind is thin, smooth, and pale reddish yellow when young, but with age it thickens, hardens, wrinkles, and turns darker with reddish veins; interior is ivory white when young—aging darkens the color to yellow-gold and forms thin blue veins
Texture	Firm but flaky when young, becoming more compact with age
Flavor	Mildly savory when young, developing a fuller, more pungent character as it ages; blue veins make the cheese even more flavorful

This well-respected cheese has been produced in the southern part of Piedmont since the twelfth century, and there's evidence that it was used as a form of payment in the thirteenth century. Castelmagno's beginnings roughly coincided with those of GORGONZOLA, with which it shares many similarities. Its name is taken from the village of Castelmagno located near Dunero in the Cuneo Mountains. DENOMINAZIONE DI ORIGINE CONTROLLATA (DOC) regulations for Castelmagno require that it be made only in Piedmont's Cuneo province in and around the towns of Castelmagno, Monterosso, and Pradleves. It's produced from partially skimmed cow's milk with small additions of sheep's and/or goat's milk. The cheese is comprised of two separate milkings (one in the evening and one the next morning). Castelmagno is aged for up to 6 months in caves that promote the growth of desirable microflora mold (or rooms providing a comparable environment) on the surface. Sometimes naturally growing *PENICILLIUM* molds in the caves create fiberlike blue streaks that give the PASTE a spicy character. Whereas longer-aged, stronger-flavored Castelmagnos were once fashionable, today younger, milder cheeses

C

are more popular. This cheese has a fat content of 44 to 52 percent.

Castelo Branco [kersh-TEH-loo BRER*N*-koo] *see* QUEIJO DE CASTELO BRANCO

Cato Corner Farm *see* DUTCH FARMSTEAD; HOOLIGAN

cave Underground area used for RIPENING cheese and appreciated for its naturally low temperature, minimal light, and high humidity. *See also* CELLAR.

Cedar Grove Cheese, Inc. *see* BUTTERKÄSE; HAVARTI

cellar A temperature- and humidity-controlled room used for RIPENING cheese. As the name suggests, a cellar is typically underground, but the name can also refer to any atmosphere-controlled cheese-ripening area. *See also* CAVE.

cendre [SAH*N*DR] French for "ASH," found on labels of cheeses with such a coating.

Cendré d'Aisy [*sahn*-DRAY day-ZEE] *see* AISY CENDRÉ

centrifugal separator (*see* SEPARATOR)

cerise [seuhr-REEZ] French for "cherry," used in the cheese world to describe both the size of the EYES in cheese and one of the many shapes into which CHÈVRE is formed.

C

Chabichou du Poitou (AOC; PDO); Chabichou/Chabis [SHAH-bee-shoo doo pwah-TOO; SHAH-bee]

Origin	France (Poitou-Charentes)
Milk	Unpasteurized and pasteurized goat's
Type	SEMISOFT; MOLDED UNCOOKED; NATURAL RIND; FARMSTEAD, COOPERATIVE, and FACTORY
Appearance	4¼- to 6-ounce drum-shaped cylinders; rind is thin and mottled with white and beige molds when young, adding blue and gray molds as it ripens; interior is white
Texture	Young versions are soft and moist; older ones are firmer and become crumbly over time
Flavor	Mild, sweet, fresh, and tangy when young, becoming rich and complex with a pungent, nutty character as they ripen

The word *chabichou* comes from *chabi,* derived from the Arabic *chebli* ("goat"). The origins of this cheese date back to at least the eighth century, when the Saracens, an Arabian people, controlled parts of France. After their defeat in 732, some remaining Saracens taught the locals how to make Chabichou from whole goat's milk. The cheese's production is connected to Poitou, a French province that's now part of the Poitou-Charentes region—France's primary area for goat breeding. The cheeses are rubbed with salt and allowed to dry for a couple of days before beginning a minimum RIPENING period of 10 days, though 3 weeks or more is not uncommon. Cheeses made from raw milk meet APPELLATION D'ORIGINE CONTRÔLÉE (AOC) regulations and may be labeled *Chabichou du Poitou.* Those made from pasteurized milk to meet United States standards (*see* UNPASTEURIZED MILK/IMPORTED CHEESE DILEMMA) are not AOC-approved and are therefore simply labeled *chabichou* or *chabis.* The FAT CONTENT for this cheese is about 45 percent.

C

chabis [SHAH-bee] *see* CHABICHOU DU POITOU

chalky *see* Glossary of Cheese Descriptors,
    page 495

Chaource (AOC; PDO) [shah-OORS]

Origin	France (Champagne-Ardenne; Burgundy)
Milk	Unpasteurized or pasteurized cow's
Type	SOFT; MOLDED UNCOOKED; BLOOMY RIND; ARTISAN and FACTORY
Appearance	7- or 16-ounce drum-shaped cylinders; rind is thin with a velvety coating of white mold that shows tinges of red as it ripens; interior is pale yellow
Texture	Young versions are light, coarse, and chalky; older examples are buttery smooth and creamy in the center, runny around the edges
Flavor	Mild, milky, tangy, and salty when young, changing to rich, nutty, fruity, mushroomy, and pungent as it ripens

Chaource was first made sometime in the Middle Ages. There are references to it in the fourteenth century and again in 1513, when inhabitants of Chaource, a small town in Champagne, gave the cheese to an important area official. Chaource is made in a manner similar to BRIE and is RIPENED for a minimum of 2 weeks but usually for 4 weeks or more. A pasteurized milk version is allowed under APPELLATION D'ORIGINE CONTRÔLÉE (AOC) rules. The FAT CONTENT of Chaource is approximately 50 percent.

Chavignol [shah-vee-NYOHL] *see* CROTTIN DE CHAVIGNOL

cheddar; Cheddar [CHED-uhr]

Origin	England (Somerset)
Milk	Unpasteurized and pasteurized cow's
Type	SEMIHARD to HARD; PRESSED COOKED; NATURAL RIND; ARTISAN, FARMSTEAD, COOPERATIVE, and FACTORY
Appearance	Farmstead cheddar versions typically come in 60- to 70-pound wheels; other cheddars are available in a variety of sizes and shapes, including rectangles and small wheels, and MAMMOTH cheddars can weigh up to 950 pounds (which are, of course, cut into small wedges or rectangles); the rind on farmstead cheese is golden brown to gray-brown with patches of white mold and is usually cloth covered; other cheddars are often rindless and come in a variety of packaging, including plastic wrap or WAX covering; farmstead cheeses have interiors that range in color from ivory to pale yellow; others range from white to orange
Texture	Smooth, tight, and firm—handmade examples are fine and crumbly or flaky, whereas factory-produced cheddars are typically slick and slightly gummy
Flavor	Farmstead versions are full and complex with a range of flavors, including caramellike, fruity, nutty, tangy, grassy, and spicy; factory versions range from bland to sharp

Cheddar takes its name from a village in southwest England's Somerset County, where production of this cheese began. The area's cheesemaking dates back to medieval times, and accurate

C

information on cheddar production can be traced to at least the end of the sixteenth century. Whereas cheddar was once a luxury, today such cheeses are readily available. In the late 1930s there were over five hundred farms in the United Kingdom producing farmstead cheddars. Today that number has dwindled to a precious few, with most cheddar production taking place in factories. Unlike the names of many European cheeses, that of cheddar is not protected—*see* PROTECTED DESIGNATION OF ORIGIN (PDO). That's due to the fact that it's now the most widely produced cheese in the world, with production in myriad countries including Australia, Canada, Ireland, New Zealand, Scotland, South Africa, Sweden, and the United States. In truth, the word *cheddar* is no longer grounded on the name of the English village, but rather on the PRESSING process by which the cheese is made. With this technique, known as *CHEDDARING,* slabs of partially drained curd are stacked on top of each other and turned and restacked every 10 to 15 minutes for up to 1½ hours, which ensures that all slabs are pressed evenly. This produces a cheese with the characteristically smooth, tight texture of cheddar, CHESHIRE, and LANCASHIRE. Cheddar's flavor develops with age, and consumers can choose their preferred style by how the cheese is labeled. Some labels indicate the length of time a cheese has been ripened. Other labeling classifies cheddars as *mild* (usually 2 to 4 months of RIPENING), *medium* (4 to 8 months aging), *sharp* (9 to 12 months old), or *extra-sharp* (cheeses aged over 1 year). It must be said, however, that the aging times for cheddars listed as mild, medium, sharp, or extra-sharp can vary widely, depending on the producer. In general, mass-produced cheddars are second-rate to traditional handmade versions. Factories simply cannot control the quality of the milk, which is almost always pasteurized, whereas handmade cheddars are typically made with raw milk. Although **British farmstead cheese production** is dwarfed by the huge amount of factory-made cheese, a

C

renaissance of traditional cheesemaking is occurring in the United Kingdom, United States, Australia, and elsewhere. One signal of handmade cheddar is that it's wrapped in cloth (*see* BANDAGING). Another is that it isn't dyed orange with ANNATTO. It's not unusual to see a streak or two of blue veining here and there in some farmstead cheddars. It's simply a sign that the mold has breached the rind and isn't harmful in the least. In fact, some people quite enjoy the flavor. The FAT CONTENT of regular cheddar is 48 percent. There are also low-fat and nonfat cheddars, as well as those seasoned with ingredients such as garlic, basil, sage, horseradish, chile peppers, and port. At this writing, only one cheddar in the United Kingdom—**West Country Farmhouse Cheddar**—has been given PDO recognition. There are more than a dozen cheesemakers in Somerset, Dorset, and Devon counties that are producing this farmstead cheese in the time-honored traditional manner. Two of England's most highly respected and award-winning farmhouse, traditionally made cheddars are Montgomery's and Keen's. **Montgomery's Cheddar** is considered by many to be the quintessential English cheddar, with its impeccably balanced nutty-fruity-grassy flavor profile. It's been made for centuries by the Montgomery family (cheesemaker James Montgomery) at their five hundred-year-old Manor Farm in Somerset. Montgomery's cheddar is produced with raw milk from the family's herd of 140 Friesian cows and aged from 1 to 2 years. **Keen's Cheddar** has been made at Moorhayes Farm in Wincanton, Somerset, since 1899. The Keens typically age their cheeses a minimum of 10 months, more likely from 12 to 18 months, and up to 2 years. Keen's Cheddar is noted for its sharp, nutty, spicy flavor. **Reade's Isle of Mull Cheddar** is another raw-milk farmstead cheese, but this one is from Scotland. The Isle of Mull lies just off the west coast of Scotland, and here Chris and Ian Reade and their sons raise Friesian-Holstein cows. They make about 20 wheels of cheese a

C

day in a method similar to that of the English farmstead cheeses, including bandaging in cloth. Isle of Mull Cheddar is RIPENED for about 1 year. The cheese is sometimes called **Tobermory,** which is the capital of the island. In the United States, many states (including California, New York, Oregon, Wisconsin, and Vermont) are producing artisanal cheddars. **Cabot Creamery Cooperative** of Monpelier, Vermont, produces Cabot Clothbound Cheddar, a single-breed, small-batch, 12-month-old cheese that was a recent "Best of Show" winner at the American Cheese Society conference. This cooperative was founded in 1919 and began making cheddar in the 1930s. **Carr Valley Cheese Company** of La Valle, Wisconsin, also consistently wins awards for several of its cheddars, including Mammoth Cheddar, made in 74-pound wheels and RIPENED for 10 months, Aged Cheddar 8-year, Aged Cheddar 10-year, and Cave Aged Cheddar. **Fiscalini Cheese Company** of Modesto, California, produces its award-winning farmstead **30-Month Bandage Wrapped Cheddar** and **18-Month Bandage Wrapped Cheddar** using unpasteurized milk and traditional production techniques, including bandaging the cheese in cheesecloth. Fiscalini's cheesemaker, Jorge "Mariano" Gonzalez, trained at England's Montgomery Farms. **Grafton Village Cheese Company** of Grafton, Vermont, makes only raw-milk cheddar cheeses for which it has won numerous awards. It produces Premium Cheddar (1 year old), Classic Reserve (2 years), 4 Star (4 years), 5 Star (5 years), and Stone House (6 years). Grafton also makes flavored cheddars such as sage and garlic and an award-winning Maple Smoked Cheddar. **Shelburne Farms** in Shelburne, Vermont, has been making award-winning cheddar since 1981. It produces several styles, including Six- to Nine-Month, One-Year, Two-Year, Three-Year, Smoked, and Clothbound Cheddar. Shelburne uses traditional farmstead production techniques and raw milk from its herd of purebred Brown Swiss

C

cows. Shelburne Farms is a 1,400-acre working farm, a National Historic Landmark, and a nonprofit environmental education center. Australia's **King Island Dairy** produces several award-winning cheddars, including the **Black Label Cloth-Matured Cheddar,** aged a minimum of 6 months; **Stokes Point Smoked Cheddar,** ripened for 9 months and smoked with Tasmanian hardwood; and **Black Label Black Waxed Cheddar,** which has at least 18 months of aging.

cheddaring An alternative form of PRESSING the CURD to create fine-textured, semifirm cheeses such as CHEDDAR, CHESHIRE, and LANCASHIRE. Cheddaring begins once the curd has become a single mass. With hand-cheddared cheeses, the curd is typically divided in half and pushed to the vat's edge so most of the WHEY can drain off. The partially drained curd is then cut into large slabs. These pieces are stacked on top of each other, usually two to four slabs to a stack. They're turned and restacked every 10 to 15 minutes for up to 1½ hours, which ensures that all slabs are pressed evenly. This technique not only extracts as much WHEY as possible but also creates chemical changes in the curd that increase the acidity, which lengthens and binds the CASEIN protein molecules into long filaments. This molecular change transforms the curd from its original fragile structure into a densely matted mass. The curd is then minced before undergoing SALTING and MOLDING. Factory cheddaring typically involves the curd slabs being stacked into a "cheddar tower," a stainless-steel tube where the curd is pressed continuously without being turned, after which it's milled (*see* MILLING). Factory-made cheddars have a dense, slightly slick consistency, whereas the texture of handmade cheddars is firm and slightly crumbly or flaky.

Cheddar squeakers *see* SQUEAKERS

cheese; cheesemaking In the simplest terms, cheese is a concentrated dairy product made from milk (cow's, goat's, sheep's, and other ruminants). The word *cheese* comes from the Latin *caseus*. In the United States, about one-third of all milk is used to make cheese. The milk may be in any of several forms— whole, reduced fat (2 percent or 1 percent fat), fat-free (also called *nonfat* or *skim*), or a combination of styles. U.S. federal regulations require all cheeses (either domestic or imported) to be made from pasteurized milk (*see* PASTEURIZATION) or RIPENED a minimum of 60 days at a temperature of at least 35°F. The **cheesemaking** process, in the most basic terms, entails (1) selecting the milk or combination of milk types; (2) ACIDIFICATION, typically by adding a STARTER; (3) adding RENNET to coagulate (*see* COAGULATION) the milk; (4) CUTTING and stirring the curd; (5) COOKING (which isn't done for all cheeses); (6) draining (separating the curds from the WHEY); (7) MOLDING the cheese into its final shape; (8) PRESSING to further encourage whey drainage; (9) SALTING to preserve, flavor, and concentrate the cheese (salting may be done before the cheese is molded); (10) RIPENING or aging the cheese; and (11) rind formation (*see* RINDS), which occurs during ripening. *See also* TYPE(S), CHEESE, and How Cheese Is Made, page 1.

cheese board (cheeseboard); cheese plate; cheese course *see* Serving Cheese, page 25

cheesecake A luscious, rich dessert typically made by combining CREAM CHEESE, RICOTTA, or COTTAGE CHEESE with eggs, sugar, and sometimes cream or other liquids. Cheesecakes can have a crust or not, and such a foundation can range from a pastry crust to a cookie crust to a simple dusting of cookie, bread, or graham cracker crumbs. They're baked in special springform pans, with sides that come off after the baked cheesecake has cooled thoroughly. Cheesecakes can range in texture from creamy, dense, and heavy to light and ethereal. Though cheesecakes are typically thought of as desserts, savory versions—made with CHEDDAR, GRUYÈRE, and so on—make a wonderful hors d'oeuvre to spread on crackers or bread.

cheese classifications *see* TYPE(S), CHEESE

cheesecloth A lightweight natural cotton cloth that won't fall apart when wet or flavor the food it touches. Cheesecloth and MUSLIN are used in cheesemaking for a host of functions, primarily as a liner for cheese molds before the CURDS are added and pressed (*see* PRESSING). For some cheeses, the curds are spooned directly into cheesecloth or muslin bags to be drained and shaped (*see* MOLDING). In Britain cheesecloth is sometimes referred to as *muslin cheesecloth*. *See also* BANDAGING; MUSLIN

cheese color *see* COLORING

cheese food *see* PROCESS(ED) CHEESES

cheese harp A long, wide rakelike device (which may or may not have a long handle) used in cheesemaking for CUTTING the CURD. The "tines" on a harp are tautly strung wires. Also called *Swiss harp*.

cheese iron *see* IRONING CHEESE

cheesemaker; cheese maker One who produces cheese, primarily professionally. A **master cheesemaker** is typically one with extensive experience who has undergone advanced training. At this writing, the Wisconsin Master Cheesemaker Program is the

C

only one of its kind in the United States. The program is modeled on European standards, administered by the Wisconsin Center for Dairy Research, and funded by Wisconsin dairy producers through the Wisconsin Milk Marketing Board.

cheesemaking *see* CHEESE; CHEESEMAKER

cheese mites Tiny insects that infest not only cheese but also corn, flour, and other foods. Just visible to the naked eye, cheese mites create tiny holes in a cheese's rind and PASTE. The surface of a mite-infested cheese is covered by a fine grayish brown powder comprised of mite skins, feces, and both living and dead mites. Appetizing, yes? That said, there are those who consider the piquant characteristic of such cheeses immensely appealing. Still, mite infestation is considered a defect, though surface damage can be brushed off or the rind peeled away. Cheeses with interior mite damage are best discarded, unless you're particularly fond of that pungent flavor and fragrance of eau-de-insect.

cheesemonger The word *monger* is defined as a dealer in a specific commodity, so a cheesemonger sells cheese.

cheese product *see* PROCESS(ED) CHEESES

cheese salt *see* SALTING

cheese sizes and shapes *see* BARREL; BLOCK; DAISY; FLAT; LOAF; LONGHORN; MAMMOTH; MOON; TRUCKLE; WHEEL

cheese spread *see* PROCESS(ED) CHEESES

cheese starter culture *see* STARTER

cheese type *see* TYPE(S), CHEESE

cheese wax *see* WAX

Chenna [CHEH-nah] *see* PANEER

Cheshire [CHEH-sher]

Origin	England (Cheshire)
Milk	Unpasteurized and pasteurized cow's
Type	SEMIHARD to HARD; PRESSED COOKED; NATURAL RIND; FARMSTEAD and FACTORY
Appearance	Tall wheels of various sizes weighing from 2 to 44 pounds, farmstead versions cloth-wrapped, sometimes with WAX covering the cloth, factory versions usually vacuum packed in plastic; rind is light gold with blue-gray mold; interior ranges from ivory (natural) to orange (dyed); blue versions have blue-green veins
Texture	Firm, moist, and flaky
Flavor	Farmstead versions are lightly salty, savory, and tangy; factory versions are blander

This cheese—thought to be England's oldest—hails from Cheshire, a county in northwestern England. Believed to pre-date the Roman occupation of England, it shows up in the *Doomsday Book* census of 1086. In the late eighteenth century, Cheshire was one of England's most popular cheeses and always stocked on Royal Navy ships. Cheshire is sometimes referred to as *Chester,* an important port from which Cheshire was shipped to London during the cheese's prominence and that today is the county seat. There are 3 varieties of Cheshire—

C

white (natural ivory in color), red (which is dyed with AN-NATTO), and blue (a BLUE-VEINED CHEESE). The milk used to produce all three styles comes from cows that graze on the Cheshire Plain's saline-rich pastures, which gives the cheese its slightly salty trait. Two milks comprise this cheese—morning milk and the prior evening's. Cheshire is typically RIPENED for 4 to 8 weeks, but farmstead versions are usually aged much longer than that—usually from 6 months to a year. **Blue Cheshire,** sometimes referred to as *Cheshire-Stilton,* is made like regular Cheshire except that curd inoculated with *Penicillium roqueforti* is mixed with fresh curd to create the mold necessary for blue-veined cheese. At the beginning stages of aging, the cheese is pierced with needles to allow oxygen access to the interior in order to feed the bacteria that creates the bluing. The resulting cheese is full flavored yet milder than STILTON. Blue Cheshire is sometimes called *Blue Fade* when created from a naturally colored cheese or *Green Fade* when produced from an orange-dyed cheese (blue plus orange produces a greenish cast). The farmstead Cheshires generally have richer, fuller flavors than factory-made versions because they're made with high-quality milk (often unpasteurized) and ripened longer for flavor development. The FAT CONTENT of Cheshire is about 48 percent.

Cheshire-Stilton *see* CHESHIRE

Chester *see* CHESHIRE

chèvre [SHEHV; SHEHV-r] French for "goat," the word *chèvre* in the cheese world refers generically to a broad and diversified family of cheeses made with goat's milk. Much of France's goat cheese production is centered along the Loire Valley, which is south and east of Paris. The history of the area's goat population goes back to the Saracens, people of Arab descent who settled first in Spain and then in parts of France. Goats and goat cheeses were an integral part of their culture. When the Saracens of the Loire Valley area were defeated in the eighth century, most of them departed, leaving behind their goats and cheesemaking techniques. The art of crafting chèvre has evolved over the ages. Today there are nine French chèvres with APPELLATION D'ORIGINE CONTRÔLÉE (AOC) and PROTECTED DESIGNATION OF ORIGIN (PDO) status—CHABICHOU DU POITOU, CROTTIN DE CHAVIGNOL, PÉLARDON, PICODON DE L'ARDÈCHE (or PICODON DE LA DRÔME), POULIGNY-SAINT-PIERRE, ROCAMADOUR, SAINTE-MAURE DE TOURAINE, SELLES-SUR-CHER, and VALENÇAY. Chèvre comes in many forms, and sometimes the shape's name is part of the name of the cheese. Among the most popular **chèvre shapes** are *besace* (beggar's purse), *bicorne* (two horns), *bondon* (bung, a wine cask stopper), *bouchon* (cork), *boule* or *boulette* (ball, as in BOULE DE LILLE), *bouton* (button), *brique* (brick), *brochette* (skewer, where the cheese is shaped around a wooden stick), *bûche* (log), *carré* (square), *cerise* (cherry), *clochette* (small bell), *coeur* (heart), *crottin* (horse droppings), *figue* (fig), *fleur* (flower), *lingot* (bar), *médaillon* (medallion), *pavé* (square paving stone), *pavé amalthée* (hexagonal paving stone), *pyramide* (pyramid), *quatre feuille* (four-leaf clover), *rond* (round), and *taupinière* (molehill). The label term *pur chèvre* ensures that the cheese is made entirely from goat's milk; *mi-chèvre* means that it's comprised of at least 50 percent goat's milk, with the remainder typically cow's milk. Chèvres can range in texture from moist, creamy, and soft to dry and semifirm. The plural is *chèvres,* which originally referred to all *French* goat cheeses but is now widely used to refer to all goat cheeses, wherever their origin. In the United States there are a few large commercial factories and numerous FARMSTEAD and ARTISANAL chèvre producers, including **Capriole Goat Cheese** in Indiana, **Haystack Mountain Goat Dairy** in Colorado, and **Laura Chenel Chèvre** in California. Laura Chenel began making goat cheese in the late seventies as the first commercial goat cheese producer in the United States and—at this writing—now sells over a million pounds of cheese annually. Chenel is widely recognized as the pioneer in generating the prototype for farmstead and artisanal chèvres, establishing the market and paving the way in the United States for today's almost ninety chèvre-producing dairies. Though almost all chèvre sales around the world were initially geared to fresh (unripened) styles, today there are numerous artisans making RIPENED goat cheeses that are becoming immensely popular. Three of these exceptional aged goat's milk American-made cheeses are MIDNIGHT MOON from California's **Cypress Grove Chèvre,** CAPRICIOUS from **California's Achadinha Cheese Company,** and LE CHÈVRE NOIR from Canada's **Fromagerie Tournevent.**

Chèvre Noir, Le [leuh shev NWAH*R*]

Origin	Canada (Quebec)
Milk	Unpasteurized and pasteurized goat's
Type	SEMIHARD to HARD; PRESSED COOKED; ARTISAN
Appearance	$4\frac{1}{2}$-ounce shrink-wrapped blocks or 9-ounce and $2\frac{1}{2}$-pound blocks coated with black wax; rindless; interior is white to off-white with a small number of tiny EYES
Texture	Smooth, tight, firm, moist, and crumbly with occasional crunchy bits
Flavor	Nutty, buttery, and savory with a sweet hint of caramel

Le Chèvre Noir is produced by **Fromagerie Tournevent** in Chesterville, Quebec. It was first made in 1989 and has been a consistent award winner ever since, taking first place in many Canadian cheese events as well as at the annual American Cheese Society competition. It's savored not only for its complex flavor but also for the crunchy bits of crystallized protein that give the cheese a pleasantly sweet characteristic. This goat's milk CHEDDAR-style cheese is produced with both raw and pasteurized milks. Raw-milk versions are RIPENED for 6 months or more. Other Chèvre Noirs are aged for 1 year, and choice lots are matured for 2 years. This cheese has a FAT CONTENT of 28 percent.

Chevrotin des Aravis (AOC) [shev-roh–TAN dayz ah-rah–VEE]

Origin	France (Rhône-Alpes)
Milk	Unpasteurized goat's
Type	SEMISOFT; PRESSED UNCOOKED; WASHED RIND; FARMSTEAD
Appearance	9- to 12-ounce wheels; rind is thin and beige to reddish orange with velvety white mold; interior is ivory with a small scattering of EYES
Texture	Smooth, creamy, and supple, becoming oozy as it ripens
Flavor	Mild, slightly musty, savory, spicy, and nutty

This type of goat's milk cheese has been made in the Savoie and the Haute-Savoie for over three centuries. It's unlike the goat's milk cheese of the Loire Valley (CROTTIN DE CHAVIGNOL, POULIGNY-SAINT-PIERRE, VALENÇAY) in that it's a washed-rind cheese that becomes runny (instead of becoming dry and firm) as it ages. It's essentially a goat's milk version of RE-BLOCHON, the renowned cow's milk cheese from the same area.

C

Both are washed-rind cheeses made with uncooked, slightly pressed CURD. Chevrotin des Aravis cheeses are ripened from 3 to 8 weeks and have a minimum FAT CONTENT of 45 percent. Because Chevrotin des Aravis is made with unpasteurized milk and most of these cheeses have less then 60 days of ripening, they cannot be imported into the United States at this writing (*see* UNPASTEURIZED MILK/IMPORTED CHEESE DILEMMA).

Chihuahua [chee-WAH-wah; chih-WAH-wah]

Origin	Mexico (Chihuahua)
Milk	Unpasteurized and pasteurized cow's
Type	SEMISOFT to SEMIHARD; PRESSED COOKED; NATURAL RIND; ARTISAN, FARMSTEAD, and FACTORY
Appearance	Various shapes and sizes including wheels, squares, rectangles, braids, and balls; rind is thin and ranges in color from off-white to pale yellow, some rindless; interior ranges from off-white to pale yellow
Texture	Young versions are creamy and elastic, becoming firmer with age
Flavor	Delicate, mild, salty, buttery, and slightly sour

Though now more popularly known as Chihuahua, this cheese was originally (and still is) called *Menonita,* a name that comes from its Mennonite history. In 1922, the president of Mexico invited Canadian Mennonites to settle in the state of Chihuahua, offering them land at reasonable prices and no taxes for a hundred years. In return, the Mennonites were to make the majority of the cheese required by the people of northern Mexico. Thousands of Mennonites moved to Chihuahua, bringing with them household goods, farm equipment, and livestock. Eventually the Mennonites established about forty villages where the women were typically the cheesemakers while their husbands ran the farms. There are still thousands of Mennonites producing this cheese in Chihuahua. It's a mild, smooth-melting cheese used throughout much of Mexico and in parts of the United States. It can be made with either whole or partially skimmed milk and is often compared to young JACK cheeses or mild GOUDA.

chile con queso [CHEE-lay kon KAY-soh] Spanish for "chiles with cheese," this warm cheese dip is, as the name implies, flavored with hot chiles, such as jalapeños. Chopped tomato, onion, and garlic are also traditionally added. The Tex-Mex version unabashedly uses Velveeta cheese (*see* PROCESS(ED) CHEESES); other renditions typically employ CHEDDAR, JACK, or a combination. Tortilla chips for dipping are the classic accompaniment.

Chimay [she-MAY]

Origin	Belgium (Chimay)
Milk	Pasteurized cow's
Type	SEMISOFT TO SEMIHARD; PRESSED UNCOOKED; WASHED RIND; ARTISAN
Appearance	5- to 7-pound wheels; rind is thin and can range in color from a mottled golden to orangey brown; interior is ivory to pale yellow to golden (depending on style) with a scattering of EYES
Texture	Smooth, creamy, and supple
Flavor	Mild, rich, creamy, and slightly nutty

C

A renowned cheese made by Trappist monks at the Abbey of Notre Dame de Scourmont (Scourmont is the hill on which the abbey perches) not far from the town of Chimay. It's located just north of the French border and surrounded by picturesque forest and farmlands. The Romanesque abbey was constructed in 1850, the dairy and brewery added in 1862. The monastery at Chimay is one of only six in the world approved by the Vatican to market and Trappist-designate the beer and food products it produces. The cheeses are made with milk from the abbey's farm and ripened in the monastery's vaulted cellars. There are several styles of Chimay cheese. **Chimay Grand Classic** is aged for 4 weeks, has a semisoft texture, and comes in various sizes— from 12-ounce to 4.4-pound wheels and 1- to 4-pound rectangular bricks. **Chimay Trappiste with Beer** is a variation on the classic version that's washed in the famous Chimay beer, which gives the cheese nuances of hops and malt. It comes in 11-ounce and 4.4-pound wheels. **Chimay Grand Cru** is aged for 6 weeks, semihard in texture, and comes in a 4.4-pound wheel. **Chimay Vieux** matures for a minimum of 6 months, which produces a flavor that's sharp yet creamy and redolent of hazelnuts. It comes in a 6.6-pound ball shape, similar in shape to a MIMOLETTE. As with most cheeses of this style, Chimays have an assertive odor but a relatively mild flavor.

Christian; Christian IX *see* DANBO

chymosin [KI-muh-sin] *see* RENNET

citrusy *see* Glossary of Cheese Descriptors, page 496

clabber [KLA-ber] **n.** Milk or cream that has soured and thickened. **v.** To COAGULATE or curdle milk.

C

classifications, cheese *see* TYPE(S), CHEESE

clean *see* Glossary of Cheese Descriptors, page 496

clean break The test to see if the CURD is ready to be cut is to insert a finger or other instrument into the curds at a 45-degree angle. If the curd forms a clean, clear separation (a clean break), it's ready.

clochette [kloh-SHEHT] French for "small bell" and one of the many shapes into which CHÈVRE is formed.

close; closed *see* Glossary of Cheese Descriptors, page 496

cloth-wrapped *see* BANDAGING; BANDAGED

clove cheese *see* NÖKKELOST

club cheese *see* COLD PACK CHEESE

coagulation; coagulate, to The transformation of a liquid into a semisolid or solid mass. In the initial stages of cheesemaking, pH-balanced milk (*see* STARTER) has RENNET added to it, which coagulates the milk protein (CASEIN) and forms the CURD. Coagulation is also called *curdling* or *curding*.

Cobble Hill *see* VERMONT BREBIS

coeur [koor] French for "heart" and one of the many shapes into which CHÈVRE is formed.

Cojack *see* COLBY

C

Colby [KOHL-bee]

Origin	United States (Wisconsin)
Milk	Unpasteurized or pasteurized cow's
Type	HARD; PRESSED UNCOOKED; NATURAL RIND and rindless; ARTISAN and FACTORY
Appearance	Various shapes (including blocks, wheels, and tall cylinders) and sizes up to 75 pounds; rind is thin or nonexistent with a color that ranges from ivory to medium yellow-orange (the latter artificial), often with wax covering; interior is ivory or medium yellow-orange in color
Texture	Slightly firm, loose texture, and elastic
Flavor	Mild and creamy

This American original was invented in 1885 by Joseph Stein-wand in his father's cheese factory near Colby, Wisconsin. It's similar to CHEDDAR but is made with the WASHED-CURD technique, which produces a milder flavor and a softer, springier texture. According to USDA standards, Colby cheeses cannot contain more than 40 percent moisture—cheddar not more than 39 percent. So Colby's softer consistency is due to the loose texture created by the washed-curd process and not because of a significantly higher moisture content. Some Colbys have added smoke flavoring; all have a minimum FAT CONTENT of 50 percent. **Longhorn** is a Colby-style cheese that's normally produced in tall cylinders but sold in thick slices that are cut into two half-moon shapes. A popular hybrid is a mixture of Colby and JACK cheese, often called **Colby Jack** or **CoJack.** It's a blend of orangish yellow and ivory cheeses, the combination of which produces a marbled effect. **Crowley Cheese Company** in Vermont makes a Colby cheese that's often referred to simply as **Crowley.** This artisan cheese is considered

C

superior to most factory versions. Other well-regarded American Colby producers are **Carr Valley Cheese** and **Widmer's Cheese Cellars,** both located in Wisconsin. Colby is also made in other countries, including Canada and Denmark, and is very popular in New Zealand, where it's been produced for over 100 years.

cold pack cheeses A blend of natural cheese (typically CHEDDAR) and other ingredients that can range from herbs to spices to wine flavoring. More than one type of cheese of the same variety can be used—mild and sharp, for example. In the production of cold pack cheese (also called *club cheese*), natural cheese is shredded and blended with seasonings, then packed into molds before being pressed (*see* PRESSING). The cheesemaking process is done without heat, which differentiates cold pack cheese from PROCESS(ED) CHEESE. The result is a firm (not soft or hard) cheese that's creamy yet crumbly when cold. It's spreadable when brought to room temperature. *See also* IMITATION CHEESE; SUBSTITUTE CHEESE.

coloring Some cheeses, such as CHEDDAR, are tinted with ANNATTO, a natural coloring that can produce shades ranging from yellow to orange.

ColoRouge

Origin	United States (Colorado)
Milk	Pasteurized cow's
Type	SOFT; MOLDED UNCOOKED; WASHED RIND; ARTISAN
Appearance	5-ounce round; rind is a reddish orange coated with a hazing of white mold; interior is ivory colored

C

Texture	Ranges from relatively firm and creamy to exceedingly soft and oozy when ultraripe
Flavor	Subtle, buttery, spicy, and beefy

ColoRouge was introduced in 2003 and a year later won the prestigious gold medal at the American Cheese Society competition. It's the second cheese to be made by **MouCo Cheese Company** (*mou* as in a cow's "moo," *co* as in "company"), whose flagship effort is a traditional French–style CAMEMBERT. MouCo is owned and lovingly operated in Ft. Collins, Colorado, by husband-and-wife team Robert Poland and Birgit Halbreiter, who met at a brewing conference when they were both in the beer business. Halbreiter, whose father, Franz, is a master cheesemaker in Germany, grew up around cheese and once worked for one of the world's largest soft-ripened cheese producers in Germany. So segueing from beer to cheese was a natural move for the couple. They use Jersey and Holstein milk from nearby farms for their handmade ColoRouge (*Colo* as in Colorado, *Rouge* as in the color red, after Colorado's red earth and rocks, as well as the color of the rind). At the start of the RIPENING period, the cheese is hand-rubbed with a secret mixture of BRINE, bacteria, and yeasts. It's turned repeatedly and ready for release at the end of 2 weeks. MouCo's third addition to its line is **Blü,** a soft-ripened blue cheese.

colostrum Also known as *beestings,* colostrum is the first "milk" (actually a thin, yellowish *foremilk*) produced by a cow for the first five milkings after calving. It's exceedingly rich in antibodies, vitamins, and minerals. In Spain's province of Léon, colostrum is used in the production of a strong, cylindrically shaped, semifirm cheese called ***Armada.***

Comté (AOC; PDO) [kawn-TAY]

Origin	France (Franche-Comté, Rhône-Alpes, Burgundy, Champagne-Ardenne, Lorraine)
Milk	Unpasteurized cow's
Type	HARD; PRESSED COOKED; NATURAL RIND; COOPERATIVE; some MOUNTAIN
Appearance	Round, 75- to 120-pound wheels with convex sides; rind is thin, hard, and rough with small pits, the color golden brown with some gray spotches; interior is off-white to pale yellow, developing small EYES and cracks as it ripens
Texture	Firm and supple
Flavor	Complex variety of sweet toffee, fruit, nuts, and savoriness

Comté, also called **Gruyère de Comté,** has almost certainly been made for several thousand years and, by the eleventh century, farmers began pooling their milk to produce these large wheels of cheese. Today there are over three thousand farms and several hundred cooperative dairies (FRUITIÈRES) scattered across APPELLATION D'ORIGINE CONTRÔLÉE (AOC)– designated areas in parts of five French regions. France produces more tons of Comté than any other cheese, and yet its strictly regulated quality remains very high. Appellation d'Origine Contrôlée (AOC) regulations state that the milk must come from Montbéliard cows that eat plant life grown only in the approved areas. Minimum aging is 4 months, but 5 to 6 months or longer is more common. Each Comté cheese must pass a 20-point grading system; those scoring 15 or more points get green labels; those with 12 to 15 points have

C

red labels. Those below 12 points (about 5 percent) are rejected and sold as GRUYÈRE. The FAT CONTENT of Comté is about 45 percent.

Constant Bliss

Origin	United States (Vermont)
Milk	Unpasteurized cow's
Type	SEMISOFT; MOLDED UNCOOKED; BLOOMY RIND; FARMSTEAD
Appearance	6- to 8-ounce cylinders, which become misshapen with age; rind is rough, rippling, and beige to light brown with a velvety coating of white mold; interior is snow white to ivory, darker near the rind
Texture	Dense, smooth, and buttery
Flavor	Rich, creamy, and earthy, with hints of mushroom, becoming more pronounced with age

Constant Bliss was named after an American Revolution scout who in 1781 was killed by Native Americans near Greensboro, Vermont, the home of **Jasper Hill Farm**. The farm is owned by the Kehler families, who raise a small herd of registered Ayrshire cows that produce a milk that's rich in protein and fat. Mateo and Andy Keyler, along with their wives, Victoria and Angela, produce Constant Bliss, which has taken a gold medal at the annual American Cheese Society competition. The Constant Bliss cheesemaking process begins even before the evening milking is completed so the milk can be used before it cools down. This evening milk has a richer FAT CONTENT—the lower-fat morning milk is used for Jasper Hill Farm's award-winning BAYLEY HAZEN BLUE. Constant Bliss, which is RIPENED for at least 60 days, develops its bloomy rind from the existing molds in the aging cave, rather than from having bacterial molds sprayed on the surface of the cheese.

cooked *see* Glossary of Cheese Descriptors, page 496

cooked cheese *see* COOKING

cooked pressed cheeses *see* PRESSED COOKED CHEESES

cooking A cheesemaking step during which the CURDS are heated in WHEY while being stirred. This process tightens the curd's protein network, firms the texture, and expels more whey. How long the curds are heated and at what temperature depends on the type of cheese being made. The higher the cooking temperature and the longer the cooking time, the firmer the resulting cheese. For example, for very hard cheeses like PARMESAN, the curds are cooked at 131°F (55°C), whereas the curds for a softer cheese like FONTINA are heated only to around 110°F (43°C). Cheeses heated at temperatures below 120°F are often referred to as *semicooked*. **Scalding** is a similar but milder heating process whereby the vat (rather than the curds) is heated, sometimes by a steam jacket. In this case, only the curd's surface is heated.

Coolea [koo-LAY]

Origin	Ireland (Cork)
Milk	Pasteurized cow's
Type	SEMIHARD to HARD; PRESSED COOKED; NATURAL RIND; ARTISAN
Appearance	9- and 19-pound wheels; rind is synthetic and golden tan in color; interior is pale gold (turning darker at the rind) with a few small EYES

C

Texture	Firm and supple, becoming denser and flaky with RIPENING
Flavor	Young versions are mild, creamy, slightly tangy, and nutty; older versions become stronger, more complex, and develop a caramellike character

A cheese developed by Dick and Helen Willems in western county Cork, Ireland. Coolea is the name of a town and surrounding area between Cork City and Killarney in county Kerry. This GOUDA-style cheese was a natural for the Willems, who moved from Holland to Ireland over 20 years ago. Coolea is a traditionally made farmstead cheese along the lines of a full-flavored BOERENKASS (farmer's) Gouda, and unlike the bland, mass-produced WAX-wrapped versions that abound. Coolea is usually ripened for 6 to 12 months and comes in two styles—plain or flavored with cumin seed. The FAT CONTENT of this cheese is approximately 45 percent.

cooperative Small local dairies that make cheese from milk provided by nearby farms.

Cornish Yarg

Origin	England (Cornwall)
Milk	Pasteurized cow's
Type	SEMIHARD; PRESSED COOKED; NATURAL RIND; FARMSTEAD
Appearance	2¼- to 6½-pound wheels; rind is wrapped in nettle leaves and develops a grayish green cast as it ripens; interior is white to ivory
Texture	Moist, loose, and crumbly when young; aged versions will be creamier near the rind while still chalky and crumbly in the center

C

Flavor   Mild, grassy, and buttery with a lemony tang,
becoming richer, creamier, less tangy, and
somewhat floral with age

Cornish Yarg is made at Lynher Dairies Cheese Company at the
century-old Netherton Farm, which is part of the Duchy of
Cornwall Estate. The Cornwall region is at England's extreme
southwest tip on a peninsula bounded by the Atlantic Ocean
and English Channel. Mike and Margaret Horrell of Netherton
Farm began making cheese in the 1980s and had success in England with their cheeses, all with *Cornish* in the name. Eventually they brought in two Welsh cheesemakers—Alan and Jenny
Gray—to create a new cheese. The Grays adapted a thirteenth-
century recipe to create what is now Cornish Yarg. *Yarg,* rather
than being Cornish dialect as many assume, is actually simply
the name *Gray* spelled backward. The Grays have since left, and
Catherine Mead is now the cheesemaker. Throughout the eons
leaves have been used to cover and protect cheeses. In the case of
Cornish Yarg, as befits a centuries-old recipe, local nettle leaves
are used—picked when fresh and frozen until required. The
freezing neutralizes the chemicals associated with the stinging
nature of nettle leaves and also makes the leaves malleable
enough to place on the cheese. The leaves are edible, though
most cheese lovers discard them. The recipe for Cornish Yarg
and the resulting cheese is similar to that of the Welsh cheese
CAERPHILLY. Cornish Yarg is RIPENED for a minimum of 3
weeks, but often for 2 to 3 months, and has a FAT CONTENT of
about 45 percent. **Cornish Wild Garlic Yarg** is covered with
wild garlic leaves, which impart an herbaceous flavor with light
onion and garlic traits. Lynher Dairies Cheese Company also
makes other semihard cheese, including Cornish Tiskey and
Cornish Garland, and SEMISOFT cheeses including Cornish Pepper, Cornish Herb, Garlic, and Cornish Tarragon.

C

Cotija; queso Cotija [koh-TEE-hah; KAY-soh]

Origin	Mexico (Michoacán)
Milk	Unpasteurized and pasteurized cow's or goat's
Type	SEMISOFT to HARD; GRANA STYLE; PRESSED COOKED; rindless; ARTISAN and FACTORY
Appearance	24- to 66-pound cylinders; rindless; exterior and interior are white to ivory, may contain a scattering of small EYES
Texture	Young versions are smooth, firm, and slightly crumbly; ripened ones are hard, dry, and granular
Flavor	Salty, milky, and tangy when young, becoming very salty and pungent with age

Named after the town of Cotija de la Paz in the state of Michoacán, this cheese is also called *queso añejo* or *queso añejado* ("aged cheese"). Cotija's popularity spread from central and southern Mexico to other parts of the country and now has a following in the United States, where some cheesemakers are producing it. Although Cojita is available in a moister form that resembles a young FETA, what's more commonly found in the marketplace is the RIPENED version. This aged cheese is hard enough for grating, which is why its nickname is "Mexican Parmesan." Traditional Mexican versions were made from raw milk, but factory-made Cojitas in both Mexico and the United States now primarily use pasteurized milk. The hard, grana-style Cotija is ripened for from 3½ months to 1 year and has a FAT CONTENT of about 45 percent. Because Cotija is extremely salty, it's used primarily as a seasoning for a variety of Mexican-style dishes.

Cotswold *see* GLOUCESTER

cottage cheese

Origin	Europe; United States
Milk	Pasteurized cow's
Type	FRESH; UNPRESSED UNCOOKED; FACTORY and FARMSTEAD
Appearance	8- to 32-ounce tubs; loose white curds ranging from small to large
Texture	Tender, moist, and sometimes creamy
Flavor	Fresh and milky, ranging from bland to slightly tangy

Made in Europe for eons, cottage cheese is now produced in many countries around the world and is immensely popular in the United States. This fresh cheese can be made from any style of milk—whole, partially skimmed, or fat free. It's an ACID CURD cheese, which means the milk is COAGULATED naturally, rather than with the aid of RENNET. Once the curd forms, it's cut into small pieces before being heated in WHEY until the desired texture is obtained. The curds are then drained completely before being thoroughly rinsed with water to remove all traces of LACTOSE that might convert to acid. Such WASHED-CURD cheeses are generally tender and have a mild flavor. At the end of the process, the curds are typically salted and amended with milk or cream. Cottage cheese is available in several CURD styles ranging from small to medium to large. The FAT CONTENT can also vary: **nonfat,** of course, has zero added fat; **low-fat** has 1 to 2 percent; and **creamed cottage cheese** may contain from 4 to 8 percent added fat (in the form of cream). California's Cowgirl Creamery produces an award-winning old-fashioned "clabbered cottage cheese," which is made with organic nonfat milk, then dressed with clabbered cream. Most cottage cheese is unflavored, though some have added seasonings, such as chives or pineapple. **Bakers'**

C

cheese is basically COTTAGE CHEESE with some of the moisture
drained off. It's similar in texture to fresh RICOTTA but has a
tangier flavor because it's slightly more acidic. It's primarily sold
for commercial use (rather than directly to consumers) and is
used extensively in preparations such as cheesecakes, pies, pastries, and blintzes. **Pot cheese** is cottage cheese that has been
drained of more moisture. It has a drier, slightly grainy texture,
which is why it's also called *dry-curd cottage cheese*. **Farmer('s)
cheese** is a form of cottage cheese that is most often pressed into
firm loaves or log shapes that can be sliced or crumbled. It has a
smooth, supple texture and a buttery, slightly acidic flavor. Farmer
cheese may be flavored with a variety of seasonings, including
basil, caraway, dill, garlic, and jalapeño. It's sometimes available
in dry curds—similar to cottage cheese without the liquid.

Coulommiers [koo-luhm-MYAY]

Origin	France (Île-de-France)
Milk	Unpasteurized or pasteurized cow's
Type	SOFT; MOLDED UNCOOKED; BLOOMY RIND; ARTISAN, FARMSTEAD, and FACTORY
Appearance	Thick ¾- to 1½-pound wheels; rind is thin and uneven with a velvety coating of white MOLD that shows patches of red as it ages; interior is pale yellow to light gold with a few EYES
Texture	Soft, smooth, and creamy; the best are *almost* oozy
Flavor	Farmstead and artisan versions are rich, buttery, and nutty with a hint of wild mushroom; factory versions are milder—not as rich and complex

Also called *Brie de Coulommiers* and *Petit Brie,* this cheese is
made in the Brie country east of Paris. It takes its name from

C

the town of Coulommiers, which lies between Meaux (where BRIE DE MEAUX is made) and Melun (of BRIE DE MELUN fame). It's much smaller than these two cheeses but is very much a Brie style and likely as old as these cheeses, which dates it back to the eighth century. Coulommiers does not have APPELLATION D'ORIGINE CONTRÔLÉE (AOC) or PROTECTED DESIGNATION OF ORIGIN (PDO) status like these other two cheeses, primarily because its production has never been uniform. Factory versions are usually made with pasteurized milk to meet U.S. standards and are generally RIPENED for 4 weeks. Raw-milk Coulommiers, aged for 6 to 8 weeks, are considered more flavorful, but they cannot be shipped to the United States at this writing (*see* UNPASTEURIZED MILK/IMPORTED CHEESE DILEMMA). The FAT CONTENT of Coulommiers ranges from 40 to 45 percent.

Coupole [koo-POHL] *see* BONNE BOUCHE

Cowgirl Creamery *see* MT. TAM; RED HAWK; ST. PAT

cow's milk cheeses *see* Index, page 519

cowy *see* BARNYARDY in Glossary of Cheese Descriptors, page 494

cracking Fissures in a cheese that can be the result of natural aging or a signal that a poorly wrapped cheese has dried out.

Crater Lake Blue *see* ROGUE RIVER BLUE

Crave Brothers Farmstead Cheese *see* MASCARPONE

cream *see* MILK

cream cheese

C

Origin	United States
Milk	Pasteurized cow's
Type	SOFT; UNPRESSED or PRESSED COOKED; FACTORY and ARTISAN
Appearance	3- and 8-ounce foil- or plastic-wrapped rectangles, 8-ounce plastic tubs or glass jars, and 3-pound loaves; rindless and white
Texture	Soft and creamy
Flavor	Milky, mildly salty, and slightly sweet and tangy

Contrary to popular belief, cream cheese does not hail from Philadelphia. It was invented in 1872 by William Lawrence, a dairyman in Chester, New York. It wasn't until a few years later, in 1880, that a New York cheese distributor began wrapping this creamy concoction in foil. It was dubbed "Philadelphia Brand Cream Cheese" because at the time that city had a reputation for top-quality dairy products. Kraft Foods purchased the brand in 1928, and so a legend was born. Today this well-known cream cheese is sold in over a hundred countries around the world with sales topping $1 billion. Cream cheese is made with a mixture of cow's milk and cream and by law must have a minimum FAT CONTENT of 33 percent and no more than 55 percent moisture. Ninety-nine percent of this soft, unripened cheese is factory-made. The CURD is typically heated (from 115°F to 125°F) and stirred in the vat until the WHEY begins to separate. The procedure for industrial cream cheese uses a centrifugal SEPARATOR to quickly drain the whey from the curds, a process that increases shelf life because the curds can be packaged hot. The curd is then mixed with salt and stabilizers—usually a combination of some of the following: carrageenan, guar gum, locust bean gum, sodium alginate, and xanthan gum. There are a few artisanal cream cheese producers in the United States, one of the most notable being the award-winning **Sierra Nevada Cheese Company**. Such producers make a product with hormone-free milk and without stabilizers. The milk is cultured and allowed to ripen for about 16 hours, whereas the milk for industrially produced cream cheese is typically COAGULATED in as little as 4 hours. After being salted and stirred mechanically for about 12 hours, the cooled curds are scooped into large bags, stacked on top of each other, and allowed to drain for about 36 hours, during which time the bags are rotated several times. This gentle, slow draining produces a lighter, silkier texture and fresher, tangier flavor. The downside is that such artisanal cream cheeses have a shorter shelf life than the mass-produced versions, but most agree that flavor trumps convenience any day. Cream cheese is available plain or may have flavorings added, such as berry or garlic. **American neufchatel cheese** (not to be confused with the French NEUFCHÂTEL) has only about 23 percent milkfat and a slightly higher moisture content than regular cream cheese. **Reduced-fat cream cheese** has a milkfat content of between 16.5 and 20 percent, **light or low-fat cream cheese** can have no more than 16.5 percent milkfat, and **nonfat cream cheese** contains, of course, no fat grams. **Whipped cream cheese** has had air whipped into it, giving it fewer calories per gram because there's less volume per serving. *See also* CREOLE CREAM CHEESE.

creamline milk *see* MILK

creamy *see* Glossary of Cheese Descriptors, page 496

crémier [kraym-YAY] French term for a small cheese producer. *See also* FRUITIÈRE; LAITIER.

C

Creole cream cheese

Origin	United States (Louisiana)
Milk	Pasteurized cow's
Type	SOFT; FRESH; MOLDED UNCOOKED; ARTISAN
Appearance	11.5-ounce tub; ivory white
Texture	Smooth, silky, some styles with soft curds throughout
Flavor	Slightly sweet-tart and nutty

This specialty of southern Louisiana has been produced since the 1800s and is thought to have roots in France's Brittany and Burgundy regions. It's essentially a mixture of cow's milk (usually skimmed) CURD and cream (generally half-and-half). The results can vary broadly from dairy to dairy, with textures ranging from a very thick, smooth sour cream to that of whole soft curds nestled in sour cream. Louisiana's **Bittersweet Plantation Dairy**'s Creole Cream Cheese is a consistent award winner in the American Cheese Society competition. Creole cream cheese is best eaten with fresh fruit and a sprinkling of sugar but can also be spread on toast.

Crescenza [kray-SHEHN-tzuh]

Origin	Italy (Lombardy, Piedmont, and Veneto)
Milk	Pasteurized cow's
Type	SOFT; MOLDED UNCOOKED; ARTISAN and FACTORY
Appearance	Milky white, 2-inch-thick squares or rectangles weighing from 2¼ to 4½ pounds; rindless and white exterior; interior is also white

Texture	Soft, smooth, moist, and creamy
Flavor	Mild, delicate, and milky with a slight tang

Crescenza belongs to the STRACCHINO family and, in fact, is sometimes called *Crescenza Stracchino* or simply *Stracchino*. This cheese is brined (*see* SALTING) and typically RIPENED for 5 to 6 days and not more than 10. The result is a moist cheese that at room temperature is buttery soft and very spreadable—similar to CREAM CHEESE. It has a FAT CONTENT of approximately 50 percent and a short shelf life that requires it to be eaten within a few days. Some American artisan cheesemakers produce high-quality Crescenza, including **Bellwether Farms** in California and MOZZARELLA COMPANY in Texas.

Crescenza Stracchino [Kray-SHEHN-tzuh Straht-CHEE-noh] *see* CRESCENZA

Crocodile Tear

Origin	United States (Indiana)
Milk	Pasteurized goat's
Type	SEMISOFT; MOLDED UNCOOKED; FARMSTEAD
Appearance	3-ounce cone; rind is slightly wrinkled and mottled red and white (paprika and mold); interior is white
Texture	Smooth, dense, and chalky, becoming slightly creamy under the rind as it ages
Flavor	Mellow and slightly acidic

This tear-shaped award-winner is produced by **Capriole Goat Cheese** company on an 80-acre farm in the rolling hills of southern Indiana. Master cheesemaker Judy Schad makes this cheese with the milk of her herd of 400 selectively bred Alpine,

Sannen, and Nubian goats. The fresh cheese is dried slightly, dusted with paprika, and transferred to a cave to RIPEN for 3 weeks. Other Capriole winners include MONT ST. FRANCIS, O'BANON, and WABASH CANNONBALL.

crottin; crottin de chèvre [crow-TAN; deuh SHEHV] The generic term for small (about 2 inches in diameter) drums of goat's milk cheese made throughout France. They may be aged for anywhere from 10 days to 6 weeks or more. Young crottins have a soft texture, mild, salty flavor, an off-white to ivory PASTE, and a pale yellow rind that may or may not have white or blue molding. Aged versions become drier and therefore firmer in texture, the interior turning golden, the rind darkening, and the flavor becoming more intense. At 8 weeks they're typically hard enough to be used for grating.

Crottin de Champcol [crow-TAN deuh SHAW*M*-kohl] *see* CROTTIN DE CHAVIGNOL

Crottin de Chavignol; Chavignol (AOC; PDO) [crow-TAN deuh shah-vee-NYOHL]

Origin	France (Burgundy; Centre)
Milk	Unpasteurized goat's
Type	SEMISOFT TO SEMIHARD; MOLDED UNCOOKED; NATURAL RIND; FARMSTEAD, ARTISAN, and FACTORY
Appearance	1½ - to 5-ounce flat drums (which shrink as they ripen and lose moisture); rind is thin, wrinkled, and mottled with white and beige molds when young, with blue and gray molds developing with age, and long-ripened versions becoming dark brown; interior is white to off-white, yellowing

C

	toward the rind; older versions become pale yellow with dark yellow near the rind
Texture	Young versions are soft and moist; older ones are firmer, becoming crumbly with time
Flavor	Mild and slightly nutty when young, becoming richer, complex, pungent, and nutty as they ripen

This type of cheese has been produced around the small village of Chavignol (near Sancerre) since goat herding began in the sixteenth century. The area is part of the Loire Valley, south of Paris. There's often a reaction to the word *crottin* because it means "horse droppings," referring to the shape of a well–ripened cheese, which becomes small, flat, and dark brown. Of course, most such cheeses are not eaten this ripe. Crottin de Chavignol, also simply called *Chavignol,* is made from whole goat's milk. The cheeses are rubbed with salt and dried for a couple of days before undergoing RIPENING for a minimum of 10 days, but more often 3 or 4 weeks and sometimes 4 or more months. Cheese made from unpasteurized milk meets APPELLATION D'ORIGINE CONTRÔLÉE (AOC) regulations and may be labeled Crottin de Chavignol but cannot be exported to the United States at this writing (*see* UNPASTEURIZED MILK/IMPORTED CHEESE DILEMMA). **Crottin de Champcol** is produced in the same area with the same techniques as Crottin de Chavignol but with pasteurized goat's milk. It meets U.S. standards but is not an AOC cheese. It's better than some of the factory-produced Crottin de Chavignol, but not as good as the farmstead cheeses, which are labeled either *Fabrication Fermière* or *Fromage Fermier.* The FAT CONTENT of these cheeses is about 45 percent.

croute fleurie [KROOT fleu-REE] French for "flowered crust," which in the cheese world refers to a BLOOMY RIND.

Crowley Cheese; Crowley Cheese Company *see* COLBY

C

Crozier Blue [KROH-zher bloo] *see* CASHEL BLUE

crumbly *see* Glossary of Cheese Descriptors, page 496

crust *see* RIND

culture(s) *see* STARTER

curd(s) When milk undergoes COAGULATION, it forms a gelatinous mass of semisolids (curds) and the watery liquid (WHEY) trapped within it. It's the addition of RENNET to the milk that makes the individual milk protein (CASEIN) cells clump together to form the curd mass. The texture of the curd can vary from soft to firm, depending on the milk's ACIDITY (pH), the temperature at which the milk is COAGULATED, and the time it's allowed to develop—anywhere from 10 minutes to 2 hours, but typically under an hour. It all depends on the type of cheese being made. Higher acidity and temperature plus longer formation time produces a firmer curd. The curd is further concentrated by techniques including CUTTING, COOKING, PRESSING, and SALTING.

curding To cause the formation of a CURD; to COAGULATE.

curdle; curdling *see* COAGULATION

curing *see* RIPENING

current *see* YOUNG in Glossary of Cheese Descriptors, page 507

cutting; cutting the curd This cheesemaking step is done right after the CURD reaches the desired texture, depending on the cheese being made. Cutting the semisolid curd exposes more surfaces and helps expel the WHEY (*see* DRAINING). Many cutting tools are used for this procedure, including a large rakelike device called a CHEESE HARP and a large swordlike knife. Cutting may be done by machine or manually. The smaller the curds, the more liquid is released, which results in denser, drier cheese. For instance, CHEDDAR is typically made from rice-size bits of curd. Conversely, larger curds hold more whey and therefore produce a softer cheese. The curd for many cheeses—such as CAMEMBERT and some CHÈVRES—isn't cut at all but simply scooped into perforated molds where draining continues. *See also* CHEDDARING.

cylinder *see* WHEEL

Cypress Grove Chèvre *see* BERMUDA TRIANGLE; HUMBOLDT FOG; LAMB CHOPPER; MIDNIGHT MOON

D

daisy A cylindrical CHEDDAR weighing approximately 20 pounds. It's also referred to as a *daisy cheddar wheel*. *See also* CHEESE SIZES AND SHAPES.

Damenkäse [DAH-mern-ki-zer (-kah-zeh)] *see* BUTTERKÄSE

Damiati; Damietta [dah-mee-YAH-tee; dah-mee-YET-tah] *see* DOMIATI

D

Danablu (PDO) [DAN-uh-bloo]

Origin	Denmark
Milk	Pasteurized cow's
Type	SEMIHARD; MOLDED UNCOOKED; BLUE-VEINED; FACTORY
Appearance	6- to 9-pound foil-wrapped wheels, squares, and rectangles; essentially rindless; interior is white to ivory with dark blue-green veining and a few irregular EYES
Texture	Creamy, moist, and crumbly
Flavor	Mild, buttery, salty, and tangy with a light spiciness that intensifies as it ages

Danablu, also called *Danish Blue* and *Marmora,* was created by cheesemaker Marius Boel in the 1920s as Denmark's answer to French ROQUEFORT. Though it didn't present quite like Roquefort—it's milder and not as complex—Danablu has become extremely popular in Denmark and other countries, where it's thought to be one of the world's better blue cheeses. It's made with milk that's been inoculated with *Penicillium roqueforti,* which creates the bluing. Danablu is usually RIPENED for 2 to 3 months. There are two versions—*full fat* has a FAT CONTENT of 50 percent, while *extra full fat* contains about 60 percent.

> Sweet cheese is the trompe l'oeil of food. It will try to trick you; it supplies both the illusion of lightness and the satisfaction of having eaten something really, really sinful.
>
> —Molly O'Neill

D

Danbo [DAN-boh]

Origin	Denmark
Milk	Pasteurized cow's
Type	SEMIHARD; PRESSED COOKED; NATURAL RIND or rindless; FARMSTEAD, COOPERATIVE, and FACTORY
Appearance	13- to 31-pound squares; rind is hard, dry, and yellow and may be covered with wax or plastic coating; interior is ivory to pale yellow with a few pea-sized EYES
Texture	Supple, elastic, and smooth
Flavor	Very mild and buttery

One of Denmark's most popular cheeses, Danbo is also called *King Christian* and *Christian IX* in honor of King Christian IX, Denmark's monarch from 1836 to 1906. Danbo, which is very similar to another Danish favorite, SAMSOE, is RIPENED for a minimum of 6 weeks and sometimes up to 5 months or more. Caraway seeds are sometimes added for flavor. The FAT CONTENT for standard Danbo is a minimum of 45 percent; there's also a low-fat version that has about 10 percent fat.

Danish Blue *see* DANABLU

Danish cheeses *see* Cheeses by Country of Origin, page 509

Danish Port Salut *see* ESROM

dates on products *see* PRODUCT DATING

D

Deep Ellum Blue

Origin	United States (Texas)
Milk	Pasteurized cow's
Type	SOFT TO SEMISOFT; MOLDED UNCOOKED; rindless; ARTISAN
Appearance	5-pound rectangular block; exterior is ivory colored with blue-green mold on the top; interior is ivory
Texture	Soft, smooth, and creamy
Flavor	Complex and earthy, with mild blue characteristics

Produced by Paula Lambert's **Mozzarella Company,** this cheese is named after the downtown Dallas neighborhood where it's produced—Deep Ellum, alternative urban home to artists, art galleries, bars, and blues clubs. Lambert describes it as "a blue cheese for people who don't like blue cheese," presumably referring to the fact that it's relatively mild and not as assertive as many of its ilk. Most blue cheeses are made by adding *Penicillium roqueforti* to the milk and piercing the formed cheese with metal skewers so oxygen can reach the interior and feed the bacteria that produces the veining. With Deep Ellum Blue, however, the cheeses are bathed in the *P. roqueforti,* which means the mold grows only on the exterior. After being RIPENED for a minimum of 2 months, the cheese is wiped with extra virgin olive oil before being packaged for market. *See also* BLANCA BIANCA; HOJA SANTA; MONTASIO FESTIVO; MOZZARELLA.

delicate *see* Glossary of Cheese Descriptors, page 497

de Murcia al Vino *see* QUESO DE MURCIA

Denominação de Origem [day-noo-mee-NAH-ker*n* der oo-REE-zher*n*] *see* PROTECTED DESIGNATION OF ORIGIN

Denominación de Origen Protegida (DO; DOP) [day-noh-mee-nah-THYON day oh-REE-khayn proh-tay-KHEE-dah] Spanish for "protected denomination of origin," this is Spain's national quality-control system for foods and wines. The DO controls where designated cheeses can be made, what type of milk can be used (including the animal's breed and grazing lands), exactly how the cheese is to be produced, and its physical characteristics, including shape and size. Name-controlled cheeses have the letters "DO" stamped on either the wrapping or the rind. It wasn't until 1981 that the first cheese was given a name-controlled distinction. At this writing, there are fifteen DO cheeses out of over eighty distinct varieties made in the country. In 1992, the European Union approved protected name standards for cheeses produced by member countries. Cheeses can be classified as either PROTECTED DESIGNATION OF ORIGIN (PDO) or PROTECTED GEOGRAPHICAL INDICATION (PGI). Countries may use these new designations with cheeses that qualify.

Denominazione di Origine Controllata (DOC) [deh-NAW-mee-nah-TSYAW-neh dee oh-REE-jee-neh con-traw-LAH-tah] Italian for "Controlled Denomination of Origin," this is Italy's system of standards of excellence for indigenous wines and foods. The original criteria were established in 1955, and at this writing DOC status has been granted to only 30 out of approximately 450 Italian cheeses. DOC tenets include precise geographical production areas, standards of cheesemaking (in part, to preserve tradition), and each cheese's composition and physical characteristics (milk used, size, rind, texture, minimum fat content, and so on). Producers are regulated by frequent

D

inspections to make sure they are complying with DOC conventions for product authenticity and quality. DOC cheeses are readily identifiable by the *DOC* designation imprinted on the wrapping or rind. In 1992, the European Union approved protected name standards for cheeses produced by member countries. Cheeses can be classified as either PROTECTED DESIGNATION OF ORIGIN (PDO) or PROTECTED GEOGRAPHICAL INDICATION (PGI). Countries may use these new designations with cheeses that qualify.

Denominazione di Origine Protetta [deh-NAW-mee-nah-TSYAW-neh dee oh-REE-jee-neh proh-TAY-tah] *see* PROTECTED DESIGNATION OF ORIGIN

Derby; Sage Derby [DER-bee; DAHR-bee]

Origin	England (Derbyshire; North Yorkshire, Warwickshire)
Milk	Pasteurized cow's
Type	SEMIHARD; PRESSED COOKED; NATURAL RIND; FARMSTEAD and FACTORY
Appearance	9- to 30-pound wheels—farmstead versions are often buttered and cloth-bound, factory versions usually waxed; the rind of regular Derby is yellow to yellow-orange, whereas that of Sage Derby is a marbled green, although some farmstead versions are yellow with green flecks of sage; the interior of regular Derby is pale to medium yellow; factory-made Sage Derby is a marbled green and white; farmstead versions have a green-flecked center sandwiched with pale yellow cheese

Texture	Traditional farmstead versions are smooth, firm, and flaky, whereas factory-produced Derbys are typically slick and slightly gummy
Flavor	Farmstead versions are mild, buttery, nutty, and tangy, becoming richer and more piquant with age; factory versions are blander; Sage Derby is lightly herbaceous

D

As with most English cheeses, for centuries Derby was made with traditional recipes and techniques on small farms. But around 1870, it was the first cheese to be made in a factory with large-scale production processes. The proliferation of factory-made CHEDDAR slowly began diminishing Derby's popularity. Today Derby is still made primarily in factories, with a scattering of farmstead producers. One of those is made by Warwickshire's Fowlers of Earlswood, who've been producing Derby traditionally since 1840. These farmstead cheeses are still wrapped in cloth and RIPENED for at least 7 months (ordinary Derby is ripened for 1 to 3 months). They also make a farmstead version of **Sage Derby,** which was introduced in the seventeenth century at a time when sage was touted as a cure for a variety of ailments. Sage Derby was initially made only for holidays but is now available year-round. Farmstead versions like the Fowlers' blend bits of sage into some of the curd, sandwiching it in the middle of two layers of regular Derby. The tops of farmstead versions are sprinkled with bits of sage. The curd for factory-made Sage Derby is typically colored with a blend of green vegetable dye and sage powder or chopped sage and spinach juice. This green curd is mixed with regular curd for a green-and-white marbled effect. The FAT CONTENT for Derby cheeses is 45 to 48 percent.

D

Despearado [dehs-pehr-AH-doh] *see* HOOLIGAN

DO Abbreviation for the appellation system of Spain—DENOMINACIÓN DE ORIGEN PROTEGIDA.

DOC Abbreviation for the appellation system of Italy—DENOMINAZIONE DI ORIGINE CONTROLLATA.

Doeling Dairy Goat Farm *see* GOUDA

Dolcelatte [dohl-chay-LAHT-tay] Italian for "sweet milk" and a brand name for a particular GORGONZOLA *dolce*.

Domiati [doh-mee-YAH-tee]

Origin	Egypt
Milk	Unpasteurized or pasteurized cow's, goat's, and water buffalo's
Type	SEMISOFT to SEMIHARD; PRESSED UNCOOKED; ARTISAN and FACTORY
Appearance	Various cylinder and loaf shapes (typically cut into smaller wedges or blocks), packed in containers and covered in salted WHEY; rindless and stark white in color, may darken with extensive ripening
Texture	Smooth, firm, and slightly crumbly
Flavor	Fresh, milky flavor with slight tang when young, becoming stronger with age; can be quite salty

Produced in Egypt for at least 2,300 years, Domiati is considered this country's national cheese and is also popular in neighboring Mediterranean countries. It's named after a small

Mediterranean seaport and is similar to FETA, though made slightly differently. An unusual cheesemaking step in Domiati production is that the milk is salted *before* the RENNET is added and the CURD develops. As with Feta, Domiati can be eaten either fresh or RIPENED. During ripening it's covered with BRINE, which is why, like Feta, its called a "pickled" cheese. After 1 to 3 months of storage, Domiati is ready for consumption, though it can be aged for up to a year or more. This cheese has a FAT CONTENT that can range from 20 to 45 percent. Local names for it include *Gibbneh Beda*, *Damiati*, and *Damietta*.

DOP *see* DENOMINACIÓN DE ORIGEN PROTEGIDA; PROTECTED DESIGNATION OF ORIGIN

double-cream (-crème)/triple-cream (-crème) cheeses Decadently lush, velvety, buttery cheeses that have been enriched with the addition of cream. This style of cheese was first created in Normandy, France, in the early 1900s. At the time, such cheeses were known as *cheeses of affluence* because the added cream was a luxury. **Double-cream cheeses** must contain a minimum of 60 percent butterfat and **triple-cream cheeses** at least 72 percent butterfat. Because double- and triple-cream cheeses can contain up to 67 percent moisture, and the fat content in cheese is measured on DRY MATTER only (*see* FAT), the *actual* fat content of such cheeses is actually between 20 and 35 percent. Double-cream cheeses include BOURSIN and PETIT SUISSE; triple-creams include BRILLAT-SAVARIN and EXPLORATEUR. *See also* TYPE(S), CHEESE.

Double Gloucester [GLOSS-ter] *see* GLOUCESTER

draining During cheesemaking WHEY is drained from the CURD in several ways, and drainage continues, little by little, throughout

D

much of the cheesemaking process. The process begins by CUTTING the curd, thereby exposing more of the surfaces and draining additional whey. Other ways to drain off the whey include COOKING (contraction from the heat forces out liquid), CHEDDARING (stacking large blocks of curd to press out whey), MOLDING (liquid drains through perforated molds), and PRESSING either mechanically or naturally.

Drunken Hooligan *see* HOOLIGAN

Drunk Monk *see* HOOLIGAN

drying The point in cheesemaking when, after the curds have been drained and (sometimes) pressed, the formed cheeses are placed in a well-ventilated room to allow further evaporation and drainage of whey. Depending on the cheese, this drying period can take anywhere from a few hours to several days.

dry Jack *see* JACK

dry matter The term used in the United States for the nonliquid components of cheese (including FAT, LACTOSE, proteins, and minerals). Depending on the cheese, the liquid constituents can range between 30 and 80 percent. The remaining portion is dry matter, also referred to as *solids*. The fat content of cheese is based only on the solid materials, sans moisture. Dry matter isn't measured until the cheese has been fully ripened (*see* RIPENING) for that style. On U.S. cheese labels the percentage of fat is indicated in one of several ways: *in dry matter* (or *IDM*), *fat on a dry basis* (*FDB*), or *butterfat content*. The synonymous term on French and other imported cheese labels is *matière grasse* or *m.g.*

dry-salting *see* SALTING

D

Durrus [DUR-ruhs]

Origin	Ireland (Cork)
Milk	Unpasteurized cow's
Type	SEMISOFT; MOLDED UNCOOKED; WASHED RIND; ARTISAN
Appearance	13-ounce and 3¼-pound wheels; rind is pinkish yellow, turning reddish orange with age; interior is white to pale yellow with a few small EYES
Texture	Soft, smooth, and creamy
Flavor	Mild, delicate, creamy, and nutty when young, becoming stronger, fruity, and earthy with ripening

Durrus is made by Jeffa Gill in county Cork's Coomkeen Valley in southwestern Ireland. Gill was one of the first modern cheese-makers to return to traditional cheesemaking methods to produce artisan cheeses. In 1979, she began making Durrus—named for the village in which it's made—and has won a number of awards since then. In 2003, Gill's Durrus won Best Irish Cheese at the British Cheese Awards competition. The cheese is sprayed with *BREVIBACTERIUM LINENS,* which RIPENS the cheese from the outside in. The cheeses are placed in a curing room, where they're turned daily and frequently hand-washed with BRINE to encourage the growth of the *B. linens* bacteria. Ripening typically takes 3 to 5 weeks, though for import into the United States the cheese must be aged over 60 days (*see* UNPASTEURIZED MILK/IMPORTED CHEESE dilemma), at which point the rind has hardened and darkened, the PASTE has turned golden, and the flavor has intensified. The FAT CONTENT for Durrus ranges from 52 to 57 percent.

Dutch cheeses *see* Cheeses by Country of Origin, page 513

D

Dutch Farmstead

Origin	United States (Connecticut)
Milk	Unpasteurized cow's
Type	SEMIHARD; PRESSED COOKED; NATURAL RIND; FARMSTEAD
Appearance	10- to 12-pound wheels; rind is thin and yellow when young, becoming darker and thicker with age; interior is pale yellow to deep gold with a scattering of irregularly shaped EYES; aged versions have crystalline white flecks
Texture	Smooth and supple when young; long-aged cheeses become hard, flaky, and brittle
Flavor	Younger cheeses are creamy, moderately complex, and well balanced with a hint of nuttiness; aged versions are richer, fuller flavored, and have nuances of butterscotch and caramel

A GOUDA-style cheese made by **Cato Corner Farm**'s mother-and-son team Elizabeth MacAlister and Mark Gillman. Their 75-acre farm is located southwest of Hartford, Connecticut, and hosts thirty Jersey cows. Dutch Farmstead is RIPENED for 3 to 5 months and was recognized by Slow Food USA in 2003 as one of the best American raw milk farmstead cheeses and chosen by *Saveur* magazine in 2005 as one of the top fifty artisanal cheeses made in America. **Block's Landing** is a version with 10 to 18 months of aging. *See also* HOOLIGAN.

Dutch Port Salut *see* ESROM

E

E

earthy *see* Glossary of Cheese Descriptors, page 497

Edam [EE-duhm]

Origin	Netherlands
Milk	Pasteurized cow's
Type	SEMISOFT TO HARD; PRESSED COOKED; NATURAL RIND; FARMSTEAD and FACTORY
Appearance	Most are sphere shaped with slightly flattened tops and bottoms (some loaves), sizes ranging from ¾ to 14 pounds; most Edams are covered with red or yellow WAX or plastic; rindless or a very thin, yellow rind; interior is pale yellow with a scattering of small irregular EYES
Texture	Smooth and elastic
Flavor	Delicate, mild, and slightly salty

> How can you be expected to govern a country [France] that has 246 kinds of cheese?
> —Charles de Gaulle

A cheese named after the small port town 12 miles northeast of Amsterdam in the province of North Holland. By the middle of the thirteenth century, this cheese was being exported from Edam and other surrounding port towns. Up until the end of the nineteenth century Edam was made by farmstead methods, but now it's primarily factory-produced. The standard size for

E

Edam spheres is $3\frac{3}{4}$ to $5\frac{1}{2}$ pounds, for loaves 11 or more pounds. Smaller versions—**Baby Edam** or **Baby Loaf Edam**—can weigh from 14 ounces to $2\frac{1}{2}$ pounds. Most factory Edams are coated in red wax and are typically RIPENED for 6 to 8 weeks. Those coated in black wax have been ripened for at least 17 weeks and sometimes up to 10 months. Factory-produced Gouda and Edam are very similar, the primary difference being that—until recently—Gouda was made exclusively from whole milk, which gave it a FAT CONTENT of about 48 percent, while Edam has only 30 to 40 percent fat because it's made from fat-free (or partially skimmed) milk. Now, however, there's a light style of Gouda with a fat content in the Edam range. PROTECTED DESIGNATION OF ORIGIN (PDO) has been granted to one Edam cheese—**Noord-Hollandse Edammer,** which can be produced only in the North Holland province and which has a lower salt content than most other Edams. Even though these are factory-produced cheeses, strict PDO regulations generate a higher-quality product than non-PDO Edams. Otherwise the name *Edam* is not protected, and this cheese is made in other countries. Several Edam cheeses are produced in the United States, primarily in New York and Wisconsin. Most are factory produced and bear a close resemblance to the Dutch imports. California's Bravo Farms produces an award-winning farmstead Edam called **Tulare Cannonball** using raw whole milk, which gives it a higher fat content than most Edam cheeses.

Édel de Cleron, l' [lay-DEHL deuh kleh-ROHN] *see* VACHERIN DU HAUT-DOUBS

18-Month Bandage Wrapped Cheddar *see* CHEDDAR

Ekte Gjetost (Geitost) [EK-teh YAYT-oost] *see* GJETOST

Emmental; Emmentaler; Emmenthal [EM-mawn-tahl]

Origin	Switzerland (Berne)
Milk	Cow's, traditionally unpasteurized and partially skimmed
Type	SEMIHARD; PRESSED COOKED; NATURAL RIND; FARMSTEAD
Appearance	200-pound wheels about 45 inches in diameter; rind is thin, hard, and pale yellow to yellow-brown in color; interior is ivory-yellow with a random scattering of EYES
Texture	Supple and smooth
Flavor	Delicately sweet, earthy, fruity, and buttery with hints of hazelnut when young, concentrated and spicy with age

The Swiss cheese after which all others were patterned, Emmental is Switzerland's most important cheese. Produced since the thirteenth century, the world-famous Emmental takes its name from its birthplace, the Emme Valley (Emme River). Today it's made throughout Switzerland's midlands, including the cantons of Aargau, Berne, Glarus, Lucerne, Schwyz, Solothurn, St. Gallen, Thurgau, Zug, Zurich, and in some parts of Fribourg. However, since the name is not protected, you'll also find so-called Emmentals produced in Austria, France, Denmark, Finland, Germany, and the United States. Swiss Emmental is made from unpasteurized milk from cows that have fed on grass and hay but never silage (fermented fodder). It takes around 265 gallons of milk to produce one Emmental wheel, which is about 45 inches in diameter and up to 9 inches thick. This cheese is made from two milkings—evening and the following morning. After the CURD is cut into very small pieces, it's heated and stirred to further extract WHEY. The curds are then gathered in a giant cheesecloth bag and lifted by pulley to drain further before being lowered into a mold. After being brined (*see* SALTING) for several days, the Emmental is ready for RIPENING. It's placed in warm rooms where the heat-loving *Propionibacter shermani* bacteria begins its fermentation, forming carbon dioxide bubbles and creating Emmental's characteristic eyes, which can range from cherry to walnut size. Final ripening takes place in cool rooms—minimum aging time is 4 months, 8 months for "mature," and 12 months or more for "fully mature." Mature and fully mature Emmentals are cellared in a damp environment, which can darken the rind to almost black. Authentic Emmentals will always have "Emmental" and "Switzerland" stamped on the rind. They are about 45 percent FAT. **French Emmental** has been made for nearly as long as Switzerland's original. It's produced in the Franche Comté region and parts of Bourgogne, Champagne-Ardenne, Lorraine, and Rhône-Alpes. The French cheeses are similar in size to those of Switzerland, except the huge wheels are bulbous rather than flat-sided. The recipes and production methods are the same in both countries, but French versions are primarily factory made. French Emmental tends to have a slightly deeper flavor than the Swiss original. It's also pricier because not as much of it is exported. France's **Emmental Grand Cru** is made with raw milk, whereas the regular French Emmental is based on pasteurized milk. In France, both **Emmental de Savoie** and **Emmental Français Est-Central** have PROTECTED DESIGNATION OF ORIGIN (PDO) designations. Germany's **Allgäuer Emmentaler** (PDO) hails from Bavaria's Allgäu region and is typically made from pasteurized milk. It's less flavorful than Swiss and French versions, in part because it's not aged as long. Emmentals made in other countries are usually factory made and don't come close to the flavor of the original. *See also* SWISS CHEESE.

Emmental de Savoie [EM-mawn-tahl deuh SAH-vwah] *see*
EMMENTAL

E

Emmental Français est-Central [EM-mawn-tahl frah*n*-SAY ehst
sah*n*-trahl] *see* EMMENTAL

enchilado [en-chee-LAH-doh]

Origin	Mexico
Milk	Unpasteurized and pasteurized cow's or goat's
Type	SEMIHARD to HARD; GRANA STYLE; PRESSED COOKED; ARTISAN and FACTORY
Appearance	11- to 22-pound cylinders with a red coating of paprika or chili powder; rindless; interior is white to ivory, with a scattering of small EYES
Texture	Younger versions are firm, dry, and crumbly; ripened ones are very hard, dry, and crumbly
Flavor	Salty, milky, tangy, and mildly spicy, becoming stronger with age

Similar to another favorite Mexican cheese, COTIJA, enchilado is
slightly milder and is distinguished by a spicy red coating of
paprika or mild chili powder. It's available in a young, firm version but is more often found in a drier, harder RIPENED form
called *enchilado añejo* or *añejo enchilado*. Such versions are ripened
for 3 months or more, have a FAT CONTENT of about 45 percent,
and are good grating cheeses.

Endeavor Blue *see* ROARING FORTIES BLUE

English cheeses *see* Cheeses by Country of Origin, page 509

Entrammes *see* PORT SALUT

E

enzymes Any of over seven hundred extraordinarily efficient organic substances that act as catalysts to speed up chemical reactions in living things. Each enzyme has a particular temperature at which it's most effective. It is also exclusive to the compound in which it creates a reaction. Some enzymes can accelerate a variety of reactions, while others control only one reaction. Enzymes are responsible for everything from fermentation (as with beer, wine, and milk for cheese) to human digestion. In the world of cheese, **proteolytic enzymes** break down proteins (proteolysis) and **lipolytic enzymes** break down lipids (fats) through lipolysis. Enzymes are responsible for many cheese-related functions, from FERMENTATION to COAGULATION to generating the volatile compounds that produce and enrich specific flavors.

Époisses de Bourgogne (AOC; PDO) [ay-PWAHSS deuh boor-GO-nyuh]

Origin	France (Burgundy; Champagne-Ardenne)
Milk	Unpasteurized and pasteurized cow's
Type	SEMISOFT; MOLDED UNCOOKED; WASHED RIND; ARTISAN and FARMSTEAD
Appearance	Flattened wheels weighing either 9 to 12 ounces or 1½ to 2½ pounds; rind is wrinkled and reddish orange; interior is off-white to pale yellow
Texture	Creamy and supple, becoming thickly fluid as it RIPENS

Flavor	Milky, yeasty, and tangy when young, developing with age into a complex mélange of strong, creamy, savory, pungent, and zesty flavors

This cheese was created in the early 1500s by Cistercian monks residing in the village of Époisses, midway between Dijon and Auxerre in the region of Burgundy. Several hundred years later when the monks departed, they left the local population with the secrets of Époisses de Bourgogne (commonly called simply *Époisses*). It's said that Napoleon loved it, and in 1825 the famous French gastronomic writer Brillat-Savarin crowned it "King of Cheeses." Its popularity waned in the 1900s, due in part to the two world wars, and Époisses essentially vanished until Robert and Simone Berthaut resurrected it in the mid-1950s. Since then it has gained a huge following and is now produced both in Burgundy and the Champagne-Ardenne region. Époisses is dry-salted (*see* SALTING) and ripened for a minimum of 4 weeks. During ripening, Époisses is frequently brushed with a mixture of water and MARC, a potent brandy distilled from skins and seeds leftover from winemaking. This washing helps spread desirable bacteria evenly over the cheese's surface. Époisses is packaged in a small wooden box to protect its soft contour. It has a minimum FAT CONTENT of 50 percent. The Berthauts also produce a "young Époisses" called *AISY CENDRÉ* and another washed-rind cheese called **Affidélice.** The latter's full name is *l'Affidélice au Chablis,* which refers to the practice of washing the rind with Chablis wine instead of marc. The resulting cheese weighs about 7 ounces and has a bright orange rind, a creamy texture, and a savory, earthy flavor.

Esrom (PDO); Esrum [EHS-rom]

Origin	Denmark
Milk	Pasteurized cow's
Type	SEMIHARD; PRESSED UNCOOKED; WASHED RIND; ARTISAN, FARMSTEAD, COOPERATIVE, and FACTORY
Appearance	Various-size loaves—standard is 2¾ to 3 pounds; rind is thin and yellow-orange to yellow-brown in color; interior is ivory to yellow and has irregularly shaped EYES
Texture	Smooth and supple
Flavor	Mild, buttery, and spicy, becoming fuller, more robust, and savory with age

In the eleventh and twelfth centuries, a cheese similar to the contemporary Esrom was produced by the monks at the area's monastery. Over time, production eventually dwindled to a stop, and it wasn't until the mid-1930s that cheesemakers began to re-create this cheese. No one claims that the resurrected Esrom is made by the monks' original recipe, but it is certainly produced in the style and spirit of that cheese. Esrom was initially called *Dutch* or *Danish Port Salut,* but that title ran into a snag with European Union laws (regarding France's PORT SALUT), so the name of the original monastery location was adopted. The surface of this cheese is washed with a mixture of BRINE and BREVIBACTERIUM LINENS, which encourages development of the characteristic rind. Esrom is RIPENED for 10 to 12 weeks, during which time it receives frequent brine washings, brushings, and turnings, all of which help spread desirable bacteria evenly over the surface. Though this cheese develops a distinctively smelly rind, its PASTE is comparatively mild in flavor. A standard Esrom weighs 2¾ to 3 pounds, a larger one between 4½ to 5½ pounds, and a mini-version is about 2 pounds. Esrom, occasionally spelled *Esrum,* is produced in two versions—*full-fat,* which has a minimum FAT CONTENT of 45 percent, and *extra full-fat,* with at least 60 percent fat.

estate cheese *see* FARMSTEAD CHEESE

Étivaz, l' (AOC) [lay-tee-VAH]

Origin	Switzerland (Vaud)
Milk	Unpasteurized cow's
Type	HARD; PRESSED COOKED; NATURAL RIND; ARTISAN, FARMSTEAD, and COOPERATIVE; MOUNTAIN
Appearance	22- to 84-pound wheels; rind is hard, dry, pitted, and golden brown to brown; interior is ivory to medium yellow with very few EYES
Texture	Very dense and compact yet supple
Flavor	Complex blend of creamy, fruity, nutty, and savory flavors

Akin to a traditional old-style GRUYÈRE, l'Étivaz was created in the 1930s when over seventy cheesemakers ceased producing Gruyère because they felt that its production regulations had relaxed so much that quality was compromised. They named their cheese after the local village, in the mountains of western Switzerland in the canton of Vaud. L'Étivaz is produced only between May 10 and October 10 from the milk of cows that graze in pastures at altitudes of about 3,300 to 6,600 feet. All of the almost eighty cheesemakers produce it by identical artisanal methods—two milkings are combined in copper cauldrons and heated over open wood fires.

E

Regular l'Étivaz is RIPENED on spruce planks in caves for a minimum of 4½ months but often for up to a year. The very rare **l'Étivaz Rebibes** is aged for 30 months and represents only about 2 percent of the annual production of 12,000 to 14,000 wheels. The flavors of both styles are influenced by the wild alpine flowers and herbs on which the cows graze and by the smoke from the open fires. This cheese has a FAT CONTENT of between 49 and 54 percent.

Etorki [eh–TOR–kee]

Origin	France (Aquitaine)
Milk	Pasteurized sheep's
Type	SEMIHARD; PRESSED UNCOOKED; NATURAL RIND; FACTORY
Appearance	1- to 10-pound wheels; rind is thin and orangish brown in color; interior is pale yellow with no EYES
Texture	Firm, supple, and faintly oily
Flavor	Mildly sweet, creamy, rich, and slightly nutty with a burnt caramel finish

Cheese has been made in France's Basque region in the Pyrénées for over 4,000 years, which makes Etorki—created in the late 1970s—a relative infant. Still, producers claim that the Etorki recipe is based on an age-old recipe, and the cheese lives up to that assertion. The milk for Etorki comes from Manech sheep, and the cheese is made only from late December to mid-July, while the sheep are lactating. The cheese is soaked in a BRINE bath for a minimum of 2 hours, then rubbed with salt and wrapped in brine-soaked cloths for the RIPENING period, which can range from 3 to 6 months. The FAT CONTENT for Etorki is around 50 percent.

Evangeline

Origin	United States (Louisiana)
Milk	Pasteurized goat's
Type	SOFT; TRIPLE-CREAM; BLOOMY RIND; ARTISAN
Appearance	4-ounce round; rind is thin with a velvety coating of white mold; interior is off-white
Texture	Soft, creamy, and moist, almost runny
Flavor	Tangy, creamy, and piquant; rind is slightly bitter

This cheese was named after the heroine of Henry Wadsworth Longfellow's epic poem that was loosely based on the 1755 exile of the Acadians from Nova Scotia and the arrival of some of them in south Louisiana. Evangeline is made by **Bittersweet Plantation Dairy** in Gonzales, Louisiana, which is located between Baton Rouge and New Orleans. This rich, tangy cheese has won first place in the annual American Cheese Society competition in the soft-RIPENED goat's milk category. Evangeline is ripened for 3 to 4 weeks and has a minimum FAT CONTENT of 75 percent. Bittersweet Plantation Dairy has also won American Cheese Society awards for some of its other cheeses, including FLEUR-DE-LIS, FLEUR-DE-TECHE, and CREOLE CREAM CHEESE.

Everona Dairy [Eh-veh-ROH-nah] *see* PIEDMONT

Évora [eh-VOH-rah] *see* QUEIJO DE ÉVORA

Ewe-F-0 *see* LAMB CHOPPER

Explorateur [ehk-sploh-rah-TEUHR]

Origin	France (Île-de-France)
Milk	Unpasteurized and pasteurized cow's

Type	SEMISOFT; TRIPLE-CREAM; MOLDED UNCOOKED; BLOOMY RIND; FACTORY
Appearance	8- to 9-ounce, 14- to 15-ounce, and 3½- to 4-pound drums; rind is soft, white, developing a downy mold as it ripens; interior is off-white to pale yellow
Texture	Soft and moist
Flavor	Rich, buttery, sweet, and mild with a slight mushroomy nuance

Explorateur was created in the late 1950s when rocket ships were in the news and the United States launched its first successful satellite, *Explorer 1*. Explorateur's creator, Fromagerie du Petit Morin, placed a spaceship on the label as a sign of the times. Cream is added to this uncooked, unpressed cheese to increase its FAT CONTENT to around 75 percent, which places it in the triple-cream category. Explorateur is RIPENED for 2 to 3 weeks. Only pasteurized-milk versions can be imported into the United States (*see* UNPASTEURIZED MILK/IMPORTED CHEESE DILEMMA).

eyes Also called *holes*, eyes are simply openings in the interior of a cheese. Their distinguishing characteristic is what makes SWISS CHEESES *Swiss*. Eyes are typically formed by carbon dioxide (CO_2) gas created by specific (natural and harmless) bacteria included in the STARTER during the initial stage of cheesemaking. For EMMENTAL cheese, for example, *Propionibacter shermanii* is added to the starter culture. Some gas-producing bacteria also occur naturally in raw milk. Eyes can be as large as a walnut and as small as a pinhead—the most common midrange is about the size of a grape. The bacteria that produce eyes in cheeses such as FONTINA and HAVARTI are less aggressive than those found in Swiss-style cheeses and subsequently produce much smaller

E

openings. In France, cheesemakers categorize and name *eyes* according to size: tiny size are called *les yeux de perdrix* (partridge eyes), small are *petit pois* (little peas), medium-size eyes are referred to as *cerises* (cherries), and large ones are *noix* (walnuts).

• • • • •

F

• • • • •

factory cheeses; factory-made A term used for mass-produced cheeses that can range in quality from dreadful to extremely good. The milk for such cheeses is typically pasteurized (*see* PASTEURIZATION) and, because cost is a primary focus, often comes from an amalgam of various herds. Many factory cheeses, also called INDUSTRIAL CHEESES, are highly processed and undergo minimum RIPENING, which translates to less time for flavor and aroma to develop.

faisselle [fays-SEHL] **1.** The French word for a perforated cheese MOLD, which comes in myriad shapes and sizes. In Europe, some cheesemakers send the fresh cheese (still exuding WHEY) in these molds directly to market, where the purveyor turns out the cheese into a plastic bag and sends it home with the buyer. CHÈVRE is one cheese that is often formed in a faisselle. **2.** The fresh cheeses that are shaped in such molds.

> People who know nothing about cheeses reel away from Camembert, Roquefort, and Stilton because the plebeian proboscis is not equipped to differentiate between the sordid and the sublime.
> —Harvey Day

F

farmer cheese; farmer's cheese *see* COTTAGE CHEESE

farmhouse cheese *see* FARMSTEAD CHEESE

farmlike *see* Glossary of Cheese Descriptors, page 497

farmstead (farmhouse) cheese In the cheese world, the terms *farmstead* (in the United States) and *farmhouse* (throughout Europe) are used to describe cheeses that are produced on a farm from milk produced exclusively by that farmer's animals. The cheese is made in an ARTISAN style with high-quality ingredients, which translates in the marketplace to better quality and higher cost. Farmstead cheese is sometimes called ESTATE CHEESE.

fat; fat content The word *fat* in the cheese world refers to the fat content of milk and, subsequently, the cheese it produces. Also called *milkfat* or *butterfat,* this element contributes greatly to the flavor and aroma of cheese. Milkfat varies from one animal species to another. For example, of all the dairy species, sheep's milk has proportionately the highest amount of fat and other nonliquid components (*see* DRY MATTER). In cheesemaking terms, the higher percentage of solids in sheep's milk means that, to make 1 pound of cheese, it takes less of it (4½ pounds) than it does cow's milk (10 pounds). The amount of fat in cheese is partially determined by the type of milk (whole, nonfat, and so on) from which it was made. Then there are examples like DOUBLE-CREAM and TRIPLE-CREAM CHEESES, which have had extra cream added to the milk. However, the final **fat content** listed on cheese labels is determined by measuring the fat in the total DRY MATTER of the finished cheese. That's because the solids stay constant, while the moisture content may vary due to the fact that cheese continues to dry out during RIPENING. Common sense tells us that rich, creamy cheeses are higher in fat than dense, hard cheeses. But remember that the percentage of fat in cheese is based *only on dry matter,* which means fat is more concentrated in low-moisture cheeses. Soft cheeses like BRIE have a higher moisture content (and, therefore, a lower percentage of solids) than hard cheeses, such as PARMIGIANO-REGGIANO. All of which means that a hard cheese with 40 percent fat (as a percentage of its solids) could provide more fat per ounce than a soft cheese with 70 percent fat but a higher moisture content. Bottom line? A cheese label that states the cheese is "50 percent fat" doesn't mean that half the cheese is actually fat, but simply that 50 percent of the dry matter (what's left after all the moisture's removed) is fat. *See also* MILK.

fat-free milk *see* MILK

faux Vacherin [foh vash-RAN] *see* VACHERIN DU HAUT-DOUBS

FDB *see* DRY MATTER

feed *see* Glossary of Cheese Descriptors, page 497

fermentation The process of producing changes in organic substances through the action of BACTERIA, ENZYMES, or yeasts. Fermentation takes place in myriad consumables, including beer, wine, bread, and cheese. In the cheesemaking process, the fermentation of milk converts carbohydrates into acids, producing lactic acid from the lactose (milk sugar). Although milk may undergo natural fermentation via its normal microbiota, today's cheesemakers typically initiate the process with lactic acid–producing microorganisms in the form of a STARTER. This balances the milk's acidity (pH level) so the CASEIN (milk protein) will COAGULATE into a CURD when RENNET is added.

F

fermier [fehr-MYAY] French for "farm," *fermier* is a descriptor for FARMSTEAD CHEESE.

Fernwood *see* VERMONT BREBIS

Feta (PDO); feta; feta-style [FEH-tuh]

Origin	Greece
Milk	Unpasteurized and pasteurized sheep's, cow's, and goat's
Type	SEMISOFT TO SEMIHARD; MOLDED UNCOOKED; ARTISAN, FARMSTEAD, COOPERATIVE, and FACTORY
Appearance	Various cylinder and loaf shapes weighing from 10 to 30 pounds (typically cut into smaller wedges or blocks), packed in large tins or wooden barrels, and covered in brine; rindless and stark white in color
Texture	Smooth, firm, and slightly crumbly
Flavor	Fresh, milky flavor with slight tang when young, becoming more complex, intense, and peppery with age; can be quite salty

Feta has been made in Greece and other Balkan countries for centuries and is one of the world's oldest cheeses. Directions for making it can be found in Homer's *Odyssey*. Initially making feta was a way for shepherds to preserve the milk of their wandering flocks. Today it's made by numerous producers in countries around the world. In October 2005, the European Union granted feta PROTECTED DESIGNATION OF

F

ORIGIN (PDO) status and acknowledged Greece as the only country that could refer to this type of cheese by the protected name *Feta*. This meant that by the end of 2006 other European countries (such as Denmark, France, and Germany), which produce tons of feta-style cheese, had to rename their cheeses. Over time the European Union will certainly press for American cheesemakers also to discontinue using the name *Feta*. PDO-approved feta must be made in designated areas in Greece primarily from sheep's milk, though up to 30 percent goat's milk may be added. It must be produced using traditional methods, may not use pressure to drain the WHEY, and must be matured and stored in BRINE (which is why feta is often referred to as a "pickled" cheese). After one to two months of brine storage, feta is ready for consumption, though it can be aged for up to a year. The FAT CONTENT of feta ranges from 40 to 50 percent. The majority of French feta-style cheeses are made with sheep's milk (an outgrowth of surplus milk from ROQUEFORT production), although a goat's milk style is also produced. The French sheep's milk version is moist, creamy, and mild—that made with goat's milk is equally mild but drier. Bulgarian "feta" is a sheep's milk product that's tangier than the French version. Israeli fetas typically use sheep's milk, and many enthusiasts favor their creamy tang over the mild French renditions. American and Danish feta-style cheeses are primarily produced from cow's milk, which results in a drier cheese. However, there are always exceptions to every rule. **Haystack Mountain Goat Dairy** produces a handmade goat's milk feta that has won an American Cheese Society award.

Feta Tis Fotias [FEH-tuh tees foh-TEE-ahss] *see* SFELA

Figaro [FIG-ah-roh] *see* NOCTURNE

F

figue [FEEG] French for "fig" and one of the many shapes into which CHÈVRE is formed.

filled cheese *see* IMITATION CHEESE

finish 1. A term describing how a cheese is packaged—covered in WAX, wrapped in muslin, encased in its natural rind, and so forth. **2.** *See also* "finish" in Glossary of Cheese Descriptors, page 497.

finishing *see* RIPENING

Fiore Sardo (DOC; PDO) [FYOH-ray SAHR-doh]

Origin	Italy (Sardinia)
Milk	Pasteurized or unpasteurized sheep's
Type	SEMIHARD to HARD; MOLDED UNCOOKED; NATURAL RIND; sometimes SMOKED; ARTISAN and FACTORY
Appearance	3- to 11-pound wheels; rind is golden yellow to dark brown, sometimes black when smoked; interior is off-white to straw yellow
Texture	Firm becoming crumbly as it's aged
Flavor	Rich, full flavored, and nutty with a hint of caramel; pungent character grows stronger with age

This type of cheese has been made on the island of Sardinia for eons and has been known as *Fiore Sardo* ("flower of Sardinia") since at least the eighteenth century. Although some references indicate Fiore Sardo is the same as PECORINO SARDO, the latter is a cooked cheese, whereas Fiore Sardo is not. The DENOMINAZIONE DI ORIGINE CONTROLLATA (DOC) regulations state that Fiore Sardo can be made only throughout Sardinia. The milk must come from Sardinian sheep, which are thought to be descended from the wild mountain sheep called *Mouflon*. The pressed cheese is wrapped in cloth and scalded with very hot water or WHEY to seal the rind. It's then brined or dry-salted (*see* SALTING). Occasionally the cheese is kept near a fire for 5 to 10 days to become slightly smoked. Fiore Sardo cheeses are generally aged from 2 to 8 months, during which time they are rubbed with olive oil, a mixture of olive oil and sheep's fat, or sometimes vinegar. If aged for 6 months or more, Fiore Sardo hardens considerably, making it better for grating. This cheese has a FAT CONTENT of about 45 percent.

FireFly Farms *see* MOUNTAIN TOP BLEU

firm cheeses *see* TEXTURE, CHEESE

Fiscalini Cheese Company *see* SAN JOAQUIN GOLD; CHEDDAR

flat 1. A cheese-tasting term for essentially insipid cheese with no sign of character in either aroma or flavor (see Glossary of Cheese Descriptors, page 497). **2.** A WHEEL-shaped CHEDDAR that ranges in weight from 30 to 40 pounds. *See also* CHEESE SIZES AND SHAPES.

flavored cheeses Also called *spiced cheeses,* this general category refers to cheeses with added seasonings such as spices, herbs, seeds, and so on. *See also* PICKLED CHEESES; SMOKED CHEESES.

fleur [fleuhr] French for "flower" and one of the many shapes into which CHÈVRE is formed.

F

Fleur-de-Lis [fleuhr-deuh-LEE]

Origin	United States (Louisiana)
Milk	Pasteurized cow's
Type	SOFT; TRIPLE-CREAM; BLOOMY RIND; ARTISAN
Appearance	7- to 8-ounce wheel; rind is thin with a velvety coating of white mold; interior is white
Texture	Soft, smooth, and moist—almost oozy
Flavor	Rich, creamy, buttery, and slightly tangy

Chef John Folse operates a diverse Louisiana food business that includes his restaurant, Laffite's Landing, and his cheesemaking operation, **Bittersweet Plantation Dairy**. The dairy venture was started in 2002 and produces a full line of fresh and aged cheeses. In 2004 Folse hired Dimcho Dimov, a veteran cheese-maker who emigrated from Bulgaria. The same year Fleur-de-Lis took third place in the soft-ripened category of the American Cheese Society competition. Since then it's also taken a gold medal at the World Cheese Awards in London. This rich cheese is named after the royal emblem of France, which founded Louisiana. It's made with milk from Guernsey cows and is RIP-ENED for 4 to 6 weeks. It has a FAT CONTENT of at least 75 per-cent, which places it in the triple-cream category. In addition to Fleur-de-Lis, Bittersweet Plantation Dairy has won Ameri-can Cheese Society awards for EVANGELINE, FLEUR-DE-TECHE, and CREOLE CREAM CHEESE, Bulgarian Style Black and Blue Drained Yogurt, and Chocolate Pecan Butter.

Fleur-de-Teche [fleuhr-deuh-TESH]

Origin	United States (Louisiana)
Milk	Pasteurized cow's

F

Type	SOFT; TRIPLE-CREAM; BLOOMY RIND; ARTISAN
Appearance	7- to 8-ounce wheel; rind is thin with a velvety coating of white mold; interior is off-white with a layer of vegetable ash running through the center
Texture	Light, creamy, and moist
Flavor	Sweet, creamy, and mild with a faint barnyard trait

Fleur-de-Teche is named in honor of Louisiana's Bayou Teche, which, according to legend, was formed when an enormous snake was killed while battling the Chetimaches Indians. As the dead snake's curved, miles-long body slowly sank into the swampland, it formed Bayou Teche. The ribbon of ASH running through the cheese's interior represents the bayou. Fleur-de-Teche is produced by the renowned **Bittersweet Plantation Dairy** in Gonzales, Louisiana. Bulgarian master cheesemaker Dimcho Dimov produces this ultra-rich cheese from Holstein cow's milk. It's RIPENED for 4 to 6 weeks and has a FAT CONTENT of approximately 80 percent, which places it well into the triple-cream category. Fleur-de-Teche is a multiple winner in the annual American Cheese Society competition. Under Dimov's guidance, Bittersweet Plantation Dairy has also won Society awards for its EVANGELINE and FLEUR-DE-LIS ripened cheeses, as well as for its CREOLE CREAM CHEESE.

Fleur du Maquis [fleuhr doo mah-KEE] *see* BRIN D'AMOUR

floral *see* Glossary of Cheese Descriptors, page 497

flowery rind *see* BLOOMY RIND

F

fondue (au fromage) [fahn-DOO oh froh-MAHZH] *Fondue* is the French word for "melt," from *fondre*. *Fondue au fromage* is a traditional melted cheese dish of Swiss heritage. The classic blend is EMMENTAL and GRUYÈRE, which are combined with white wine, Kirsch, and seasonings such as garlic and nutmeg, then stirred together over low heat until melted and smooth. Bite-sized chunks of French bread are dipped into the hot, gooey cheese mixture. Heating the last bit of fondue coating the pan toasts and crisps it. This delicacy, known as *la religieuse,* can be broken into pieces for a crunchy treat. *See also* FONDUTA; QUESO FUNDIDO.

fonduta [fahn-DOO-tah] Italy's answer to FONDUE, the word *fonduta* comes from *fondere,* which means "to melt." Fonduta is a homogenous mélange of FONTINA, cream, butter, and egg yolks, heated and beaten together until silky and smooth. It's more complex and versatile than its French cousin in that, though it may be used as a dip for bread chunks, it's also employed as a sauce over myriad dishes such as pasta, rice, boiled potatoes, and polenta. Fonduta Piemontese gilds the lily with the addition of fresh white truffles. *See also* FONDUE; QUESO FUNDIDO.

Fontina; Fontina Valle d'Aosta (DOC; PDO) [fahn-TEE-nah; VAHL-lay D'AOW-stah]

Origin	Italy (Valle d'Aosta)
Milk	Unpasteurized cow's
Type	SEMISOFT to SEMIHARD; PRESSED COOKED; NATURAL RIND; some MOUNTAIN; ARTISAN, FARMSTEAD, and FACTORY
Appearance	18- to 40-pound wheels; rind is thin, rigid, and ranges in color from yellow-gold to reddish

brown; interior varies from pale yellow to dark
yellow and has a scattering of small EYES

Texture   Supple, smooth, and firm

Flavor   Full flavored, sweet, and buttery with nutty
nuances

While "fontina" cheese is produced in Denmark, France, Sweden, and the United States, genuine Fontina can be produced
only in the Valle d'Aosta region in northern Italy near the French
and Swiss borders. By most accounts, it's been made in this
Italian-Alps region for at least 700 years. Of the many Fontina
imitations, none match the quality of the cheese from this region,
and most fall far short. Genuine DENOMINAZIONE DI ORIGINE
CONTROLLATA (DOC) Fontina has a round label with the capitalized word *FONTINA* in the middle and a graphic of the Alps
above it. Although Fontina is made year-round, the best cheese is
produced during the summer from the cows that graze in mountain pastures. DOC regulations require the milk to come from
Pezzata Rossa Valdostana cows, internationally known as *Aosta
Red Spotted*. Fontina is made twice daily, each time from a single
milking. The pressed cheese is placed in forms and rubbed with
salt or washed with brine (*see* SALTING) numerous times until the
rind develops. Fontina cheese is generally aged for 3 to 7 months.
It has a minimum FAT CONTENT of 45 percent.

force(d) ripening *see* RIPENING

foremilk *see* COLOSTRUM

Formaella Arachovas Parnassou (PDO); Formaella of Parnassos
[for-mah-EHL-lah ah-rah-KOH-vahs pahr-NAH-soo]

Origin   Greece (Boeotia)

Milk   Unpasteurized sheep's or goat's

F

Type	SEMISOFT to HARD; PRESSED COOKED; NATURAL RIND; ARTISAN, FARMSTEAD, and COOPERATIVE
Appearance	Small 9-ounce cylinders; rind is thin and beige with markings of the wicker mold; interior is off-white
Texture	Young versions are firm and supple; aged versions can be very hard and good for grating
Flavor	Sweet and milky, becoming strong and piquant with age

For centuries Greek cheesemakers have been producing Formaella Arachovas Parnassou, the formal PROTECTED DESIGNATION OF ORIGIN (PDO) name, although it's also called *Formaella of Parnassos* and simply *Formaella*. This cheese comes from central Greece's Arachova Parnassou area in the Boeotia prefecture. During production, the cut CURD is packed into small, woven molds (*tirivoli*) and immersed in 140°F WHEY for 1 hour. The cheese is then allowed to dry in the mold for 24 hours before being removed to dry and drain for 4 days. At this point the young Formaella is most often used for fried cheese (*SAGANAKI*). For longer aging, the cheeses are taken to caves in the Parnassos mountains to RIPEN for at least 3 months. During aging Formaella dries and hardens and develops much stronger flavors. The FAT CONTENT of this cheese is 30 to 35 percent.

formaggio [for-MAH-zhoh] Italian for "cheese."

Formai de Mut dell'Alta Valle Brembana (DOC; PDO) [FOR-mi day MOOT dell-AWL-tah braym-BAH-nah]

Origin	Italy (Lombardy)
Milk	Unpasteurized cow's

Type	SEMISOFT to SEMIHARD; PRESSED COOKED; NATURAL RIND; MOUNTAIN, ARTISAN, and FARMSTEAD
Appearance	17- to 27-pound wheels; rind is thin, smooth, and rigid and varies in color from pale yellow to gray, depending on age; interior is off-white to pale yellow, depending on age, and has a scattering of small EYES
Texture	Supple, smooth, and firm
Flavor	Mild with light herbal aroma

Formai de Mut (the abbreviated form that's typically used) is made only in the Val Brembana, which lies north of Milan near the medieval hilltop city of Bergamo. The name derives from the local dialect—*formai* ("cheese"), *mut* ("mountain"), and *dell'alta* ("of the high one")—resulting in "mountain cheese of the high Brembana Valley" or simply "mountain cheese." The pastures in this alpine valley are at 4,000 to 8,200 feet. The herds are traditionally all Brown Alpine cattle (also known as Swiss Brown). Until 1988, cheese was made only during the 5 months surrounding summer when the cattle could graze in the mountain pastures. Although most cheese is still made in the summer season, some is now also made year-round. DE-NOMINAZIONE DI ORIGINE CONTROLLATA (DOC) rules are relaxed during the nonsummer seasons, allowing cattle to consume food sources other than the mountain grasses. Formai de Mut is similar to FONTINA in that it's handcrafted and follows many of the same production techniques. For Formai de Mut, both morning and evening milk is used. The pressed CURD is placed in circular molds called *fassere* and repeatedly sprinkled with salt for 8 days or until the rind develops. The cheese is aged for at least 40 to 45 days and often for over 6 months. The distinctive label features the words *Formai de Mut* in large letters that surround the artistic image of a wheel of cheese inside a cowbell and, in smaller letters, the words *Dell'Alta Valle Brembana*. The FAT CONTENT of this cheese is a minimum of 45 percent.

Fourme d'Ambert; Fourme de Montbrison (AOC; PDO) [FOORM dah*n*-BEH*R*; FOORM deuh maw*n*-bree-saw*n*]

Origin	France (Rhône-Alpes; Auvergne)
Milk	Unpasteurized cow's
Type	SEMISOFT TO SEMIHARD; MOLDED UNCOOKED; BLUE-VEINED; NATURAL RIND; FARMSTEAD, ARTISAN, COOPERATIVE, and FACTORY
Appearance	Tall, slim $3\frac{1}{2}$- to $5\frac{1}{2}$-pound drum-shaped wheel; rind is dry, pitted, and coated with beige and gray molds with occasional red and blue splotches; interior is ivory colored and marbled with blue veins
Texture	Moist and creamy
Flavor	Mild, earthy, and slightly pungent with nuances of nuts and fruit

According to legend, Fourme d'Ambert–type cheeses have been produced for over 2,000 years and were known to the Druids who came to worship in the area. Whatever its origins, Fourme d'Ambert has clearly been made for centuries by small farms scattered around the town of Ambert on the western side of Mont du Forez in central France. The word *fourme* is from the Latin *forma,* which means "form" or "shape." **Fourme de Montbrison** is a nearly identical cheese produced around the town of Montbrison, which is on the eastern side of Mont du Forez. In 1972, both cheeses were combined under the same

APPELLATION D'ORIGINE CONTRÔLÉE (AOC) but were separated into individual AOC designations in 2002. The cows that produce the milk for these cheeses graze at altitudes of 2,000 to 5,000 feet. During production, *Penicillium glaucum* is added to the CURDS. Once the cheese is firm enough, it's dry-salted or brined (*see* SALTING). Thick needles are used to pierce the cheese so air can feed the bacteria that creates the bluing. RIPENING takes a minimum of 1 month and up to 5 months. The FAT CONTENT is about 50 percent.

Fourme de Cantal [FOORM day kahn-TAHL] *see* CANTAL

Fourme de Montbrison [FOORM deuh mawn-bree-sawn] *see* FOURME D'AMBERT

Fourme de Salers [FOORM day sah-LEHR] *see* SALERS

frais [FRAY] French for "fresh." *Fromage frais* means "FRESH CHEESE." *See also* FROMAGE BLANC.

French cheeses *see* Cheeses by Country of Origin, page 509

fresh cheeses Young cheeses that have not undergone COOKING or RIPENING at all (or only for a few days), which is why they're also called *unripened cheeses*. Fresh cheeses, which are moist, mild, and sometimes slightly tart, include COTTAGE CHEESE, CREAM CHEESE, RICOTTA, and water-packed fresh MOZZARELLA. Because there are invariably exceptions to every rule, a few fresh cheeses, such as FETA, have been slightly ripened. Others, such as MURAZZANO, undergo MOLDING. All are rindless. According to U.S. federal regulations, fresh cheeses transported interstate must be produced from milk pasteurized not less than

F

30 minutes at a temperature of at least 145°F. *See also* CHEESE; TYPE(S), CHEESE.

friability [fry-uh-BIH-lih-tee] *see* Glossary of Cheese Descriptors, page 498

Fribourgeois [free-boor-ZHWAH] *see* VACHERIN FRIBOURGEOIS

frico; fricco [FREE-koh] Italian for "little trifles," frico are lacy, crisp cheese wafers. In Italy, they're classically made with MONTASIO, but many other cheeses may be used, including ASIAGO, CHEDDAR, and PARMESAN. Frico can be made either in a nonstick stovetop skillet or on a lightly greased baking sheet in the oven. Spoonfuls of grated cheese (sometimes mixed with herbs and a soupçon of flour) are sprinkled on the cooking surface and cooked over medium heat until melted and bubbly. After cooling for a couple of minutes, a spatula is used to transfer the frico from the cooking surface to paper towels. When completely cool, the crispy treats can be eaten as appetizers or used to garnish soups, salads, or other dishes.

Frieskaas [FREES-kahss] *see* KANTERKAAS; KANTERNAGELKAAS; KANTERKOMIJNEKAAS

fromage [froh-MAHZH] French for "cheese." *Le fromage fondu* is "cheese spread."

fromage à pâte persillé [froh-MAHZH ah paht pehr-see-YAY] *see* PERSILLÉ

Fromage à Raclette [froh-MAHZH ah rah-KLEHT)

see RACLETTE

fromage blanc [froh-MAHZH BLAH*N*)

Origin	France
Milk	Pasteurized or unpasteurized cow's, goat's, or sheep's—or a mixture
Type	SOFT; FRESH; FARMSTEAD
Appearance	White; sold in 8-ounce tubs or disks
Texture	Creamy, soft, and smooth, with a texture ranging from that of a very thick sour cream to ricotta or cream cheese
Flavor	Fresh and faintly tangy, though not as much so as sour cream

A simple blend of milk and STARTER that's uncooked and un-molded, fromage blanc ("white cheese") has its origins in France, where it's called *fromage frais* ("fresh cheese"). In its pure form, this unripened cheese is fat free; however, some cheesemakers add cream, which can increase the fat content to around 40 percent. On French labels, you'll see the terms *maigre* (for very low fat) and *allege* (very high fat). Fromage blanc can be used as a spread (in which case herbs and other flavorings may be added), in cooking, or as an adjunct or top-ping for fruit. One of the top fromage blanc producers in the United States is **Vermont Butter & Cheese Company,** which has won World Cheese Awards for their **Vermont Fromage Blanc.** Cheesemaker and cofounder Allison Hooper modeled their fat-free version after the fromage blanc she enjoyed as an apprentice at a farm in Brittany, France.

F

fromage de brebis [froh-MAHZH deuh breuh-BEE]

see BREBIS

Fromage de Herve (AOC; PDO) [froh-MAHZH deuh ehr-VAY]

Origin	Belgium (Liège)
Milk	Unpasteurized and pasteurized cow's
Type	SEMISOFT; PRESSED UNCOOKED; WASHED RIND; ARTISAN, FARMSTEAD, COOPERATIVE, and FACTORY
Appearance	$1^3/_4$- to 14-ounce cubes or rectangles; rind is sticky, wrinkled, and pinkish orange to reddish brown in color; interior is off-white to pale yellow
Texture	Firm and supple, becoming creamy as it ages
Flavor	Complex and rich array of sweet, spicy, savory, and tangy

This cheese has been produced on the Herve plateau around the town of Herve (between Liège and Verviers) since the fifteenth century. Early names for this strong, richly flavored cheese include *remoudous*, *quatre saisons,* and *bizeux*—cheeses all made with some variation but primarily in the same manner as modern-day Fromage de Herve. During RIPENING, this cheese is washed (usually with beer) every couple of days for a minimum of 5 weeks, though 2 to 3 months of aging is not uncommon. The minimum FAT CONTENT for Fromage de Herve is 45 percent. **Plateau de Herve,** a washed-rind cheese made in this same area, is dome shaped and has a much milder flavor. It has neither an APPELLATION D'ORIGINE CONTRÔLÉE (AOC) or PROTECTED DESIGNATION OF ORIGIN (PDO) accreditation.

Fromage de Savoie [froh–MAHZH deuh SAH–vwah]
see REBLOCHON

fromage fort [froh–MAHZH FAWR] French for "strong cheese,"
fromage fort is a combination of leftover cheese scraps, wine,
butter, and sometimes seasonings such as herbs and garlic.
Traditionally, the French would let this mélange ferment until
good and stinky. Today, fromage fort is more likely to be
blended together and either allowed to mellow in the refrigerator for a couple of days or served immediately as a spread for
bread or crackers.

fromage frais [froh–MAHZH FRAY] French for "fresh cheese."
See FROMAGE BLANC.

fromager [froh–mah–ZHAY] French term for a cheesemaker;
sometimes also a cheese wholesaler or retailer.

Fromager d'Affinois [froh–mah–ZHAY dah–fee–NWAH]

Origin	France
Milk	Pasteurized cow's, some sheep's
Type	SOFT; MOLDED UNCOOKED; BLOOMY RIND; some DOUBLE–CREAM; FACTORY
Appearance	4½-pound wheels and 1- and 5⅓-ounce squares; rind is thin with a velvety coating of white MOLD; interior is ivory colored
Texture	Very soft and smooth
Flavor	Delicate, creamy, and grassy with a nuance of mushrooms

F

Fromager d'Affinois is produced by Fromagerie Guilloteau using a process called ultrafiltration, which was developed by Jean-Claude Guilloteau and the French National Agronomy Research Agency. Ultrafiltration removes water from pasteurized milk, which minimizes the WHEY-elimination steps. This results in a cheese with a higher nutrient content and a creamier presence on the palate. It also speeds cheesemaking, allowing Fromager d'Affinois to be ready in 2 weeks as opposed to 6 to 8 weeks for most BRIE, a cheese with which it's often compared. Whereas Brie has a 45 percent FAT CONTENT, that of Fromager d'Affinois is 60 percent. Many opine that it tastes more like a TRIPLE-CREAM, which contains at least 72 percent fat. **Fromager d'Affinois Poivre** is flavored with black pepper and **Fromager d'Affinois Ail et Fines Herbes** contains garlic and herbs. **Fromager d'Affinois Léger** is a reduced-fat (25 percent) version. **Pavé d'Affinois** refers to 1- and 5⅓-ounce square formats of this cheese, the fat content of which may be 25, 45, or 60 percent. **Pavé d'Affinois Brebis** is the sheep's milk version of this cheese.

fromagerie [froh-mah-zheuh-REE] French for a cheese dairy, though the term can also sometimes refer to a cheese shop.

Fromagerie Tournevent *see* LE CHÈVRE NOIR

fruitière [free-tee-YAIR] French term for a small cheese producer or co-op. *See also* CRÉMIER; LAITIER.

fruity *see* Glossary of Cheese Descriptors, page 498

fundido *see* QUESO FUNDIDO

furry *see* Glossary of Cheese Descriptors, page 498

G

Gabrielson Lake *see* BIG HOLMES

Gailtaler Almkäse (PDO); Gailtaler Alpkäse
[GAYL-tah-ler AHLM-ki-zer;
AHLP-ki-zer (-kah-zeh)]

> Poets have been mysteriously silent on the subject of cheese.
> —G. K. Chesterton

Origin	Austria (Carinthia)
Milk	Unpasteurized cow's and goat's
Type	SEMIHARD; PRESSED COOKED; NATURAL RIND; ARTISAN, FARMSTEAD, and COOPERATIVE; MOUNTAIN
Appearance	1- to 77-pound wheels; rind is dry, smooth, and golden yellow in color; interior is pale yellow to medium yellow with a small number of EYES
Texture	Smooth and supple
Flavor	Mild, delicate, and slightly sweet, becoming stronger, savory, tangy, and more aromatic with additional ripening

Gailtaler Almkäse is a MOUNTAIN CHEESE produced in the Gailtal alpine region in Carinthia, Austria's southernmost state, which borders on Italy and Slovenia. Historical documents show that cheese has been made in this alpine region since the fourteenth century. Although the term *Gailtaler Alpkäse* ("Gailtal alpine cheese") has been in common use for centuries, today the accepted name is *Gailtaler Almkäse* ("Gailtal *mountain* cheese").

G

PROTECTED DESIGNATION OF ORIGIN (PDO) regulations state that the milk for this cheese can come only from animals that graze in alpine pastures—no valley-produced milk can be used. Most of the milk comes from cows, but up to 10 percent goat's milk may be used. This cheese is made with evening milk that's been skimmed, then poured into *stotzen* (round wooden containers) and placed in a cool (53°F to 62°F) room to RIPEN overnight. The next day the ripened milk is combined with that of the morning's milking. The cut CURD is cooked in WHEY, drained, placed in molds, and pressed for about 2 days, during which time it's turned several times. The cheese is then placed in a BRINE bath for 2 to 3 days to encourage proper rind development. Gailtaler Almkäse is ripened for a minimum of 7 weeks; if the cheese is to be vacuum-packed, the minimum is 11 weeks.

Gamonedo [gah-moh-NAY-doh] *see* QUESO GAMONEDO

Gamoneú [gah-moh-NAY-yoo] *see* QUESO GAMONEDO

gamy; gamey *see* Glossary of Cheese Descriptors, page 498

Gaperon [gah-peuh-ROH*N*]

Origin	France (Auvergne)
Milk	Unpasteurized and pasteurized cow's
Type	SEMISOFT to SEMIHARD; PRESSED UNCOOKED; NATURAL RIND; ARTISAN and FARMSTEAD
Appearance	9- to 12-ounce flat-bottomed dome, sometimes tied with raffia; rind is often very wrinkled and soft with white downy mold when young, becoming hard and dry with blue, gray, and white molds after ripening; interior is off-white with specks of garlic and peppercorn

Texture	Young cheeses are supple, creamy, and soft; older versions are denser
Flavor	Milky, tangy, garlicky, and peppery when young, becoming more piquant with age; some have a smoky trait

G

Gaperon has been made in central France's Auvergne region since at least the seventh or eighth century. Its name is derived from *gape,* which in the Auvergne dialect means "buttermilk." In the past this cheese was made by combining the liquid left over from churning butter with fresh milk to produce a low-fat cheese. Today Gaperon is made primarily from partially skimmed cow's milk, though whole milk is occasionally used. During production, salt, peppercorns, and garlic bits are added to the curd. Some cheeses are hung or placed by the fire to dry and absorb a smoky quality. Gaperon is RIPENED for 1 to 2 months and has a FAT CONTENT between 30 and 45 percent.

garlic; garlicky *see* Glossary of Cheese Descriptors, page 498

Garrotxa [gahr-ROH-chah]

Origin	Spain (Catalonia; Garrotxa)
Milk	Pasteurized or unpasteurized goat's
Type	SEMISOFT; PRESSED UNCOOKED; NATURAL RIND; FARMSTEAD
Appearance	2-pound rounds; rind is light golden marked with pale gray mold; interior is chalk white
Texture	Firm, buttery smooth, and velvety
Flavor	Mild, tangy, with nuances of nuts, flowers, and fresh grass.

G

Made for centuries in Catalonia, Garrotxa (also called *Queso de la Garrotxa*) is a rustic cheese that has been revived by modern cheesemakers using the original recipe. This lightly pressed cheese undergoes a brief brining (*see* SALTING) before it's cave-RIPENED in high humidity for a minimum of 20 days. It has a FAT CONTENT of about 50 percent.

Geitost [YEHT-ohst] *see* GJETOST

German cheeses *see* Cheeses by Country of Origin, page 511

Géromé [zhay-roh-MAY] *see* MUNSTER

Gibbneh Beda [GIHB-neh BED-ah] *see* DOMIATI

Girolle [zhee-ROHL] A clever device invented by Swiss precision engineer Nicolas Crevoisier in the 1980s specifically to cut TÊTE DE MOINE. Tired of shaving the cheese with a knife in the traditional way, Crevoisier developed a tool consisting of a stainless-steel rod on which is mounted a downward-facing blade with attached handle. The rod is pushed through the center of the cheese and, as the handle is turned, the blade slowly lowers on the rod while shaving off a very thin layer of cheese, forming rosettes. Crevoisier's ingenuity has paid off—in the last quarter century almost 2½ million Girolles have been sold.

Gjetost; Geitost [YAYT-oost; YEHT-oost]

Origin	Norway
Milk	Pasteurized cow's and goat's
Type	SEMISOFT to SEMIHARD; MOLDED COOKED; rindless; FACTORY

Appearance	Various-sized blocks ranging from 9 ounces to 9 pounds or more; rindless; color is light to deep golden brown
Texture	Smooth, firm, and fudgelike
Flavor	Sweet and caramellike, but somewhat sour and salty; the 100 percent goat's milk version is slightly tangier; darker-colored styles usually exhibit stronger nuances of caramel or burnt sugar

G

Gjetost, also commonly spelled *geitost,* means "goat cheese." However, unless it's labeled *Ekte Gjetost* or *Ekte Geitost* ("authentic goat cheese"), this cheese is usually made with a blend of goat's milk, cow's milk, and WHEY. This cheese is based on an ancient process for spreadable cheese (called *prim* or *primost*), whereby the whey is simmered until the moisture evaporates and the milk sugars caramelize. Today's Gjetost is believed to have been made first in 1863 in Norway's Gubrands Valley when a farmer's wife named Anne Hov added cream to the whey and created a richer, firmer version. It's said that Gjetost cheeses from Gubrands Valley (known then and now as *Gudbrandsdalsost*) commanded high prices, which helped the valley through tough financial times in the 1880s. Today many versions of this style of cheese are made throughout Scandinavia. Once the cream-milk-whey mixture is cooked, the sticky reduction is placed in molds and allowed to cool. Because of the diversity of production techniques, Gjetost comes in a broad range of consistencies, flavors, and colors. It's widely popular, particularly among children because of its sweet, caramellike flavor. Other names that apply to this style of cheese include **brunost** ("brown cheese") and **mysost** (a version made only with cow's milk). Although the FAT CONTENT of Gjetost is generally 30 to 35 percent, there are lower-fat versions that are identified by the word *lett* ("light") on the label.

Glarnerkäse [GLAHR-ner-KI-zer (-kah-zeh)] *see* SAPSAGO

Gloucester [GLOSS-ter]

Origin	England (Gloucestershire)
Milk	Unpasteurized and pasteurized cow's
Type	SEMIHARD; PRESSED COOKED; NATURAL RIND; ARTISAN, FARMSTEAD, COOPERATIVE, and FACTORY
Appearance	Single Gloucester comes in 7- to 12-pound wheels, and Double Gloucester comes in 8- to 18-pound wheels—farmstead versions are cloth covered or have the imprint of cloth covering; rinds are thick, hard, and dark beige with blue and gray mold; interiors are pale yellow to yellow-orange
Texture	Single Gloucesters are light, dry, and crumbly; Double Gloucesters are firmer and denser
Flavor	Single Gloucesters are mild, milky, and slightly sweet with hints of vanilla and caramel; Double Gloucesters are richer flavored and more mellow with savory and nutty traits

Gloucester cheeses are thought to have originated in the eighth century but didn't become popular outside the local area until the eighteenth century. There are two styles—**Single Gloucester** and **Double Gloucester**—both of which originated around the city of Gloucester in southwestern England's County Gloucestershire. It's believed the two types originated because on certain days the cream was skimmed from some of the milk for butter production. On skimmed-milk days, Single Gloucester was produced, and on days when whole milk was available Double Gloucester was made. Some say the word *double* refers to the use of whole milk. Others think it comes from the fact that the cheese is made in larger wheels. Single Gloucester, which has been granted PROTECTED DESIGNATION OF ORIGIN (PDO) status, is made entirely from milk from Gloucester cows, which at one point were near extinction. PDO regulations require it to be produced by traditional farmstead methods. Milk is taken from the evening milking and the next morning's milking; one or both may be skimmed. The CURDS are pressed for up to 5 days. Unlike Double Gloucester, Single Gloucester cannot be dyed. It also has a lower FAT CONTENT, the texture is lighter and more crumbly, and the taste is milder. Single Gloucester is generally RIPENED anywhere from 10 weeks to 9 months. Double Gloucester, which doesn't have PDO status at this writing, is made in a similar fashion from whole milk, which produces a richer flavor. It's usually ripened for 6 months or more and has a FAT CONTENT of about 48 percent. Most Double Gloucesters are factory produced, fairly bland tasting, and the wheels are plastic coated. The few farmstead versions are richer and more complex in flavor and have either a cloth covering or markings made by cloth during ripening. **Cotswald,** also known simply as *pub cheese,* is a Double Gloucester flavored with bits of chive and onion.

goat cheeses; goat's milk cheeses *see* CHÈVRE and Cheeses by Milk Type, page 522

goaty *see* Glossary of Cheese Descriptors, page 498

Gorgonzola (DOC; PDO) [gor-gahn-ZOH-lah]

Origin	Italy (Lombardy and Piedmont)
Milk	Unpasteurized or pasteurized cow's

G

Type	SEMISOFT to SEMIHARD; MOLDED UNCOOKED; BLUE-VEINED; NATURAL RIND; ARTISAN and COOPERATIVE
Appearance	13- to 29-pound wheels; rind is thick, rough, moist, and reddish (darkening with age); interior ranges from white to ivory with bluish green streaks
Texture	Moist and creamy when young, firmer and more crumbly when aged
Flavor	Ranges from mild, fresh, and sweet with a piquant touch in younger cheese to sharper, more acidic, and stronger flavored in aged versions

Gorgonzola is known to have been produced since the tenth century and probably predates that. There are myriad stories but no real certainty as to how or when Gorgonzola was first produced. However, at some point a local cheese was discovered to have been infected with PENICILLIUM spores, and thus was born one of Italy's most famous cheeses. The early name of this cheese was **Stracchino** and later **Stracchino di Gorgonzola.** In the Lombardy region, *stracco* means "tired," purportedly in reference to the cows being weary after making the long trek from the alpine meadows to the Po Valley. The town of Gorgonzola, which lies northeast of Milan, was one of the main stops along the way, and eventually its name became tied to this style of cheese. Interestingly, this cheese is no longer made in the town of Gorgonzola, which, along with the surrounding farmlands, has been absorbed into Milan's urban sprawl. DENOMINAZIONE DI ORIGINE CONTROLLATA (DOC) standards state that Gorgonzola can be produced only in two Italian regions—Lombardy's provinces of Bergamo, Brescia, Como, Cremona, Lecco, Lodi, Milan, Pavia, and Varese and Piedmont's provinces of Novara, Vercelli,

G

Cuneo, Biella, Verbania, and the territory of Casale Monferrato. Historically, Gorgonzola was produced only in the fall because that's when favorable RIPENING conditions existed. Now it's produced year-round in caves and manmade facilities with an environment that encourages proper aging. There are two types of Gorgonzola—**one-layer curd** (*una pasta*) and **two-layer curd** (*due paste*), though the latter is rarely seen today. Both types are made similarly with whole milk except that the one-layer curd uses milk from only one milking, whereas the two-layer CURD uses milk from an evening milking to which *PENICILLIUM* spores have been added, plus a morning milking. The two-layer version is created by alternating layers of curd from the two different milkings. Both processes use thin nails or thick needles to pierce the cheese, first on one side and then, several days later, on the other. This encourages development of the flavorful blue-green mold. Gorgonzola is aged for 2 to 3 months and sometimes up to 6 months. Younger cheeses are sold as **Gorgonzola dolce,** while longer-aged cheeses are sold as **Gorgonzola naturale** or **Gorgonzola piccante.** The FAT CONTENT generally ranges from 39 to 49 percent. Most producers belong to the *Consorzio per la Tutela del Formaggio Gorgonzola* (Consortium for the Protection of the Gorgonzola Cheese), whose inspectors ensure compliance with DOC regulations. These producers wrap their cheeses in foil labeled with the combined letters *CG,* which appears as **g.** Though the only true Gorgonzola comes from Italy's Lombardy and Piedmont regions, there are numerous pretenders (including American and Danish), which for the most part are simply not as good.

Gouda [HOW-dah; GOO-dah]

Origin	Netherlands
Milk	Unpasteurized and pasteurized cow's

G

Type	SEMIHARD to HARD; PRESSED COOKED; NATURAL RIND; some SMOKED; ARTISAN, FARMSTEAD, COOPERATIVE, and FACTORY
Appearance	Primarily wheels ranging in size from less than 1 pound to 88 pounds; some have a natural rind that's thin and yellow when young, becoming darker and thicker with age; others are covered with various-colored waxes; interior is pale yellow to deep gold with a scattering of irregularly shaped EYES; aged versions have crystalline flecks of white
Texture	Smooth and supple when young; long-aged cheeses become hard, flaky, and brittle
Flavor	Ranges from delicate and mild for young factory cheeses to full, rich, fruity, and nutty in FARMSTEAD cheeses; aged versions are rich, intense, and have nuances of butterscotch and toffee

Gouda is named after a small city located between Utrecht and Rotterdam in the South Holland province of the western part of the Netherlands. It was produced as far back as the sixth century and in the thirteenth century was exported to England, where it was quite popular. Today, Gouda is one of the best-known cheeses in the world and represents 60 to 65 percent of cheese production in Holland. This Dutch hallmark is now primarily factory produced with pasteurized milk and can weigh anywhere from 6 to 50 pounds. Most Goudas are in the form of wheels, though some 8-pound loaves are produced. **Baby Gouda** comes in wheels weighing from 6 ounces to 3¼ pounds. Most factory Gouda comes coated in red WAX, which extends its longevity. Other wax colors signify additions—green wax indicates the addition of herbs, while an orange color tells you the cheese is flavored with cumin. Most Gouda is RIPENED for 1 to 6 months, but a black wax coating indicates an **aged Gouda,** which has been ripened for at least 12 months and some for up to 5 or 6 years. The label will state the age of the cheese. Gouda aged for 2 years or more has a deep golden color, a drier, harder texture with bits of crystallized protein that add a sweet characteristic, and a flavor replete with rich toffee and butterscotch notes. Some of the most widely recognized aged Goudas are **Beemster, Rembrandt,** and **Saenkanter.** Another prized Gouda is **Boe-renkaas** (Dutch for "farmer's cheese"), which is farmstead produced in wheels weighing up to 88 pounds. It's made with raw milk, which gives it a rich, full flavor at 4 to 6 months, though it's often ripened for 6 to 7 years, which intensifies the flavor and makes it more complex. The single PROTECTED DESIGNA-TION OF ORIGIN (PDO) Gouda is **Noord-Hollandse Gouda,** which can be produced only in the North Holland province and has a lower salt content than most other Goudas. Even though Noord-Hollandse Goudas are factory produced, strict PDO regulations generate a higher quality than in many non-PDO relatives. Because Gouda is not a protected name, it can be made in other parts of the world. COOLEA is a full-flavored Boerenkass-style Gouda produced in Ireland's western county Cork. Pen-bryn is another Gouda-style cheese made in Wales. And there are many American Goudas, most of which are factory produced, coated with red wax, and bear a close resemblance to the Dutch imports. Among the award-winning, raw-milk, farmstead producers making Gouda in the United States are **Prima Käse** in Wisconsin, **Smith's Country Cheese** in Massachusetts, and **Winchester Cheese Company** in California. Jules Wesselink, owner of Winchester Cheese Company in Winchester, California, produces an award-winning Boerenkaas-style Gouda. Wesselink ran dairy farms for over 40 years but in his mid-sixties returned to his native Netherlands to learn to

G

make cheese and in 1996 produced his first Gouda. His Super Aged Gouda is made with raw cow's milk and RIPENED for 15 months, which produces a cheese that's rich, fruity, and nutty with notes of butterscotch. **Doeling Dairy Goat Farm** in Arkansas makes an unusual farmstead Gouda from unpasteurized goat's milk. The FAT CONTENT for standard Gouda is approximately 48 percent. **Double Cream Gouda** (or **Roomkaas**) has cream added, which pushes its fat content to 60 percent. A relatively recent addition is **Light Gouda,** made with partially skimmed milk, which puts its fat content in the 30 to 40 percent range.

gougère [goo-ZHEHR] A cheese-flavored choux pastry (from which cream puffs are made) that is typically piped into a ring or into small mounds before being baked. Ring-shaped gougères may be filled with a meat or vegetable mixture and served as a main dish, whereas mound-shaped pastries are typically split, filled with a savory mixture, and served as an hors d'oeuvre. Gougère is classically flavored with GRUYÈRE, though CHEDDAR or any like-textured cheese may be used.

Gräddost [GRAHD-oost]

Origin	Sweden
Milk	Pasteurized cow's
Type	SEMISOFT; PRESSED COOKED; rindless; ARTISAN and FACTORY
Appearance	14-ounce to 2¼-pound barrel-shaped wheels; rindless; interior is ivory to pale yellow with a large number of irregular EYES
Texture	Supple and elastic, higher-fat versions are creamier
Flavor	Mild, buttery, and tangy

Gräddost is Sweden's version of HAVARTI, the popular Danish cheese. *Grädde* is Swedish for "cream," and *ost* means "cheese," which is why this cheese is sometimes referred to as *butter cheese*. This cheese was introduced in the early 1960s and quickly became a Swedish favorite. Gräddost is cave ripened for about 2 months and can have a FAT CONTENT as high as 60 percent.

Grafton Village Cheese Company *see* CHEDDAR

grainy *see* Glossary of Cheese Descriptors, page 499, and GRANA CHEESES

grana cheeses; grana-style cheeses [GRAH-nah] In the cheese world, the Italian word *grana* refers to finely grained hard cheeses that, when grated, have a granular or flaky texture, depending on the style of grater used. Such cheeses undergo COOKING, PRESSING, and MOLDING. During RIPENING, the cheese is turned frequently from top to bottom. Two of the most widely acclaimed grana-style cheeses are PARMIGIANO-REGGIANO and GRANA PADANO. *See also* TYPE(S), CHEESE.

Grana Padano (DOC; PDO) [GRAH-nah pah-DAH-noh]

Origin	Italy (Emilia-Romagna, Lombardy, Piedmont, and Veneto regions)
Milk	Unpasteurized cow's
Type	SEMIHARD to HARD; GRANA STYLE; PRESSED COOKED; NATURAL RIND; ARTISAN, FARMSTEAD, and FACTORY
Appearance	Very large 53- to 88-pound wheels; rind is rigid and smooth and ranges in color from gold to golden brown; interior ranges in color from yellow to deep gold

G

Texture	Finely grained, becoming flaky and crumbly as the cheese ages
Flavor	Mellow, delicate, fruity, and aromatic, intensifying as the cheese ages

Grana Padano is thought to have originated early in the eleventh century in northern Italy's Po Valley region. The name *grana* comes from its "grainy" consistency, which was unusual in the eleventh century. By the late 1400s, Grana Padano had become Italy's most popular cheese, primarily because it could be kept for long periods without losing its superior flavor or nutrition. Today, though Grana Padano is still more widely sold, PARMI-GIANO-REGGIANO has become the most recognized name in the GRANA CHEESE category. The DENOMINAZIONE DI ORIGINE CON-TROLLATA (DOC) regulations for Grana Padano allow it to be produced over a fairly large area of only four regions—Emilia Romagna (the provinces of Bologna, Ferrara, Forli, Piacenza, Ravenna), Lombardy (Bergamo, Brescia, Como, Cremona, Mantua, Milan, Pavia, Sondrio, and Varese), Piedmont (Alessandria, Asti, Cuneo, Novara, Turin, and Vercelli), and Veneto (Padua, Rovigo, Trento, Treviso, Venice, Verona, and Vicenza). This cheese is made from partially skimmed cow's milk, which produces a lower FAT CONTENT of about 32 percent. The cooked CURD is molded and bathed in brine (*see* SALTING) until the rind forms. During the aging process (1 to 2 years) the wheels are inspected constantly and turned frequently. Grana Padano goes through a rigorous inspection process, and acceptable wheels are stamped with the Grana Padano Consortium mark. The words *Grana* and *Padano* are alternated around the circumference of the wheel so that any wedge cut from the wheel will have an identifying mark on it.

Grand Cru Gruyère [grah*n* KROO groo-YEHR] *see* GRUYÈRE

GranQueso; Solé GranQueso [grahn KAY-soh; SOH-lay]

Origin	United States (Wisconsin)
Milk	Pasteurized cow's
Type	SEMIHARD; PRESSED UNCOOKED; NATURAL RIND; ARTISAN
Appearance	4-pound wheels; rind is thin, has a tight basket-weave pattern, and is reddish to reddish brown in color; interior is compact with a small scattering of EYES, and color ranges from ivory to pale yellow, depending on age
Texture	Firm and compact; aged versions can become crumbly
Flavor	Buttery and sweet yet tangy and zesty

GranQueso is an original cheese created by **Roth Käse USA, Ltd.** of Monroe, Wisconsin. It's patterned after a Spanish QUESO MANCHEGO and has received numerous awards, including multiple golds from the World Cheese Awards in London and both state and national awards in the United States. GranQueso, which is part of Roth Käse's Sole! line of Spanish cheeses, is made using traditional artisanal methods and RIPENED for about 6 months. It has a FAT CONTENT of about 50 percent. Roth Käse USA traces its cheesemaking beginnings to Switzerland in 1863. In the early 1900s the Roth family decided to set up shop in the United States and began importing European cheeses. Eventually the company began making cheese in the United States and in 2001 built a new state-of-the-art cheese plant in Monroe, Wisconsin. The plant includes some traditional European cheese-making equipment, including large copper vats. The company has been very successful and produces a number of award-winning cheeses, including **Braukäse** (a rich, buttery, semi-soft cow's milk cheese), **Butterkäse** (a mild and delicate

G

semisoft cow's milk cheese), **Grand Cru Gruyère** (see GRU-YÈRE), **Lace Käse** (a reduced-fat, low-sodium cow's milk cheese made with imported Swiss EMMENTAL cultures), **Paniña** (a rich, buttery, semisoft, Spanish-style cow's milk cheese), and **Rofumo** (a semisoft, hickory-smoked cow's milk cheese with a mild, delicate flavor).

grassy; grassiness *see* Glossary of Cheese Descriptors, page 499

grating cheeses A term used for very hard cheeses (*see* HARD CHEESES) that are best suited for grating. Such cheeses also do well when thinly shaved and used as a garnish. Grating cheeses include aged ASIAGO, FIORE SARDO, GRANA PADANO, JACK (dry), IDIAZÁBAL, MANCHEGO, PARMIGIANO-REGGIANO, PECORINO ROMANO, PECORINO SARDO, PECORINO SICILIANO, PECORINO TOSCANO, PROVOLONE (sharp), ROMANO, RONCAL, and SAPSAGO.

Gratte-Paille [graht-PIE]

Origin	France (Île-de-France)
Milk	Unpasteurized and pasteurized cow's
Type	SEMISOFT; DOUBLE-CREAM; MOLDED UNCOOKED; BLOOMY RIND; ARTISAN
Appearance	11- to 12-ounce brick; rind is soft, white, and develops a downy mold as it ripens; interior is off-white to pale yellow
Texture	Soft, creamy, and moist
Flavor	Rich, creamy, sweet, mild, and lightly mushroomy with a slight tang

Gratte-Paille was created in the 1960s by **Robert Rouzaire,** founder of **Fromagerie Rouzaire** in the Seine-et-Marne *départe-*

ment just east of Paris, where a great deal of BRIE is made. The name *gratte* ("scrape") *paille* ("straw") comes from the town of Meaux, which had such narrow streets that the straw-laden wagons would scrape the walls of houses as they passed, leaving straw on the walls and in the streets. During production of this cheese, cream is added to increase the FAT CONTENT to 70 percent, which places it in the double-cream category. Gratte-Paille is usually RIPENED for 2 to 4 weeks but sometimes longer. *See also* PIERRE ROBERT.

Graukäse [*GROW*-ki-zer (-kah-zeh)] *see* TIROLER GRAUKÄSE

Graviera [grah-VYEH-rrah]

Origin	Greece
Milk	Unpasteurized or pasteurized cow's, sheep's, and/or goat's
Type	SEMIHARD to HARD; PRESSED COOKED; NATURAL RIND; ARTISAN, FARMSTEAD, COOPERATIVE, MOUNTAIN, and FACTORY
Appearance	4- to 40-pound wheels; rinds are thin, hard, and often show cheesecloth marks; interiors range from ivory to deep gold (depending on age and milk type) with a scattering of small EYES
Texture	Ranges from smooth and supple when young to firm when aged
Flavor	Complex blend of buttery, savory, toffee, fruit, and nuts

Graviera, introduced in Greek cheesemaking circles in the early 1900s, was modeled after Switzerland's GRUYÈRE. Originally made from sheep's milk, Graviera has now become the generic

G

name for Gruyère-style cheeses produced throughout Greece from cow's, sheep's, and/or goat's milk. In fact, after FETA, it's Greece's second-most-popular cheese and one of its highest-quality products. To make Graviera, the wheels are pressed (with gradually increasing pressure) over a 12- to 16-hour period. It's then dry-salted (*see* SALTING) frequently during RIP-ENING, which lasts a minimum of 3 months but often for over a year. Graviera's FAT CONTENT is between 40 and 50 percent. Since the European Union implemented its PROTECTED DESIG-NATION OF ORIGIN (PDO) program, three Greek Graviera cheeses have received PDO certification. **Graviera Agrafon (PDO)** is produced in the Agrafon area of the Karditsa prefecture (county) in central Greece's Thessaly region. It's traditionally made from sheep's milk and can be produced from a mixture of sheep's and goat's milk. **Graviera Kritis (PDO)** is produced on the island of Crete in the prefectures of Hania, Iraklion, Lasithio, and Rethymnos. It's also traditionally made from sheep's milk or from a mixture of sheep's milk and goat's milk. **Graviera Naxou (PDO)** is produced on Naxos, the largest island in the Cyclades prefecture, located southeast of Athens in the Aegean Sea. This Graviera is traditionally made from cow's milk or with a mixture of at least 80 percent cow's milk with the balance either sheep's or goat's milk. *See also* KEFALOGRA-VIERA.

Great Hill Blue

Origin	United States (Massachusetts)
Milk	Unpasteurized cow's
Type	SEMISOFT; MOLDED UNCOOKED; BLUE-VEINED; NATURAL RIND; ARTISAN
Appearance	6-pound wheels; rind is ivory to pale yellow with bluish green mold; interior is ivory to pale

	yellow with bluish green striations and small pockets
Texture	Creamy, moist, and firm yet somewhat crumbly
Flavor	Smooth, buttery, creamy, and slightly tangy with a mild spiciness

Great Hill Dairy is located in Marion, Massachusetts about 50 miles south of Boston. After the dairy-farming Stone family sold their dairy herd, they began investigating ideas for a new nonconventional business. It took about a year of research before they decided to get into cheesemaking and focus on blue cheese. Tim Stone took a cheesemaking course, they bought equipment and set it up in an old barn, and they produced their first Great Hill Blue in 1996. Only three years later it took a gold medal at the American Cheese Society competition. The cheese is unique because it's made from unhomogenized cow's milk, which means the cheese RIPENS more slowly, resulting in a creamier, smoother flavor. Whereas some blue cheeses age in 2 to 6 weeks, Great Hill Blue takes 6 to 10 months to ripen. Production methods include inoculating the milk with *Penicillium roqueforti* (the same mold used for producing ROQUEFORT, GORGONZOLA, and STILTON) and piercing the cheese with needles so air can access the interior to encourage the proper mold growth. Great Hill Blue has a FAT CONTENT that can range from 45 to 55 percent.

Greek cheeses *see* Cheeses by Country of Origin, page 511

Green Fade *see* CHESHIRE

Grünerkäse [GROO-ner-KI-zer (-kah-zeh)] *see* SAPSAGO

G

Gruyère (AOC) [groo-YEHR; gree-YEHR]

Origin	Switzerland (Fribourg)
Milk	Cow's, traditionally unpasteurized
Type	SEMIHARD to HARD; PRESSED COOKED; NATURAL RIND; ARTISAN, FARMSTEAD, COOPERATIVE, and some MOUNTAIN
Appearance	55- to 88-pound wheels; rind is hard, dry, pitted, and golden brown to brown; interior is ivory to medium yellow (today there are very few EYES)
Texture	Very dense and compact yet supple
Flavor	Complex flavor blend of creamy, fruity, nutty, earthy, and mushroomy

Taking its name from Gruyères, a small town in the Fribourg canton in western Switzerland, this cheese has been made in this area for centuries. Records dated 1115 show that farmers were using it to tithe to the area's abbeys. The word *gruyères* is a term from Charlemagne's era for "forests," *gruyer* for "forestry official." Besides Switzerland, "Gruyère" cheeses can be found in various parts of France and Germany. In France large cheeses like COMTÉ, BEAUFORT, and EMMENTAL are referred to as "Gruyère cheeses." The word is also used in the name of cheeses like GRUYÈRE DE COMTÉ. In July 2001, the Swiss gained APPELLATION D'ORIGINE CONTRÔLÉE (AOC) name-protection status for Gruyère, which should put an end to the intercountry clash over the name. Of course, because of Gruyère's reputation, the name is used for cheeses made in other nations, including Austria, Denmark, Germany, and the United States. If and when the Swiss obtain the European Union's PROTECTED DESIGNATION OF ORIGIN (PDO) status, other European countries will have to discontinue using the name. At some point the United States may also agree not to use the name Gruyère on its cheeses. In general, and with the exception of the French cheeses dubbed "Gruyère," cheesemongers agree that most Gruyère-style cheeses can't compete with Switzerland's high-quality examples. That's because the majority of non-Swiss versions are factory produced with pasteurized milk, which typically doesn't deliver the full flavor of raw-milk cheeses. Gruyère with an AOC designation can be produced solely in the cantons of Fribourg, Vaud, Neuchâtel, Jura, and Berne. The cows must be fed grass or hay—no silage. Gruyère is made from two milkings and can be prepared only in copper pots. It's brined (*see* SALTING) for a day before RIPENING begins. During the first 3 weeks of aging the surface of the cheese is wiped every other day with brine, which encourages the growth of beneficial molds. There are three types of Gruyère AOC: Classic (ripened for a minimum of 5 months), Réserve (10 to 16 months), and d'Alpage, which is made only from April through October from milk produced by cows grazing in high alpine pastures. Gruyère has a FAT CONTENT of between 49 and 53 percent. In America, **Roth Käse USA, Ltd.,** of Monroe, Wisconsin, makes an award-winning version called **Grand Cru Gruyère.** In 2001, this company—which has Swiss origins—built a new state-of-the-art cheese factory that includes some traditional Swiss cheesemaking equipment such as large copper vats. They produce three versions of Gruyère: Grand Cru Gruyère—aged a minimum of 4 months; Grand Cru Gruyère Reserve—at least 6 months of ripening; and Grand Cru Gruyère Surchoix—with a minimum of 9 months in the curing cellars.

Gruyère de Comté [groo-YEHR day kaw*n*-TAY] see COMTÉ

Gubbeen [goo-BEAN]

Origin	Ireland (Cork)
Milk	Pasteurized cow's
Type	SEMISOFT; PRESSED UNCOOKED; WASHED RIND; FARMSTEAD
Appearance	1¼- and 2½-pound wheels; rind is thin and beige to reddish orange with white mold; interior is ivory to golden with a small scattering of EYES
Texture	Smooth, creamy, and supple, becoming oozy as it ripens
Flavor	Creamy, savory, mushroomy, and nutty

Gubbeen is produced by Giana and Tom Ferguson, who run a coastal farm near the town of Schull in the far southwestern corner of Ireland's county Cork. As a child, Giana was introduced to cheesemaking at her uncle's home in France. After marrying, she and Tom decided to produce cheese from some of the rich milk from their herd of Friesian, Guernsey, Simmenthal, and the local black Kerry cows. The name *Gubbeen* is a derivative of the Gaelic *gobin,* meaning "small mouthful," which relates to the bay west of Schull. The Fergusons originally made Gubbeen with raw milk but now use pasteurized milk. It's made with vegetarian RENNET, washed with brine (see SALTING), and turned frequently during its 2-month RIPENING period. The end result is a pungent cheese similar to LIVAROT or MUNSTER. Son Fingal Ferguson established a smokehouse on the property where he smokes some of his parents' Gubbeen, along with his own line of cured meats. Young Ferguson uses oak to lightly smoke the Gubbeen, which is then coated with yellow WAX and aged for 3 months.

Gudbrandsdalsost [GUD-brahnds-dahls-oost] *see* GJETOST

G

Guilde des Fromagers; Guilde des Fromagers/Confrérie de St Uguzon
A not-for-profit professional association founded in 1969 and based in Orly, France. According to the group's mission statement, its purpose is "to support the tradition of quality cheesemaking, to facilitate professional networking, to educate consumers, and encourage cheese consumption." *See also* MAÎTRE FROMAGER.

gummy *see* Glossary of Cheese Descriptors, page 499

H

half moon *see* MOON

Halloumi; Haloumi; Hallumi [hah-LOO-mee]

Origin	Greece (Cyprus)
Milk	Unpasteurized and pasteurized sheep's and goat's (sometimes cow's)
Type	SEMISOFT; PRESSED COOKED; FARMSTEAD and FACTORY
Appearance	8- to 12-ounce half-moon shapes or bars, typically wrapped in plastic; rindless

> A perfect Brie cannot be produced by standardized methods; it is the end product of a series of miracles. Essays are writ by fools like me, but only God can make a Brie.
> —Clifton Fadiman

H

exterior is white, moist, and smooth; interior is
pure white

Texture	Firm but soft and springy
Flavor	Mild, tangy, salty, and slightly minty

Popular throughout Greece, Turkey, and the Middle East, Halloumi has been produced for centuries. Its myriad fans included nineteenth-century Turkish writer Sidqui Effendi, who wrote that Halloumi is "good food which enhances sex." Halloumi's origins can be traced back to Cyprus, where it's part of that Mediterranean island's national history. Thanks to Cypriot regulatory efforts, this cheese is now name protected, and the only cheeses that may be called "Halloumi" are those made on Cyprus. Though traditionally a sheep's milk cheese, Halloumi today is produced primarily with a mixture of sheep's and goat's milk. Some mass-produced Halloumis are now being made with cow's milk, though such cheeses are considered mediocre by comparison. Halloumi has a texture akin to that of MOZZARELLA but is slightly softer and not as stringy. Its springy texture comes from a PASTA FILATA–style production technique whereby the cut CURDS are molded, pressed, then removed from their molds and reheated in hot water or WHEY until pliable. The warm cheese is then kneaded (sometimes with chopped mint) before being shaped. Some producers simply sprinkle the fresh mint over the cheese before folding it over into the traditional half-moon shape. Halloumi is stored in BRINE, which is why it's been referred to as a PICKLED CHEESE. It can be consumed within a day or so but is sometimes ripened for up to a month. It has a FAT CONTENT of about 47 percent. To desalt this cheese, soak ½-inch slices in lukewarm water for an hour or so; blot dry before using. Halloumi is one of those rare cheeses that can be heated without losing its shape. In Lebanon it's known as the "kebab cheese," and chunks of it are skewered and grilled in street stalls. When slices are sautéed or grilled, the exterior gets browned and crusty, the inside warm and soft.

hâloir [ah-LWAH] The French word for a ventilated RIPENING room, typically for SOFT CHEESES.

hard cheeses *see* TEXTURE, CHEESE

harp, cheese *see* CHEESE HARP

Harvest Cheese *see* HILLTOWN WHEEL

Havarti [hah-VAHR-tee]

Origin	Denmark
Milk	Pasteurized cow's
Type	SEMISOFT tO SEMIHARD; PRESSED COOKED; NATURAL RIND, WASHED RIND, and rindless; ARTISAN and FACTORY
Appearance	Wheels, rectangles, and squares weighing from 7 ounces to 10 or more pounds, often wrapped in foil, also 14-ounce tubs; rind is thin and reddish yellow to reddish brown, although many are rindless; interior is ivory to pale yellow with a large number of irregular EYES
Texture	Supple and elastic; higher-fat versions are creamier
Flavor	Mild, buttery, and tangy, developing stronger, more pungent flavors with ripening

This cheese was named after *Havartigaard,* the experimental "Havarti Farm" where in the nineteenth century Hanne Nielsen

H

created what is now one of Denmark's most popular cheeses. Havarti is often called "the Danish TILSIT" because of its similarity to that cheese, though it's milder in both aroma and flavor. Like Tilsit, Havarti is cooked, pressed, and bathed in BRINE. During RIPENING the rind is washed and brushed regularly; rindless versions do not go through this process. Ripening typically takes from 2 to 4 months, the timing varying depending on the size and weight of the cheese. Regular Havarti has a FAT CONTENT of approximately 45 percent; the low-fat version contains 30 percent, and the creamy version (enriched with added cream) contains 60 percent fat. Havarti comes plain or flavored with any of a variety of seasonings, including dill, caraway seeds, chives, jalapeño peppers, and blends of herbs and spices. This cheese is also produced in other countries, including Australia and the United States. American versions are almost identical to the Danish originals and primarily factory produced, mostly in New York and Wisconsin. There are, however, a few artisanal producers scattered around the country, including Wisconsin's **Cedar Grove Cheese, Inc.**, which has won awards for its farmstead Havarti.

Havarti Tilsit [hah–VAHR-tee TIHL-ziht] *see* TILSIT; TILSITER

Hawes Dairy *see* WENSLEYDALE

Haystack Mountain Goat Dairy *see* CHÈVRE FETA; HAYSTACK PEAK; QUESO DE MANO

Haystack Peak

Origin	United States (Colorado)
Milk	Pasteurized goat's
Type	SOFT to SEMISOFT; MOLDED UNCOOKED; BLOOMY RIND; ARTISAN

Appearance	2-pound truncated pyramid; rind is coated with vegetable ash topped by snowy white mold; interior is off-white
Texture	Creamy and smooth
Flavor	Delicate, rich, and slightly tangy with a faint mineral trait

One of several cheeses produced by **Haystack Mountain Goat Dairy** in Niwot, Colorado, not far from Boulder. This venture was started by Jim Schott in 1989 and has now expanded into a second facility in Longmont, Colorado. At this writing, Schott is in the process of working with the Pontotoc Area Vocational Technical School in Ada, Oklahoma, to build an on-campus cheesemaking teaching facility for production of small-batch artisanal goat's milk cheeses under the Haystack Mountain Goat Dairy label. The milk for Haystack cheeses comes from over a hundred of the dairy's own Alpine, La Mancha, Oberhasli, Nubian, and Saanen goats, plus another eight hundred goats from a nearby herd. Haystack Peak has a truncated pyramid shape similar to the French POULIGNY-SAINT-PIERRE and VALENÇAY goat cheeses. However, unlike its French cousins, Haystack Peak has a bloomy rind created by the use of *Penicillium candidum* during production. The cheese is coated with salt and vegetable ash before being RIPENED for 1½ to 2 weeks. It has a FAT CONTENT of 45 to 50 percent. Haystack Peak has won several awards over the years at the American Cheese Society competition. Other winners from this dairy include Haystack Feta (see FETA) and QUESO DE MANO.

heat-treated milk *see* PASTEURIZATION

herbaceous *see* Glossary of Cheese Descriptors, page 499

Herve [ehr-VAY] *see* FROMAGE DE HERVE

Hillman Farms *see* HILLTOWN WHEEL

Hilltown Wheel

Origin	United States (Massachusetts)
Milk	Unpasteurized goat's
Type	SEMIHARD to HARD; PRESSED UNCOOKED; NATURAL RIND; FARMSTEAD
Appearance	7- to 9-pound wheels; thin, rough rind is beige to reddish gold with mold marks; interior is ivory to light gold
Texture	Firm, smooth, and supple
Flavor	Mild, creamy, fresh, and nutty with a hint of caramel, becoming more piquant with age

Hilltown Wheel is made by Joe and Carolyn Hillman at their **Hillman Farm** in the Berkshire foothills of western Massachusetts. The milk is produced from spring through fall from the farmstead's herd of over forty Alpine goats. The animals graze on rolling pastures replete with organic grasses, herbs, and berries, all of which flavor the milk. The Hillmans use labor-intensive small-batch production techniques to handcraft the cheeses. Hilltown Wheel is RIPENED for 5 to 8 months, during which time the rind is frequently turned and brushed with BRINE. This cheese has won several awards (including gold) in the annual American Cheese Society competition and "best of class" honors at London's World Cheese Awards. **Harvest Cheese,** another Hillman award winner, is made similarly to Hilltown Wheel but aged from 3 to 7 months.

Hock Ybrig [HOKH ee-brig]

Origin	Switzerland (Schwyz)
Milk	Unpasteurized cow's
Type	SEMIHARD; PRESSED COOKED; NATURAL RIND; ARTISAN and MOUNTAIN
Appearance	16-pound wheels; rind is hard, dry, and reddish gold, darkening with age and showing a delicate dusting of white mold; interior is ivory to gold with a few irregular EYES, developing white protein crystals with age
Texture	Very dense and compact yet supple
Flavor	Complex and savory blend of toffee, fruit, and nuts

Hailing from Switzerland, this relative newcomer was created in the 1980s. Like many cheeses, it's patterned after the famous Swiss GRUYÉRE but in a much smaller format—16 versus 88 pounds. Hoch Ybrig is named after a 6,100-foot mountain and popular skiing location just outside of Zurich. The cheese is a special version of the generic Küssnachter cheese made in this area. The milk for Hoch Ybrig comes from local Simmental cows, and the cheese is made by Josef Barmettler and RIPENED by AFFINEUR Rolf Beeler. Hoch Ybrig is aged for a minimum of 8 months, though many aficionados prefer them ripened for a year. The FAT CONTENT of Hoch Ybrig is about 45 percent.

Hoja Santa [OH-hah SAHN-tah]

Origin	United States (Texas)
Milk	Pasteurized goat's
Type	SOFT; MOLDED UNCOOKED; rindless; ARTISAN
Appearance	5-ounce rounds; exterior is wrapped in leaves and tied with raffia; interior is white

H

Texture	Soft and smooth
Flavor	Mildly tangy and zesty with accents of mint, anise, and sassafras

Yet another award winner from Paula Lambert, founder of the famed **Mozzarella Company** in Dallas, Texas. Lambert has over twenty-five cheeses in her popular line, which ranges from Italian notables including RICOTTA, SCAMORZA, and her flagship fresh MOZZARELLA to south-of-the-border favorites like QUESO BLANCO and QUESO OAXACA, to originals such as BLANCA BI-ANCA, DEEP ELLUM BLUE, and MONTASIO FESTIVO. Her hand-molded Hoja Santa cheese is a Lambert creation distinguished by the eponymous heart-shaped leaf in which it's wrapped after having been salted and turned for several days. The edible leaves (*hoja santa* is Spanish for "holy leaves") are blanched in boiling water, plunged into ice water, then stretched out on a plastic mat. Each disk of cheese is wrapped in half of a giant leaf, then secured with raffia and finished with a bow on top. The fragrant hoja santa leaf imparts an herbal character that flavors the cheese with nuances of sassafras, mint, and anise.

holes *see* EYES

homogenization [huh-MAHJ-uh-ni-ZAY-shuhn] The process of emulsifying a mixture. In the case of MILK, for instance, the cream, which would naturally rise to the top, is integrated into the milk by mechanically breaking down the fat globules until they're evenly and imperceptibly distributed throughout. This means that less fat is lost in the WHEY when the CURD is drained during the cheesemaking process. The majority of milk in the United States is homogenized. An exception is creamline milk, in which the cream rises to the top because the mixture hasn't undergone homogenization.

H

Hooligan

Origin	United States (Connecticut)
Milk	Unpasteurized cow's
Type	SEMISOFT; PRESSED COOKED; WASHED RIND; FARMSTEAD
Appearance	1¼- to 1½-pound wheels; rind is pinkish orange with basket marks; interior is off-white to straw colored with a scattering of eyes
Texture	Smooth, creamy, and supple
Flavor	Mild, savory, and mushroomy flavors with a hint of sweetness

Hooligan is produced by **Cato Corner Farm** in Colchester, Connecticut, which is about 30 miles southwest of Hartford. Here mother-and-son team Elizabeth MacAlister and Mark Gillman tend to thirty Jersey cows and produce a wide array of cheeses. Hooligan is washed twice a week with a buttermilk-BRINE mixture, and its flavors develop fully during the 2- to 3-month RIPENING period. Cato Corner produces several washed-rind cheeses from the same base. The rind of **Desperado** is washed with pear juice and Pear William, an eau-de-vie from a Connecticut distillery. **Drunken Hooligan** is washed with wine from a nearby winery, and **Drunk Monk** is bathed in ale from Connecticut's Willimantic Brewing Company. Each of the various washing solutions lends a slightly different and distinctive nuance to the cheese. And, though these cheeses all have a moderately stinky smell, their respective flavors are relatively mild. *See also* DUTCH FARMSTEAD.

hoop *see* MOLD (3)

hooping *see* MOLDING

Hudson Valley Camembert *see* CAMEMBERT

Humboldt Fog

Origin	United States (California)
Milk	Pasteurized goat's
Type	SEMISOFT; MOLDED UNCOOKED; BLOOMY RIND; ARTISAN
Appearance	14-ounce round or 5-pound wheel; rind is coated with ASH topped with a layer of white mold; interior is ivory colored near the rind and bright white in the center
Texture	Creamy, soft, and oozy near the rind, becoming firmer and crumbly-smooth toward the middle, with a fine layer of ASH running through the center
Flavor	Mild, tangy, clean, and lemony

The flagship cheese of the award-winning **Cypress Grove Chèvre,** located in the Humboldt County town of Arcata amid the towering California redwoods. This famed cheese company is owned and operated by mother-and-daughter team Mary Keehn and Malorie McCurdy. Humboldt Fog is named after the thick morning fog so prevalent in Humboldt County. Keehn is the cheesemaker, and nearby farms provide her with premium milk, which must meet stringent quality requirements. The milk undergoes the gentle heat-treatment PASTEURIZATION rather than the 15-second high-heat method. Keehn uses a combination of cultures to create the complexity for which Cypress Grove Chèvre cheeses are known. Humboldt Fog has a thin line of vegetable ash running through its center, emulating the look of France's MORBIER. This distinguishing feature is obtained by filling the molds halfway with the CURDS, sprinkling the surface with a vegetable ash mixture, then topping off with more curds. Depending on the size of the cheese, RIPENING takes from 3 to 4 weeks. At the 2005

American Cheese Society competition, Cypress Grove Chèvre won 12 awards, making it the year's most decorated goat cheese company. The 14-ounce Humboldt Fog won a blue ribbon at that competition and has won several times before. It's also taken a gold medal at the annual World Cheese Awards. Cypress Grove Chèvre produces a wide variety of cheeses, including fresh CHÈVRE, FROMAGE BLANC, and a goat's milk CHEDDAR. *See also* BERMUDA TRIANGLE; LAMB CHOPPER; MIDNIGHT MOON.

Hungarian cheese *see* Cheeses by Country of Origin, page 512

. . . .

I

. . . .

Ibérico [ee-BHAY-ree-koh]

Origin	Spain (central)
Milk	Pasteurized blend of cow's, goat's, and sheep's
Type	HARD; PRESSED UNCOOKED; NATURAL RIND; FARMSTEAD and FACTORY
Appearance	From 2½- to 7-pound wheels; rind is hard, dark yellow-brown, and bears the hatched imprint of the molds in which it drains; interior is golden flecked with tiny EYES
Texture	Creamy, smooth, and slightly oily
Flavor	Rich, buttery, nutty, and slightly tangy

This cheese (also called *Queso Ibérico*) combines the best of all worlds with its combination of cow's, goat's, and sheep's milk in a blend of not less than 25 percent or more than 40 percent of any one milk. It's made in the MANCHEGO style, using the cross-hatch mold, which, though typically made of plastic today, is patterned to replicate the fiber (*esparto*) molds of old. Some Ibérico cheeses may be labeled "Manchego blend," referring to the milk mix. This cheese contains a minimum of 54 percent fat and may be RIPENED for anywhere from 2 weeks to 6 months. Of course, the younger the cheese, the softer the texture.

Ibores [ee-BOHR-ays] *see* QUESO IBORES

Idiazábal (DO; PDO) [ee-dee-ah-ZAH-bahl]

Origin	Spain (Basque Country and Navarre)
Milk	Unpasteurized sheep's
Type	SEMIHARD; PRESSED COOKED; NATURAL RIND; ARTISAN and FACTORY
Appearance	3- to 7-pound wheels; rind is thin, smooth, and yellow to pale orangey brown; interior is pale yellow with a scattering of minuscule EYES
Texture	Firm and slightly dry, though supple and agreeably oily on the palate
Flavor	Robust, somewhat sharp and lightly smoky (though some Idiazábals are not smoked)

As between mice and men, man is easily the more devoted to cheese, and always has been. The mouse, scientists have found, will content himself with cheese for want of something better, but his real passion is for gumdrops.
—Vivienne Marquis and Patricia Haskell, *The Cheese Book*

Considered one of Spain's great cheeses, Idiazábal can be made only from the milk of Latxa or Carranzana sheep. The DENOMI-NACIÓN DE ORIGEN PROTEGIDA (DO) permits external smoking of the cheese (typically with beechwood, birch, cherry wood, or hawthorn), a tradition that hails from shepherds storing their cheeses near their fires. Unsmoked versions are also produced, primarily in the lower regions. Even factory-made versions of this cheese must be made by traditional methods. Idiazábal undergoes SALTING (usually in brine) for up to 48 hours and is typically RIPENED for 2 (and up to 6) months. Its fat content ranges from 45 to 50 percent.

IGP *see* PROTECTED GEOGRAPHICAL INDICATION

imitation cheese Sometimes called *filled cheese* or *analog cheese,* imitation cheese is fundamentally a PROCESS(ED) CHEESE with all the butterfat removed and replaced by nonfat milk, WHEY solids mixed with water, or vegetable oil. It is less expensive than real cheese, has a long shelf life, and often requires no refrigeration. It also has a rubbery texture and paltry flavor and is higher in sodium and lower in nutrients. Other than that, it's great. *See also* SUBSTITUTE CHEESE.

Indian cheeses *see* Cheeses by Country of Origin, page 512

industrial cheeses *see* FACTORY CHEESES

industriel [ahn-doo-stree-EHL] French for "industrial," used in the cheese world to describe mass-produced FACTORY CHEESES.

intense *see* Glossary of Cheese Descriptors, page 499

Iranian cheeses *see* Cheeses by Country of Origin, page 512

Iraty [ee-rah-TEE] *see* ARDI-GASNA; OSSAU-IRATY

Irish Cashel Blue *see* CASHEL BLUE

Irish cheeses *see* Cheeses by Country of Origin, page 512

ironing cheese A technique used by some cheesemakers to test the flavor, texture, and aroma of a RIPENING cheese. A small metal corer known as a *cheese iron* is inserted into the interior to obtain a plug of cheese. After the cheese has been evaluated, the cheese plug is replaced and the "scar" covered with a dab of cheese. Mold can sometimes grow around the plug, but often the rind simply grows over it and no one's the wiser. Still, many cheesemakers consider this practice a desecration of the cheese.

Isle of Mull Cheddar *see* CHEDDAR

Italian cheeses *see* Cheeses by Country of Origin, page 512

J

Jack cheese

Origin	United States (California)
Milk	Unpasteurized and pasteurized cow's
Type	SEMISOFT, SEMIHARD, HARD, and GRANA STYLE; PRESSED COOKED; NATURAL RIND; ARTISAN, FARMSTEAD, and FACTORY
Appearance	Wheels, squares, and rectangles weighing between 6 and 12 pounds; thin rind ranges from pale yellow to dark brown, some rindless; interior ranges from pale yellow to deep golden
Texture	Fresh versions are creamy and elastic; dry versions are hard, crumbly, and almost brittle
Flavor	Young Jack cheeses are delicate, mild, and fresh; fully ripened, dry versions are rich, sweet, and full flavored with fruit and caramel traits

> Cheese that is compelled by law to append the word "food" to its title does not go well with red wine or fruit.
> —Fran Lebowitz

Although the origin of Jack cheese is sometimes attributed to 1890s Monterey, California, businessman David Jacks, it appears the true source is Spain. There's evidence that the Jack cheese we know today was based on a recipe for *queso del país* ("country cheese"), which was brought via Mexico into California by the

J

Franciscan monks in the 1700s. Furthermore, a Spanish family headed by Dona Juana Cota de Boronda is known to have produced and sold queso del país in 1800s Monterey County prior to Jacks's involvement. However, David Jacks can be credited for creating a large following for this cheese when he started shipping it to San Francisco and other parts of the United States. This wealthy businessman owned a number of dairies and was the first to produce this cheese on a large scale. One theory for today's name is that he stamped "Jacks Cheese" on the shipping crates and eventually the s was dropped. Another theory suggests the name comes from a vise (or "jack") that was used to press the cheese. Since the production was originally centered in Monterey County, the name Monterey Jack was eventually associated with such cheeses. Ultimately, other areas began to associate their names with this style of cheese, such as Sonoma Jack, from California's Sonoma County. Today Jack cheese is made in many other parts of the United States. Dry Jack is said to have been created by accident when a San Francisco wholesaler, D. F. DeBernardi, had too much inventory, so he allowed his Monterey Jack cheese to age much longer than normal, which resulted in a drier, hard cheese. This occurred during World War I, when imports of hard, aged European cheeses were limited, prompting a ready market for Dry Jack. Today, Dry Jack producers include California's Rumiano Cheese Company, Sonoma Cheese Factory, and **Vella Cheese Company,** the last started in 1931 by Tom Vella. Son Ignacio "Ig" Vella has continued the cheesemaking tradition, and Vella Dry Jack—one of America's original artisan cheeses—is the most prominent of the Dry Jacks. Ig also maintains an ongoing relationship with the **Rogue Creamery** (see ROGUE RIVER BLUE), which was also founded by his father. While fresh Jack cheese is ripened for only a few weeks, Dry Jack is aged for 7 to 10 months and sometimes longer. The high-moisture regular Jack cheese comes plain or with added flavorings, including herbs,

J

horseradish, chile peppers, garlic, and onion. The fat content for Jack cheese ranges from 32 percent to over 50 percent.

Jarlsberg [YAHRLZ-berg]

Origin	Norway
Milk	Pasteurized cow's
Type	SEMIHARD; PRESSED COOKED; NATURAL RIND, some rindless; FACTORY; some SMOKED
Appearance	20- to 24-pound wheels and 10-pound loaves, often covered with yellow wax; rind is thin, hard, and pale yellow to yellow-brown in color; can be rindless; interior is ivory-yellow with a random scattering of large irregular EYES
Texture	Supple and smooth
Flavor	Sweet, buttery, and slightly nutty

Jarlsberg-style cheese was first produced in the 1830s in Norway's Jarlsberg and Laurvig County, which is now part of Vestfold County. Swiss cheesemakers came to this area to teach the locals about cheesemaking, and Jarlsberg appears to be patterned after Switzerland's EMMENTAL. However, Jarlsberg production was stopped at some point, and it wasn't until the 1960s that it resumed. Professor Ole Martin Ystgaard led a group at the University of Norway in researching the cheese and redeveloping the recipe, including determining the bacteria (*Propionibacter shermani*) required for the unique EYE formations. Jarlsberg has since become extremely popular and is now exported worldwide. In the United States the Alpine Cheese Company of Millersburg, Ohio, has been licensed to make Jarlsberg using special bacterial cultures sent from Norway. Although Jarlsberg is patterned after Emmental, the wheels are only about a tenth the size of that huge cheese, and most cheese lovers don't feel Jarlsberg has Emmental's flavor depth.

J

Regular Jarlsberg has a FAT CONTENT of about 45 percent and is generally RIPENED for about 6 months, though some are aged for 12 months or more. There are also low-fat (usually rindless) and smoked versions. The latter are typically flavored with liquid smoke and not by smoking the cheese over a wood fire.

Jasper Hill Farm *see* BAYLEY HAZEN BLUE; CONSTANT BLISS; LEICESTER

Joe Matos Cheese Company *see* ST. GEORGE

Juniper Grove Farm *see* TUMALO TOMME

K

kaas [KAHSS] Dutch for "cheese."

Kanterkaas; Kanternagelkaas; Kanterkomijnekaas (PDO) [KAHN-ter-kahss; KAHN-ter-NAH-gerl-kahss; KAHN-ter-KOH-mayn-kahss]

Origin	Netherlands (Friesland)
Milk	Pasteurized cow's milk
Type	SEMIHARD to HARD; PRESSED COOKED; NATURAL RIND; FACTORY
Appearance	6½- to 19-pound wheels; rind is smooth

> It is a bit of a mystery why so many aspiring American hosts—gourmet and otherwise—came to think of mass quantities of cheese before dinner as an appropriate hors d'oeuvre; but cheese for dessert was strictly for the sophisticated set.
> —Jane and Michael Stern

K

and yellow to gold with darker specks of clove and/or caraway seed; interior is ivory to greenish yellow with dark flecks of clove and/or caraway seed and a scattering of small EYES

Texture Firm and somewhat elastic, becoming hard and granular as it ripens

Flavor Nutty, creamy, and spicy flavors dominated by caraway seeds and/or clove

Three PROTECTED DESIGNATION OF ORIGIN (PDO) cheeses that can be produced only in the Friesland province and the neighboring Westerkwartier area in the northern part of the Netherlands. Roman records indicate that this was a pastureland area perfect for both cattle raising (the renowned black and white Friesians originated here) and cheesemaking. Additional documents show that by the sixteenth century cheese from Friesland was being exported to other countries and was called both *Kanterkaas* and *Frieskaas*. This cheese comes in three styles: **Kanterkass**—the plain version, **Kanternagelkaas**—flavored with cloves and sometimes a few caraway seeds, and **Kanterkomijnekaas**—flavored with cumin seeds. The molds used for these cheeses have a rounded edge where the sides meet the top but a very sharp, angular edge where the sides join the base. The angular rim is called a *Kanter*, and such molds are used exclusively for these traditional cheeses. All three styles are ripened for at least 4 weeks and sometimes up to a year. There are two classifications: "20+," which has a minimum FAT CONTENT of 20 percent, and "40+," with a minimum of 40 percent.

Käse [KI-zer (-kah-zeh)] German for "cheese."

Kasseri (PDO); Kaseri [kah-SEHR-ree]

Origin Greece

Milk Unpasteurized and pasteurized cow's, sheep's, and goat's

K

Type	SEMISOFT to SEMIHARD; PRESSED UNCOOKED; PASTA FILATA; NATURAL RIND; ARTISAN, FARMSTEAD, COOPERATIVE, and FACTORY
Appearance	2- to 20-pound wheels; rind is thin, smooth, glossy, and pale to golden yellow in color; interior ranges from off-white to pale yellow
Texture	Smooth, elastic, and firm
Flavor	Younger versions are delicate, sweet, and tangy; older styles become more piquant and saltier

Kasseri, sometimes spelled *Kaseri,* has been made in Greece since the nineteenth century. Production is restricted to the regions of Macedonia, Thessaly, and the prefectures of Xanthi and Lesbos. Kasseri is a PASTA FILATA CHEESE, which means it's immersed in hot water and kneaded and stretched until it has a consistent stringlike quality. It's thought to have been modeled after the Italian CACIOCAVALLO cheeses and is similar to PROVOLONE. PROTECTED DESIGNATION OF ORIGIN (PDO) regulations require a minimum RIPENING period of 3 months, though most Kasseri cheeses are aged for 6 months to a year. The FAT CONTENT ranges from 32 to 52 percent, depending on whether the milk is partially skimmed or not. Although Greek Kasseri is traditionally made with sheep's and goat's milk, there are non-Greek versions made with cow's milk, particularly in the United States. Because Kasseri has PDO status in Greece, no other European Union members can call their Kasseri-style cheeses by that name. However, until the protected name of Kasseri is accepted by other non–EU countries and the United States, there will continue to be non–Greek versions by that name.

Keen's Cheddar *see* CHEDDAR

Kefalograviera (PDO) [keh–FAH–loh–grah–VYEH–rrah]

Origin	Greece (Macedonia, Epirus, and Sterea Ellada)
Milk	Pasteurized sheep's and goat's
Type	HARD; PRESSED COOKED; NATURAL RIND; ARTISAN, FARMSTEAD, and COOPERATIVE
Appearance	12- to 22-pound wheels wrapped in plastic; rinds are thin, hard, and yellow to tan, often with cheese cloth marks; interiors range from ivory to pale yellow with many small EYES
Texture	Smooth and firm
Flavor	Salty, savory, piquant, and nutty

Created in the 1960s, Kefalograviera is one of Greece's most popular cheeses. Its style ranges somewhere between that of KEFALOTYRI and GRAVIERA, and its name is a combination of the two. Kefalograviera is made in the western Macedonia and Epirus regions and the Etoloakarnania and Evritania prefectures in the Sterea Ellada region. It's produced from sheep's milk or a mixture of sheep's and goat's milk. This cheese is soaked in BRINE for several days before beginning a minimum RIPENING period of 3 months, during which time the cheese is dry-salted (see SALTING) many times. The FAT CONTENT of Kefalograviera is about 40 percent.

Kefalotyri; Kefalotiri [keh–fah–loh–TEE–rree]

Origin	Greece
Milk	Unpasteurized and pasteurized sheep's and goat's

K

Type	HARD; PRESSED COOKED; NATURAL RIND; GRANA STYLE; ARTISAN, FARMSTEAD, COOPERATIVE, and FACTORY
Appearance	13- to 23-pound wheels; rind is hard, smooth, and pale to deep yellow; interior ranges in color from ivory to pale yellow with many irregular EYES
Texture	Firm and dry, becoming flaky and brittle with age
Flavor	Salty and piquant, intensifying as the cheese ages

Kefalotyri is believed to date back to at least the third or fourth century. It's produced throughout Greece and in other surrounding countries. In Greece it's often the practice to attach the name of the region (such as Crete, Naxos, or Thessaly) to the word *Kefalotyri*. To satisfy the demand for hard cheeses, some countries make a cow's milk "Kefalotyri," but this nontraditional version is not considered as good. True Kefalotyri is the Greek's version of PECORINO ROMANO and is often used as a grating cheese. It's soaked in BRINE for several days before beginning a minimum RIPENING period of 3 months. During this time the cheese is dry-salted (*see* SALTING) as many as twenty-five times. Some Kefalotyris are aged for 2 years or more. This cheese has a FAT CONTENT of 40 to 50 percent.

King Christian *see* DANBO

King Island Dairy *see* CHEDDAR; ROARING FORTIES BLUE

kosher cheeses Known as *gvinas Yisroel* ("cheese made by a Jew"), kosher cheeses are strictly controlled and produced under Kosher law—Jewish biblical rules that include the type of food that may be eaten, the kinds of food that may be combined at one meal (for example, meat and dairy products may not be mixed), and so on. This means that animal-origin RENNET, an enzyme used for COAGULA-TION in the beginning stages of cheesemaking, cannot be used as it's considered a meat product, which conflicts with the milk. Today a wide selection of kosher cheeses is available because most kosher cheese producers use biotech-produced microbial rennet, obtained with kosher procedures and ingredients. Kosher cheeses are made in myriad countries including Denmark, England, France, Israel, and the United States. There are many types, including Brie, Camembert, Danish Blue, Edam, Emmental, Gouda, Gruyère, and Raclette. Currently, the Brooklyn-based World Cheese company is said to control 70 percent of the kosher cheese market. Kosher cheeses are clearly marked as such and can be found in supermarkets as well as specialty cheese stores.

Krauterkäse [KROW-ter-KI-zer (-kah-zeh)] *see* SAPSAGO

Kuminost [KOO-mihn-oost] *see* NÖKKELOST

kvarg [KVARG] *see* QUARK

L

Lace Käse [ki-zer (–kah-zeh)] *see* GRANQUESO

A bad accent is the cinematic equivalent of a festering Limburger cheese planted on a sumptuous dinner table, making it pointless for the gourmand to try thinking about anything other than that peculiar odor.

—Joe Queenan

lactic The word itself is an adjective for things relating to or derived from milk. *See also* Glossary of Cheese Descriptors, page 499.

lactic acid An acid found in sour milk, molasses, various fruits, and wines, generated by the breakdown of LACTOSE (milk sugar). In cheese-making, lactic acid is produced when a STARTER is added to the milk. The starter's bacteria feed on the milk sugar and thereby produce lactic acid.

lactose The natural sugar found in MILK, which is why it's also called *milk sugar*. Lactose can constitute up to 5 percent of the milk's total weight.

lactose intolerance; lactose sensitivity The inability to digest LACTOSE, the primary natural sugar found in dairy products. The intolerance is due to the small intestine not producing enough lactase, the enzyme needed for lactose digestion. Lactase is responsible for breaking down milk sugar into glucose and galactose, which are then absorbed into the bloodstream. The degree of the intolerance depends on the individual—some may be able to ingest larger quantities of milk-based products than others. Cheese contains less lactose than milk, with hard cheeses such as extra-sharp CHEDDAR or aged GOUDA typically containing only a trace amount.

L

Ladotyri Mytilinis (PDO) [lah-thoh-TEE-ree mee-tih-LIH-nihs]

Origin	Greece
Milk	Unpasteurized and pasteurized sheep's and/or goat's
Type	HARD; PRESSED COOKED; NATURAL RIND; ARTISAN, FARMSTEAD, and COOPERATIVE
Appearance	2- to 2½-pound cylinders; ivory-colored rind has basket-mark ridging and is coated with olive oil, sometimes paraffin; interior is ivory colored with a scattering of EYES
Texture	Firm and dry
Flavor	Slightly salty and piquant, intensifying with age

Though typically referred to as simply *Ladotyri,* the official PRO-TECTED DESIGNATION OF ORIGIN (PDO) name for this cheese is *Ladotyri Mytilinis.* The Greek translation for *Ladotyri* is "olive oil cheese"—*lado* ("olive oil") and *tyri* ("cheese"), the name referring to the fact that the RIPENED cheese was traditionally preserved in olive oil. *Mytilinis* refers to Mytilini (or Mytilene), the capital city of Lesbos (or Lesvos), the Greek island in the Aegean Sea where this PDO cheese is produced. Although there are non-PDO Ladotyri cheeses (all akin to a very small KEFALOTYRI), Ladotyri Mytilinis can be produced only on Lesbos from local sheep's and goat's milk. RIPENING takes a minimum of 3 months. This hard cheese (40 percent moisture) is stored in olive oil or coated with paraffin until sold. Its FAT CONTENT ranges from 35 to 45 percent.

La Fleurie [lah fleur-EE] *see* VERMONT BREBIS

Laguiole (AOC; PDO) [lay-YOHL; lah-YOHL]

Origin	France (Auvergne, Midi-Pyrénées, Langeudoc-Roussillon)
Milk	Unpasteurized cow's
Type	SEMIHARD; PRESSED UNCOOKED; NATURAL RIND; COOPERATIVE
Appearance	Tall wheels that weigh from 66 to 100 pounds; rind is thick and rough, beige with patches of orange, brown, and gray, the color darkening with age; interior is light yellow to gold, depending on age
Texture	Younger versions are firm and supple, older versions brittle and crumbly
Flavor	Tangy, savory, and nutty, becoming more complex with age

Cheesemaking in the Aubrac Mountains dates back to the fourth century, and Laguiole is said to have been made here since at least the eleventh century. It's believed that the first Laguiole was produced in a mountain monastery. Today this cheese is made in the town of Laguiole and about thirty other communes in this area of central France. Laguiole is very similar to the CANTAL and SALERS cheeses made to the north in the Cantal Mountains. However, unlike Cantal, Laguiole is always made from raw milk. Historically, the cheese was made in stone huts (*burons*), but production fell off, the number of burons dwindled, and in 1960 most of the cheesemaking shifted to the Coopérative Fromagère Jeune Montagne. Over the years the local Aubrac cows were supplemented with Holstein and Pie-Rouge-de-l'Est cattle in an effort to increase cheese production. Like Cantal, Laguiole goes through a double pressing, unique for French cheeses. Once the CURD is formed, it's cut into ½-inch cubes, wrapped in cloth, and pressed. It's then allowed to rest for about 8 hours before being ground into small pieces, salted (*see* SALTING), molded, and pressed a second time. For the next month the cheese is frequently turned and rubbed with salt. Laguiole is RIPENED longer than Cantal—from a minimum of 4 months to 10 months or more. The FAT CONTENT of this cheese is 45 percent. The town of Laguiole may be better known for its expensive, handcrafted knives and corkscrews than for its cheese.

lait [LAY] French for "milk."

lait cru [lay KROO] French for "RAW MILK."

laitier [lay-tee-YAH] French term for cheese manufactured in a large dairy. The opposite of small cheese producers (CRÉMIER or FRUITIÈRE).

Lamb Chopper

Origin	United States (California)
Milk	Pasteurized sheep's
Type	SEMIHARD; PRESSED COOKED; NATURAL RIND; ARTISAN
Appearance	10-pound wheels; rind is ivory and coated with wax; interior is pale yellow with occasional EYES
Texture	Firm and smooth
Flavor	Mellow, buttery, and nutty with a nuance of sweetness

Another offering from the inventive mind of master cheese-maker Mary Keehn, owner of **Cypress Grove Chèvre,** a leader in the goat cheese industry since the 1980s. Lamb Chopper, however, is not a CHÈVRE but an organic (*see* ORGANIC CHEESE) sheep's milk GOUDA. And it's not made in California, but rather in Holland from Dutch milk. *And* it doesn't have a conventional label but rather one depicting a cool sunglass-sporting sheep dude on a motorcycle cruising down a flower-lined lane. This isn't the only cheese Keehn is having made in Holland to her exacting specifications—she also produces MIDNIGHT MOON, an aged goat cheese. Why make Lamb Chopper in Holland? Because that's where Keehn could find enough organic sheep's milk (which is scarce in the United States), not to mention a Dutch cheesemaking partner who specialized in Gouda. She also chose to RIPEN Lamb Chopper in Holland so it wouldn't be infected with the molds that create magic in her BLOOMY-RIND cheeses. It's aged from 4 to 6 months before being sent to market. Lamb Chopper won the 2004 Winter Fancy Food Show's "Best Product of Aisle" award. Besides the Dutch-made Midnight Moon and Lamb Chopper, Keehn also created **Ewe-F-O,** an aged sheep's milk cheese produced in Sardinia and marketed in the United States. Cypress Grove Chèvre produces a wide variety of other cheeses, including fresh CHÈVRE, FROMAGE BLANC, and a goat's milk CHEDDAR. *See also* BERMUDA TRIANGLE and HUMBOLDT FOG.

l'âme [LAAHM] *see* ÂME, L'

Lancashire [LANG-kah-shur; LANG-kuh-sheer]

Origin	England (Lancashire)
Milk	Unpasteurized and pasteurized cow's

Type	SEMIHARD to HARD; PRESSED COOKED; NATURAL RIND; FARMSTEAD and FACTORY
Appearance	Tall 9- to 55-pound wheels; farmstead versions are often buttered and cloth-bound; factory versions are usually waxed; rind is light gold with blue-gray mold; interior is pale yellow
Texture	Loose and crumbly when young, becoming soft and creamy with additional ripening
Flavor	Mild, buttery, nutty, and tangy, becoming richer and more piquant with age

Lancashire, a county in northwest England along the Irish Sea, has been producing this CHEDDAR-family cheese for hundreds of years. Sadly, farmstead production has diminished significantly since World War II and, whereas there were once hundreds of British cheesemakers making raw-milk Lancashire with traditional methods, today there is only one—fourth-generation cheesemaker Graham Kirkham. For the time-consuming farmstead Lancashire, the CURD from two different days (three days' curd for Kirkham's Lancashire) is combined—the previous day's curd has already been drained, salted, and pressed—then finely milled before undergoing SALTING and MOLDING. After being lightly pressed, the formed cheese is buttered and wrapped in cloth (or sometimes waxed) before being RIPENED for 1 to 10 months. This technique results in a delicate, soft, and crumbly texture that slowly firms but becomes creamy as the cheese ages. The Beacon Fell vicinity in western Lancashire's Flyde area has been awarded PROTECTED DESIGNATION OF ORIGIN (PDO) status for its **Beacon Fell Traditional Lancashire,** which is made with farmstead methods. Unfortunately, the majority of today's Lancashire (also called *New Lancashire*) is factory produced. It's made with curds from a single day, which produces an entirely different flavor and texture. Lancashire's FAT

CONTENT is about 48 percent. Because it melts beautifully, this cheese is a favorite for Welsh Rabbit (also called *Welsh Rarebit*).

Langres (AOC; PDO) [LAHN-gruh]

Origin	France (Champagne-Ardenne; Lorraine; Burgundy)
Milk	Unpasteurized and pasteurized cow's
Type	SEMISOFT; MOLDED UNCOOKED; WASHED RIND; ARTISAN and FARMSTEAD
Appearance	Small drums with concave tops—small size a minimum of 5 ounces, large size a minimum of 1¾ pounds; rind is sticky and wrinkled with a reddish orange color; interior is off-white to pale yellow
Texture	Firm and supple, becoming creamy as it ripens
Flavor	Complex array of smoky, creamy, savory, tangy, and zesty

This cheese has been made in and around the town of Langres on the Langres plateau in France's Champagne region since at least the eighteenth century. Langres is a washed-rind cheese similar to EPOISSES DE BOURGOGNE, though not as strong. Small Langres are RIPENED for a minimum of 2 weeks but generally for a month; large versions are aged a minimum of 3 weeks, with 2 to 3 months being more common. During ripening, Langres is frequently brushed with a mixture of water and ANNATTO (*rocou*), which tints the rind a reddish orange color. This cheese is sometimes also brushed with MARC, a potent brandy distilled from skins and seeds left over from winemaking. These washings help spread desirable bacteria evenly over the cheese's surface. The FAT CONTENT for Langres is a minimum of 50 percent.

La Peral [lah pay-RAHL] *see* QUESO DE LA PERAL

la religieuse [lah reuh-lee-ZHEUHZ] *see* FONDUE (AU FROMAGE)

Largo [LAHR-goh] *see* NOCTURNE

late blowing A negative bacterial activity that can occur during the final stages of cheese RIPENING, caused by the bacterium *Clostrium tyrobutyricum*. Late blowing produces unwanted gases, which can affect the cheese's flavor and aroma. The natural enzyme lysozyme, extracted from egg albumen, attacks the bacteria without affecting the cheese's aging process or flavor potential.

Latin American cheeses *see* Cheeses by Country of Origin, page 513

La Tur [la TOOR]

Origin	Italy (Piedmont)
Milk	Pasteurized cow's, sheep's, and goat's
Type	SEMISOFT; MOLDED UNCOOKED; BLOOMY RIND; ARTISAN
Appearance	8- to 9-ounce wheels packaged in ruffled cupcake holders; rind is fluffy, wrinkled, and cream to pale yellow in color; interior is ivory to pale yellow
Texture	Creamy and velvety near the rind, becoming slightly firmer in the middle; becomes oozy with additional ripening
Flavor	Rich, creamy, savory, and tangy with earthy and mushroomy traits

L

La Tur is produced by Caseificio dell'Alta Langa, a dairy located near the town of Bosia, just south of Alba in the Piedmont region. It's made from a balanced blend of cow's, sheep's, and goat's milk, which has been pasteurized at a low temperature. The curd is placed in small molds and allowed to drain naturally, without pressing. La Tur is RIPENED for only 10 to 15 days before being shipped to market. It has a FAT CONTENT of 55 to 60 percent, placing it almost in the DOUBLE-CRÈME category.

Laura Chenel Chèvre *see* CABÉCOU; CHÈVRE

l'Édel de Cleron [lay-DEHL deuh kleh-ROHN] *see* VACHERIN DU HAUT-DOUBS

Leicester [LESS-ter]

Origin	England (Leicestershire)
Milk	Pasteurized cow's
Type	SEMIHARD to HARD; PRESSED COOKED; NATURAL RIND; FARMSTEAD, COOPERATIVE, and FACTORY
Appearance	Farmstead versions come in 9- to 40-pound wheels; others are available in various-sized blocks; the rind on farmstead cheese is thin, hard, reddish orange to reddish brown with patches of gray mold, and cloth-covered—other Leicesters are often rindless and covered variously, most often with plastic wrap or WAX covering; interior is a deep reddish orange color
Texture	Smooth, tight, firm, and flaky
Flavor	Farmstead versions are mild but complex with a range of flavors including savory, caramel, nutty, citrusy, and grassy; factory versions range from bland to sharp

Leicester was created in the eighteenth century as a means of using the milk surplus from STILTON production. Both cheeses are thought to have originated in Leicestershire County in central England near Nottingham. Though commonly known simply as *Leicester,* the official name of this cheese is **Red Leicester.** Originally it was colored with beet or carrot juice, then with ANNATTO, and was simply known as *Leicester.* During World War II, however, the use of annatto was discontinued and Leicester cheese took on a naturally light color. When the use of annatto was reinstated after the war, the word *red* was appended to *Leicester* to differentiate the pale style from the dyed version. And the name *Red Leicester* stuck with many, though to distinguish it as such isn't necessary today because all Leicester is the same color—a deep reddish orange. Leicester's texture resembles that of CHEDDAR but is flakier, the flavor slightly milder. Leicester is RIPENED for from 4 to 9 months, and the FAT CONTENT is about 48 percent. Only a few farmstead producers produce traditional, handmade cheeses today; most Leicester is now factory produced. In the United States, **Jasper Hill Farm** of Greenboro, Vermont, produces **Aspenhurst,** which is a rendition of a traditional English Leicester. It's made with raw cow's milk, cloth bound, and RIPENED for at least 12 months.

Leiden; Leidenkaas [LAY-den; LI-den (-kahss)] *see* BOEREN-LEIDSE MET SLEUTELS

les yeux de perdrix [layz-yeuh deuh pehr-DREE] French for "partridge eyes" (*see* EYES)

l'Étivaz *see* ÉTIVAZ, L'

Leyden [LAY-den; LI-den] *see* BOEREN-LEIDSE MET SLEUTELS

Liederkranz [LEE-der-kranz] *see* LIMBURGER; SCHLOSS

Limburger [LIHM-ber-ger]

Origin	Belgium (Liège)
Milk	Unpasteurized and pasteurized cow's
Type	SEMISOFT to SEMIHARD; PRESSED UNCOOKED and MOLDED UNCOOKED; WASHED RIND; FACTORY
Appearance	1- to 2½-pound cubes or loaves; rind is sticky, wrinkled, and pinkish orange to reddish brown in color; interior is off-white to pale yellow with a few EYES
Texture	Firm and supple, becoming softer as it ages
Flavor	Sweet, spicy, savory, and tangy—much milder than its aroma

Limburger was first made in Belgium by Trappist Monks and is named after the town of Limburg in Belgium's easternmost province of Liège. Origin aside, today Limburger is most associated with Germany, where the majority of it is now produced. It's also made in Austria and in Wisconsin at the Chalet Cheese Cooperative (currently the only United States producer) by master cheesemaker Myron Olson. Limburger has the reputation of being one of the smelliest of the washed-rind cheeses, though its flavor is mild by comparison. It's ripened for at least 3 to 4 weeks but often for longer. Because it's made from whole milk, it has a relatively high FAT CONTENT of at least 50 percent. In the late 1800s New Yorker Emil Frey created **Liederkranz,** which was patterned after Limburger but was truly an American original. Frey named the cheese, which meant "wreath of song," after the glee club in which he sang. Sadly for Liederkranz lovers, this American creation has since disappeared from the cheese scene.

Lincolnshire Poacher

Origin	England (Lincolnshire)
Milk	Unpasteurized cow's
Type	HARD; PRESSED COOKED; NATURAL RIND; FARMSTEAD
Appearance	44-pound wheels; the rind is golden brown to gray brown with light patches of white mold; interior is ivory to golden yellow with occasional irregular EYES and cracks
Texture	Smooth, tight, and firm, becoming crumbly or flaky with age
Flavor	Sweet, rich, and creamy with a range of flavors including caramel, fruit, nuts, and spice

As with many dairy farmers, Simon Jones turned to cheesemaking to diversify when milk prices fell. He's a fourth-generation farmer in Lincolnshire, a county in England's East Midlands, not an area well known for dairy farming or cheesemaking. Jones's mentor when he began cheesemaking was Dougal Campbell, who makes Tyn Grug, a Welsh cheese loosely based on CHEDDAR. His first Lincolnshire Poacher was produced in 1992—four years later it was crowned the Supreme Champion at the British Cheese Awards and has since won Best British Cheese at the World Cheese Awards. Lincolnshire Poacher follows many of the classic cheddar-making techniques, including MILLING the cheese into rice-sized bits and CHEDDARING, where slabs of partially drained curd are stacked on top of each other and turned and restacked. This technique ensures that all slabs are evenly pressed of WHEY and produces a cheese with a smooth, tight texture. The cheese is also pressed for about 2 days. However, unlike farmstead ched-dars, which are clothbound, Lincolnshire Poacher is coated with a synthetic rind called *Plasticote,* which allows the cheese to breathe while RIPENING. This artificial rind eventually decomposes, making way for the natural rind to form. Lincolnshire Poacher is ripened for 12 to 24 months and even longer. It has a FAT CONTENT of about 45 percent.

lingot [lan-GOH] French for "bar" and one of the many shapes into which CHÈVRE is formed.

lipase [LIP-ays] Any of a group of ENZYMES that act as catalysts in the breaking down of fats into glycerol and fatty acids. Lipase is found in raw milk (*see* MILK) and can be added to the STARTER of some cheeses to lend a tangy quality. *See also* RANCID in the Glossary of Cheese Descriptors, page 502.

lipolysis [lih-PAHL-ih-sis] The breakdown of lipids (fats) into glycerol and fatty acids. *See also* ENZYMES.

lipolytic enzymes [lip-uh-LIHT-ick] *see* ENZYMES; LIPASE

Liptauer [LIP-tow-er]

Origin	Hungary
Milk	Unpasteurized sheep's, sometimes with cow's
Type	FRESH; MOLDED UNCOOKED; FARMSTEAD and COOPERATIVE
Appearance	Sold in various-sized pots, boxes, or other containers; color ranges from stark white to orangish red
Texture	Soft and creamy
Flavor	Varies widely, depending on the added flavorings

L

Liptauer, also called *Liptoi,* is a traditional Austro-Hungarian cheese spread that's hard to find outside of Hungary. It hails from the Lipto region in the picturesque Tatra Mountains. The name *Liptauer* is derived from the word *Liptov,* once a historic county of Hungary and now an informal territory in northern Slovakia. The shepherds typically RENNET the milk from their sheep daily, breaking up and pressing the CURDS before hanging them to drain in cloth sacks. Sometimes a small amount of cow's milk is mixed in. Once a week the shepherds trek down to the dairies, where the drained curds RIPEN for about 2 weeks before being mashed, salted, sometimes blended with paprika, and turned into pots or small barrels. Liptauer has a FAT CONTENT of about 45 percent. There are almost as many versions of this cheese as there are cooks, with each family flavoring it differently. Some Liptauers contain more than twenty ingredients, and additions can include anchovies, beer, butter, capers, caraway seed, chives, mustard, onions, paprika (mild or hot), and salt. Liptauer is traditionally served as a spread, accompanied by pumpernickel or rye bread and frosty cold beer.

Liptoi [LIP-toy] *see* LIPTAUER

liquescent [lih-KWEHS-ent] *see* Glossary of Cheese Descriptors, page 500

Little Holmes *see* BIG HOLMES

Livarot (AOC; PDO) [lee-vah-*ROH*]

Origin	France (Normandy, Lower)
Milk	Unpasteurized and pasteurized cow's
Type	SEMISOFT; MOLDED UNCOOKED; WASHED RIND; ARTISAN and FACTORY
Appearance	Various-sized wheels with 5 strips of sedge

L

leaves, raffia, or paper encircling the wheel; rind is smooth, moist, and reddish orange to reddish brown with white mold streaks; interior is pale to medium yellow with a scattering of EYES

Texture Smooth, dense, and supple

Flavor Strong, meaty, nutty, pungent, and slightly tangy

Livarot is one of Normandy's oldest cheeses, dating back to at least the thirteenth century. It comes from the area around Livarot, a small town in the Calvados département. Large quantities of this cheese were being produced by the mid-1800s, when Livarot was called *la viande du pauvre* ("meat of the poor"). This exceedingly pungent cheese has 5 strips of raffia (though today orange paper or plastic is used more often) encircling the rind's circumference, initially to make sure the cheese didn't collapse. These strips earned Livarot the nickname "The Colonel" because they resemble the stripes of a French military officer of that rank. Livarot is made from partially skimmed cow's milk and RIPENED for at least 3 weeks, but more commonly for 2 months. During the aging period Livarot is washed frequently with BRINE. The final wash is mixed with ANNATTO, which has an orange pigment that contributes to the rind's reddish orange color. These frequent washings help spread desirable bacteria evenly over the cheese's surface. APPELLATION D'ORIGINE CONTRÔLÉE (AOC) regulations allow Livarot to be made in three sizes, based on the internal diameter of the molds: *Quart-Livarot,* just under 3 inches; *Petite-Livarot,* 3½ inches; and *Trois Quarts Livarot,* 4 inches. The FAT CONTENT of this cheese is 40 to 45 percent.

Livingstone Gold *see* WINDSOR BLUE

Llangloffan [lang-LAWF-fuhn]

Origin	Wales (Pembrokeshire)
Milk	Unpasteurized cow's
Type	SEMIHARD; PRESSED COOKED; NATURAL RIND; FARMSTEAD
Appearance	3- to 30-pound wheels; rind is thin, rough, imprinted with cloth, and beige with patches of gray mold; interior is ivory to yellow or orange-red (dyed)
Texture	Dry and slightly flaky
Flavor	Full, buttery, and grassy, becoming richer and more piquant with age

Similar to CAERPHILLY and CHESHIRE, this cow's-milk cheese is produced by Joan and Leon Downey on the Pembrokeshire coast in western Wales. In 1977 they moved from the Cheshire, England, area, where Leon was an accomplished viola musician in the famous Hallé Orchestra, to live in the country and make handcrafted farmstead cheeses. The Downeys get their milk from Brown Swiss and Jersey cows and produce their cheese with morning milk combined with the prior evening's milk. The Downeys make a natural colored cheese, a **Red Llangloffan** (dyed with ANNATTO to create a bright yellow-orange cheese), and a version with chives and garlic. Llangloffan is RIPENED for 2 to 12 months and has a FAT CONTENT of about 45 percent.

loaf A 5-pound piece of cheese cut from a BLOCK and available in a variety of cheeses, including BRICK, MOZZARELLA, and MUNSTER. *See also* CHEESE SIZES AND SHAPES.

longhorn Traditionally a half-moon-shaped COLBY; however, the longhorn shape can also be found in CHEDDAR and JACK. *See also* CHEESE SIZES AND SHAPES.

LoveTree Farmstead *see* BIG HOLMES; TRADE LAKE CEDAR

Low-fat milk *see* MILK

L

M

Mahón; Mahón-Menorca (DO; PDO) [mah-OWN; mah-HONE]

> The world's great cheeses have always been made from raw milk. No one is dying from them. No one is getting sick from them. They are the healthiest, most delicious, and most nearly perfect foodstuff that exists.
> —Steven Jenkins

Origin	Spain (Menorca; Minorca)
Milk	Pasteurized or unpasteurized cow's, some sheep's (up to 5 percent sheep's)
Type	SEMIHARD to HARD; PRESSED UNCOOKED; NATURAL RIND; ARTISAN, FARMSTEAD, and FACTORY
Appearance	5- to 6-pound, 8-inch rounded-edged squares about 2 inches thick; rind is oily, compact, smooth, and burnished gold in color—it bears the imprint of the cloth in which the cheese is formed; interior has myriad small EYES and ranges in color from ivory to deep gold, the deeper color indicating age

M

Texture	Slightly hard and crumbly, yet meltingly smooth on the palate
Flavor	Somewhat acidic and salty, with buttery, nutty nuances; the flavor and aftertaste intensify and become sharper with age

Hailing from Menorca, the outermost of Spain's Balearic Islands, Mahón has been dated back to 3,000 B.C. Its name derives from the island's capital and port, through which this cheese was first exported. The milk comes from Friesian, Mahónan, or Brown Alpine cows; up to 5 percent of Menorquian sheep's milk may also be included. Wild thistle pistils are used for CO-AGULATION. The CURDS are wrapped in a cloth square, the corners tautly tied, and the cheese pressed for 2 to 3 hours. This technique gives this cheese its classic "fat cushion" shape. Mahón then undergoes a day of brining (*see* SALTING) before beginning its RIPENING process, which can range anywhere from 10 days to 10 months. Mahóns RIPENED over a month are rubbed with oil and/or paprika. This cheese may be sold in several stages of maturity: *fresco* (fresh) has 10 days of aging, *semi-curado* (medium-ripe) is aged at least 2 months, *curado* (cured) for 5 months, and *viejo* (old) for 10 months. As with all cheese, the older the Mahón, the more assertive the flavor. The FAT CONTENT of this cheese ranges from 38 to 45 percent.

maître fromager [MAY-truh froh-mah-ZHAY] French for "master of cheese" or "master cheesemaker," referring to a professional cheese expert. *See also* CHEESEMAKER; GUILDE DES FROMAGERS.

Majorero (DO) [mah-hoh-REH-roh] *see* QUESO MAJORERO

mammoth The largest CHEDDAR size available, a mammoth can range from 75 to 950 pounds. *See also* CHEESE SIZES AND SHAPES.

Manchego (DO; PDO) [mahn-CHAY-goh] *see* QUESO MANCHEGO

Manouri [mah-NOO-rree] *see* MIZITHRA

Manoypi [mah-NOH-pee] *see* MIZITHRA

manteca [mahn-TAY-kah] *see* BURRINO

marc [MARK; *Fr.* MAHR] **1.** The residue (skins, seeds, etc.) remaining after the juice has been pressed from fruit, usually grapes. **2.** A potent *eau de vie* (the counterpart to Italy's *grappa*) distilled from this mixture.

Marin French Cheese Company *see* BRIE; CAMEMBERT; QUARK; ROUGE ET NOIR; SCHLOSS

Marmora [mahr-MOH-rah] *see* DANABLU

Maroilles; Marolles (AOC; PDO) [mah-RWAHL; mah-ROHL]

Origin	France (Picardie; Nord-Pas-de-Calais)
Milk	Unpasteurized and pasteurized cow's
Type	SEMISOFT; MOLDED UNCOOKED; WASHED RIND; FARMSTEAD and FACTORY
Appearance	various sizes from 4½ ounces to 1½ pounds, square and from 1 to 2 inches deep; rind is ridged and yellow to dark gold in color with reddish tinges; interior is off-white to pale yellow with numerous small EYES
Texture	Smooth, dense, and supple
Flavor	Strong, savory, meaty, pungent, and slightly tangy

M

This cheese was created over 1,000 years ago at the monastery at Mariolles, a town in northern France's Nord-Pas-de-Calais region. Nicknamed *vieux puant* ("old stinker"), this exceedingly smelly cheese has a flavor that's strong but still milder than its aroma. Made like ÉPOISSES DE BOURGOGNE, LANGRES, and LIVA-ROT, Mariolles is BRINE-washed during RIPENING. The smallest size is aged a minimum of 3 weeks and the larger sizes for at least 5 weeks, although 2 to 4 months is more common. Pasteurized versions are typically ripened longer than raw-milk cheeses. Maroilles, also called *Marolles,* has a minimum FAT CONTENT of 45 percent.

Marolles [mah-ROHL] *see* MAROILLES

mascarpone [mah-skar-POH-nay]

Origin	Italy (Lombardy)
Milk	Pasteurized cow's
Type	SOFT; DOUBLE-CREAM to TRIPLE-CREAM; ARTISAN and FACTORY
Appearance	White and creamy, sold in small to medium-size containers
Texture	Like whipped butter
Flavor	Mild, creamy, and buttery

Mascarpone dates back to the sixteenth century, and its origins are thought to be in Lombardy from an area outside of Milan near the towns of Abbiategrasso and Lodi. There are several theories on the source of its name. One suggests that it comes from *mascarpa,* a term referring to a WHEY by-product from making other cheeses. Another version proposes that the name comes from *mascarpia,* local dialect for RICOTTA (mascarpone and ricotta are made similarly). The most popular

M

premise dates to Spain's occupation of Italy when a Spanish official supposedly said it was *más que bueno* ("more than good"). Mascarpone, sometimes called *mascharpone,* is not technically a cheese, because citric or tartaric acid is used rather than RENNET to thicken the warmed cream. The un-salted COAGULATED cream is then placed in cheesecloth and allowed to drain and thicken further (large-scale factories may use centrifuge equipment to perform this operation). The result is a dense cream similar to condensed crème fraîche or English clotted cream. Mascarpone's FAT CONTENT is be-tween 70 and 75 percent. Rarely found is a version from southern Italy made from water buffalo's milk. This cheese is made in several other countries, including the United States, where respected award-winning producers include **Blue Ridge Dairy Company** in Leesburg, Virginia; **Cantaré Foods** in San Diego, California; **Crave Brothers Farmstead Cheese** in Waterloo, Wisconsin; **Mozzarella Company** in Dallas, Texas; and **Vermont Butter & Cheese Company** in Webster-ville, Vermont. Many people know mascarpone because it is a key ingredient in the popular Italian-inspired dessert tira-misù.

master cheesemaker *see* CHEESEMAKER

matière grasse [mah-TYEHR grahss] French for "fat matter," this term is used on French and other imported cheese labels to indicate the percentage of FAT in DRY MATTER. Also referred to simply as *m.g.*

maturing *see* RIPENING

Maytag Blue

Origin	United States (Iowa)
Milk	Unpasteurized cow's
Type	SEMISOFT; MOLDED UNCOOKED; BLUE–VEINED; NATURAL RIND; ARTISAN
Appearance	2- and 4-pound wheels; rind is ivory with blue, gray, and white mold; interior is ivory with blue-green to blue-gray veining and scattered EYES
Texture	Dense, creamy, moist, and crumbly
Flavor	Creamy, salty, and tangy with a zesty spiciness that increases as it ripens

In 1919, E. H. Maytag, son of the founder of Maytag Appliances, began establishing a herd of Holstein cattle at the family's Iowa farm in Newton, outside of Des Moines. Even with this prize-winning herd, milk sales weren't very profitable. So in 1940 his son Fred obtained a recipe from Iowa State University and began making blue cheese in a style similar to ROQUEFORT. In 1941 the first Maytag Blue was released and was an immediate success. Though today Maytag Dairy Farms no longer has its own herd (the milk comes from neighboring farms), the cheese is made using traditional artisanal techniques. As with Roquefort, STILTON, and GORGONZOLA, *Penicillium roqueforti* is used to create the desirable blue molds. It's added both to the milk and to the CURDS. When the cheese is ready, thick needles are used to pierce each wheel to allow oxygen into the interior to feed the mold's growth. Maytag Blue is RIPENED for a total of 4 to 6 months in hillside caves. Partway through ripening, the cheeses are covered in wax, which is removed at the end of the ripening process. Before being sent to market, the cheeses are wrapped in foil. Over the years Maytag Dairy Farms has added CHEDDAR, BRICK, SWISS, and EDAM

M

to its line of cheeses. This concern is still a family-run business with grandchildren and great-grandchildren helping to produce over a million pounds of cheese a year. Another grandson, Fritz Maytag, produces the popular Anchor Steam beer at his San Francisco brewing company.

médaillon [may-dih-YON] French for "medallion" and one of the many shapes into which CHÈVRE is formed.

Menonita [mee-non-NEE-tah; meh-noh-NEE-tah] *see* CHIHUAHUA

Merry Goat Round *see* MOUNTAIN TOP BLEU

mesophilic cultures *see* STARTER

metallic *see* Glossary of Cheese Descriptors, page 500

Metronome [MEHT-ruh-nohm] *see* NOCTURNE

Metsovone (PDO) [meht-soh-VOH-neh]

Origin	Greece (Epirus)
Milk	Unpasteurized cow's and some sheep's or goat's
Type	SEMIHARD to HARD; PASTA FILATA; NATURAL RIND; SMOKED; ARTISAN, FARMSTEAD, and COOPERATIVE
Appearance	4- to 10-pound oblong sausage shape, usually tied with twine; rind is thin, smooth, glossy, tan to brownish gold, and usually paraffin-covered; interior ranges from off-white to pale yellow with scattering of EYES, developing pits and cracks with age

Texture	Firm, smooth, and silky when young, becoming crumbly with age
Flavor	Smoky, buttery, and mildly tangy; older styles become more piquant and somewhat saltier

M

This cheese is named after Metsovo (or Metsovon), a town in northern Greece's Epirus region high on the slopes of the Pindus Mountains. It's been produced in this mountainous region since the 1960s. Metsovone is similar to a small smoked Italian PROVOLONE. PROTECTED DESIGNATION OF ORIGIN (PDO) regulations state that it must be made with at least 80 percent whole cow's milk, which can be combined with up to 20 percent sheep's or goat's milk. Metsovone is a PASTA FILATA CHEESE, which means it's immersed in hot water and kneaded and stretched until it has a consistent stringlike quality. Once the cheese is set, it's soaked in BRINE for a period of days (depending on its weight), then dried and tied with twine. This cheese is RIPENED for 3 to 5 months, after which it's smoked for 1 to 2 days before being coated with paraffin. Metsovone has a FAT CONTENT of about 45 percent.

Mexican cheeses *see* Cheeses by Country of Origin, page 513

Mexican Mozzarella *see* QUESO OAXACA

Mexican Parmesan *see* COTIJA

m.g. *see* MATIÈRE GRASSE

Midnight Moon

Origin	United States (California)
Milk	Pasteurized goat's

M

Type	SEMIHARD; PRESSED COOKED; NATURAL RIND; ARTISAN
Appearance	9-pound wheel; rind is pale golden and covered with black wax; interior is ivory colored
Texture	Firm, dense, and smooth with traces of graininess on the palate
Flavor	Nutty and tangy with notes of brown butter and caramel

Midnight Moon is the inspiration of Mary Keehn, proprietor of **Cypress Grove Chèvre** and the genius behind the multi-award-winning HUMBOLDT FOG. Almost a decade ago, Keehn—known for her fresh goat's milk cheeses—decided she wanted to produce an aged cheese and so began working with a cheese-maker in Holland to learn more about the process. The ultimate goal was to produce a GOUDA-style goat cheese made from Dutch milk. In the end, Keehn formed an alliance with the Dutch dairy to produce her Midnight Moon, which was launched at the Fancy Food Show in the summer of 2002, where it was named "outstanding new product." Midnight Moon is aged a minimum of 1 year. Besides the Dutch-made Midnight Moon and LAMB CHOPPER, Keehn created **Ewe-F-O,** an aged sheep's milk cheese produced in Sardinia and marketed in the United States. Cypress Grove Chèvre produces a wide variety of cheeses, including fresh CHÈVRE, FROMAGE BLANC, and a goat's milk CHEDDAR. *See also* BERMUDA TRIANGLE.

mild *see* Glossary of Cheese Descriptors, page 500

milk The genesis, the very essence, of cheese is milk, whether cow's, sheep's, goat's, or other ruminant's. Among the milk-related factors that determine the taste and smell of cheese are the animal (and even the breed) it came from; what the animal

M

grazed on prior to being milked; the locale, climate, and elevation of the grazing grounds; and the season and time of day the animal was milked. The FAT CONTENT is also a consideration in flavor and texture of cheese. By weight, cow's milk consists of an average of 3¾ percent fat, goat's milk 3½ percent, sheep's milk 6¾, and water buffalo's milk a hefty 9 to 10 percent fat. HOMOGENIZED **whole milk** has nothing (such as fat in the form of cream) removed or added. **Fat-free milk** (also called *nonfat* or *skimmed*) has had *almost* all of the cream removed—by U.S. law it must contain less than ½ percent MILKFAT. In between these two categories are **2 percent** (reduced fat) **and 1 percent** (low-fat) **milks**, which produce low-fat cheeses. Such cheeses are often referred to as partially **skimmed**. **Creamline milk** is unhomogenized (and may or may not have undergone PASTEURI-ZATION) so the cream naturally rises to the top of the milk. Whether the milk is raw or has undergone PASTEURIZATION (heat treatment) also contributes greatly to the way a cheese tastes. Cheeses made from **raw (unpasteurized) milk**—the pure milk as it comes from the animal—typically have a more complex flavor than those made with pasteurized milk. Raw milk has simply been filtered and cooled, which means its vitamin content is higher than heat-treated milk. In the United States, federal regulations require that all cheeses (domestic or imported) either be made from pasteurized milk or RIPENED for a minimum of 60 days at a temperature of not less than 35°F. *See also* LACTOSE; UNPASTEURIZED MILK/IMPORTED CHEESE DILEMMA.

milkfat The fat content of MILK, also called *butterfat*. *See* FAT for information on fat relating to cheese.

milk serum Another term for WHEY.

milk sugar *see* LACTOSE

M

milling A mechanical cheesemaking process whereby the CURD is torn or cut into pieces before undergoing MOLDING, PRESSING, and SALTING.

millstone *see* WHEEL

Mimolette; Mimolette Française [mee-moh-LEHT; frah*n*-SEZ]

Origin	France (Nord-Pas-de-Calais)
Milk	Pasteurized cow's
Type	SEMIHARD to very HARD; PRESSED COOKED; NATURAL RIND; FACTORY
Appearance	7- to 8-inch ball shape slightly flattened on the top and bottom and weighing 4½ to 9 pounds; rind is dry, hard, and yellow-orange to brown in color, becoming pitted with age; interior is yellowish orange to deep reddish orange with a few small EYES
Texture	Compact, firm, and waxy when young, becoming harder and more brittle with age
Flavor	Mild, lightly fruity, and nutty when young; older versions are fuller flavored and have a tangy character

The beginnings of Mimolette appear to trace back to the Middle Ages, when the area called *Flanders* encompassed parts of northern France, Belgium, and the Netherlands. This cheese is also known as *Mimolette Française*, *Boule de Lille*, and *Vieux Lille*, the last being the original ("old") city of Lille in northern France near the Belgian border where many of the cheeses were originally RIPENED. Mimolette undergoes a minimum

RIPENING of 6 weeks but is usually aged for much longer. There are various ripening stages: *jeune* ("young") is aged 3 months, *demi-étuvée* or *demi-vieille* ("half old") for 6 months, *vieille en étuvée* ("old") for 12 months, and *très vieille* ("very old") for 2 years. The bright orange color of the PASTE is attributed to AN-NATTO, a natural dye derived from the achiote tree. Mimolette, which is also produced in the Netherlands and in Normandy, has a FAT CONTENT of 40 to 45 percent.

M

Minuet [mihn-yoo-EHT] *see* NOCTURNE

Mitzithra [mih-ZEE-thrrah] *see* MIZITHRA

Mizithra; Myzithra; Mitzithra; Mytzithra [mih-ZEE-thrrah]

Origin	Greece
Milk	Unpasteurized sheep's and goat's
Type	SOFT (for FRESH versions), to SEMISOFT to HARD, GRANA STYLE; rindless; ARTISAN, FARMSTEAD, COOPERATIVE, and FACTORY
Appearance	A variety of shapes, packaging, and sizes including balls, small wheels, and truncated cones, some weighing as little as 7 ounces; exterior and interior are milky white; some versions have a scattering of EYES
Texture	Fresh Mizithra is moist to semimoist, loose, and slightly granular; pressed versions range from compact and malleable to very dense
Flavor	Fresh versions are delicate, sweet, and nutty; pressed versions range from mild, milky, slightly sweet, and salty to quite pungent and sour for those with more age

M

A cheese produced from WHEY left over from making sheep's and goat's milk cheeses. Its production is similar to that of the more familiar Italian RICOTTA, which is made with cow's whey. History suggests the Italians learned how to make this style of cheese from the Greeks, who sought ways to use milk by-products eons ago. The word *Mizithra* is used in a general way to describe a class of whey-based cheeses. That's because Mizithra production methods and RIPENING times can vary, which affects both texture and flavor. **Fresh Mizithra** is seasonal because sheep's and goat's milk is available only from December to June. It's made by reheating the whey to about 185°F, at which point it separates and tiny clumps of protein rise to the surface. The solids are skimmed off, strained, and placed in perforated molds or baskets to finish draining. The end result is a white, creamy, firmly moist, ready-to-eat mound of "cheese." In principle, of course, Mizithra is not a cheese but rather a "dairy product," because no STARTER or RENNET is used. This fresh form of Mizithra has a low FAT CONTENT of 10 to 20 percent. Some producers add whole milk to the whey, which naturally boosts the fat content. **Dried Mizithra,** which is similar to ricotta salata (*see* RICOTTA), is made by SALTING and PRESSING fresh Mizithra, then ripening it for about 3 months. The result is a snow-white, firm, smooth, and pliable cheese with a sweet, milky, slightly nutty flavor. **Longer-aged Mizithra** cheeses are ripened for a year or more, at which point they're hard enough to use for grating. **Anthotiro** (or Anthotyro) is a type of Mizithra that was originally produced only on the island of Crete but is now made in other regions, including the Aegean and Ionian islands, Epirus, Macedonia, Peloponnesus, Sterea Hellas, Thessaly, and Thrace. It's made from whey left over from making KEFALOTYRI, combined with whole sheep's or goat's milk. This style of Mizithra has a fat content of around 65 percent. In the past the term *Anthotiro* referred only to the dried version, but today it describes both

M

fresh and dried styles. **Xinomizithra** (or Xynomizithra) is another Mizithra that originated on Crete. It's pressed and RIP-ENED in cloth sacks for several months at warm temperatures (40° to 50°F). This technique produces a sour taste (*Xino* means "sour"), which is more pronounced in higher-fat versions. Xinomizithra was traditionally made in limited numbers at small dairies, but today factories use nontraditional methods to produce mediocre versions in vast quantities. This has resulted in the establishment of the PROTECTED DESIGNATION OF ORIGIN-approved **Xynomyzithra Kritis,** which follows strict regulations for quality production. **Manouri (PDO)**—also called *Manoypi*—is made in central and western Macedonia and Thessaly. It's known as the "fat" Mizithra because whole milk and sometimes cream are added, which boosts the fat content into the 36 to 38 percent range. Manouri is salted minimally, and the result is a velvety-textured cheese that's often used in desserts.

mold; Br. mould; molding 1. Any of various fungi that grow off both living and dead organisms and cause organic matter to break down. Mold that forms on the outside of old or poorly wrapped cheese can be cut away and discarded and the cheese consumed. However, if mold develops on fresh cheese (such as COTTAGE CHEESE or RICOTTA), the cheese cannot be salvaged. **2.** In the cheesemaker's realm, beneficial mold is often encouraged to develop on or in cheese. Mold spores can be added via a STARTER to the milk or CURDS, or the surface of the cheese may be inoculated or sprayed with the spores. **Interior molds,** such as those used for BLUE-VEINED CHEESES, ripen throughout the cheese. **Surface molds,** such as those that coat BRIE and CAMEMBERT, are completely harmless and entirely edible. In either case, beneficial *PENICILLIUM* mold contributes greatly to a cheese's character and flavor development. The type called *white mold* (*P. candidum*) is cultivated on cheeses such as Brie

M

and Camembert, giving both their characteristic pungency. That known as **blue mold** (*P. glaucum, P. gorgonzola,* and *P. roqueforti*) produces the blue to blue-black veins in cheeses such as BLEU DE BRESSE, GORGONZOLA, and ROQUEFORT.

3. Cheese molds (also called *hoops*) come in myriad sizes and shapes and, for many cheeses, are used to hold the CURDS during PRESSING. Some cheese molds are similar to colanders or sieves, with holes or other openings. Others are simple hoops or bands, without bottom or top. Still others are simple muslin or nylon bags, which can be tied into specific shapes, depending on the style of cheese. All molds serve to drain off the WHEY from the curds and determine the final shape of the product. *See also* BACTERIA; MOLDING; MOLD–RIPENED CHEESES; SOFT–RIPENED CHEESES.

molded cheese *see* MOLDING

molded uncooked cheeses Cheese that hasn't undergone cooking or pressing. The unheated (uncooked) curds are simply scooped or poured into a mold, drained to expel WHEY, then RIPENED in accordance with their style. Notable molded uncooked cheeses include MUNSTER, PÉLARDON, QUESO IBORES, and BLUE–VEINED CHEESES such as BLEU D'AUVERGNE and GORGONZOLA. *See also* PRESSED COOKED CHEESES; PRESSED UNCOOKED CHEESES.

molding; Br. moulding Also called *hooping*, molding is the cheesemaking step during which the CURDS are either hand-ladeled or poured into a MOLD (3), which may or may not be lined with CHEESECLOTH or MUSLIN. Sometimes a mold is simply a muslin or nylon bag, which can be tied into a specific form, depending on the style of cheese. Some molds are perforated, while others are simply hoops that hold the sides of the cheese. During molding the WHEY drains from the curds and the cheese takes its final shape. *See also* BANDAGING; PRESSING.

M

mold-ripened cheeses A style of cheese that matures through the induction of PENICILLIUM mold spores, either interior or exterior. Examples include CAMEMBERT, which has been coated with *P. candidum* to produce its characteristic BLOOMY RIND, and *P. roqueforti*, which creates the blue veining throughout cheeses like ROQUEFORT.

monastery cheeses A style of WASHED-RIND, SEMISOFT cow's-milk cheese that historically originated with Christian religious orders, primarily in France, Belgium, and Switzerland. Although monasteries still produce this style of cheese, the bulk of the production comes from nonsectarian factories. Monastery cheeses, known for their pronounced flavor and aroma, are also called *monk's cheeses* and *Trappist cheeses*. Among the better-known examples are CHIMAY, MAROILLES, and MUNSTER.

Mondegueiro [mon-day-GAY-roh] *see* QUEIJO SERRA DA ESTRELA

monk's cheeses *see* MONASTERY CHEESES

Montasio (DOC; PDO) [mohn-TAH-zyoh]

Origin	Italy (Friuli-Venezia Giulia and parts of Veneto)
Milk	Unpasteurized or pasteurized cow's
Type	SEMISOFT to HARD; PRESSED COOKED; NATURAL RIND; FARMSTEAD, ARTISAN, and FACTORY
Appearance	14- to 25-pound wheels; rinds range from very thin, elastic, and pale yellowish brown to hard, thicker, and dark yellow with brownish gray shading, depending on age; interiors range from ivory to dark yellow with a scattering of small EYES

M

Texture	Ranges from smooth and supple when young to hard and grainy with age
Flavor	Younger versions have a delicate, slightly sweet, fruity flavor; aged versions are full-flavored, nutty and pungent

As early as the thirteenth century, cheeses similar to Montasio were being made by the monks at the Abbey of Moggio in the Friuli-Venezia Giulia region. The techniques for making Montasio were passed down through the centuries and eventually incorporated into today's regulations for DENOMINAZIONE DI ORIGINE CONTROLLATA (DOC). Montasio, which is often compared to ASIAGO, can be produced only throughout the Friuli-Venezia Giulia region and in the provinces of Belluno, Padua, Treviso, and Venice in the Veneto region. The milk comes from Italian Red Spotted, Brown Alpine (also known as *Swiss Brown*), and Holstein-Friesian cows. Two milkings (one of them partially skimmed) are used for Montasio, which is RIPENED to produce three different styles: "fresh" is aged for about 2 months, "medium" for 5 to 10 months, and the "aged" version for 1 to 4 years. Montasio's fat content ranges from 32 to 34 percent.

Montasio Festivo [mohn-TAH-zyoh fehs-TEE-voh]

Origin	United States (Texas)
Milk	Pasteurized goat's
Type	HARD; PRESSED COOKED; NATURAL RIND; ARTISAN
Appearance	5-pound wheel; rind is thin and dark red; interior is ivory colored with a scattering of small EYES
Texture	Smooth, firm, and supple
Flavor	Assertive, nutty, and pungently mellow

Master cheesemaker Paula Lambert, founder of the **Mozza-rella Company** in Dallas, created this original based on Italy's MONTASIO. It's unique, however, in that it's made with goat's milk rather than cow's milk, as with the classic version. And in her inimitable style, Lambert has also given this cheese a southwestern touch by slathering the aged cheese with an ancho chile–olive oil paste, an accent that adds aroma, flavor, and color. Montasio Festivo is aged a minimum of 2 months—usually longer and often up to a year. It's an excellent grating cheese.

Montbriac; Mont Briac [mawn-bree-YAHK]

Origin	France (Auvergne)
Milk	Pasteurized cow's
Type	SEMISOFT; MOLDED UNCOOKED; BLUE-VEINED; NATURAL RIND; FACTORY
Appearance	8½- to 20-ounce wheels; rind is thin, rough, pitted, and coated with ASH covered with splotches of white mold; interior is ivory with flecks of blue
Texture	Moist, smooth, and creamy, becoming runny when perfectly ripe
Flavor	Mild, fresh, and creamy with a slight tang

Montbriac was created in 1995 as a lusciously rich, mild-flavored blue cheese. It's similar to a BRIE with bluing and is made in the Velay Mountains of south-central France's Auvergne region. Production methods include adding cream to the milk and inoculation with *Penicillium roqueforti,* the same mold used for producing ROQUEFORT, GORGONZOLA, and STILTON. Stainless-steel needles are used to pierce the cheese, first on one side and then, several days later, on the other. This allows air to reach the interior to promote desirable mold growth. Montbriac is RIPENED for 2 to 4 weeks and has a FAT CONTENT of about 55 percent. It's also referred to as *Roche Baron, Rochebaron*, or *Montbriac Rochbaron*.

Mont d'Or [maw*n* DOR] *see* VACHERIN DU HAUT–DOUBS

Monte Enebro; Montenebro [MON-tay ay-NAY-broh]

Origin	Spain (Castile and León)
Milk	Pasteurized goat's
Type	SEMISOFT; MOLDED UNCOOKED; NATURAL RIND; FARMSTEAD
Appearance	Large flattened loaves with rounded corners; rind is thin with a light coating of ASH and mottled with white, beige, brown, and bluish gray molds; interior is white to off-white, becoming darker near the rind
Texture	Dense, creamy, and chalky
Flavor	Full, creamy, and herbaceous with a lemony tang, becoming more intense and somewhat pungent with age

Monte Enebro, also spelled *Montenebro,* is made by Rafael Baez, a legendary Spanish cheesemaker, who created it at the age of sixty-four. The cheese is made from milk from goat herds in the Ávila province located southwest of Madrid in the Castile and León region. This award-winning cheese is inoculated with *Penicillium roqueforti,* the same mold used for producing ROQUE-FORT, GORGONZOLA, and STILTON. However, Monte Enebro is not pierced with needles, which encourage the mold to grow in the interior of cheeses. Instead, the mold grows only on the exterior, with the interior remaining pale and without the veining found in blue cheeses. The exterior mold contributes to the flavor complexity of this cheese, which is RIPENED for about 3 weeks and has a FAT CONTENT of approximately 45 percent. Monte Enebro has been voted one of the 100 Best Food Products in Spain.

Monterey Jack *see* JACK

Monte Veronese (DOC; PDO) [MOHN-tay vay-roh-NAY-say]

Origin	Italy (Veneto)
Milk	Unpasteurized cow's
Type	SEMISOFT to SEMIHARD; PRESSED COOKED; NATURAL RIND; ARTISAN; MOUNTAIN
Appearance	Small wheels; rinds range from pale yellow and elastic to yellowish brown and hard, depending on age; interiors range from ivory to medium yellow (age-dependent) with a scattering of small EYES
Texture	Ranges from smooth and supple when young, to firm when aged
Flavor	Younger versions have a mild, slightly sweet, milky flavor whereas longer aged versions are full flavored, sharp, and pungent

A form of this cheese has been made in the Verona province of the Veneto region since the 1100s, but the name *Monte Veronese* was not used until early in the twentieth century. There are two types of Monte Veronese—one made with whole milk and one made with partially skimmed milk, the latter called *d'allevo*. Both have DENOMINAZIONE DI ORIGINE CONTROLLATA (DOC) status and are made only in the Monti Lessini range in the Verona

M

province. The d'allevo version can be aged for anywhere from 3 months to 3 years. Shorter-aged d'allevo is called *mezzano,* while those with longer aging are called *vecchio.* The FAT CONTENT of the d'allevo is about 35 percent. The whole-milk version is a newer creation and is similar to an Asiago Pressato (*see* ASIAGO). It has a relatively short 1- to 2-month aging period, a fresher, sweeter flavor, and a fat content of about 44 percent. Monte Veronese d'allevo mezzano comes with blue labeling, the d'allevo vecchio with black, and the whole milk version with green.

Montgomery's Cheddar *see* CHEDDAR

Mont St. Francis [mawn saynt FRAN-sis]

Origin	United States (Indiana)
Milk	Unpasteurized goat's
Type	SEMIHARD; MOLDED COOKED; WASHED RIND; FARMSTEAD
Appearance	4- to 5-pound wheel; rind is wrinkled, slightly moist, and reddish orange in color, sometimes with patches of mold; interior is ivory
Texture	Smooth and compact with a very few small EYES
Flavor	Rich, hearty, and pungent

A multiple winner in the annual American Cheese Society competitions, Mont St. Francis is produced by **Capriole Goat Cheese** by master cheesemaker Judy Schad. Her 80-acre farm is located in the lush rolling hills of Greenville, Indiana, where her four-hundred-head herd of Alpine, Sannen, and Nubian goats graze on rich grasslands. Mont St. Francis is named after a nearby Franciscan monastery, which is now a retreat. This washed-rind cheese undergoes frequent washings with BREVI-BACTERIUM LINENS for about the first week and continues to RIPEN for at least 3½ and up to 8 months. As the cheese ages, the PASTE takes on a semisoft texture. *See also* CROCODILE TEAR; O'BANON; WABASH CANNONBALL.

moon Description of a cross section slice of a LONGHORN (a cylindrical shape); a **half moon** is a half slice of a cross section. *See also* CHEESE SIZES AND SHAPES.

Morbier (AOC; PDO) [mohr-bee-AY]

Origin	France (Franche-Comté)
Milk	Unpasteurized and pasteurized cow's
Type	SEMISOFT; PRESSED UNCOOKED; NATURAL RIND; ARTISAN, FARMSTEAD, COOPERATIVE, and FACTORY
Appearance	Flat 11- to 20-pound wheels; rind is thick, leathery, and golden brown with white and gray splotches; interior is ivory with a scattering of irregular EYES and a thin layer of ASH (now probably vegetable coloring) in the middle
Texture	Supple, smooth, and firm
Flavor	Lightly piquant with nutty, yeasty, fruity, and fresh grass traits

Morbier is named after a small village in eastern France's Franche-Comté region. It was originally created in the nineteenth century as a way of using up surplus CURD from making the 100-pound wheels of COMTÉ. Leftover Comté curd from the morning milking was topped with a layer of ash, which performed two functions—preventing a rind from forming and keeping pests away. Later the ash would be

M

topped with the excess curd from the evening milking, then the curds were pressed and RIPENED. Today Morbier is made on its own from one milking. To create the classic look, cheesemakers halve the cheese horizontally and sprinkle the ash or vegetable coloring over the bottom portion. Morbier is ripened for at least 30 days and more commonly for 2 to 4 months. It has a minimum FAT CONTENT of 45 percent. Although most of today's Morbiers are made with pasteurized milk, raw-milk versions are more highly regarded. Some cheesemakers even make a goat's milk "Morbier," which of course isn't a Morbier at all.

morge [MORG] A mixture of wine and cheese scraps (and occasionally WHEY) that's used to bathe WASHED-RIND CHEESE.

mottled *see* Glossary of Cheese Descriptors, page 500

MouCo Cheese Company *see* COLOROUGE

mould *see* MOLD

mountain cheeses A general term referring to RAW-MILK CHEESES produced from animals (typically cows) that have grazed in alpine meadows. Mountain cheeses are characteristically assertively flavored HARD CHEESES that have been pressed, cooked (*see* PRESSED COOKED CHEESES), and RIPENED. The majority of SWISS CHEESES are mountain cheeses, although there are a wide variety of styles throughout Europe and some in the United States. At this writing, Europeans have taken steps to authenticate mountain cheeses by establishing the European Center Caseus Montanus (CIFMO), the aim of which is to legally define mountain cheeses through clear and controlled standards, specifically: such cheeses must be made from milk

M

produced solely in mountainous zones not less than 600 meters high and be produced and aged in the aforesaid area by the regulations pertaining to that specific cheese. The finalized regulations may also include tenets regarding summer and winter temperatures, quantity of rain and snow, and certain mountainous flora.

Mountain Tomme *see* VERMONT BREBIS

Mountain Top Bleu

Origin	United States (Maryland)
Milk	Pasteurized goat's
Type	SEMISOFT; MOLDED UNCOOKED; BLUE-VEINED; FARMSTEAD
Appearance	8- to 11-ounce truncated pyramid; rind is thin and covered with blue, gray, and white molds; interior is off-white with slight blue veining
Texture	Moist, smooth, and creamy
Flavor	Creamy and tangy with a slight spiciness, intensifying with age

Mountain Top Bleu is made by **FireFly Farms** of Bittinger, Maryland. The farm, which is a venture formed in 2000 by Mike Koch, Pablo Solanet, and Ron and Beth Brenneman, is located on Meadow Mountain, part of western Maryland's Allegheny Plateau. Mountain Top Bleu is unique in that it's made with both *Penicillium roqueforti* (used for producing ROQUEFORT, GORGONZOLA, and STILTON) and *Penicillium candidum* (used to make CAMEMBERT). It's made in truncated pyramidal molds (like the ones used to make VALENÇAY) imported from France and RIPENED for 5 to 8 weeks. Mountain Top Bleu has won honors

M

from both the American Cheese Society competition and the World Cheese Awards. Another award winner from FireFly Farms is **Merry Goat Round,** a goat's milk cheese that resembles a firmer, slightly tangier BRIE and is also ripened for 5 to 8 weeks.

mouthfeel The textural experience of a cheese on the palate. It might feel buttery and smooth dense and grainy, or creamy and full-bodied—the permutations are endless. *See also* TEXTURE.

mozzarella; Mozzarella di Bufala Campana (DOC; PDO) [maht-suh-REHL-lah, moht-suh-REHL-lah; dee BOO-fah-lah]

Origin	Italy
Milk	Pasteurized cow's or water buffalo's
Type	SOFT to SEMISOFT; PASTA FILATA; ARTISAN, FARMSTEAD, and FACTORY; some SMOKED
Appearance	2- to 17-ounce round or egg-shaped balls, loaves, and sometimes braided or knotted; rindless exterior is white and glossy, smoked versions are brown; interior is pure white
Texture	Elastic, soft, and spongy
Flavor	Mild and delicate with a fresh milky character and just a hint of grassy tang

Mozzarella originated in southern Italy near Naples but is now made in other countries, including the United States. Historically mozzarella was made from water buffalo's milk, and no one's really clear as to when these powerful creatures first came to Italy—some say that they were used as draft animals as far back as the second century. Cheese produced from the milk of water buffalo was not recorded until about the twelfth century, and widespread consumption didn't begin until the eighteenth century. Demand for this soft white cheese increased, and it wasn't long before cow's milk (or a mixture of cow's and water buffalo's) was the norm. Most cheese experts agree that mozzarella made from the milk of water buffalo is superior to that made with cow's milk. **Mozzarella di Bufala Campana,** which has DENOMINAZIONE DI ORIGINE CONTROLLATA (DOC) status, can be made only from whole water buffalo's milk. The designated area of production for this cheese is in southern Italy's Campania and Lazio regions and includes the entire provinces of Caserta and Salerno and parts of the provinces of Benevento, Frosinone, Latina, Naples, and Rome. Though not required to do so, other areas of Italy also make mozzarella from water buffalo's milk. It's rare to find American mozzarellas made from the milk of water buffalos because there's so little of it available in the United States. There are two styles of mozzarella: **Fresh mozzarella** (Mozzarella di Bufala Campana being a prime example) is made with whole milk and typically packaged in whey and/or salted or unsalted water; sometimes the packaging is vacuum-sealed. In Italy it's called *il fiore di latte* ("the flower of the milk"). This style has a soft texture that often oozes milky liquid when cut, and the flavor is sweet, mild, and delicate. **Regular mozzarella,** on the other hand, is drier, more elastic, and typically rather bland. It's factory produced, comes in low-fat and nonfat as well as whole-milk forms, and is often called the "pizza cheese" because of its good melting properties and nondescript flavors, which provide a perfect palette for other ingredients. All mozzarella is made by the PASTA FILATA process, which means the CURD is immersed in hot whey or water and continually stretched until it reaches the desired pliable consistency. It's then cut into the desired sizes and formed into various shapes, depending on local tradition—small balls, larger rounds, loaves, knots, or braids. To set the shape, the cheese is immersed in cold water.

M

Little cherry-sized balls are called *ciliegini;* slightly larger 1-inch versions are called *bocconcini*. **Mozzarella affumicata** is a smoked version that usually comes in larger spheres with brown exteriors. **Mozzarella manteca** is shaped around a lump of fresh butter. There are also loaves of mozzarella layered with fillings such as sun-dried tomatoes, chopped olives, or pesto. In the United States, Paula Lambert pioneered the way for fresh American mozzarella when she founded the renowned **Mozzarella Company** in 1982 after falling in love with the cheese during an extended stay in Italy several years previous. Lambert learned how to create this handmade specialty from Mauro Brufani, owner of a cheese factory near Perugia, Italy. The Mozzarella Company now produces 250,000 pounds of cheese annually and, at this writing, has a broad-spectrum line of about twenty-five cheeses, including BLANCA BIANCA, DEEP ELLUM BLUE, HOJA SANTA, MASCARPONE, MONTASIO, and QUESO OAXACA. One of the most popular cheeses Lambert produces is **Capriella,** a tangy fresh mozzarella made with half goat's milk and half cow's milk. The name comes from *capri* (Italian for "goat") and "ella" (from "mozzarella"). Lambert has won myriad awards for her handcrafted fresh mozzarella and other cheeses over the years at American Cheese Society and other competitions, and in 2005 the Southern Foodways Alliance named her fresh mozzarella one of its top ten best cheeses.

Mozzarella Company *see* BLANCA BIANCA; CRESCENZA; DEEP ELLUM BLUE; HOJA SANTA; MASCARPONE; MONTASIO FESTIVO; MOZZARELLA; QUESO OAXACA

Mt. Tam

Origin	United States (California)
Milk	Pasteurized cow's

Type	SEMISOFT; TRIPLE-CREAM; MOLDED UNCOOKED; BLOOMY RIND; ARTISAN
Appearance	10-ounce round; rind is bloomy, thick, and snowy white; interior is ivory colored
Texture	Firm but supple, smooth, and silky
Flavor	Milky, mellow, earthy, and buttery, with a nuance of white mushrooms

Mt. Tam is the signature cheese of **Cowgirl Creamery,** which is located on California's stunning Pt. Reyes Peninsula. Owners Sue Conley and Peggy Smith opened the creamery in 1994, debuting with fresh ORGANIC CHEESES, including clabbered COTTAGE CHEESE, FROMAGE BLANC, and QUARK. Mt. Tam was their first aged cheese, and it's become a highly successful award winner, taking first prize in the soft-ripened cheese category at an American Cheese Society competition. The name is a tribute to Mt. Tamalpais, just north of the San Francisco Bay. This WASHED-CURD, triple-cream cheese is made with organic milk from the Straus Family Dairy, where the cows graze on hundreds of acres of organic pastureland. Mt. Tam is aged a minimum of 3 weeks and is perfectly ripe at 4 to 5 weeks. This cream-enriched cheese has a FAT CONTENT of about 75 percent. *See also* RED HAWK; ST. PAT.

Muenster [MUHN-stehr] *see* MUNSTER

Munster; Munster-Géromé (AOC; PDO) [mewn-STEHR; MUHN-stehr; zhay-roh-MAY]

Origin	France (Alsace; Lorraine; Franche-Comté)
Milk	Unpasteurized and pasteurized cow's
Type	SEMISOFT; MOLDED UNCOOKED; WASHED RIND; FARMSTEAD, COOPERATIVE, and FACTORY

M

Appearance	Flat, 4½-ounce, 1-pound, and 3-pound wheels; rind is sticky and wrinkled and pinkish orange to reddish brown in color; interior is off-white to pale yellow
Texture	Firm and supple, becoming creamy as it ages
Flavor	Complex and rich array of sweet, beefy, savory, and tangy

This cheese takes its name from the village of Munster in the upper Munster Valley of Alsace's Vosges Mountains. The word *Munster* is derived from the local dialect for "monastery." The cheese's origin can be traced to the monks of Munster Abbey, who began producing it in the Middle Ages and eventually taught the technique to local villagers. Munster is made on the east side of the Vosges Mountains in Alsace, and an identical cheese, called *Géromé,* is made on the west side in Lorraine. In 1978 these two cheeses were united under the Munster-Géromé APPELLATION D'ORIGINE CONTRÔLÉE (AOC). The milk comes from Vosges cattle, brought to the region in the seventeenth century by Swedish soldiers. This is a stinky washed-rind cheese loaded with flavor. Once the cheese is formed, it's BRINE-washed every couple of days during RIPENING—a minimum of 2 weeks for small cheeses and 3 weeks for large ones, but 2 to 3 months of aging is fairly common. The Alsatians have always enjoyed eating cumin with their Munster and produce some cheeses embedded with cumin seeds. The minimum FAT CONTENT for Munster is 45 percent. Unpasteurized-milk Munsters are more highly regarded, but those with less then 60 days of ripening cannot be imported into the United States at this writing (*see* UNPASTEURIZED MILK/IMPORTED CHEESE DILEMMA). There are also French Munsters made in areas outside the AOC-defined territory, but they're generally not considered as good as AOC

M

versions. Other countries make "Munsters," but none come close to having the rich, complex flavors of the French AOC originals. Danish and German versions (spelled *Münster*) have a firmer texture than the French original, and their flavor is not nearly as distinctive or assertive. American renditions (spelled *Muenster*) are bland, soft, rindless, and sold in loaves rather than wheels.

Münster [mewn-STEHR] *see* MUNSTER

Murazzano (DOC; PDO) [moo-rah-TZAH-noh]

Origin	Italy (Piedmont)
Milk	Unpasteurized cow's and sheep's
Type	SOFT; MOLDED UNCOOKED; ARTISAN, FARM-STEAD, and COOPERATIVE
Appearance	10- to 14-ounce rounds; rind is smooth, very thin, and white to golden reddish brown; interior is ivory to light yellow with a scattering of tiny EYES
Texture	Firm but soft
Flavor	Mellow, delicate, and slightly savory, becoming more pungent when aged

Murazzano is made primarily by small cooperatives that must be located in and around forty-three towns and villages in the Cuneo province of northern Italy's Piedmont region—Murazzano is named after one of these villages. Originally made only from Langhe sheep's milk, Murazzano is now allowed to be augmented with cow's milk, but no more than 40 percent. Because it's unpressed, Murazzano retains a high degree of moisture. Most Murazzano cheeses are ready in only 4 to 10 days, though

M

some may be RIPENED slightly longer. This cheese has a FAT CONTENT of around 45 percent. A distinctive triangular paper with the logo of the Consorzio Tutela Formaggio Murazzano must be used to wrap this cheese.

Murcia al Vino *see* QUESO DE MURCIA

mushroomy *see* Glossary of Cheese Descriptors, page 500

muslin [MUHZ-lihn] A lightweight finely woven cotton fabric used in cheesemaking to line molds and for myriad other functions. *See also* BANDAGING; CHEESECLOTH.

musty *see* Glossary of Cheese Descriptors, page 500

mysost [MEES-oost] *see* GJETOST

Mytzithra [mih-ZEE-thrrah] *see* MIZITHRA

Myzithra [mih-ZEE-thrrah] *see* MIZITHRA

N

An apple pie without some cheese Is like a kiss without a squeeze.
—American proverb

naboulsi; nabulsi; nabulsieh; nabulsiyye [nah-BOOL-see] *see* AKAWI

Nata de Cantabria [NAH-tah day kahn-TAH-bree-ah] *see* QUESO DE CANTABRIA

N

natural rind; natural-rind cheeses Unlike BLOOMY-RIND and WASHED-RIND cheeses, which require some sort of treatment for rind formation, natural rinds form normally from air contact. The air dries the surface, which hardens and protects the interior of the cheese. In a few cases, such as PARMIGIANO-REGGIANO, the exterior is rubbed with salt to encourage rind formation. Natural-rind cheeses characteristically have a denser texture than other cheeses. Other natural-rind cheeses include CANTAL, EMMENTAL, PECORINO, and RONCAL. *See also* RIND(S).

needling A process used in making BLUE-VEINED CHEESES where cheese that has been inoculated with mold spores is pierced with metal skewers. The holes allow oxygen to feed the bacteria, thereby forming the characteristic veining throughout the cheese's interior. Also sometimes called *spiking*.

nerveux [nehr-VEUH] *see* Glossary of Cheese Descriptors, page 501

Netherlands cheeses *see* Cheeses by Country of Origin, page 513

Neufchâtel (AOC; PDO); neufchatel [NEUHF-sha-tell]

Origin	France (Normandy, Upper; Picardie)
Milk	Unpasteurized and pasteurized cow's
Type	SOFT; PRESSED UNCOOKED; BLOOMY RIND; FARMSTEAD, COOPERATIVE, and FACTORY
Appearance	Various shapes—hearts, cylinders, rectangles, and squares—sized from $3\frac{1}{2}$ to 7 ounces; rind is thin with a velvety coating of white mold that shows patches of red as it ages; interior is off-white to golden yellow
Texture	Soft and smooth but slightly grainy

N

Flavor	Delicate but piquant, mushroomy, and savory, gaining strength as it RIPENS

This cheese has been made for over 1,000 years in the area around Neufchâtel, a town in the north of Normandy. Neufchâtel is uncooked and lightly pressed. It's sprayed with *Penicillium candidum* and/or ripened in rooms permeated with this mold. Neufchâtel is ripened for a minimum of 10 days but often for 3 weeks or more. It's known for its many various shapes— *bonde* (a small cylinder), *double bonde* (a large cylinder), *carré* (square shaped), *briquette* (a small brick shape), *coeur* (heart shaped), and *grand-coeur* (large heart). The cheeses have a minimum FAT CONTENT of 45 percent. The American cheese called *neufchatel* is essentially a lower-fat CREAM CHEESE with a slightly higher moisture content. It's nothing like Normandy's APPELLATION D'ORIGINE CONTRÔLÉE (AOC) original.

Nevat [nay-BAHT (-VAHT)]

Origin	Spain (Catalonia)
Milk	Pasteurized goat's
Type	SOFT to SEMISOFT; MOLDED UNCOOKED; BLOOMY RIND; ARTISAN
Appearance	5-pound irregular, lumpy round with deep creases from the cheesecloth molding and a tiny peak at the center top; rind is snowy white, with some golden mold patches in older versions; interior is off-white
Texture	Creamy and smooth
Flavor	Delicate and rich with a slightly sweet tanginess

A cheese invented and produced by cheesemaker Josep Cuixart. The name *Nevat* comes from Catalan for "snowy," a reference to the velvety white mold that blankets this cheese and its shape, which resembles the snow-covered foothills of the Barcelona Mountains. The milk for Nevat comes from Murcia and Grenadine goats, a breed whose output is richer than that of most goats. The CURDS are scooped into a cheesecloth bag, tied at the top, and drained. Once firm, the cheesecloth is removed and the cheese's surface is treated with *Penicillium candidum*, which produces the downy white coating. Nevat is RIPENED for 2 to 3 months and has a FAT CONTENT of 55 percent.

New Lancashire *see* LANCASHIRE

New Zealand cheeses *see* Cheeses by Country of Origin, page 514

Nisa [NEE-sah] *see* QUEIJO DE NISA

Nocturne [NAHK-turn]

Origin	United States (California)
Milk	Pasteurized cow's
Type	SOFT; MOLDED UNCOOKED; BLOOMY RIND; ARTISAN
Appearance	4-ounce truncated pyramid; rind is thin and mottled gray with powdered charcoal and white mold; interior is ivory colored
Texture	Firm and smooth, becoming creamy, buttery, and spreadable with age
Flavor	Milky, fresh, and pleasantly tart when young, taking on faintly nutty, mushroomy traits as it ripens

Handmade by Korean-born Soyoung Scanlan at her tiny **Andante Dairy,** Nocturne was so named because the cheese's

N

color reminded Scanlan of Whistler's *Nocturne* paintings, its slow cheesemaking process and delicate flavor reminiscent of Chopin's piano Nocturnes. This music aficionado named her company Andante—a term used primarily relating to music to mean a moderately slow tempo—to describe her longing for a more leisurely pace, both in life and in traditional cheesemaking. Although Scanlan makes a variety of cheeses, Nocturne was her first. It's made with Jersey cow's milk from a neighboring dairy, and Scanlan's andante method of cheesemaking takes 18 hours to set the CURD, compared to the usual hour or less for many cheeses. This slow COAGULATION produces a cheese with a more complex flavor and finer texture. Nocturne is RIPENED for 3 to 4 weeks and has a FAT CONTENT that ranges between 40 to 50 percent, depending on the season. Among Andante Dairy's other musically named cheeses are **Pianoforte** and **Cadenza** (cow's milk); **Rondo** and **Metronome** (mixture of goat's and cow's milk); **Adagio, Acapella,** and **Figaro** (goat's milk); and **Minuet, Picolo,** and **Largo** (TRIPLE-CREAM CHEESES).

noix [NWAH] French for "walnuts" (*see* EYES).

Nökkelost; Nøkkelost [NUH*R*-kehl-oost]

Origin	Norway
Milk	Unpasteurized and pasteurized cow's
Type	SEMIHARD; PRESSED UNCOOKED; NATURAL RIND; FARMSTEAD and FACTORY
Appearance	11- to 33-pound wheels and blocks; thin rind is pale yellow to golden yellow, sometimes covered with red wax; interior is ivory to pale yellow with seeds and clove buds distributed throughout
Texture	Supple, elastic, and smooth

N

Flavor	Nutty, creamy, tangy, and spicy, intensifying with age

Nökkelost, also called *Kuminost*, is similar to Dutch Leiden cheese (*see* BOEREN-LEIDSE MET SLEUTELS). The word *nökkelost* literally means "key cheese" and refers to the two crossed keys that are the coat of arms for Leiden, Netherlands. In the early 1900s Norwegian timber was exchanged for Dutch cheeses, including EDAM and Leiden. Norwegians developed a taste for these cheeses and began making their own version, keeping the keys as part of the equation. The spiciness of this cheese comes from the addition of cumin seeds, cloves, and/or caraway seeds, which is why Nökkelost is sometimes referred to as "clove cheese." It's generally RIPENED for about 3 months, though some styles are aged longer. Regular Nökkelost has a FAT CONTENT of approximately 45 percent; low-fat versions are also available.

nonfat milk *see* MILK

Noord-Hollandse Edammer [nord HOL-lahnd-see EE-dam-mer] *see* EDAM

Noord-Hollandse Gouda [nord HOL-lahnd-see HOW-dah] *see* GOUDA

Norwegian cheeses *see* Cheeses by Country of Origin, page 514

nutty *see* Glossary of Cheese Descriptors, page 501

O

Oaxaca [wuh-HAH-kah] *see* ASADERO

O'Banon

Origin	United States (Indiana)
Milk	Pasteurized goat's
Type	SOFT TO SEMISOFT MOLDED UNCOOKED; NATURAL RIND; FARMSTEAD
Appearance	6-ounce wheels wrapped in chestnut leaves; cheese is wrapped in chestnut leaves and then vacuum-wrapped in plastic; interior is white
Texture	Dense and creamy
Flavor	Milky, lightly tangy, savory, and complex

> My favorites [cheeses] are authentic, the real thing, palpably linked to the milks from which they are made and to their geographic origins. To taste them is to appreciate the link that must take place for a cheese to achieve greatness—a concomitance of soil and herbage, beast and human, climate and the passage of time.
> —Steven Jenkins

Produced by the **Capriole Goat Cheese** company by master cheesemaker and owner Judy Schad, O'Banon is a multiple-year winner in the annual American Cheese Society competition. It was inspired by the BANON produced in France's Haute Provence region and takes its name from a family friend who was a former governor of Indiana, the late Frank

O'Bannon. However, whereas the Provençal original is briefly RIPENED, this one isn't, and while the French original is wrapped in chestnut leaves and soaked in eau de vie, in Schad's rendition the leaves are soaked in fine artisanal bourbon, which gives the flavor a kick. Schad produces her cheeses from the rich milk of her four hundred-head herd of Alpine, Sannen, and Nubian goats that graze on the rolling grasslands of southern Indiana's Kentuckiana. O'Banon is handmade in small batches. *See also* CROCODILE TEAR; MONT ST. FRANCIS; WABASH CANNONBALL.

Oka; Oka Classique; Oka Léger [OH-kah; klah-SEEK; lay-ZHAY]

Origin	Canada (Quebec)
Milk	Unpasteurized and pasteurized cow's
Type	SEMISOFT; PRESSED UNCOOKED; WASHED RIND; COOPERATIVE
Appearance	5-pound wheel; rind is slightly moist and beige to reddish orange; interior is ivory with a scattering of small EYES
Texture	Soft and creamy to slightly firmer
Flavor	Mellow, creamy, slightly nutty, and fruity, becoming stronger with additional aging

Oka takes its name from a small village in Canada's province of Quebec. It originated in the 1890s after a band of eight Trappist monks were expelled from the Abbaye de Bellefontaine in France and invited to immigrate to Quebec. They established a monastery at Oka and began making cheese based on the recipes they'd brought with them. **Oka** is made from pasteurized milk and RIPENED for 30 days. **Oka Classique** is a raw-milk cheese ripened for 60 days. Both have a FAT CONTENT

O

of approximately 50 percent. **Oka Léger** (light) is a lower-fat version made with pasteurized milk. All three Okas have the characteristic pungent aroma of washed-rind cheeses but flavors that are relatively mellow.

Old Chatham Sheepherding Company *see* CAMEMBERT

oniony *see* Glossary of Cheese Descriptors, page 501

oozy *see* Glossary of Cheese Descriptors, page 501

open *see* Glossary of Cheese Descriptors, page 501

Oregon Blue Vein *see* ROGUE RIVER BLUE

Oregonzola *see* ROGUE RIVER BLUE

organic cheeses Cheeses made from organic milk taken from animals that graze on open pastureland or consume organically grown feed, untainted by fertilizers, pesticides, or other chemicals. Organic herds are free of growth hormones and preventive antibiotics. Apart from the use of organic milk, the cheesemaking process is the same for organic cheeses as it is for others. Organic cheeses will be clearly labeled as such and can be found at natural foods stores and many supermarkets. *See also* RBGH; RBST.

Ossau-Iraty; Ossau-Iraty Brebis Pyrénées (AOC; PDO) [OH-soh ee-rah-TEE; breuh-BEE PIHR-ay-nay]

Origin	France (Béarn and Pays Basque regions in the western Pyrénées)
Milk	Unpasteurized or pasteurized sheep's
Type	SEMIHARD; PRESSED UNCOOKED; NATURAL RIND; ARTISAN

Appearance	Rounded 10-pound wheel; rind is thick and brownish orange; interior is pale ivory yellow with tiny scattered EYES
Texture	Supple yet firm; high butterfat makes it somewhat oily
Flavor	Richly aromatic with nutty, slightly herbal nuances

O

The Ossau-Iraty banner unites two of France's western Pyrénées regions—Ossau, a valley and river in Béarn, and Iraty in the Pays Basque forests. Cheeses made under the Ossau-Iraty APPELLATION D'ORIGINE CONTRÔLÉE (AOC)—formally entitled *Ossau-Iraty Brebis Pyrénées*—can be produced only from the milk of Manech and Basc-Béarnaiser sheep from local herds. The milk must be transformed into cheese within 48 hours of milking. This cheese must be RIPENED for at least 90 days and has a FAT CONTENT of 45 to 50 percent. Although classically made with unpasteurized milk in a farmstead tradition (often in mountain huts), pasteurized-milk Ossau-Iratys are now being produced by some French creameries. This cheese is also known simply as *Iraty,* which can be confusing as ARDI-GASNA is also sometimes shortened to that name. *See also* ABBAYE DE BELLOC.

oveja [oh-BHAY-khah] Spanish for "sheep," seen on some labels of sheep's milk cheeses from Spain.

ovelha [oo-VAY-lyer] Portuguese for "sheep," found on sheep's milk cheeses from Portugal.

overripe *see* Glossary of Cheese Descriptors, page 501

P

pack date *see* PRODUCT DATING

> For full persuasion Camembert, like a good orator, should stop short just this side of fluency.
> —Clifton Fadiman

Pakistani cheeses *see* Cheeses by Country of Origin, page 514

Palmero [pahl-MEH-roh] *see* QUESO PALMERO

paneer; panir; paner; panneer [pah-NEER]

Origin	India, Iran, Pakistan
Milk	Unpasteurized and pasteurized cow's and water buffalo's
Type	FRESH; SEMISOFT; PRESSED UNCOOKED; FACTORY and FARMSTEAD
Appearance	Various sizes usually in squares or blocks; rindless; exterior and interior are white to off-white
Texture	Tender, moist, soft, and elastic (like tofu)
Flavor	Fresh, mild, milky, and lightly tangy

Paneer, Hindi for "cheese," is the dominant cheese found in Indian, Pakistani, and other cultures of the Indian subcontinent. It's also very popular in Iran, and in fact it's thought that the cheese was first introduced to India by Persian traders. Paneer (also spelled *panir* and occasionally *paner* and *panneer*) is a simple cheese to produce, and the Internet abounds with recipes for doing so. A small amount of citrus juice (such as lemon or lime) is added to whole cow's or water buffalo's milk that's been heated. As the juice is stirred in, the milk begins to curdle, and once the CURD forms it's transferred to a cheesecloth bag so the WHEY can drain. Once firm, the curd is shaped into a ball or square and pressed with a heavy weight for several hours. The result is similar to QUESO BLANCO, although generally not salty. Some recipes call for salt and cumin powder, but commercially available products are not at all salty. Paneer is used in myriad Indian dishes as a means of providing protein in a vegetarian-oriented diet. Cow's milk paneer has a FAT CONTENT of about 53 percent, the version made with milk from water buffalo slightly higher. **Chenna,** a close relative of paneer, is made in a similar fashion except that it's not pressed. Instead, the final step for Chenna is to knead the curd until it achieves the consistency of a soft, light CREAM CHEESE. Chenna is used primarily for making desserts.

panela [pah-NAY-lah] *see* QUESO BLANCO

Paniña [pah-NEE-nyah] *see* GRANQUESO

paraffin; paraffin wax *see* WAX

Parmesan [PAHR-muh-zahn]

Origin	Italy, Argentina, Australia, and the United States
Milk	Pasteurized cow's
Type	HARD; PRESSED COOKED; NATURAL RIND; GRANA STYLE; FACTORY
Appearance	15- to 16-pound wheels; rind is thick, rigid, and smooth, ranging in color from yellow to

	golden, and is typically covered with WAX; interior ranges from light to medium yellow
Texture	Finely grained, flaky, and brittle
Flavor	Full and sharp, sometimes nutty

For the most part, cheeses labeled *Parmesan* are mediocre imitations of Italy's PARMIGIANO-REGGIANO, one of the world's great cheeses. Parmesan is made in several countries outside Italy, including Argentina, Australia, and the United States (chiefly in Wisconsin, Michigan, and New York). The name *Parmigiano* is also used in parts of Italy for GRANA CHEESES that don't meet DENOMINAZIONE DI ORIGINE CONTROLLATA (DOC) requirements for Parmigiano-Reggiano. Whereas Parmigiano-Reggiano cheeses are subject to strict regulations regarding areas of production, what the cattle eat, lengthy aging, and so on, regulations for Parmesan cheeses in other countries are comparatively lax. The one thing they have in common is that the cheese is made from partially skimmed or fat-free cow's milk, which delivers a cheese with a FAT CONTENT of around 32 percent. At this writing, American Parmesans are RIPENED for a minimum of 10 months, but Food and Drug Administration officials are being petitioned by giant cheese producers to reduce the aging period to 6 months (Parmigiano-Reggianos are aged for 1 to 2 years or more). There are a few exceptions to lackluster American Parmesans. One producer—Wisconsin's **Antigo Cheese Company**—makes a critically acclaimed, award-winning Stravecchio ("very old") Parmesan, which is aged for 20 months and comes as close to Parmigiano-Reggiano as any Parmesan has gotten. Argentina produces a **Reggianito** (also called *Reggianito Argentino*), which means "little Reggiano" and refers to its smaller 15-pound profile compared to Parmigiano-Reggiano's over-50-pound wheels. Reggianito must be ripened for a minimum of 6 months. As grana-style cheeses, Parmesans are best suited for grating, and much of this product is found pregrated, a process that further diminishes what flavor the cheese had to begin with.

Parmigiano-Reggiano (DOC; PDO) [pahr-muh-ZHAH-noh reh-zhee-AH-noh]

Origin	Italy (Emilia-Romagna and Lombardy)
Milk	Unpasteurized cow's
Type	HARD; PRESSED COOKED; GRANA STYLE; NATURAL RIND; ARTISAN and FACTORY
Appearance	53- to 88-pound wheels; rind is thick, rigid, smooth, slightly oily, and ranges in color from gold to golden brown; interior ranges in color from light yellow to gold with little flecks of white
Texture	Finely grained, flaky, and brittle
Flavor	Full, rich, fruity, and aromatic, intensifying as the cheese ages

One of the world's great cheeses, Parmigiano-Reggiano has been made in northern Italy for centuries. It can be dated back to the 1300s, but historians believe it's been made for much longer than that. Although GRANA PADANO appears to have been originated earlier and is still more widely sold, Parmigiano-Reggiano has now become the most recognized name in the GRANA CHEESE category. Today there are myriad imitations (labeled simply *Parmigiano* or PARMESAN), and most fall far short of the original in flavor, texture, and character. Parmigiano-Reggiano takes its name from the provinces of Parma and Reggio Emilia. The DENOMINAZIONE DI ORIGINE CONTROLLATA (DOC) regulations for this cheese confine production to areas in two regions—Emilia Romagna (the provinces of Modena,

P

Parma, and Reggio Emilia and part of Bologna) and Lombardy (part of the Mantua province). Parmigiano-Reggiano is made from partially skimmed cow's milk, which produces a cheese with a FAT CONTENT of about 32 percent. The CURD undergoes MOLDING and PRESSING before being bathed for 3 to 4 weeks in brine (*see* SALTING) until the rind forms. During the aging process the wheels are inspected constantly and turned frequently. Aging for Parmigiano-Reggiano ranges from 1 year (*giovane*) to 2 years (*vecchio*) to 3 years (*stravecchio*) to 4 years or more (*stravecchione*). Parmigiano-Reggiano goes through a rigorous DOC inspection process, and, if acceptable, the wheels are stamped with the Parmigiano-Reggiano Consortium mark. The words *Parmigiano-Reggiano* are stenciled into the rind around the wheel's circumference so that any wedge will bear the identifying mark. The strict DOC rules for feeding the cattle (no silage), regulations for making the cheese, and the fact the production comes from over eight hundred small farms has allowed Parmigiano-Reggiano to maintain its high-quality standards and its esteemed reputation even though over 2 million cheeses are produced annually.

part-skim A label term signifying that the cheese (such as MOZZA-RELLA) was made with reduced fat (partially skimmed) milk.

pashka; paskha [PAHSH-kuh; PAHS-kuh] A traditional cheese mold made for Russian Orthodox Easter. Pashka combines sweetened POT CHEESE, regular COTTAGE CHEESE, or sometimes QUARK, with chopped nuts, candied fruit, and lemon rind. The mixture is turned into a cheesecloth-lined mold and refrigerated overnight. The classic shape of a pashka mold is a four-sided pyramid embossed with *XB,* which stands for "Christ has risen." A good substitution for the embossed mold is a clean 6-inch flowerpot. Once the flowerpot pashka has been unmolded, it may be decorated with nuts or candied fruit to form the XB.

Passendale Classic [PAHS–sen–dayl]

Origin	Belgium (West Flanders)
Milk	Pasteurized cow's
Type	SEMISOFT; PRESSED UNCOOKED; NATURAL RIND; ARTISAN
Appearance	6½- to 8-pound rounded loaf; rind is rough, hard, and golden brown with a light coating of white mold; interior is ivory to light gold with a scattering of tiny EYES
Texture	Soft and springy
Flavor	Creamy, mellow, and slightly tangy with a hint of sweetness

Passendale (once known as *Passchendaele*), a village in the West Flanders province of Belgium, was the site of a major World War I battle between the Allied Forces and the Germans, resulting in a huge loss of life. The cheese, which takes its name from this village using the current spelling, has been produced only since 1932, though its roots are based on older recipes and traditions used by the area's Trappist Monks. Passendale Classic is RIPENED for about 4 weeks and has a FAT CONTENT of around 50 percent.

pasta filata cheeses [PAH-stah fee-LAH-tah] Italian for "spun paste," pasta filata cheeses are produced by being kneaded and stretched while the CURD is still warm. This process may be done either by hand or by machine. Stretching the curd in this manner produces the distinctively elastic, stringlike quality common to pasta filata cheeses. After the cheese has been

P

stretched, it's formed or molded into the desired shape. Other names for this type of cheese are *plastic-curd, pulled-curd, spun curd,* and *stretched-curd*. Pasta filata cheeses include ASADERO; CACIOCAVALLO, MOZZARELLA, PROVOLONE, SCAMORZA, and STRING CHEESE.

paste The interior of a cheese, as opposed to the exterior or RIND. In France, the paste is called *pâte*.

pasteurization Nineteenth-century French scientist Louis Pasteur invented pasteurization, the technique of heating an ingredient for a specific period of time to kill potentially harmful microorganisms. Cheesemakers typically use one of two types of pasteurization. **Standard pasteurization** (high temperature/short time—HTST), the faster, more economical method, heats the milk to 161°F and holds it there for 15 seconds before quickly cooling it to between 45° and 55°F. Sadly, this flash pasteurization of milk often results in a telltale "cooked" flavor and slows down the RIPENING process, which typically affects a cheese's complexity, character, flavor, and texture. Some cheesemakers use **heat** (or **batch**) **treatment pasteurization**, which gently warms the milk for 30 minutes at 145°F. This method produces a cheese with a more natural flavor. **Thermalization** (also spelled *thermization* and *thermisation*) is another heat treatment whereby milk is heated at 145° to 150°F for 15 to 20 seconds. This technique significantly reduces bacterial counts while preserving the milk enzymes so crucial to a superior end product. The FDA, however, categorizes thermalized milk right along with raw milk, and such cheeses must be aged for 60 days before being released (*see* UNPASTEURIZED MILK/IMPORTED CHEESE DILEMMA). Pasteurization kills 99 percent of the bacteria in milk. Unfortunately for cheese lovers, it also destroys the natural enzymes that impart much of a cheese's complexity and character in both flavor and aroma. That's not to say that an expert cheesemaker can't produce a perfectly wonderful cheese with pasteurized milk by reintroducing strains of lactic acid bacteria and through ripening techniques. However, to do so is a more intricate and time-consuming process. *See also* MILK.

pasteurized milk *see* PASTEURIZATION

pasteurized process(ed) cheeses *see* PROCESS(ED) CHEESES

pasty *see* Glossary of Cheese Descriptors, page 501

pâte [PAHT] French for "paste" or "dough," used in cheese parlance to describe the interior. *See also* PASTE.

Pau [POW]

Origin	Spain (Catalonia)
Milk	Pasteurized goat's
Type	SEMISOFT; PRESSED COOKED; WASHED RIND; ARTISAN
Appearance	2-pound wheels; rind is dry and dark orange mottled with brown mold; interior is pale ivory with a scattering of EYES
Texture	Firm yet soft and supple
Flavor	Mildly sweet, nutty, and complex

Winner of the 2003 Specialty Food Trade show's "outstanding cheese" award, this cheese (also called *Picos de España Pau*) is a relative newcomer to the cheese world. Pau is made in a small factory using artisan techniques. It's BRINE washed before being RIPENED for a minimum of 45 days and up to 2 months. This cheese has a FAT CONTENT of 45 percent.

pavé; pavé amalthée [pah-VAY; ah-mahl-TAY] French for "square paving stone" and one of the many shapes into which CHÈVRE is formed (as in PAVÉ D'AUGE). *Pavé amalthée* refers to the shape of a hexagonal paving stone.

Pavé d'Affinois *see* FROMAGER D'AFFINOIS

Pavé d'Auge [pah-vay DOHZH]

Origin	France (Normandy, Lower)
Milk	Unpasteurized and pasteurized cow's
Type	SEMISOFT; MOLDED UNCOOKED; NATURAL or WASHED RIND; ARTISAN and FARMSTEAD
Appearance	1½- to 1¾-pound squares; rind can be sticky or dry, has a ridge pattern, and is light to medium yellow in color, developing white and red patches of mold as it ripens; interior is pale yellow and has irregularly shaped EYES
Texture	Smooth and supple, turning creamy as it ripens
Flavor	Rich, slightly sweet, and nutty, becoming more piquant, earthy, and savory with age

Pavé d'Auge has been produced in the Normandy region for centuries. The name comes from *pavé*—the word for the rough square cobblestones in the center of many old French towns—and refers to the shape of the cheese. Pays d'Auge is an area in Normandy that encompasses portions of the *départements* of Calvados, Orne, and Eure, where this cheese is made. Pavé d'Auge resembles and appears to be related to the more renowned

PONT-L'ÉVÊQUE from the same area. Both are square shaped washed-rind cheeses. Pavé d'Auge is RIPENED for 2 to 3 months and has a FAT CONTENT of about 50 percent. It's also called *Pavé de Moyaux* and *Pavé du Plessis*.

Pavé de Moyaux [pah-vay deuh mwah-YOH] *see* PAVÉ D'AUGE

Pavé du Plessis [pah-vay doo pleh-SEES] *see* PAVÉ D'AUGE

PDO *see* PROTECTED DESIGNATION OF ORIGIN

pecora [PEH-koh-rah] Italian for "sheep," seen on some cheese labels made from that milk.

pecorino [peh-koh-REE-noh] In Italy a cheese made from sheep's milk is generically referred to as *pecorino*. The most widely known is PECORINO ROMANO, followed by PECORINO SARDO, PECORINO SICILIANO, and PECORINO TOSCANO—all of which have DENOMINAZIONE DI ORIGINE CONTROLLATA (DOC) status. There are myriad non-DOC pecorinos, including Pecorino Abruzzese, Pecorino Baccellone, Pecorino del Sannio, Pecorinodi Norcie, and Pecorino Veneto. Pecorino styles range from SOFT to GRANA STYLE.

Pecorino Romano (DOC; PDO) [peh-koh-REE-noh roh-MAH-noh]

Origin	Italy (Lazio, Sardinia, Tuscany)
Milk	Unpasteurized sheep's
Type	HARD; PRESSED COOKED; NATURAL RIND; GRANA STYLE; ARTISAN and FACTORY
Appearance	48- to 73-pound wheels; rind is hard, smooth, and pale yellow (unless rubbed with oil, suet, or

P

	umber, which darkens it); interior ranges in color from ivory to pale yellow
Texture	Finely grained, flaky, and brittle
Flavor	Salty, fruity, and piquant, intensifying as the cheese ages

This ancient sheep's milk cheese has been in existence for over two millennia. As early as the first century, written mention hints at its production methods, which are very similar to today's process. Pecorino Romano originated in the farmlands around Rome (hence the name) and is thought to have been a staple of Roman armies. In the late 1800s, demand for Pecorino Romano was so high that some producers started relocating their cheesemaking facilities to Sardinia, where today the majority of this cheese is made. The DENOMINAZIONE DI ORIGINE CONTROLLATA (DOC) regulations for Pecorino Romano say it can be made in the Lazio region (in the provinces of Frosinone, Latina, Rieti, Rome, and Viterbo), in the entire region of Sardinia, and in Tuscany's Grosseto province. The milk comes from sheep raised in these areas, and the cheese is made from November through June. After the curds undergo MOLDING and PRESSING, the cheese is rubbed frequently with salt (*see* SALTING) over a 2-month period. Aging lasts for at least 8 and often for 12 months. Pecorino Romano has a FAT CONTENT of approximately 29 percent.

Pecorino Sardo (DOC; PDO) [peh-koh-REE-noh SAHR-doh]

Origin	Italy (Sardinia)
Milk	Unpasteurized sheep's
Type	SOFT to HARD depending on type and aging; PRESSED COOKED; NATURAL RIND; some GRANA STYLE; ARTISAN and FACTORY; some SMOKED

Appearance	2- to 9-pound wheels; rind is thin, smooth, and pale yellow in younger cheeses, becoming hard, thick, and brown in aged examples; interior ranges in color from white to pale yellow with a scattering of EYES
Texture	Soft and elastic when young, becoming hard and granular in aged versions
Flavor	Sweet, delicate, and faintly acidic in younger examples, gaining piquant characteristics and a butterscotch finish as the cheeses age

Though Sardinians have been making cheese for many centuries, Pecorino Sardo is a relatively recent entry in the cheese world—historical references date it only to about the late eighteenth century. The DENOMINAZIONE DI ORIGINE CONTROLLATA (DOC)–approved area of production for Pecorino Sardo covers all of Sardinia. The milk must come from Sardinian sheep, which are thought to be descended from the wild mountain sheep called *Mouflon*. There are two types of Pecorino Sardo—*dolce* (mild) and *maturo* (mature), both of which are made in a similar fashion. For the *dolce* style, the CURD is broken into small chunks, for *maturo* into tiny granules. The mild versions are aged for only 20 to 60 days and have a delicate, sweet flavor and soft texture. They're made in small wheels weighing up to about 5 pounds and have a green label. The mature cheeses are aged from 4 to 12 months and have a tangy, spicy flavor and a denser, harder texture, with older versions becoming granular. Mature Pecorino Sardo is sometimes smoked, and the wheels can weigh 8 or 9 pounds. The labeling for *maturo* styles is blue. There's a great deal of confusion about Pecorino Sardo because some references say that it's the same cheese as FIORE SARDO. True, both are made from Sardinian sheep's milk, but Pecorino Sardo is a semicooked cheese (*see* COOKING) and Fiore Sardo is

P

uncooked. To muddy the issue further, many references say Pecorino Sardo and PECORINO ROMANO are the same, perhaps because a majority of the latter is also produced in Sardinia. But PROTECTED DESIGNATION OF ORIGIN (PDO) regulations identify them separately, and there are distinct differences. Pecorino Romano comes in wheels of up to 73 pounds and isn't made in a mild (shorter-aged) version. It should be noted, however, that the aged versions of both cheeses are very similar in flavor and texture.

Pecorino Siciliano (DOC; PDO) [peh-koh-REE-noh see-see-lee-AH-noh]

Origin	Italy (Sicily)
Milk	Unpasteurized or pasteurized sheep's milk
Type	HARD; GRANA STYLE; PRESSED COOKED; NATURAL RIND; ARTISAN and FACTORY
Appearance	9- to 33-pound wheels sometimes marked by indentations caused by rush baskets; rind is hard and pale yellow unless rubbed with oil, suet, or umber that darkens it; interior ranges from ivory to pale yellow with minimal EYES and may have a scattering of black peppercorns
Texture	Finely grained, flaky, and brittle
Flavor	Salty, fruity, and piquant, intensifying as the cheese ages

Pecorino Siciliano was mentioned in Homer's *Odyssey*, giving credence to the idea that this cheese is at least 2,800 years old. This DENOMINAZIONE DI ORIGINE CONTROLLATA (DOC) cheese is produced throughout the region of Sicily. It's made in different ways, but the most common version is formed in rush baskets (*canestre*), which is why this cheese is sometimes

P

called *Canestrato Siciliano*. The CURDS are scooped up in the *canestre,* pressed, cooked in WHEY for 3 hours, and then drained. Occasionally whole black peppercorns are added to the curds before they're placed in the basket. The cheese then goes through several dry SALTINGS—one initially, another 10 days later, and possibly a third after about 2 months. Pecorino Siciliano must be RIPENED for a minimum of 4 months. It has a minimum FAT CONTENT of 40 percent. **Pecorino Tuma** is a style that's unsalted and unaged. **Pecorino Primo Sale** (or Primosale) gets only one salting and is aged for about 2 weeks. **Pecorino Secondosale** (or Secondo Sale) has gone through a second salting and is aged about 2 months.

Pecorino Toscano (DOC; PDO) [peh-koh-REE-noh toh-SKAH-noh]

Origin	Italy (Tuscany)
Milk	Unpasteurized and pasteurized sheep's
Type	SOFT TO SEMIHARD, depending on type and aging; PRESSED COOKED; NATURAL RIND; ARTISAN, FARMSTEAD, and FACTORY
Appearance	2- to 7-pound wheels; rind is pale yellow to dark yellow but can be orange, dark brown, or black if rubbed with tomato paste; interior is white to ivory to pale yellow, depending on age
Texture	Firm and supple when young, becoming hard and crumbly in older versions
Flavor	Young cheeses are mild, creamy, with a hint of nuttiness and become more nutty, piquant, and mildly peppery as they age

Pecorino Toscano cheeses date back more than 2,500 years. The approved production area for this DENOMINAZIONE DI ORI-

GINE CONTROLLATA (DOC) cheese includes all of Tuscany and
a few neighboring villages in the Lazio and Umbria regions.
However, most of the production is centered in southwestern
Tuscany's wild countryside of Maremma. This cheese can be
made only from the following pure breeds of sheep: Apen-
ninian, Comisana, Massese, Sardinian, and Sopravissana.
The best cheeses are made from milk collected during the
spring when new grasses proliferate, which is why in the fifteenth century this cheese was called *Cacio Marzolino* ("March
cheese"). Pecorino Toscano comes in a **soft** and **semihard**
version, both of which are made similarly. The CURD is broken into small chunks for the soft version or tiny granules for
the semihard. Reheating the curd for the semihard version is
allowed. The soft version is RIPENED for a minimum of 20
days, the semihard cheese for at least 4 months.

Pélardon (AOC; PDO) [pay-lahr-DAWN]

Origin	France (Languedoc-Roussillon)
Milk	Unpasteurized goat's
Type	SOFT to SEMISOFT; MOLDED UNCOOKED; NATURAL RIND; ARTISAN and FARMSTEAD
Appearance	2¼- to 3¾-ounce wheels; thin rind becomes wrinkled and changes from off-white to pale yellow and develops light mold as it ripens; interior is white to pale yellow
Texture	Soft and creamy, becoming drier as it ripens
Flavor	Milky and lightly tangy and savory with nutty traits

Pélardon originated in the Cévennes Mountains in the
Languedoc-Roussillon region of southern France and has been

made there for at least 2,000 years. The term *pélardon* is used generically for all small goat cheeses made in this area. Previously known as *Pélardon des Cévennes,* this cheese was awarded its APPELLATION D'ORIGINE CONTRÔLÉE (AOC) in 2000 and, in accordance with those standards, may be produced only in the Gard and Lozère *départements.* Though other Pélardon cheeses are made throughout the region, this is currently the only one with AOC and PROTECTED DESIGNATION OF ORIGIN (PDO) status. It's either sold fresh or RIPENED for up to 3 weeks and has a FAT CONTENT of about 45 percent.

Penicillium [pen-ih-SIHL-ee-uhm] Any of various fungi of the genus *Penicillium.* These characteristically blue to green fungi are used in the production of penicillin and grow as MOLDS on RIPENING cheese, decaying fruit, old bread, and so on. Several *Penicilliums* are used in cheesemaking, the most popular being **Penicillium camemberti** and **Penicillium candidum,** used for SOFT-RIPENED CHEESES like CAMEMBERT and BRIE; **Penicillium glaucum,** used for BLUE-VEINED CHEESES such as BLEU D'AUVERGNE and BLEU DE BRESSE; **Penicillium gorgonzola,** used for GORGONZOLA; and **Penicillium roqueforti,** used for ROQUE-FORT and recently in gorgonzola.

Pepato [peh-PAH-toh] *see* CARMODY

peppery *see* Glossary of Cheese Descriptors, page 501

Pérail; Pérail de Brebis [pay-RI; deuh breuh-BEE]

Origin	France (Midi-Pyrénées)
Milk	Unpasteurized and pasteurized sheep's

Type	SOFT; MOLDED UNCOOKED; BLOOMY RIND; ARTISAN and FARMSTEAD
Appearance	3- to 4-ounce wheels; rind is soft, delicate, and beige with patches of white mold; interior is off-white to pale yellow
Texture	Soft, smooth, and creamy
Flavor	Rich, sweet, caramellike, and nutty

Pérail is made in southern France's Aveyron *département,* the same region that produces the renowned ROQUEFORT. It was originally made when sheep's milk production dwindled in the late summer and fall—instead of making the large Roquefort wheels farmers made the diminutive Pérail. Today a large following demands that it be made all year. Also called *Pérail de Brebis*, this is one of the few bloomy-rind cheeses made with sheep's milk. Pérail must be RIPENED for at least 1 week and has a FAT CONTENT that ranges between 45 and 50 percent.

Peral [pay-RAHL] *see* QUESO DE LA PERAL

perfumy *see* Glossary of Cheese Descriptors, page 502

persillé [pehr-see-YAY] From the French *persil* ("parsley"), *persillé* means "parsleyed," or green-tinged. In the cheese world, it describes some BLUE-VEINED CHEESES, particularly ROQUEFORT, the veins of which are green to begin with, evolving with age to blue-gray. Also referred to as *fromage à pâte persillé*.

Petit Brie [peh-TEE BREE] *see* COULOMMIERS

Petit Cantal [peh-TEE kahn-TAHL] *see* CANTAL

petit lait [peh-TEE LAY] The French term for WHEY.

petit pois [peh-tee PWAH] French for "little peas," a term used in the cheese world to describe small EYES in cheese.

Petit-Suisse [peh-TEE SWEES]

Origin	France (Normandy)
Milk	Pasteurized cow's
Type	SOFT; DOUBLE-CREAM; ARTISAN and FACTORY
Appearance	1- to 2-ounce cylinder or square; rindless; exterior and interior are white
Texture	Very soft and smooth
Flavor	Delicate, creamy, sweet, and tangy

In the 1800s it was common for farmers to tend to the animals and for their wives to make the cheese. Petit-Suisse was created in the 1850s in Normandy by a farmer's wife who was acting on a suggestion from one of the Swiss farmworkers—therefore the Swiss link. She produced a cream-enriched, UNRIPENED cheese that she sent to Charles Gervais at Les Halles in Paris to sell. The rich, fresh cheese was a huge success and is now made throughout France. One of the most popular brands is Gervais, now owned by the French company Danone. Petit-Suisse is usually found in packages of 6 small containers. It has a minimum FAT CONTENT of 60 percent.

PGI *see* PROTECTED GEOGRAPHICAL INDICATION

pH A chemical term indicating the measure of a solution's ACIDITY.

Pianoforte [pee-a-noh-FOR-tay] *see* NOCTURNE

P

Piave [PYAH-vay]

Origin	Italy (Veneto)
Milk	Pasteurized cow's
Type	SEMISOFT TO HARD; PRESSED COOKED; NATURAL RIND; COOPERATIVE
Appearance	11- to 15-pound flat wheels; rind is pale yellow to yellowish brown; interior is pale yellow
Texture	Dense texture that ranges from smooth and supple for young examples to hard for older cheeses
Flavor	Younger versions have a delicate, slightly sweet, fruity flavor; aged versions are full-flavored, nutty, and piquant with hints of caramel

Piave was created in the 1960s by the Cooperativa Latte Brusche, a dairy cooperative located in the Veneto region in northeastern Italy. The cheese takes its name from the Piave River, which runs from the Alps down to the plains north and east of Venice. The milk comes from Bruna Alpina or Brown Alpine (also known as Swiss Brown) cows that graze in the alpine pastures in areas around the river. Piave is often compared to MONTASIO, ASIAGO, and younger versions of PARMIGIANO-REGGIANO. Two milkings (one of them partially skimmed) are used, and Piave is RIPENED to produce different styles: *fresco* is aged for 20 to 60 days, *mezzano* for 60 to 180 days, *vecchio* for over 180 days, and *stravecchio* (or *vecchio Oro del Tempo*) for more than a year. The FAT CONTENT of Piave ranges from 35 to 40 percent.

Picante da Beira Baixa [pee-KERN-ter dah BAY-rer BI-shah] *see* QUEIJO PICANTE DA BEIRA BAIXA

pickled cheeses A descriptor for cheeses, such as FETA and HALLOUMI, that have been packed in BRINE, which acts as a preservative. *See also* FLAVORED CHEESES.

Picodon de l'Ardèche; Picodon de la Drôme (AOC; PDO) [pee-koh-DAWN deuh lahr-DESH; DROHM]

Origin	France (Rhône-Alpes; Province–Alpes–Côte d'Azur; Languedoc-Roussillon)
Milk	Unpasteurized and pasteurized goat's
Type	SOFT TO SEMISOFT; MOLDED UNCOOKED; NATURAL RIND; ARTISAN, FARMSTEAD, and FACTORY
Appearance	2- to 3¾-ounce wheels; thin rind becomes wrinkled and changes from off white to pale yellow and develops splotches of white and blue mold as it ripens; interior is white to ivory
Texture	Soft and creamy, becoming drier and very firm as it ripens
Flavor	Sweet and mild when young, becoming lightly tangy, piquant, and spicy when fully ripened

The APPELLATION D'ORIGINE CONTRÔLÉE (AOC) area for Picodon lies south of Lyons in the mountainous Rhône-Alpes region on both sides of the Rhône River. L'Ardèche is situated on the west side and la Drôme on the east. Small zones touching them on the south from the Province-Alpes-Côte d'Azur and the Languedoc-Roussillon regions are also part of the AOC-approved areas. Goat herding and cheesemaking have existed in these regions for centuries. The name *picodon* comes from *picau,* an old regional dialect for "piquant," referring to the stinging sensation an aged Picodon imparts on the palate. During RIPENING,

P

plain water is rubbed over the cheese's surface, an aging technique referred to as *affinage méthode Dieulefit*. Ripening requires at least 12 days, but 3 to 4 weeks is more common. Some ARTISANAL producers age their Picodons by soaking them in wine, brandy, or eau de vie. Picodon has a minimum FAT CONTENT of 45 percent. Non-AOC Picodon cheeses are typically made by factories, often with cow's milk instead of goat's, and can't compare to the original in character or flavor.

Picolo [PIH-koh-loh] *see* NOCTURNE

Picón Bejes-Tresviso; Picón (DO; PDO) [pee-KOHN bay-KHES trah–BEE-soh]

Origin	Spain (Cantabria)
Milk	A mixture of cow's, sheep's, and goat's (pasteurized and unpasteurized)
Type	SEMISOFT; MOLDED UNCOOKED; BLUE-VEINED; NATURAL RIND; FARMSTEAD
Appearance	3- to 8-pound wheels wrapped in maple leaves; rind is thin, soft, and golden with gray splotches; interior is ivory colored with indigo veins and a scattering of EYES
Texture	Compact, smooth, and crumbly
Flavor	Nutty, grassy, spicy, and piquant

This DENOMINACIÓN DE ORIGEN PROTEGIDA (DOP)–designated cheese can be produced only in the district of Liebana (Potes, Pesaguero, Cabezon de Liebana, Camaleno, Castro Cillorigo, Tresviso, and Vega de Liebana) and the Penarrubia council. It must be made with the milk from approved breeds and, although traditionally prepared with a mixture of milks (cow's, goat's, and sheep's), 100 percent cow's milk versions can also be

P

found. The formed cheeses are dry-salted (*see* SALTING) and pierced with long needles to form holes so air can feed the natural *PENICILLIUM* spores that creates the bluing. Picón Bejes-Tresviso is RIPENED for 3 to 4 months in natural limestone caves at altitudes ranging between 1,650 and 6,560 feet. The cheeses are moistened and turned every 2 weeks to allow even penetration of the bacteria. *Picón* is marketed wrapped in maple leaves and has a FAT CONTENT of 45 percent.

Picos de España Pau [PEE-kohs day ays-PAH-nyah POW] *see* PAU

Picos de Europa [PEE-kohs day ay-ROH-pah] *see* QUESO DE VALDEÓN

Piedmont [PEED-mahnt]

Origin	United States (Virginia)
Milk	Unpasteurized sheep's
Type	SEMIHARD; PRESSED UNCOOKED; NATURAL RIND; FARMSTEAD
Appearance	1½- and 6-pound wheels; rind is hard and brownish gold; interior is ivory with a scattering of irregular EYES
Texture	Firm yet creamy
Flavor	Rich, buttery, and nutty with a floral trait

Piedmont is made by the **Everona Dairy** in Rapidan, Virginia, northwest of Richmond at the foot of the Blue Ridge Mountains. The owner, Dr. Pat Elliott, says she impulsively bought a border collie and later bought a few sheep to keep the dog busy. All of which led to the idea of producing cheese so the sheep could earn their keep. The end result is a dairy with close to 100 sheep and a reputation for award-winning

P

cheeses. Piedmont, Everona Dairy's signature cheese, has won several awards at the annual American Cheese Society competitions. It's RIPENED for 6 months and has a FAT CONTENT of 50 to 55 percent. There are several versions of Piedmont with added flavors, including one with chives and one with cracked pepper. Everona also makes **Pride of Bacchus,** a cheese soaked in red wine, which gives it an aromatic, fruity quality.

Pierre Robert [pee-YEHR roh-BEHR]

Origin	France (Île-de-France)
Milk	Pasteurized cow's
Type	SEMISOFT; TRIPLE-CREAM; MOLDED UNCOOKED; BLOOMY RIND; ARTISAN
Appearance	17-ounce wheels; rind is soft and white, developing a downy mold as it ripens; interior is off-white to pale yellow
Texture	Soft, creamy, and moist
Flavor	Rich, buttery, sweet, and mild with a slight tang

Pierre Robert was created in the 1970s when **Robert Rouzaire,** renowned AFFINEUR and founder of **Fromagerie Rouzaire,** began to experiment with TRIPLE-CREAM cheeses by RIPENING them for 3 to 4 weeks, much longer than the usual 1 to 2 weeks. This produced Pierre Robert, a cheese with a rich, full flavor and a decadently soft texture—it was an immediate success. During production of this cheese, cream is added to increase the FAT CONTENT to 75 percent, which places it in the triple-cream category. *See also* GRATTE-PAILLE.

piquant *see* Glossary of Cheese Descriptors, page 502

piticelle [pee-tee-CHEHL-lay] *see* BURRINO

plastic-curd cheeses *see* PASTA FILATA CHEESES

P

Plateau de Herve [pla-TOH deuh ehr-VAY] *see* FROMAGE DE HERVE

Pleasant Ridge Reserve

Origin	United States (Wisconsin)
Milk	Unpasteurized cow's
Type	HARD; PRESSED COOKED; NATURAL RIND; FARMSTEAD
Appearance	10-pound wheels; rind is thin and a dusty red color with a mottling of gray mold; interior is pale golden, darkening toward the rind, with a scattering of small EYES
Texture	Firm, smooth, and supple
Flavor	Complex, buttery, nutty, and slightly tangy, becoming more complex as it ages

This American original has won numerous awards and is the only cheese to win two national competitions—"Best of Show" twice at annual American Cheese Society conferences and United States Champion at a United States Championship competition. Pleasant Ridge Reserve is made by **Uplands Cheese Company** in southwestern Wisconsin in the old Pleasant Ridge area north of Dodgeville. This area is known as the Uplands because it was left untouched by the glaciers. The company is owned and operated by Mike and Carol Gingrich and Dan and Jeanne Patenaude. These two families began their partnership in 1994 and have 300 acres of lush ridge-top land replete with grasses, herbs, and wildflowers. In accordance with time-honored tradition, the Uplands cows

P

have their calves in the springtime, produce milk from summer through fall, and are dry for most of the winter. The Uplands team selectively chooses the milk used for cheesemaking based on quality and flavor—in short, they select "designer milk" so the cheese will develop the desired flavor. The handmade Pleasant Ridge Reserve is reminiscent of French Gruyère-style cheeses. The Uplands team ripens the cheese in a temperature- and humidity-controlled room built to the same specifications as the limestone caves of southeastern France. The cheeses are turned daily and the rinds washed with a special BRINE solution that contains the natural bacteria found in those caves. Pleasant Ridge Reserve is RIPENED for a minimum of 4 months but can be aged for up to 18 months.

Plymouth

Origin	United States (Vermont)
Milk	Unpasteurized cow's
Type	SEMIHARD to HARD; PRESSED COOKED; NATURAL RIND; ARTISAN
Appearance	$2\frac{1}{2}$- to 3-pound and 40-pound wheels; rind is yellow to golden; interior is pale yellow to yellow and replete with EYES
Texture	Moist and granular when young, drier and harder as it ripens
Flavor	Rich and tangy, gaining depth and becoming more piquant with age

Plymouth Cheese was first produced in the 1890s by John Coolidge, father of future president Calvin Coolidge. The Plymouth Cheese Corporation remained in operation until 1934, when milk shortages forced it to close. In 1960, the factory was refurbished and reopened by Calvin Coolidge's son, John, only to be closed again in 1998 when John, at age 92, sold the factory to the state of Vermont. Parts of the town of Plymouth Notch, Vermont, where the factory is located, had been established as the President Calvin Coolidge State Historic Site, and the factory became part of it. In 2004, the Frog City Cheese Company leased the factory and once again began to make this historic cheese using the original recipe. Plymouth Cheese is RIPENED to various stages: after 2 months it's sold as "mild," at 8 to 12 months it's called "getting there," and at 12 months it's "sharp," though Frog City Cheese Company and Plymouth aficionados consider it best at 15 to 18 months. There's a smoked version, as well as several flavored with herbs and spices such as caraway, rosemary, and crushed red peppers. Plymouth has a FAT CONTENT of about 45 percent.

Point Reyes Original Blue [RAY-ehs]

Origin	United States (California)
Milk	Unpasteurized cow's
Type	SEMISOFT; MOLDED UNCOOKED; BLUE-VEINED; FARMSTEAD
Appearance	6-pound wheel or 6-ounce wedges wrapped in foil; rindless; interior is ivory with greenish blue-gray veins
Texture	Moist, dense, and smooth
Flavor	Creamy, slightly salty, rich, and tangy

In 1998, third-generation dairyman Bob Giacomini had decided he needed a change after 40 years as a dairy farmer. He had long dreamed of creating a handcrafted farmstead cheese, and his wife, Dean, and their four grown daughters encouraged him to do it. Two years later, in August 2000, Point Reyes Farmstead Cheese Company produced its first wheels of

P

Original Blue, California's only artisanal blue-veined cheese, and the raves were immediate. Three of his daughters take an active role in the business, and Giacomini hired master cheese-maker Monte McIntyre (who'd previously produced MAYTAG BLUE cheese in Iowa) to create a premium California blue. Their closed herd of Holsteins (with a few Jerseys and Brown Swiss) graze on 700 acres of lush pastureland overlooking Tomales Bay, complete with coastal fog and salty Pacific breezes—a TER-ROIR reflected in this special cheese. Cheesemaker McIntyre uses raw, HOMOGENIZED milk that begins its transition into cheese barely 4 hours after the cows are milked. Every step of the cheesemaking process is done by hand. The wheels are punched with needles so air can reach the interior for the ben-eficial mold to grow. The cheese is repeatedly salted to accom-plish three things: to expel moisture, to act as an antibacterial, and to contribute flavor. McIntyre RIPENS the cheese for a mini-mum of 6 months and describes Original Blue as just that—an original: it's moister than STILTON, sweeter than GORGONZOLA, less pungent than ROQUEFORT, and very much like a mild, rich Danish-style blue. Point Reyes Farmstead Cheese Company also produces Original Blue Dip and Dressing, which comes in 7-ounce containers.

Pont-l'Évêque (AOC; PDO) [PAWN-lay-VEHK]

Origin	France (Normandy; Pays-de-la-Loire)
Milk	Unpasteurized and pasteurized cow's
Type	SEMISOFT; MOLDED UNCOOKED; WASHED RIND; ARTISAN, FARMSTEAD, COOPERATIVE, and FACTORY
Appearance	Various-size squares—standard is 12 to 14 ounces; rind is soft, sticky, ridged, and light to medium gold, developing patches of gray and

P

red mold as it ripens; interior is ivory to pale yellow and has irregularly shaped EYES

Texture   Smooth and supple, turning creamy as it ages

Flavor   Rich, slightly sweet, and nutty, becoming more piquant and savory with age

Pont-l'Évêque, one of Normandy's oldest cheeses, was known as *Angelot* (or *Augelot*) during medieval times. Its current name derives from the village of Pont-l'Évêque, which lies near Le Havre in northern Normandy. APPELLATION D'ORIGINE CONTRÔLÉE (AOC) regulations state that milk for this cheese must come from Normandy cattle in the area of Pont-l'Évêque village and the *départements* of Calvados, Eure, Manche, Mayenne, Orne, and Seine-Maritime. After the CURD is kneaded, molded, and drained, it must be RIPENED for at least 2 weeks, though 6 to 8 weeks is more common. During ripening this cheese receives frequent BRINE washings, brushings, and turnings, all of which help spread desirable bacteria evenly over the surface. Though this washed-rind cheese develops a smelly rind, its PASTE has a comparatively mild flavor. It comes in four sizes: standard (simply labeled *Pont-l'Évêque*), small (*Petit Pont-l'Évêque*), half (*Demi-Pont-l'Évêque*), and large (*Grand Pont-l'Évêque*). The cheeses are packed in wooden boxes for protection and are best from summer to early winter. Pont-l'Évêque has a minimum FAT CONTENT of 45 percent.

Port Salut; Port-du-Salut [POHR sah-LOO; deu sah-LOO]

Origin   France (Brittany)

Milk   Pasteurized cow's

Type   SEMISOFT; PRESSED UNCOOKED; WASHED RIND; FACTORY

P

Appearance	5-pound wheels; rind is slightly moist and orange-colored; interior is ivory colored with occasional EYES
Texture	Smooth and pliable
Flavor	Mild, creamy, and slightly tangy

The origin of this cheese dates back to the mid-1800s, when it was created by Trappist monks at the abbey of Notre Dame du Port-du-Salut at Entrammes in Brittany on France's west coast. Throughout the decades, Port Salut (also known as *Port-du-Salut*) became immensely popular throughout France as well as other countries. However, the quality of the cheese began to decline in the 1950s, when the abbey allowed outside companies to begin producing it. Eventually the trade name was sold, and now this cheese is produced primarily by SAFR—a giant dairy company in Lorraine. The monks produce their own FARMSTEAD cheese under the name of *Entrammes.* Port Salut is aged for 4 weeks and has a FAT CONTENT of 45 percent.

Portuguese cheeses *see* Cheeses by Country of Origin, page 514

pot cheese *see* COTTAGE CHEESE

Pouligny-Saint-Pierre (AOC; PDO) [POO-lee-nyee sa*n* pee-YEHR]

Origin	France (Centre)
Milk	Unpasteurized goat's
Type	SEMISOFT to SEMIHARD; MOLDED UNCOOKED; NATURAL RIND; FARMSTEAD and FACTORY
Appearance	9-ounce, 4- to 4¾-inch-tall truncated pyramid; rind is wrinkled and knobby with color ranging from ivory to gold, developing

	blue, white, and gray mold as it ripens; interior is white to ivory
Texture	Young versions are soft and moist; older ones are firmer, becoming hard and crumbly over time
Flavor	Mild, tangy, slightly nutty when young, becoming more complex and piquant as they ripen

Pouligny-Saint-Pierre is named after a small village in central France's Centre region. Because of its flat-topped pyramidal shape, it's nicknamed the "Pyramid" and the "Eiffel Tower." The shape is said to have been modeled after the village's belfry during the eighteenth century. To obtain it, the cheese is formed in perforated, pyramid-shaped molds. Pouligny-Saint-Pierre is RIPENED for at least 10 days but often for 4 to 6 weeks. It has a minimum FAT CONTENT of 45 percent.

Prästost; Präst [PRAST-oost]

Origin	Sweden
Milk	Pasteurized cow's
Type	SEMIHARD; PRESSED COOKED; NATURAL RIND; FACTORY
Appearance	25- to 33-pound wheels; rind is hard, dry, and pale yellow in color, sometimes covered with yellow wax; interior is ivory to pale yellow with numerous irregular EYES
Texture	Smooth and supple
Flavor	Sweet, mellow, buttery, fruity, and slightly tangy

P

Swedish for "priest cheese," Prästost takes its name from the sixteenth-century practice of tithing milk to the local priest. Because milk doesn't store well, it was made into cheese, part of which was sold at the local market. This practice lasted for several centuries, and Prästost became a well-known and popular cheese. Today this cheese, the name of which has been shortened to Präst ("cheese"), is primarily factory made. It's RIPENED for at least 2 months but often for 12 to 18 months. Prästost cheese comes in two styles—one with a FAT CONTENT of about 30 percent, the other with 45 percent. This cheese is sometimes flavored by soaking it or washing it with spirits such as whiskey or aquavit or by mixing juniper berries into the curd.

Prättigauer; Prattigauer [PRAH-tee-gow-er]

Origin	Switzerland (Graubünden)
Milk	Unpasteurized cow's
Type	SEMIHARD to HARD; PRESSED COOKED; NATURAL RIND; ARTISAN and FARMHOUSE; MOUNTAIN
Appearance	10- to 12-pound wheels; rind is hard and reddish brown; interior is ivory to pale yellow with a scattering of irregularly sized EYES
Texture	Smooth, dense, firm, and supple
Flavor	Nutty, savory, smoky, and tangy, becoming more intense with age

A cheese made in the Prättigau Valley, which is located in Graubünden, a large mountainous canton in eastern Switzerland famous for its ski areas. Prättigauer is produced only in the summer from the milk of cows grazing in high alpine pastures,

P

which is why it's also known as *Alpage Prättigau*. It's cooked in copper kettles over wood-burning fires that add a smoky trait to the cheese. Prättigauer is RIPENED for from 7 months to a year and has a FAT CONTENT of 45 to 50 percent. It resembles APPEN-ZELLER except the wheels are smaller.

pressed cooked cheeses A style of cheese created by heating (COOKING) the CURDS before MOLDING and PRESSING them to expel the WHEY. Examples of these firm-textured cheeses include EMMENTAL, GOUDA, and PARMIGIANO-REGGIANO. *See also* PRESSED UNCOOKED CHEESES.

pressed uncooked cheeses For this type of cheese, the unheated (uncooked) CURDS are simply pressed (*see* PRESSING) in a mold to expel the WHEY, then RIPENED in accordance with their style. This family of cheeses can range in texture from creamy (MORBIER) to firm (some MANCHEGO cheeses). Their flavor may range from mild (some CHEDDARS) to full-flavored (ETORKI). *See also* PRESSED COOKED CHEESES.

pressing A process by which WHEY is expelled from the CURDS, which helps knit the curds together and produces a consistent texture in the final cheese. Once cheese is placed in a mold, it can be pressed in several ways—by hand, mechanically (with hydraulic presses), or by stacking the molds so the weight does the pressing. Not all cheeses are pressed. For example, soft cheeses like CHÈVRE are simply poured into a perforated mold, and gravity does the draining. *See also* CHEDDARING.

Pride of Bacchus *see* PIEDMONT

prim [PREEM] *see* GJETOST

Prima Donna [pree-mah DAH-nah]

P

Origin	Netherlands
Milk	Pasteurized cow's
Type	SEMIHARD; PRESSED COOKED; NATURAL RIND; ARTISAN
Appearance	25- to 30-pound wheels; exterior is covered by a red or dark blue wax coating; interior is pale yellow to deep gold with a scattering of irregularly shaped EYES; aged versions have white crystalline flecks
Texture	Smooth and supple when young (dark blue label); long-aged cheeses (red wax) are harder, flaky, and brittle
Flavor	Ranges from full, rich, fruity, and nutty in younger cheeses (dark blue label) to rich, full flavored, and intensely butterscotch- and caramel-like in longer-RIPENED versions (red label)

In the early 1990s, the Vandersterre Groep of the Netherlands set about making a cheese that combined the best attributes of GRU-YÈRE and PARMIGIANO-REGGIANO. The result was Prima Donna. Though it's not a GOUDA because it's made with partially skimmed milk and has a FAT CONTENT below the minimum 48 percent required for Gouda, Prima Donna resembles that cheese in many ways. It weighs about the same as a medium-size Gouda, and the flavors of the red-wax-covered **Prima Donna Maturo** (which is RIPENED for 16 months or more) are akin to those of aged Goudas such as Beemster, Rembrandt, and Saenkanter. As with those classics, aged Prima Donna is full of crunchy bits of sweet, crystallized protein and has rich caramel and butterscotch flavors. The Prima Donna covered with dark blue wax is the younger version, which is aged for 6 months or more and is similar in texture and flavor to younger Goudas.

Prima Käse [PREE-mah kah-zeh] *see* GOUDA

primost [PREEM-ost] *see* GJETOST

process(ed) cheeses Mass-marketed products known for their long
shelf life, ordinary flavor, a texture that's often rubbery, and—
thanks to emulsifiers—the fact that they melt smoothly
without separating. Such products are also known as *pasteurized
process(ed) cheese* and *American cheese,* although the latter name is
sometimes also used in other ways, such as to refer to mild
CHEDDARS that haven't been artificially colored orange.
Processed cheese was invented by Swiss citizens Walter Gerber
and Fritz Stettler in 1911. In 1916, American James L. Kraft
was granted a patent for processed cheese, and in 1950 Kraft
Foods introduced it in presliced form. And so a legend was
born, with wrapped cheese slices now ubiquitous for grilled
cheese sandwiches and burgers. Today processed cheeses are
made by blending and heating shredded or ground pasteurized
cheeses (one or more of a similar variety) with any of various
ingredients including salt and other seasonings, water,
coloring, emulsifiers, and preservatives. Cheeses with minor
defects in rind, texture, and flavor may be used in the mix as
such faults will be minimized during processing. After being
cooked in giant vats at temperatures ranging from 150°F to
160°F, the cheese becomes homogenous, smooth, and glossy.
The mixture is then molded, after which the cheese may
further be cut into slices or bite-sized pieces. After processing,
process cheeses are practically sterile and don't undergo further
RIPENING, which means neither flavor nor texture will
improve. By law, such cheeses must contain no more than 43
percent moisture—except processed Colby (40 percent), Swiss
or Gruyère (44 percent), and process Limburger (51 percent).
Process cheese FAT CONTENT must be at least 47 percent—except

P

Swiss (43 percent) and Gruyère (45 percent). **Process cheese** *food* contains less real cheese (minimum of 51 percent) because water, WHEY solids, dry milk, or dehydrated milkfat may be added. Its moisture content must be no more than 44 percent, its fat content at least 23 percent. Undoubtedly the most popular cheese food in America is Kraft's **Velveeta,** which has been around since 1928. **Process cheese** *spread* is even lower on the cheese food chain. This variation of process cheese food has less milkfat (minimum of 20 percent), a higher moisture content (between 44 and 60 percent), and must be spreadable at 70°F. **Process cheese** *product* is at the bottom of the barrel, being simply a process cheese with lower moisture and milkfat percentages. *See also* CHEESE, CHEESEMAKING; COLD PACK CHEESE; IMITATION CHEESE; SUBSTITUTE CHEESE.

product dating Several types of dates are found on product packaging. The dates are used primarily to help stores determine the product's display life. **Pack date** refers to when the product was packaged. **Sell-by date** advises the purveyor how long to display a product. If the date on the package has passed, choose another cheese. **Pull date** designates when the product should be pulled from stock because it's too old. The **use-by date** is determined by the manufacturer and is the date after which the food is no longer at peak quality.

proper break During the production of SWISS CHEESES, while the CURDS are being cooked (*see* COOKING), the cheesemaker scoops a handful of curds, squeezing it into a ball. If the clump easily breaks into individual curds, the cheese has been cooked long enough to achieve the "proper break."

protease [PRO-tee-ays] Any of a group of ENZYMES that act as catalysts in the hydrolytic breakdown of proteins.

Protected Designation of Origin (PDO; DOP; AOP) A program designed
by the European Union to protect and recognize indigenous
agricultural products, foodstuffs, wine, and spirits. In 1992, the
EU approved two categories of protected names—PROTECTED
GEOGRAPHICAL INDICATION (PGI) and Protected Designation of
Origin (PDO), the latter having more restrictions on its use.
Before applying for a PDO, a group of producers must first
apply for approval by their country's national system of
standards—AOC in France, DOC in Italy, DO in Spain, and so on.
Once approved, they can apply to the European Union for
PDO status. Qualifying for a PDO requires adherence to
rigorous production regulations and quality standards set by
the country of origin. The quality or traits of the cheese must
be fundamentally or completely attributable to the particular
geographical environment where it's produced. This includes
intrinsic factors including local traditions, soil attributes, water,
and climate—factors that cannot be duplicated elsewhere. All
production of the cheese must occur in this geographical area,
and there must be a very close connection between the
prominent characteristics of the cheese and the environment.
An exception to pairing the cheese to the geographic name is
made if a traditional name for it can be substantiated. For
example, BLEU D'AUVERGNE is a blue cheese made in the region
of Auvergne and uses that name. On the other hand, RE-
BLOCHON is made in the Savoie and Haute-Savoie regions but
isn't required to use those indications because its traditional
name has been used for centuries. There are also a few
exceptions where, by tradition and national law, the milk is
allowed to come from a locale outside the area where the
cheese is produced. The PDO designation is referred to as
DOP (*Denominazione di Origine Protetta* in Italy and *Denominação de Origem* in Portugal) and **AOP** (*Appellation d'Origine
Protégé*) in France. **For purposes of consistency, PDO is the**

P

acronym used throughout *Cheese Lover's Companion. See also*
APPELLATION D'ORIGINE CONTRÔLÉE; DENOMINACIÓN DE ORIGEN
PROTEGIDA; DENOMINAZIONE DI ORIGINE CONTROLLATA.

Protected Geographical Indication (PGI; IGP) In 1992 the European
Union approved two categories of protected names—
PROTECTED DESIGNATION OF ORIGIN (PDO) and Protected
Geographical Indication (PGI, though sometimes the initials
IGP are used). The PGI category is not as restrictive as that of
the Protected Designation of Origin. Like those with PDO
designations, PGI cheeses must be produced in the geographic
area used in the name. However, unlike PDO cheeses, they're
not required to have all the production steps occur in that
geographic area. The connection of a PGI cheese's quality or
attributes to the geographic area is also more flexible. All
that's required is that these characteristics be a result of the
geographical area or the cheese has earned its reputation
because of the area. *PGI is the acronym used throughout
Cheese Lover's Companion. See also* APPELLATION D'ORIGINE
CONTRÔLÉE; DENOMINACIÓN DE ORIGEN PROTEGIDA; DENOMIN-
AZIONE DI ORIGINE CONTROLLATA.

proteolysis [proh-tee-AHL-ih-sihs] The enzymatic breakdown of
proteins into simpler, soluble substances. *See also* ENZYMES;
PROTEASE.

proteolytic enzymes [proh-tee-uh-LIHT-ick] *see* ENZYMES;
PROTEASE

provole [pro-VOH-lay] *see* BURRINO

Provolone; Provolone Valpadana (DOC; PDO) [proh-voh-LOH-nay
(-nee); vahl-pah-DAH-nah]

P

Origin	Italy (Basilicata, Emilia-Romagna, Lombardy, Trentino–Alto Adige, Veneto)
Milk	Unpasteurized or pasteurized cow's
Type	SEMIHARD; PASTA FILATA; NATURAL RIND; ARTISAN, FARMSTEAD, and FACTORY; some SMOKED
Appearance	This cheese can weigh from 1 to 220 pounds, is usually tied with rope or twine, and comes in various sizes and shapes including those of sausages, melons, pears, truncated cones, and bottles, often with a knob at the top where the cheese has been tied; rind is thin, smooth, glossy, and pale to golden yellow or brownish gold if smoked and sometimes covered with WAX; the interior ranges from off-white to pale yellow with a scattering of EYES, developing pits and cracks with age
Texture	Firm, smooth, and silky when young, becoming crumbly with age
Flavor	Younger versions are delicate, slightly spicy, and mildly tangy, older styles become more piquant and somewhat saltier

Provolone-style cheeses were originally produced in southern Italy, almost certainly in the Basilicata region. But by the late nineteenth century, cheesemakers in northern Italy had also learned the techniques for producing this style of cheese. Large quantities of Provolone were soon produced in the cattle-rich region of the Valpadana (the Po Valley), especially the area between Brescia and Cremona, west of Milan in the Lombardy region. So though this cheese originated in southern Italy and is still made there, it's this northern version, Provolone Valpadana,

P

that has DENOMINAZIONE DI ORIGINE CONTROLLATA (DOC) status. The approved area for producing Provolone Valpadana includes provinces in four of northern Italy's regions: Emilia-Romagna (all of the Piacenza province), Lombardy (all of Brescia and Cremona provinces and parts of Bergamo, Mantua, and Milan provinces), Trentino–Alto Adige (part of Trento province), and Veneto (all of Padua, Rovigo, Verona, and Vicenza provinces). Provolone Valpadana is a PASTA FILATA cheese, the elasticity of which allows it to be formed into a variety of shapes. Sausage shapes have many names, including *panchetta, pancettone, saleme,* and *salamino.* Among the melon- or pear-shaped cheeses are *mandarino, mandarone,* and *provoletta.* Those shaped like truncated cones are described as *gigante, gigantino,* or *gigantone.* Bottle-shaped cheeses are sometimes called *fiashetta.* There are two types of Provolone Valpadana—*dolce* (mild) and *piccante* (strong). *Dolce* is aged for only 2 to 3 months and has a more delicate flavor and supple texture—it's used primarily as a table cheese. The piccante style uses lamb's or kid's (instead of calf's) rennet, which gives it a stronger flavor. It's aged for at least 3 months and often for a year or more. Piccante has a stronger, tangier flavor and is slightly saltier. It's often used as a grating cheese. Both styles are sometimes smoked. The FAT CONTENT for Provolone Valpadana is about 45 percent. Most **American Provolones** are made in Wisconsin and Michigan and the majority are factory made, lackluster imitations of the original. There are a few exceptions, such as the award-winning Provolones from Wisconsin's BelGioioso Cheese, Inc. This company makes several styles (many of them handmade) from mild to aged and with both pasteurized and raw milk.

pub cheese *see* GLOUCESTER

pull date *see* PRODUCT DATING

pulled-curd cheeses *see* PASTA FILATA CHEESES

pungent *see* Glossary of Cheese Descriptors, page 502

Purple Moon *see* SAN JOAQUIN GOLD

Pyramid *see* TUMALO TOMME

pyramide [pee-rah-MEED] French for "pyramid" and one of the many shapes into which CHÈVRE is formed. POULIGNY-SAINT-PIERRE and VALENÇAY are two pyramid-shaped chèvres.

Q

quarg [QWARG] *see* QUARK

quark [KWARK, KVARK]

Origin	Germany and other central European countries
Milk	Pasteurized or unpasteurized cow's
Type	SOFT; FRESH; UNCOOKED, sometimes MOLDED; FACTORY and ARTISAN
Appearance	White; sold in small tubs or disks
Texture	Creamy, soft, and smooth, with a

Never commit yourself to a cheese without having first examined it.
—T. S. Eliot

Q

	texture ranging from that of a very thick sour cream to a ricotta or cream cheese
Flavor	Fresh and faintly tangy

German for "curd," quark—a soft, unripened cheese—is a staple in the diet of many Central Europeans. Historians tell us that it was first produced some 4,000 to 5,000 years ago. In Germany today it represents almost half the total cheese production. Quark can be made from whole, partially skimmed, or fat-free milk. Depending on the milk's FAT CONTENT and how much WHEY is removed during production, quark's texture may be similar to that of sour cream, COTTAGE CHEESE, FROMAGE BLANC, CREAM CHEESE, POT CHEESE, or RICOTTA. Quark can be found plain or flavored with anything from herbs to fruit to garlic. In the United States, California's **Marin French Cheese Company** won an American Cheese Award for both its jalapeño and its sweet red pepper quarks. **Vermont Butter & Cheese Company** has won World Cheese Awards for its **Vermont Quark**, which cheesemaker and cofounder Allison Hooper developed for a chef making pastries and desserts in a traditional German style. Although most quark is fat-free or reduced fat, some versions have a FAT CONTENT that can range up to 60 percent. This cheese goes by many different names: *Topfen* in Austria and Bavaria and *Quarg* and *Kvarg* in other parts of central Europe. It's also sometime referred to as simply "white cheese," as in *Weisskäse* (*Weißkäse*).

Quartirolo Lombardo (DOC; PDO) [kwar-tee-ROLL-oh lom-BAHR-doh]

Origin	Italy (Lombardy)
Milk	Unpasteurized and pasteurized cow's

Type	SEMISOFT; PRESSED UNCOOKED; NATURAL RIND; ARTISAN and FACTORY
Appearance	7- to 8½-inch squares or rectangles with flat tops, bottoms, and sides, weighing between 3 and 8 pounds; rind of young cheeses is thin (almost nonexistent) and white to pale pinkish yellow, becoming thicker and turning reddish gold with gray-green tinges with age; interior is white to ivory
Texture	Creamy when young, becoming denser and flaky when aged
Flavor	Young versions are mild and sweet with a slight tang, older cheeses are stronger, more piquant, and have a fruity trait

This style of cheese has been made in Italy's Lombardy region since the tenth century and was historically referred to as *Stracchino Quadro*. That name and its current name *Quartirolo* refer to the traditional production method using only milk from cows that grazed on fresh grasses from the season's fourth cutting (in the autumn), which gave the cheese its unique flavor. Today Quartirolo Lombardo is made year-round, but autumn cheeses are still considered the best. Quartirolo Lombardo has DENOMINAZIONE DI ORIGINE CONTROLLATA (DOC) status and the approved area of production encompasses Lombardy's provinces of Brescia, Bergamo, Como, Cremona, Milan, Pavia, and Varese. Much of this cheese is now produced in modern factories, which facilitates a very consistent product. **Quartirolo Di Monte** is an artisanal version produced in mountain huts. The factories use pasteurized milk, whereas artisans use raw milk. Although the use of partially skimmed milk is traditional, today whole milk is sometimes substituted. During the RIPENING

Q

period, cheeses are placed in squarish wooden boxes that often have reed bottoms for air circulation. Young Quartirolo Lombardos are aged for 5 to 30 days, whereas mature (*maturo*) cheeses have been ripened for over 30 days. This cheese has a minimum FAT CONTENT of 30 percent.

quatre feuille [kahtr foy] French for "four-leaf clover," and one of the many shapes into which CHÈVRE is formed.

queijo [KAY-zhoo] Portuguese for "cheese."

Queijo Amarelo da Beira Baixa (PDO) [KAY-zhoo er-mah-REH-loo dah BAY-rer BUY-shah]

Origin	Portugal (Beira Baixa)
Milk	Unpasteurized sheep's and goat's
Type	SEMISOFT TO SEMIHARD; PRESSED UNCOOKED; NATURAL RIND; FARMSTEAD, ARTISAN, and COOPERATIVE
Appearance	About 2-pound wheels; rind is tan and thin, occasionally faintly mottled with mold; interior is pale golden with small, irregular EYES
Texture	Ranges from soft to firm to slightly gooey, depending on the producer
Flavor	Earthy, herbal, and slightly tangy—some versions are assertively pungent with a bitter edge

Beira Baixa is an area located between Portugal's central mountain range and the Spanish border. Queijo Amarelo da Beira Baixa is also simply referred to as *Amarelo,* Portuguese for "yellow." It's part of the triumvirate of cheeses under the

PROTECTED DESIGNATION OF ORIGIN (PDO) umbrella of QUEI-JOS DA BEIRA BAIXA. Amarelo is made from a blend of sheep's milk and goat's milk, the proportions depending on the producer. Whereas the majority of Portugal's cheeses use an extract of dried cardoon thistle for COAGULATION, this one is made with animal RENNET. Amarelo cheeses are generally aged for a minimum of 40 days. Because PDO rules don't regulate all production methods, these cheeses can vary widely in flavor and texture, contingent on the cheesemaker. The FAT CONTENT for Amarelos ranges around 45 to 50 percent.

Queijo de Azeitão (PDO) [KAY-zhoo der ah-zhey-TAWN (-TERN)]

Origin	Portugal (Palmala, Setubal, and Sesimbra)
Milk	Unpasteurized sheep's
Type	SEMISOFT; PRESSED UNCOOKED; WASHED RIND; ARTISAN and FACTORY
Appearance	8-ounce rounds about 3 inches wide; rind is slightly wrinkled, crusty, and pale orange sometimes mottled with mold; interior is off-white to pale yellow, occasionally with scattered EYES
Texture	Creamy and softly oozy to firmly supple, depending on age
Flavor	Earthy, herbal, pungent, and slightly piquant

This cheese originated in the nineteenth century and is eponymously named after the village of its origin, in the foothills of Portugal's Serra da Arrabida Mountains. Though the official PROTECTED DESIGNATION OF ORIGIN (PDO) name is Queijo de Azeitão, this cheese is typically simply called *Azeitão*. The milk must come from Serra da Arrabida sheep, which graze on a variety

Q

of herbaceous plants that give the milk its distinguishing rich and herbal flavor. The milk is COAGULATED with an extract of dried cardoon thistle, which acts like RENNET and produces a subtle pleasantly bitter note. The CURDS are molded and drained in cloth before being gently pressed. The BRINE-washed cheese is RIPENED for a minimum of 60 days. Azeitão has a minimum FAT CONTENT of 45 percent. When perfectly ripe and at room temperature, the top may be cut off and the creamy PASTE scooped out with a spoon.

Queijo de Castelo Branco (PDO) [KAY-zhoo der kersh-TEH-loo BRERN-koo]

Origin	Portugal (Beira Baixa)
Milk	Unpasteurized sheep's and/or goat's
Type	SEMISOFT to SEMIHARD; PRESSED UNCOOKED; NATURAL RIND; FARMSTEAD and ARTISAN
Appearance	1-pound wheels; rind is pale yellow and thin; interior is off-white with small, irregular EYES
Texture	Ranges from soft to firm, depending on the producer and aging
Flavor	Mild and slightly tangy

Also called simply *Castelo Branco,* this cheese is one of the trio of cheeses under the PROTECTED DESIGNATION OF ORIGIN (PDO) umbrella of QUEIJOS DA BEIRA BAIXA. It can be made from sheep's milk, goat's milk, or a mixture of the two. Castelo Branco is also sometimes referred to simply as *cabreiro* ("goat cheese"). The milk for this cheese is COAGULATED with an extract of dried cardoon thistle, rather than animal RENNET. Castelo Brancos are typically aged for 40 days, but longer isn't unusual. They have a FAT CONTENT of about 45 percent.

Queijo de Évora; Évora De L'Alentejo (PDO) [KAY-zhoo day eh-VOH-rah]

Origin	Portugal (Alentejo)
Milk	Unpasteurized sheep's
Type	SEMIHARD to HARD; MOLDED, UNCOOKED; NATURAL RIND; FARMSTEAD
Appearance	3½- and 6-ounce rounds; rind is pale yellow with a crosshatch pattern on the top and bottom; interior is ivory with a scant scattering of small EYES
Texture	Firm and compact, becoming crumbly as it ages
Flavor	Fruity, creamy, and slightly acidic

A cheese that hails from and is named after Évora, a fortified medieval town about 65 miles east of Lisbon. Though the official PROTECTED DESIGNATION OF ORIGIN (PDO) name is *Queijo de Évora*, this cheese is also called *Évora De L'Alentejo,* after the region, and sometimes simply *Évora*. As with so many Portuguese cheeses, the coagulant used is extract of dried thistle, rather than animal RENNET. Évora can be RIPENED for anywhere from 6 to 12 months and has a FAT CONTENT of 50 percent.

Queijo de Nisa (PDO) [KAY-zhoo day NEE-sah]

Origin	Portugal (Alentejo)
Milk	Unpasteurized sheep's
Type	SEMIHARD to HARD; MOLDED UNCOOKED; NATURAL RIND; FARMSTEAD and ARTISAN
Appearance	12-ounce rounds; rind is golden brown and uneven; interior is ivory colored with plentiful small EYES

Q

Texture	Firm and supple
Flavor	Earthy, buttery, and nutty

This cheese hails from the small village of Nisa in the northern portion of Portugal's Alentejo region. Queijo de Nisa (also simply called *Nisa*) is produced from the milk of Merino sheep, which is COAGULATED with extract of dried thistle. The CURDS are molded, pressed, then the cheese turned out and salted. Queijo de Nisa is aged for a minimum of 45 days and usually longer. Its FAT CONTENT is 45 to 50 percent.

Queijo Picante da Beira Baixa (PDO) [KAY-zhoo pee-KER*N*-ter dah BAY-rer BUY-shah]

Origin	Portugal (Beira Baixa)
Milk	Unpasteurized sheep's and/or goat's
Type	SEMIHARD to HARD; PRESSED UNCOOKED; NATURAL RIND; FARMSTEAD and COOPERATIVE
Appearance	4-pound wheels; rind is tan; interior is straw colored with a scattering of small, irregular EYES
Texture	Firm and compact
Flavor	Strong, goaty, and tangy

One of three cheeses under the PROTECTED DESIGNATION OF ORIGIN (PDO) umbrella of QUEIJOS DA BEIRA BAIXA. It can be made from sheep's milk, goat's milk, or a mixture of the two. Unlike many Portuguese cheeses, Picante da Beira Baixa relies on animal RENNET for COAGULATION, rather than dried cardoon thistle. It's RIPENED for 120 days and has a FAT CONTENT of 45 to 50 percent.

Queijo São Jorge (PDO) [KAY-zhoo saow ZHOOR-zhih]

Origin	Portugal (Azores)
Milk	Unpasteurized cow's
Type	SEMIHARD to HARD; PRESSED UNCOOKED; NATURAL RIND; FARMSTEAD
Appearance	17½- to 26½-pound wheels; rind is hard, dry, dark yellow in color, sometimes with reddish brown mottling; interior is yellow with small, irregular eyes scattered throughout
Texture	Firm yet crumbly
Flavor	Strong, tangy, and slightly spicy and nutty

Made since the 1400s, this popular regional cheese is produced in São Jorge ("Saint George"), one of the Azores archipelago's nine volcanic islands and the home to only 10,000 people. Cheesemakers use animal RENNET to COAGULATE the milk. This cheese, which is also called *São Jorge,* is aged a minimum of 3 months and often for 5 months. It looks similar to GOUDA, tastes more like CHEDDAR, and has a FAT CONTENT of about 50 percent.

Queijos da Beira Baixa (PDO) [KAY-zhoos dah BAY-rer BUY-shah]
Portugal's Beira Baixa region is located between the country's central mountain range and the Spanish border. Three cheeses fall under the PROTECTED DESIGNATION OF ORIGIN (PDO) banner of Queijos da Beira Baixa: QUEIJO AMARELO DA BEIRA BAIXA, QUEIJO DE CASTELO BRANCO, and QUEIJO PICANTE DA BEIRA BAIXA. All DO cheeses from the Beira Baixa region are made with sheep's milk, goat's milk, or a combination of the two. The animals must graze only on natural pastures—no processed fodder is allowed. Cheeses from the Beira Baixa region are rustic, rugged, and full of flavor.

Queijo Serpa (PDO) [KAY-zhoo SERR-pah]

Origin	Portugal (Alentejo)
Milk	Unpasteurized sheep's
Type	SOFT to SEMISOFT; PRESSED UNCOOKED; NATURAL RIND; ARTISAN and FARMSTEAD
Appearance	3- to 4-pound wheels with slightly bulging sides and top; rind is thin, leathery, and tan; interior is ivory colored with a scattering of EYES
Texture	Smooth, creamy, and spoonable when fully ripe
Flavor	Rich and strong, with bitter, piquant, and slightly fruity notes

Hailing from Serpa, near Portugal's southeastern border, this cheese has been made with traditional methods for centuries. The milk comes from Merino sheep and is coagulated with dried thistle extract rather than animal RENNET. The cheese is RIPENED for a minimum of 60 days and has a FAT CONTENT of about 45 percent. A perfectly ripe Queijo Serpa (also simply called *Serpa*) is unctuously soft at room temperature and is typically eaten by cutting off the top of the rind and scooping out the PASTE. Longer-aged versions become firmer and exceedingly pungent.

Queijo Serra da Estrela (PDO) [KAY-zhoo SEHR-rrer dah ish-TRAY-ler (ehs-TRAY-lah)]

Origin	Portugal (Beira)
Milk	Unpasteurized sheep's
Type	SOFT to SEMISOFT; PRESSED UNCOOKED; NATURAL RIND; ARTISAN

Q

Appearance	3- to 4-pound wheels with slightly bulging sides and top; rind is thin, leathery, and tan; interior is ivory colored with occasional EYES
Texture	Creamy, satiny, and spoonable when fully ripe
Flavor	Buttery rich, nutty, herbaceous, salty, and tangy, with a pleasantly bitter undertaste

The word *serra* is Portuguese for "mountain range" and this cheese has been produced for over 800 years in the Beira region's Serra da Estrela Mountains. Serra da Estrela is considered by many to be the ultimate of Portuguese cheeses. It's entirely handmade by artisans whose techniques have been passed down through the ages. Bordaleira sheep provide the rich concentrated milk that's COAGULATED with extract of dried cardoon thistle. The cheese undergoes RIPENING for between 30 and 40 days and has a FAT CONTENT of 45 percent. The traditional way to eat it is to bring it to room temperature, slice off the rind's top, and scoop out the PASTE. Many Portuguese age this cheese until it becomes quite firm, chewy, and pungent. **Mondegueiro**, the baby sister of Serra da Estrela, weighs in at about 1¼ pounds. It's made by the same cheesemaker with identical techniques and with milk from the same sheep.

quesillo [kay-SEE-yoh] *see* QUESO OAXACA

queso [KAY-soh] Spanish for "cheese"; *quesuco* is "small cheese."

queso añejo; queso añejado *see* COTIJA

Queso Azul Asturiano [KAY-soh ah-THOOL ahs-too-RYAH-noh]
see QUESO DE LA PERAL

queso blanco [KAY-soh BLAHN-koh]

Q

Origin	Latin America
Milk	Unpasteurized and pasteurized cow's; although sometimes a mixture of sheep's and goat's milk is used
Type	FRESH, SOFT to HARD; PRESSED UNCOOKED and MOLDED UNCOOKED; usually rindless; ARTISAN, FARMSTEAD, COOPERATIVE, and FACTORY; some SMOKED
Appearance	Various sizes from 8 ounces to 100 pounds or more, usually in squares or blocks but sometimes in cylinders or half-moons; rindless; exterior and interior are white to off-white
Texture	Tender, moist, and crumbly, to soft and elastic, to hard
Flavor	Fresh, mild, milky, slightly salty, and lightly tangy, becoming stronger if ripened

Queso Blanco ("white cheese") is really a family of cheeses that can be found all over Latin America in diverse forms and by various names. Such cheeses were likely introduced by the Spaniards and particularly the cheesemaking monks that settled in the new world. Traditionally these cheeses were made by heating milk and adding an acid like lemon juice or vinegar to cause COAGULATION, but today RENNET is often used. An interesting trait shared by many of these cheeses in this family is that they don't melt completely when heated, but rather soften while holding their basic shape. Some of the fresh queso blanco cheeses are akin to a dry, crumbly COTTAGE CHEESE, and can be made from whole, partially skimmed, or fat-free milk. One prime example of this style is **queso fresco,** which is immensely popular in Latin cuisines. Fresh cheese made from either whole or partly skimmed milk and drained in a basket is called **panela** or **queso de canasta.** Fresh, pressed, uncooked cheese made from whole or partially skimmed milk is known by many names including **queso de prensa** ("pressed cheese"), **queso del pais** ("country cheese"), **queso de la tierra** ("native cheese"), and **queso estera** ("matted cheese"). Most queso blanco cheeses are unaged and eaten within a few days of being produced; these fall into the category of **queso blanco fresco** ("fresh white cheese"). But the queso blanco family also includes cheeses that are briefly RIPENED. Two examples are **queso de bagaces** and **queso de crema**—pressed cheeses that may be aged anywhere from 2 weeks to 2 months. Queso de bagaces is firmly pressed and can become hard enough to grate, while queso de crema is lightly pressed and becomes firm but supple. Some queso blanco cheese undergoes a few days of smoking, which produces a darker color and a smoky flavor. Others have added flavorings such as green chiles. The cheeses in this family are used in myriad dishes such as enchiladas, burritos, and quesadillas, crumbled as a garnish for everything from tacos to salads, and are good for frying (fried cheeses are called **queso para freír**). Naturally the FAT CONTENT of these cheeses varies depending on the type of milk used.

queso Cotija [KAY-soh koh-TEE-hah] *see* COTIJA

queso de bagaces [KAY-soh day bah-GAH-chays] *see* QUESO BLANCO

queso de canasta [KAY-soh day kah-nas-tah] *see* QUESO BLANCO

Queso de Cantabria (DO; PDO) [KAY-soh day kahn-TAH-bree-ah]

Origin	Spain (Cantabria)
Milk	Pasteurized cow's

Q

Type	SEMISOFT; PRESSED COOKED; NATURAL RIND; COOPERATIVE
Appearance	1- to 6-pound wheels or rectangular shape; rind is yellow, soft, and smooth; interior is pale yellow, typically without EYES
Texture	Soft, smooth, and supple
Flavor	Fresh, rich, and meltingly buttery with a pleasant tinge of bitterness

This cheese hails from a region in northern Spain adjacent to the sea known as *el Mar Cantábrico*. Before being awarded its DENOMINACIÓN DE ORIGEN PROTEGIDA (DO), Cantabria was known simply as *Queso de Nata* (cream cheese) *de Cantabria*. The DO regulations for this lightly pressed, cooked cheese require that it be made from the whole milk of Friesian or Santanderian cows and RIPENED for a minimum of 15 days, although some are aged for up to 2 months. Cantabria has a FAT CONTENT of 45 percent.

queso de crema [KAY-soh day kreh-mah] *see* QUESO BLANCO

Queso de Fuerteventura [KAY-soh day FWAYER-tay-bayn-TOO-rah] *see* QUESO MAJORERO

Queso de la Garrotxa [KAY-soh day lah gahr-ROH-chah] *see* GARROTXA

Queso de l'Alt Urgell y la Cerdanya (DO; PDO) [KAY-soh day lahlt oor-KHEL ee lah thayr-DAHN-yah]

Origin	Spain (Alto Urgel, Cerdaña, Lérida, Gerona)
Milk	Pasteurized cow's
Type	SEMISOFT; PRESSED UNCOOKED; WASHED RIND; COOPERATIVE

Appearance	1- to 2-pound wheels; rind is thin and pale golden; interior is ivory colored with a smattering of tiny EYES
Texture	Creamy and supple
Flavor	Mild and slightly herbal

Although commonly known as *l'Alt Urgell*, the full DENOMINACIÓN DE ORIGEN PROTEGIDA (DO) name for this cheese is *Queso de l'Alt Urgell y la Cerdanya*. Both designations have been shortened even further to *Urgelia* by the cooperative that makes the cheese with the milk from two hundred local farms. This is a specialty of several Catalan Pyrénées provinces. It's BRINE washed frequently during the 45-day RIPENING period and has a minimum FAT CONTENT of 45 percent.

Queso de la Palma [KAY-soh day lah PAHL-mah] *see* QUESO PALMERO

Queso de la Peral [KAY-soh day lah pay-RAHL]

Origin	Spain (Asturias)
Milk	Primarily pasteurized cow's, though some sheep's milk may be added
Type	SEMIHARD; MOLDED UNCOOKED; BLUE-VEINED; NATURAL RIND; FARMSTEAD
Appearance	$2\frac{1}{4}$- to $6\frac{1}{2}$-pound wheels, wrapped in foil; rind is pinkish gold to light reddish brown; interior is ivory to pale yellow with grayish blue-green veining and a scattering of cracks and EYES
Texture	Smooth and creamy yet slightly granular
Flavor	Rich, creamy, meaty, savory, and complex

Q

Queso de la Peral, or simply *La Peral*, is produced in the Principality of Asturias, a mountainous region situated along the Bay of Biscay in northern Spain. This cheese was first made in the early 1920s and is still produced by members of the León family. Queso de la Peral is milder and not as piquant as some of Spain's other blue cheeses. The CURD is inoculated with PENICILLIUM, and the cheeses are pierced with needles so oxygen can reach the interior to feed the bacteria that produces the veining. Queso de la Peral is RIPENED in natural caves for 2 to 5 months. This cheese, also known as *Queso Azul Asturiano*, has a FAT CONTENT of around 45 percent.

Queso de la Serena (DO; PDO) [KAY-soh day lah she-RAY-nah]

Origin	Spain (Extremadura)
Milk	Pasteurized and unpasteurized sheep's
Type	SOFT to SEMISOFT; PRESSED UNCOOKED; NATURAL RIND; FARMSTEAD, ARTISAN, and FACTORY
Appearance	2- to 4-pound flattened wheels with slightly bulging sides and uneven top; rind can range from yellow and waxy to dry, slightly wrinkled, and tannish orange, depending on age; interior is ivory colored (turning pale golden with age) with scattered EYES
Texture	Creamy, supple, and spoonable when fully ripe
Flavor	Buttery rich, nutty, and tangy, with a pleasantly bitter note

This cheese hails from the environs of La Serena, an area of almost 750,000 acres located in the northeastern portion of Badajoz province in southwestern Spain's Extremadura region. A cousin of TORTA DEL CASAR, Queso de La Serena (also simply called *Serena*) is one of Spain's most valued and expensive cheeses. DENOMINACIÓN DE ORIGEN PROTEGIDA (DO) parameters state that it be made only from the whole milk of the rugged Merino sheep, a rustic breed that produces exceedingly rich milk in relatively small amounts. The milk is COAGULATED with an extract of a dried wild thistle (*Yerbacuajo*), which gives the cheese a subtle hint of bitterness. The cheese is formed in molds that are either esparto-grass baskets or plastic lookalikes. Serena is RIPENED and turned daily for a minimum of 2 months. It has a FAT CONTENT of 45 to 50 percent. Although chilled Serena can be sliced when young, it becomes spoonable when fully ripe and at room temperature. The traditional way to eat it then is to slice off the rind's top and scoop out the PASTE.

queso de la tierra [KAY-soh day lah tee-EHR-rah] *see* QUESO BLANCO

Queso de los Ibores *see* QUESO IBORES

queso del pais [KAY-soh del pah-EESS] *see* JACK; QUESO BLANCO

Queso del Valle del Roncal [KAY-soh day BAH-lay day ROHNG-kahl] *see* RONCAL

Queso de Mano [KAY-soh day MAH-noh]

Origin	United States (Colorado)
Milk	Unpasteurized goat's
Type	SEMIHARD; PRESSED UNCOOKED; WASHED RIND; ARTISAN
Appearance	5-pound wheel; rind is off-white to beige with pale gray mold; interior is white
Texture	Firm, buttery smooth, and velvety

Q

| Flavor | Complex, tangy, and slightly herbal with notable nuttiness |

Queso de Mano, which means "hand cheese," is entirely hand-made at **Haystack Mountain Goat Dairy** in Niwot, Colorado, not far from Boulder. This concern has a second facility in Longmont, Colorado, and is working with the Pontotoc Area Vocational Technical School in Ada, Oklahoma, to build an on-campus cheesemaking facility for small-batch artisanal goat's milk cheeses. The texture of Queso de Mano resembles that of a Spanish GARROTXA, though the flavors are slightly different. This cheese is RIPENED for at least 4 months and has a FAT CONTENT of 45 to 50 percent. Queso de Mano has been an award winner at the American Cheese Society competition. Other Haystack Mountain Goat Dairy award winners include Haystack Feta (*see* FETA) and HAYSTACK PEAK.

Queso de Murcia; Queso de Murcia al Vino (DO; PDO) [KAY-soh day moor-SEE-ah (ahl VEE-noh)]

Origin	Spain (Murcia)
Milk	Pasteurized goat's
Type	SEMIHARD; PRESSED UNCOOKED; NATURAL RIND; FARMSTEAD
Appearance	2- to 4-pound disks; rind is thin, buff-colored (except for the *al Vino* style, which is dark magenta), sometimes smooth, other times with surface striations where the cheese rested on wooden platforms; interior is chalk white with numerous small EYES
Texture	Dense, creamy, and elastic
Flavor	Mild, herbal, slightly salty, with a slight acidic edge

This popular Spanish cheese has two DENOMINACIÓN DE ORI-GEN PROTEGIDAS (DOP)—*Queso de Murcia fresco* (FRESH CHEESE) and *Queso de Murcia curado* ("cured" or RIPENED). The DOP regulations state that the cheese must be made with milk from Murcian goats. The RIPENING process takes from 30 to 45 days, depending on the size of the cheese. The **Queso de Murcia al Vino** is made by bathing the cheese in the local red wine, which gives it a fruity, spicy nuance. These cheeses have a minimum FAT CONTENT of 45 percent.

Q

Queso de Perilla [KAY-soh day pay-REE-yah] *see* QUESO TETILLA

queso de prensa [KAY-soh day PREN-sah] *see* QUESO BLANCO

queso de San Simón de la Cuesta *see* SAN SIMÓN

Queso de Teta; Queso de Teta de Vaca [KAY-soh day TAY-tah (day BAH-kah] *see* QUESO TETILLA

Queso de Ulla; Queso de Ulloa [KAY-soh day OOH-lyah; OOL-lyoh-ah] *see* ARZÚA ULLOA

Queso de Valdeón (PGI) [KAY-soh day vahl-day-OHN]

Origin	Spain (Picos de Europa)
Milk	Primarily cow's (raw or pasteurized), though some goat's milk may be added
Type	SEMIHARD; MOLDED UNCOOKED; BLUE-VEINED; NATURAL RIND; FARMSTEAD
Appearance	4½- to 6½-pound wheels, some wrapped in sycamore leaves; rind is thin and light gray in color; interior is ivory colored with prevalent grayish blue-green veining and plentiful EYES

Q

Texture	Smooth and creamy yet a little gritty on the palate
Flavor	Rich, earthy, salty, sharp, and complex

Queso de Valdeón is produced in northwestern Spain's León region on the southern slopes of the Picos de Europa Mountains. This PROTECTED GEOGRAPHICAL INDICATION (PGI) cheese is made primarily in local dairies, particularly in the Posada de Valdeón area. Though slightly milder and creamier than some of Spain's other blue cheeses, it's still a powerhouse. The CURD is inoculated with *PENICILLIUM,* and the cheeses are pierced with needles so oxygen can reach the interior to feed the bacteria that produce the veining. RIPENING in natural caves ranges from a minimum of 1½ months for pasteurized versions to 2 to 3 months for raw-milk cheeses. This cheese, also known as *Picos de Europa* and *Valdeón,* has a FAT CONTENT of around 45 percent.

Queso de Varé [KAY-soh day vah-RAY] *see* VARÉ

queso enchilado [KAY-soh en-chee-LAH-doh] *see* ENCHILADO

queso estera [KAY-soh eh-STEH-rah] *see* QUESO BLANCO

queso fresco [KAY-soh FRES-koh] *see* QUESO BLANCO

queso fundido [KAY-soh fuhn-DEE-doh] A south-of-the-border rendition of FONDUE, *queso fundido* is Spanish for "melted cheese." CHIHUAHUA or MONTEREY JACK is the cheese most often used for this warm concoction, which may or may not include a variety of additions from chopped tomato, onion, garlic, and jalapeño to cooked ground sausage (usually chorizo) or beef. Queso fundido is typically served with tortilla chips for dipping. *See also* FONDUE; FONDUTA.

Queso Gallego [KAY-soh gahl-LYAY-goh] *see* ARZÚA ULLOA

Queso Gallego de Teta [KAY-soh gahl-LYAY-goh day TAY-tah] *see* QUESO TETILLA

Q

Queso Gamonedo (DO) [KAY-soh gah-moh-NAY-doh]

Origin	Spain (Asturias)
Milk	Traditionally a mix of unpasteurized cow's, sheep's, and goat's; now primarily cow's
Type	SEMIHARD; PRESSED UNCOOKED; BLUE-VEINED; NATURAL RIND; ARTISAN and FARMSTEAD
Appearance	5- to 11-pound wheels; rind is rough, dry, and grayish buff-colored with dark brown and orangey mottling; interior is pale golden with faint blue-green veins and a scattering of small EYES
Texture	Compact and buttery yet crumbly
Flavor	Earthy, piquant, complex, and faintly smoky

This cheese is produced in the areas of Onis and Cangas de Onis, towns in northwestern Spain's Asturias region, south of the Bay of Biscay. Traditionally Queso Gamonedo (also called Gamonedo, *Queso Gamoneú*) is made with a blend of cow's, sheep's, and goat's milk, though most modern-day production typically uses 100 percent cow's milk. The molded CURDS undergo a gentle PRESSING, after which the cheese is smoked lightly with applewood for 10 to 20 days. RIPENING takes place in caves for a minimum of 2 months and typically 4 to 5 months. Unlike other blue-veined cheeses, Queso Gamonedo blues naturally, without the injection of *PENICILLIUM* mold cultures. The FAT CONTENT of this cheese is about 45 percent.

Queso Gamoneú [KAY-soh gah-moh-NAY-yoo] *see* QUESO
GAMONEDO

Q

Queso Ibérico [KAY-soh ee-BHAY-ree-koh] *see* IBÉRICO

Queso Ibores (DO) [KAY-soh ee-BOHR-ays]

Origin	Spain (Extremadura/Cáceres)
Milk	Unpasteurized or pasteurized goat's
Type	SEMISOFT to SEMIHARD; MOLDED UNCOOKED; NATURAL RIND; FARMSTEAD and COOPERATIVE
Appearance	1- to 2-pound wheels; rind is hard and can range in color from dark yellow to deep orange (the latter paprika rubbed); interior is off-white with a scattering of tiny EYES
Texture	Smooth and creamy
Flavor	Rich, aromatic, and pleasantly GOATY

Made from the milk of Verata and Retinta goats that graze on
the abundant pastures of the Extremadura region of southwestern Spain, Ibores is a simple full-flavored cheese that re-
flects its native soil. It's RIPENED for a minimum of 2 months,
during which time the rind is typically rubbed with olive oil
or smoked paprika, the latter producing a deep orangish red
color and spicy finish. When aged longer, Ibores develops a
sharper flavor and firmer texture. Its FAT CONTENT ranges from
45 to 50 percent. This cheese is also called *Queso de los Ibores*.

Queso Majorero (DO) [KAY-soh mah-hoh-REH-roh]

Origin	Spain (Fuerteventura, Canary Islands)
Milk	Unpasteurized and pasteurized goat's, some sheep's (up to 15 percent sheep's)

Type	SEMIHARD; PRESSED UNCOOKED; NATURAL RIND; FARMSTEAD and FACTORY
Appearance	6½- to 15-pound flattened wheels; rind is thin, patterned, and beige to orange to pale brown, depending on age and processing; interior is off-white to pale butter-colored with a few EYES
Texture	Compact and creamy smooth
Flavor	Toasty, slightly sweet, and spicy, with a lively acidity and slight tang

Q

One of Spain's finest goat cheeses, Queso Majorero is produced on Fuerteventura, a volcanic island in the southeastern portion of the Canary Island archipelago, just 60 miles off the coast of Africa. The word *Majorero* comes from ancient names for the island and its inhabitants—*Maxorata, Majorata,* and *Mahorata,* all stemming from the goatskin sandal (known as *majos* or *mahos*) worn by shepherds. Farmstead Majoreros are made with raw milk, factory-produced renditions from pasteurized milk. DENOMINACIÓN DE ORIGEN PROTEGIDA (DO) regulations state that the milk used for this cheese must come from Majorero goats and that up to 15 percent of Canarian sheep's milk may also be added. The region's goat shepherds have formed the Gran Tarajal cooperative to improve and increase Majorero production. In general, CURD is cut (into smaller pieces if intended for aging) and placed in braided palm-leaf molds to drain before undergoing light PRESSING. It's these molds (or plastic or stainless-steel replicas) that give the rind its distinctive diamond pattern. Majorero is then salted—either by brining (*see* SALTING) for factory-made cheeses or by dry-salting for ARTISANAL cheeses. The cheeses are RIPENED at mild temperatures for various periods: young (*joven*), 8 to 20 days; semiaged (*semicurado*), 20 to 60 days; and aged (*curado*), over 60 days. During the ripening period, cheese may be rubbed with oil,

Q

paprika (which gives the rind an orangey color), or roasted corn-meal (*gofio*). Majorero has a FAT CONTENT of 45 to 50 percent. It's also called *Queso de Fuerteventura*.

Queso Manchego (DO; PDO) [KAY-soh mahn-CHAY-goh]

Origin	Spain (La Mancha)
Milk	Unpasteurized or pasteurized sheep's
Type	SEMIHARD to HARD; PRESSED UNCOOKED; NATURAL RIND; FARMSTEAD and FACTORY
Appearance	4- to 8-pound wheels; rind is thin and has a tight crosshatch pattern and can range in color from pale yellow to brown to charcoal gray; interior is compact with a small scattering of EYES, and color ranges from ivory to pale yellow, depending on age
Texture	Firm and compact; aged versions can become crumbly
Flavor	Buttery yet zesty and piquant with a sheep's milk aftertaste; aged versions have a sharper, nuttier nuance

Known as the cheese of Don Quixote because it was mentioned by Cervantes in his *Don Quixote of La Mancha*, Queso Manchego (typically called simply *Manchego*) is undoubtedly Spain's most well-known sheep's milk cheese. It comes from the La Mancha region, a vast 13,500-square-mile plateau almost 2,000 feet high. Official DENOMINACIÓN DE ORIGEN PROTEGIDA regulations require that this cheese be made with whole milk from the region's hardy Manchega sheep. Today Manchego is produced with both raw milk (by farmstead production) and pasteurized milk (by factories). Traditionally, Manchego was formed in plaited esparto grass molds, which imparted their distinctive

Q

crosshatch pattern. For modern production, however, specially designed plastic molds are used for the same effect. Manchego is RIPENED for a minimum of 60 days (some are aged for 3 years or more). Cheese aged the minimum 2 months is called *fresco,* that cured for 3 to 13 weeks is called *Manchego curado,* and it's considered *viejo* ("old") with 9 to 12 months of aging. There's also *Manchego en aceite* ("in oil"), which has been ripened for 1 year, during which time it's bathed in olive oil. Manchego has a FAT CONTENT of about 50 percent. Sheep's milk cheeses with the same crosshatch pattern made outside La Mancha are referred to as "Manchego-style" cheeses.

queso Oaxaca [KAY-soh wuh-HAH-kah]

Origin	Mexico (Oaxaca)
Milk	Pasteurized cow's
Type	SOFT to SEMISOFT; PASTA FILATA; ARTISAN and FACTORY
Appearance	various weights, typically a 1-pound ball; rindless exterior is glossy and white; interior is pure white
Texture	Elastic and soft
Flavor	Mild and slightly tangy, with a fresh milky character

Also known as *quesillo* and *Mexican mozzarella*, this cheese originated in Oaxaca, a city of southeast Mexico. It's made by the pasta filata process, which means the CURD is immersed in hot whey or water and continually kneaded and stretched until it reaches a pliable consistency. For queso Oaxaca, the curd is typically hand-stretched into long, thin, wide ribbons that are wound into a yarnlike ball. Sometimes the cheese is simply formed into a solid ball, which can be separated into strands. When melted, queso Oaxaca strings like MOZZARELLA and is popular for quesa-dillas and queso fundido, the Mexican version of FONDUE. Paula Lambert's **Mozzarella Company** makes an excellent queso Oaxaca that's an American Cheese Society award winner.

Queso Palmero (DO; PDO) [KAY-soh pahl-MEH-roh]

Origin	Spain (Isle of La Palma, Canary Islands)
Milk	Unpasteurized goat's
Type	SEMISOFT to SEMIHARD; PRESSED UNCOOKED; NATURAL RIND; ARTISAN and FARMSTEAD
Appearance	5- to 30-pound wheels; rind is thin and pale yellow, with some splotching of white mold in aged cheeses—smoked versions will have brown bands across the top; interior is off-white (shading to ivory with age) with occasional EYES
Texture	Firm, smooth, and elastic
Flavor	Fresh, fruity, and grassy; smoked versions reflect the wood used

The Canary Islands have been a part of Spain since 1479; how-ever, Queso Palmero dates back long before that. This cheese is made in the fourteen municipalities of La Palma Island, which is why it's also called *Queso de la Palma*. Statistics tell us that more cheese is consumed in the Canary Islands than in any other Spanish region. The DENOMINACIÓN DE ORIGEN PROTE-GIDA (DO) regulations require that Queso Palmero be made only from the milk of the island's hardy Palm goats. The RIPEN-ING period for this cheese can range from 8 to 20 days for "fresh" cheese (which does not have DO certification) to 21 to 60 days for "semicured" cheese and over 60 days for "cured" cheese. Artisan cheeses weigh less than 17½ pounds and have a green label; farmstead cheeses can be much larger and have a red label. Some Queso Palmeros are lightly smoked with either dried almond shells, prickly pear, or canary pine. This cheese typically has a FAT CONTENT of 45 percent.

queso para freír [KAY-soh PAH-rah fray-EER] *see* QUESO BLANCO

Queso Tetilla (DO; PDO) [KAY-soh tay-TEE-yah]

Origin	Spain (Galicia)
Milk	Pasteurized and unpasteurized cow's
Type	SEMISOFT; PRESSED UNCOOKED; NATURAL RIND; FARMSTEAD and FACTORY
Appearance	2- to 3-pound pear shape; rind is almost nonexistent and golden yellow in color; interior is an ivory-yellow color with abundant, irregular EYES
Texture	Supple, soft, and smooth; aged versions become firmer
Flavor	Lightly acidic, mild, and buttery with a fresh grassy note; aging intensifies the flavor

A notable cheese that hails from northwestern Spain's Galicia region, south of the Bay of Biscay. The word *tetilla* means "nipple," in reference to the classic shape of this cheese, which resembles a woman's breast. Americans will easily identify the shape as being akin to that of a Hershey's Kiss. The milk for Queso Tetilla comes from Friesian and Rubia Gallega cattle and is typically from two milkings. With the artisanal method the milk is salted, whereas factory versions dry-salt or brine (*see* SALTING) the formed cheese. Queso Tetilla is aged for a minimum of 1 week. Some are immersed briefly in scalding water, which seals the rind and gives it a waxy texture. This cheese is also called *Queso de Perilla, Queso de Teta, Queso de Teta de Vaca, Queso Gallego de Teta, Tetilla,* and *Tetilla de Vaca.* It has a FAT CONTENT of 40 to 45 percent.

Queso Zamorano (DO; PDO) [KAY-soh thah- moh-RAH-noh; sah-moh-RAH-noh]

Origin	Spain (Castille-León/Zamora)
Milk	Unpasteurized sheep's
Type	HARD; PRESSED UNCOOKED; NATURAL RIND; ARTISAN
Appearance	2- to 9-pound wheels; rind is hard, dark yellow to dark grayish brown, somewhat oily, and has a crosshatch pattern; interior is golden yellow with a scattering of tiny EYES
Texture	Dense and firm yet creamy on the palate
Flavor	Distinctively nutty, aromatic, and complex

Northwestern Spain's province of Zamora has been famed for its artisanal cheesemakers for centuries, and Queso Zamorano is an imposing example of their craft. The quality and character of this cheese can be compared with some of the world's finest. Zamora province is Spain's major producer of prime sheep's milk, and the milk for Queso Zamorano comes from the local Castilian and Churra breeds, both of which are known for their high-quality, high-fat milk. The official DENOMINACIÓN DE ORIGEN PROTEGIDA (DO) name of this cheese is *Queso Zamorano,* but it's commonly known simply as *Zamorano.* The CURDS are molded and pressed in esparto-grass molds, which give this cheese its distinctive crosshatch pattern. Zamorano is RIPENED for 3 weeks at moderate temperatures, then in cold, humid caves for a minimum of 100 days and up to a year. It has a FAT CONTENT of 53 percent.

quesuco *see* QUESO

Quesucos de Liébana (DO; PDO) [kay-SOO-kohs day lyay-BAH-nah]

Origin	Spain (Cantabria)
Milk	Pasteurized cow's (primarily), although a mix of cow's, goat's, and sheep's may be used
Type	SEMIHARD; MOLDED UNCOOKED; NATURAL RIND; FARMSTEAD
Appearance	1- to 2-pound irregular wheels; rind is rough and uneven—color ranges from ivory to pale gray to light brown (the latter in smoked versions); interior ranges from beige to pale yellow with a plentitude of small EYES
Texture	Smooth and firm
Flavor	Mild, buttery, with a slight tang; the smoked style is more pungent

Quesucos is Spanish for "small cheeses," and such cheeses abound in the area, with village households each producing their own. Most of the area's production of Quesucos de Liébana is made with cow's milk, but the herds in this region are often an amalgam of cows, goats, and sheep, which is why cheeses made under this DENOMINACIÓN DE ORIGEN PROTEGIDA (DO) have the distinction of being able to use any of these three milks or a mixture of them. According to DO standards, the cheeses must undergo a minimum RIPENING period of 2 weeks. The FAT CONTENT of Quesucos de Liébana ranges from 45 to 50 percent. The smoked version is called *Ahumado de Áliva,* or simply *Áliva.*

R

Raclette (AOC); raclette [rah-KLEHT, ra-KLEHT]

Origin	Switzerland (Valais)
Milk	Unpasteurized and pasteurized cow's
Type	SEMIHARD; PRESSED COOKED; NATURAL RIND; ARTISAN, FARMSTEAD, COOPERATIVE, FACTORY, and some MOUNTAIN
Appearance	13- to 24-pound wheels and squares; rind is light reddish brown to dark reddish brown; interior is ivory to pale yellow with a light scattering of EYES
Texture	Very dense and compact yet supple
Flavor	Complex flavor blend of creamy, fruity, nutty, earthy, and mushroomy

> Majestic Roqueforts looking down with princely contempt upon the others, through the glass of their crystal covers.
> —Émile Zola

1. Dating back to the Middle Ages with its origins in Switzerland's Valais canton, Raclette is similar to GRUYÈRE but much smaller in size. Until the nineteenth century, it wasn't widely known outside the canton, where it was often associated with the name of the village that produced it (such as Bagnes, Conches, Gomser, or Orsières). It was also sometimes called *Valais*, or simply *Fromage à Raclette*. This cheese is now made throughout Switzerland and in other countries, including Australia, Canada, France, and the United States. In 2003, Switzerland's Department of Agriculture approved APPELLATION D'ORIGINE CONTRÔLÉE (AOC) status for **Ra-clette du Valais,** a cheese that can be documented back to the mid-1500s. This accreditation was applauded in the Valais canton but strongly criticized by Swiss outside that region, who produce more Raclette than Valais-area cheesemakers. The French, who've made Raclette for centuries, are also vehemently objecting to the AOC. Appeals have been launched, but at this writing the issue has not been resolved. Traditional Raclette du Valais is produced in small batches by farmstead or artisan methods with raw milk. It's ripened for a minimum of 2 months but typically for 4 to 6 months. (In many other areas Raclette is factory produced with pasteurized milk and has minimal aging.) The minimum FAT CONTENT of Raclette is 45 percent. **2.** The word *raclette* also refers to a dish made with a chunk of the same cheese, which is heated, scraped off as it melts, and served with boiled potatoes, dark bread, and cornichons. The word *raclette* comes from the French *racler,* which means "to scrape."

Ragusano (DOC; PDO) [rah-goo-SAH-noh]

Origin	Italy (Sicily)
Milk	Unpasteurized cow's
Type	SEMIHARD tO HARD; PRESSED UNCOOKED; NATURAL RIND; PASTA FILATA; ARTISAN, FARMSTEAD, and COOPERATIVE; some SMOKED
Appearance	26- to 35-pound 16- to 18-inch brick-shaped loafs; rind is thin and firm, varying in color from pale yellow to golden brown, depending on age; interior is pale yellow to light golden
Texture	Firm and somewhat elastic, becoming stiff and granular as it ages
Flavor	Sweet and delicate when young, turning savory and pungent in aged versions

R

Ragusano has played an important role in Sicily's cheesemaking history. It's been around at least since the fourteenth century and was being traded in the Mediterranean region in the sixteenth century. It's a CACIOCAVALLO-style cheese but has an uncharacteristically large brick shape compared to the mostly gourdlike shapes of regular Caciocavallo. In fact this cheese is sometimes called *Caciocavallo Ragusano* or *Ragusano Caciocavallo*. The unappended *Ragusano* is the name under which this cheese was granted its DENOMINAZIONE DI ORIGINE CONTROLLATA (DOC) status. The approved production area is limited to parts of the Ragusa and Siracusa provinces on Sicily's southeastern end. Ragusano is made from whole milk taken only from Modicana cows. This is a PASTA FILATA cheese that undergoes brining (*see* SALTING) before being aged for 4 to 6 months for younger cheeses and 1 year or more for a GRATING CHEESE. Some Ragusanos are regularly rubbed with olive oil during their aging cycle. The word *affumicato* on the label tells you the cheese is smoked. The fat content of Ragusano is 26 to 28 percent.

rancid; rancidity *see* Glossary of Cheese Descriptors, page 502

rarebit *see* WELSH RAREBIT

Raschera (DOC; PDO) [rah-SKAY-rah]

Origin	Italy (Piedmont)
Milk	Unpasteurized or pasteurized cow's (may have sheep's or goat's added)
Type	SEMISOFT; PRESSED UNCOOKED; NATURAL RIND; FARMSTEAD and COOPERATIVE
Appearance	Either small wheels weighing 11 to 18 pounds or irregular squares weighing 15 to 22 pounds;

	rind is thin and reddish with tinges of yellow and gray; interior is white to grayish yellow with a scattering of small, uneven EYES
Texture	Dense and elastic
Flavor	Mild, delicate, and slightly sweet when young, growing stronger, more pungent, and savory with age

The name of this cheese comes from Lake Raschera, which lies at the base of Mount Mongioie in southern Piedmont's Cuneo province. According to DENOMINAZIONE DI ORIGINE CONTROLLATA (DOC) regulations, regular Raschera may be produced anywhere in the province, whereas **Raschera d'Alpeggio** may be produced and aged only in a small number of villages at altitudes of over 3,000 feet where cows graze in the alpine pastures. Raschera from the lower elevations sports a green label, while that of d'Alpeggio is yellow. These cheeses are made from partially skimmed cow's milk, though small amounts of goat's or sheep's milk may be added. The cheeses come in both round wheels and irregular squares. Squares are more traditional and more widely found, a holdover from when they were stacked on the backs of donkeys to be hauled down mountainsides. Both shapes of this cheese are made similarly, except the square ones are pressed longer and tend to have more flavor. Raschera is aged for a minimum of 1 month and sometimes for as long as 5 or 6 months. It has a minimum FAT CONTENT of 32 percent.

Rauchkäse [RAUK-ki-zer (-kah-zeh)] German for "smoked cheese." *See also* BRUDER BASIL.

raw milk Synomym for unpasteurized milk, referring to milk that hasn't undergone PASTEURIZATION. *See also* MILK.

R

raw-milk cheeses Those made from milk that hasn't been pasteurized (*see* PASTEURIZATION), also called *unpasteurized-milk cheeses*. *See also* MILK.

rbGH; rbST The naturally occurring protein hormone bovine somatotropin (**bST**) is secreted by the pituitary glands of cattle (as well as human beings, dogs, etc.) and influences the metabolism of proteins, carbohydrates, and lipids, which is why it's referred to as a "growth hormone." Science has discovered a way to genetically engineer this hormone for injection into cattle for an end result that increases milk production by anywhere from 10 to 40 percent. The full clinical name of this artificial hormone is *recombinant bovine growth hormone* (also called *recombinant bovine somatotropin*), though the acronyms *rbGH* and *rbST* are commonly used. Although rbGH is banned in Canada, it is used in the United States. The European Union allows member countries to use it or not. This controversial synthetic hormone can produce health problems in cows and, the presumption being, in humans who consume milk products from injected cattle. To date, there are no long-term studies to prove substantively whether or not rbGH milk is harmful to people. That said, health advocates are leading the way to have this artificial hormone banned in the United States. In the meantime, those who are concerned about health factors should look for milk products labeled *rbGH-free* or *rbST-free*.

Reade's Isle of Mull Cheddar *see* CHEDDAR

Reblochon; Reblochon de Savoie (AOC; PDO) [reuh-bluh-SHOH*N*; deuh SAH-vwah]

Origin	France (Rhône-Alpes)
Milk	Unpasteurized cow's

Type	SEMISOFT; PRESSED UNCOOKED; WASHED RIND; FARMSTEAD, COOPERATIVE, and FACTORY
Appearance	Flat 8½-ounce to 1¼-pound wheels; rind is thin and beige to reddish orange with a velvety white mold; interior is ivory with a small scattering of EYES
Texture	Smooth, creamy, and supple, becoming oozy as it ripens
Flavor	Complex, rich, and savory array of sweet, beefy, bacony, and nutty flavors

The derivation of Reblochon's name has a couple of explanations. One is that it comes from the word *reblocher*, which means "to pinch a cow's udder again" or "to milk again." The other is that the word is based on *reblessa*, local dialect for "to steal" or "to engage in thievery." Both renditions point to the late Middle Ages, when farmers paid rent and/or taxes in the form of milk. When the tax collector or landlord arrived, the farmer would pretend to milk the cows until they were dry and pay up. Later in the day or evening, after there was no sign of any officials, the farmer would remilk the purportedly dry cows. This second milking had a higher butterfat content, which produced rich, creamy cheeses. The milk used for Reblochon traditionally comes from the Abondance, Montbéliard, and Tarentaise cattle breeds. This washed-rind cheese is made with uncooked, slightly pressed CURD and RIPENED for a minimum of 2 weeks but often for 7 to 8 weeks. The minimum FAT CONTENT for Reblochon is 45 percent. Farmstead versions have green labels; cooperative and factory cheeses are labeled in red. Because Reblochon is made with unpasteurized milk and most are ripened for less than 60 days, they cannot be imported into the United States at this writing (*see* UNPASTEURIZED MILK/IMPORTED CHEESE DILEMMA). Even if the cheeses are ripened for more than

R

2 months, Reblochon is categorized as a "soft" cheese, forbidden by the Food and Drug Administration unless made with pasteurized milk. Some producers are making a firmer non-AOC version of Reblochon and labeling it **Fromage de Savoie,** but it can't compare to the soft, oozy original.

recombinant bovine somatotropin [ree-KOM-buh-nuhnt BOH-vine soh-mat-uh-TROH-pin] *see* RBGH

red bacteria *see BREVIBACTERIUM LINENS*

Red Hawk

Origin	United States (California)
Milk	Pasteurized cow's
Type	SEMISOFT; TRIPLE-CREAM; WASHED RIND; ARTISAN
Appearance	12-ounce rounds; rind is reddish orange; interior is a pale straw color
Texture	Soft, supple, creamy, and sticky
Flavor	Pungent, beefy, musky, and complex

Produced by the renowned **Cowgirl Creamery** in Pt. Reyes, California, Red Hawk is a triple-cream cheese that vies for the same kind of attention given to France's ÉPOISSES DE BOURGOGNE. It took the "Best in Show" title at an American Cheese Society competition. The organic milk used to produce Red Hawk comes from the Straus Family Dairy and is a mix of milk from both Holstein and Jersey cows. This BRINE-washed cheese is aged for 6 weeks, at which time the rind takes on a beautiful sunset orange cast. The FAT CONTENT of Red Hawk is about 75 percent. Cowgirl Creamery produces several other notable aged cheeses, including MT. TAM, ST. PAT, and Pierce Pt. Its fresh cheeses include a FROMAGE BLANC and a clabbered COTTAGE CHEESE (which is dressed with clabbered cream and won a blue ribbon at the 2005 American Cheese Society competition).

Red Leicester [LESS-ter] *see* LEICESTER

redressing In cheese parlance, this term refers to changing the CHEESECLOTH or MUSLIN on a cheese during DRAINING or PRESSING. Redressing prevents the cloth from sticking to the cheese. *See also* BANDAGING.

red smear; red-smear cheese *see* WASHED RIND

Redwood Hill Farm *see* CAMILLIA

Reggianito; Reggianito Argentino [reh-jee-ah-NEE-toh ahr-jen-TEE-noh] *see* PARMESAN

religieuse, la [lah reuh-lee-ZHEUHZ] *see* FONDUE (AU FROMAGE)

Rembrandt [REM-brant] *see* GOUDA

rennet; renneting [REHN-it] The cheesemaking step where rennet is added to milk to stimulate COAGULATION is called *renneting*. The type of rennet used plays an intrinsic role in the cheese's flavor. For centuries cheesemakers have used **animal rennet,** which is comprised primarily of the enzyme rennin (also called *chymosin* and *rennet*) and obtained from the gastric juice found in the fourth stomach (*abomasum*) of young ruminants. Traditionally, the rennet comes from the same animal family that produces the milk from which the cheese will be made— from a calf for cow's milk cheese, a kid for goat's milk cheese, and so on. The animal-rennet market, however, often

R

fluctuates widely in price. Add that to the fact that the use of animal products is a problem for Jews (*see* KOSHER CHEESES) and vegetarians—the latter a burgeoning consumer market. This combination of factors is why, although most European cheeses are still made from animal rennet, the majority of cheesemakers in some countries (including the United States, Britain, and New Zealand) are now using concentrated **vegetable-based "rennets."** These vegetarian versions are organically extracted from a variety of plants including thistles, nettles, fig leaves, and safflowers and are almost as powerful as their animal-derived counterparts. There are also **bioengineered rennets,** made by introducing the animal's rennin-encoding DNA into a yeast or bacterial microorganism, which can then be cultured to create rennin. Alternatively, biosynthesis can be used to do the same thing without the use of animal cells. Last, there are coagulants made from **microbial enzymes,** which are relatively inexpensive, act like rennet, and are made from the fermentation of fungi or bacteria. *See also* VEGETARIAN CHEESES.

rennin *see* RENNET

rheology [ree-AHL-uh-jee] Cheeses are sometimes classified according to rheology, the study of a matter's deformation and flow. In the cheese world this relates to the consistency of a cheese, which can range from soft to hard.

rich *see* Glossary of Cheese Descriptors, page 502

ricotta [rih-KAHT-tuh; ree-KOH-tah]

Origin	Italy (thoughout)
Milk	Unpasteurized or pasteurized cow's and/or sheep's and/or goat's; and sometimes water buffalo's

R

Type	SOFT (FRESH versions) to SEMISOFT to HARD, GRANA STYLE; fresh are rindless whereas SMOKED and RIPENED versions can have thin NATURAL RINDS; ARTISAN, FARMSTEAD, and FACTORY
Appearance	There are a variety of shapes, packaging, and sizes, including squares or cylinders in paper or plastic wrap and ricotta in round plastic containers, some weighing as little as 7 ounces, others as much as 7 pounds; for fresh versions the exterior and interior are milky white; for smoked examples the exterior ranges from grayish white to reddish gold to brown and interiors white to brownish white; for baked types the exterior is dark brown and the interior is gold-brown
Texture	Fresh ricotta is moist to semimoist, loose, and slightly granular; other versions range from compact and malleable to very dense, some with a scattering of eyes
Flavor	Fresh versions are delicate, sweet, and nutty; smoked ricottas taste of whatever wood or herb was used; baked examples also take on a slightly smoky tinge; long-aged ricottas can be quite pungent

There are several theories about ricotta's origins, one dating back to the ancient Romans, another crediting early Sicilians. One premise suggests that ricotta came about to use the prodigious amounts of WHEY produced by Italy's cheesemaking industry—a dilemma causing environmental problems. There are numerous styles of ricotta, all distinctly different. The most common version is made with whey that, when reheated (*ricotta,* from the Latin *re-cocta,* means "recooked") to about 185°F, separates, causing tiny clumps of protein particles to rise to the surface. The solids are

R

skimmed off, strained, and placed in perforated molds or baskets to drain further. The end result is a creamy, white, firm but moist ready-to-eat mound of "cheese." Of course, technically ricotta isn't a cheese at all, but a "dairy product" because neither STARTER nor RENNET is used in the process. This form of ricotta has a low fat content of from 10 to 20 percent. **Ricotta Romana,** also called *ricotta gentile*, is made in this style but uses sheep's whey left over from making PECORINO ROMANO. Some ricotta producers use partially skimmed milk in lieu of whey or add milk to the whey— such versions have a higher fat content. Sometimes citric acid or salt and vinegar are added to the whey-and-milk mixture to encourage COAGULATION. These diverse approaches to making regular ricotta result in myriad variations in both texture and flavor, though all versions are generally fresh, soft, and moist. But various other techniques can change the end result more noticeably. One example is **ricotta salata,** which is produced in Sicily, Sardinia, and several regions of mainland Italy. *Salata* means "salty," and this cheese is made by SALTING and PRESSING fresh ricotta before aging it for about 3 months. The result is a firm, snow-white cheese that's smooth, pliable, and somewhat similar to FETA, though not as salty. It has a sweet, milky, slightly nutty flavor. Some ricotta salatas are aged for a year or more, until they are hard enough to be GRATING CHEESES. The word *affumicata* in the name means the ricotta has been smoked. There are myriad smoked versions, and smoking can last for 24 hours to a week or more; the wood used depends on the cheesemaker. The longer the cheese is smoked, the firmer and denser the result. Because of the smoke and some aging, the exterior color of *affumicata* cheeses varies from grayish white to reddish gold to brown. Occasionally an outer rind will form. **Ricotta fumo di ginepro,** produced in Abruzzo and Molise from sheep's milk whey, is distinctively smoked with juniper wood. In Sardinia, **ricotta mustia** is smoked over aromatic

R

herbs, which uniquely flavor the cheese. **Ricotta forte** is made by taking leftover fresh ricotta (made from any combination of cow's, goat's, or sheep's ricotta) and kneading it periodically for several months before placing it in small clay pots to age for about a year. This results in a soft creamy-brown paste that's exceedingly pungent and piquant. **Ricotta infornata** is made by draining ricotta for several days before baking it in a greased pan or clay pot for about a half hour, or until the surface begins to brown. The cheese's interior turns pale golden and the exterior a deep golden brown. Ricotta infornata is traditionally eaten fresh, but it's also allowed to age and become hard enough to be used as a grating cheese. **American ricottas** are typically made with fat-free or whole cow's milk, sometimes combined with whey, which usually produces a wetter, creamier style of ricotta than Italian versions. Award-winning **Bellwether Farms** makes what many consider America's finest ricotta—both sheep's and cow's whey versions.

Ridder [REED-der; RIHD-der]

Origin	Norway
Milk	Pasteurized cow's
Type	SEMISOFT; PRESSED UNCOOKED; WASHED RIND; ARTISAN, FARMSTEAD, and FACTORY
Appearance	4- to 7-pound wheels; rind is moist, sticky, and beige to orangey-gold in color; interior is ivory to light yellow with occasional EYES
Texture	Soft, creamy, and supple
Flavor	Buttery, sweet, savory, and slightly nutty, becoming stronger with additional aging

Ridder was thought to have originated in Sweden and then gained popularity throughout Norway and many other countries. Today

R

it's considered a Norwegian cheese by most—*Ridder* is the Norwegian word for "knight." This cheese is made with whole cow's milk, and the wheels are dipped in BRINE and sometimes in ANNATTO, which adds color. It's ripened for 2 to 3 months and has a FAT CONTENT of about 60 percent.

rind(s) The rind (also called *crust*) is a cheese's outer covering, the purpose of which is to protect the interior and enable RIPENING. Rinds come in many forms—thick, thin, hard, soft, coated with ASH or herbs, or covered with cloth or WAX. There are many styles of rind, which develop during RIPENING. BLOOMY RINDS are a soft surface mold found on cheeses like BRIE and CAMEMBERT. Cheeses such as ÉPOISSES have WASHED RINDS, formed by brushing or washing the surface with liquid, which encourages development of a friendly bacteria that colors the rind from orange to red. Both of these styles of rind help ripen cheese from the outside in. Whereas many rinds are created by the cheesemaker, NATURAL RINDS form from normal air contact, creating a hardened surface that can range from thin to thick. Some cheeses have an ARTIFICIAL RIND, such as WAX, ash, and so on. Of course FRESH CHEESES are rindless—they're meant to be consumed young and aren't RIPENED long enough to develop a rind. Examples are COTTAGE CHEESE (CURDS coated with milk) and FETAS, most of which are protected by being soaked in BRINE. Most rinds are edible except, of course, wax rinds and the BANDAGING found on some cheeses like CHEDDAR. That's not to say that you'll want to eat the rind, some of which may be quite thick and tough (as on older cheeses) and others of which may simply be too pungent, earthy, or moldy tasting for your palate. *See individual listings of specific rinds for more information.*

ripe *see* Glossary of Cheese Descriptors, page 502

R

ripening; ripen, to; ripening room 1. Ripening milk refers to the process of adding a STARTER to increase milk's ACIDITY level. **2. Ripening cheese** is the final and, for most cheeses, most important step in cheesemaking. This ripening period is also referred to as *aging, curing,* or *finishing*. It allows the cheese to reach the optimal and distinctive flavor, texture, and aroma for its type; and the RIND develops during this time. The environment for ripening cheese is monitored carefully to keep the temperature and humidity constant. Because most cheesemakers don't have cool, moist limestone caves, such as France's Cambalou caverns (the locus of ROQUEFORT), most rely on special **ripening rooms,** where temperature, humidity, and air circulation are controlled. To reach perfect maturity, each cheese type needs an exacting combination of these factors. The length of time a cheese ripens is also part of the process, and balancing the right temperature and humidity with the perfect number of ripening days is part of the art. For example, SOFT-RIPENED CHEESES, such as CAMEMBERT, need relatively low temperatures and high humidity (around 95 percent) because they ripen quickly. On the other hand most hard cheeses, which take longer to ripen, do best with lower humidity—usually no more than around 80 percent. **Force(d) ripening** is a process whereby aging is hastened by either curing the cheese in a warmer environment than customary or adjusting the ENZYMES. This practice is often used for PROCESS(ED) CHEESE. During ripening, cheese goes through numerous processes—both natural and assisted—to produce its final character. For example, some STARTERS contain specific bacteria that naturally produce particular characteristics—the EYES in EMMENTAL are generated by *Propionibacter shermanii,* the blue veins in ROQUEFORT are formed by *Penicillium roqueforti* (*see PENICILLIUM*), and so on. Other cheeses achieve their characteristics with cheesemaker assistance. Prime examples are the WASHED-RIND cheeses where the rinds are brushed with a liquid (from saltwater to wine), which feeds the surface bacteria of a cheese and ultimately produces the distinctive aroma and flavor that exemplify its style. Other cheeses require frequent turning to allow the redistribution of BUTTERFAT. The time a cheese is allowed to ripen depends on its style and can take from a few days to several weeks to up to 2 years or more. During long ripening periods the cheese loses moisture, which intensifies its flavors and aromas. Add the combination of time and labor costs to a cheese's weight loss during long-term aging and you have the reason why such cheeses are more expensive than mass-produced examples. It should be noted that in the United States ripened cheese either must be made from pasteurized milk (*see* PASTEURIZATION) or must be aged for a minimum of 60 days at a temperature of not less than 35°F. *See also* AFFINÉ; MOLD-RIPENED CHEESES.

Roaring Forties Blue

Origin	Australia (King Island)
Milk	Pasteurized cow's
Type	SEMISOFT; MOLDED UNCOOKED; BLUE-VEINED; ARTISAN
Appearance	7-ounce or 2½-pound wheels covered with dark blue wax; rindless and ivory colored; interior is ivory to pale orange-yellow with plentiful blue-green veins throughout
Texture	Moist, smooth, and creamy
Flavor	Sweet, rich, and slightly nutty, intensifying with age

Roaring Forties Blue takes its name from the gale-force westerly winds that rage along the fortieth parallel in the southern latitudes. These winds gust across the King Island, which is located just off the northwestern tip of Tasmania, Australia's island state 120 miles off the mainland's southeastern tip. Created in 1994 at **King Island Dairy**, this cheese is made only from the milk of cows that graze local pastures. The milk is inoculated with *Penicillium roqueforti,* the same mold used for producing ROQUEFORT, GORGONZOLA, and STILTON. The cheese is pierced with thick stainless-steel needles to create holes so oxygen can reach the interior and feed the bacteria that create the bluing. Roaring Forties Blue is RIPENED for 4 to 5 weeks, after which time it's coated with dark blue wax to halt the blue-mold development. Ripening continues for a few more weeks before the cheese is ready for market. Roaring Forties Blue has a FAT CONTENT of about 50 percent. King Island Dairy's master cheesemaker, Ueli Berger, also produces the complexly flavored GORGONZOLA-style **Endeavour Blue,** which won the Grand Champion Cheese award (out of over four hundred entries) for three years running at the Australian Grand Dairy Awards.

Robert Rouzaire; Fromagerie Rouzaire *see* GRATTE-PAILLE; PIERRE ROBERT

Robiola [roh-bee-OH-lah]

Origin	Italy (Lombardy, Piedmont)
Milk	Unpasteurized or pasteurized cow's, goat's, and/or sheep's
Type	SOFT; FRESH or slightly RIPENED; NATURAL, BLOOMY, or WASHED RINDS, depending on the region and producer; FARMSTEAD and COOPERATIVE
Appearance	6- to 14-ounce wheels or squares, depending on the region; nonexistent to very thin rind, which

	can range from white and bloomy to pale golden to pinkish in washed-rind versions; interior varies from snowy white to ivory
Texture	Ranges from creamy and delicate to drier and supple
Flavor	Ranges from delicate, mild, and tangy to more pungent

A large number of Robiolas are made throughout northern Italy, and, though a wide range of styles is produced, the cheeses have many similarities, such as all being small and soft. They're made by scooping the CURD (large-cut, if cut at all) into molds and letting it drain naturally, without PRESSING. Robiolas undergo short aging periods—some as little as 3 to 8 days, although 3 weeks is more typical and some can be aged for up to 3 months. Occasionally Robiolas are wrapped in pine boughs, rosemary, or cabbage, fig, grape, or walnut leaves. Some contain flavorings, such as truffles. **Robiola Piedmont** is a generic name for Robiola cheeses made throughout Piedmont in a style very similar to the ROBIOLA DI ROCCAVERANO. **Robiola Lombardia** is a generic name for TALEGGIO-style washed-rind cheeses made throughout the Lombardy region—they're typically square and range in weight from 6 to 14 ounces. Smaller versions of Robiola are sometimes called **Robiolina**.

Robiola di Roccaverano (DOC; PDO) [roh-bee-OH-lah dee roh-kah-veh-RAH-noh]

Origin	Italy (Piedmont)
Milk	Unpasteurized or pasteurized cow's, goat's, and/or sheep's
Type	SOFT; FRESH or slightly RIPENED; NATURAL RIND; FARMSTEAD and COOPERATIVE

Appearance	9- to 14-ounce wheels; nonexistent to very thin rind that's off-white to pale yellow with tinges of brown and red; interior varies from snowy white to ivory
Texture	Ranges from creamy and delicate to coarse grained
Flavor	When young it's delicate, nutty, and sweet with a slight tang; aged versions are bolder and more pungent; unpasteurized versions are more flavorful and complex

Robiola di Roccaverano is the only member of the Robiola family to be granted DENOMINAZIONE DI ORIGINE CONTROLLATA (DOC) status. It's made in a contiguous area encompassing a group of towns and villages in Piedmont's Alessandria and Asti provinces. The name of this cheese comes from ⁓ ⁓-caverano, a small hillside town that's part of this group. This cheese has been made in this area for at least 2,000 years and probably longer. It's thought that the name *Robiola* comes from the Latin *robium,* which relates to the reddish hue of the rinds of aged versions of this style of cheese. Robiola di Roccaverano was traditionally made from goat's milk, but today it can be produced with up to 85 percent cow's milk and 15 percent or more goat's or sheep's milk. Hence it can still be made totally from goat's milk but not from 100 percent cow's milk. The cheese is aged for as little as 3 days but sometimes for another 2 to 3 weeks. The FAT CONTENT for this cheese is about 45 percent. **Robiola di Roccaverano Classica,** though not an official PDO designation, *is* made exclusively of raw goat's milk—a return to tradition by a small group of artisanal-style producers.

robust *see* Glossary of Cheese Descriptors, page 503

R

Rocamadour (AOC; PDO)

Origin	France (Midi-Pyrénées)
Milk	Unpasteurized goat's
Type	SEMISOFT to SEMIHARD; MOLDED UNCOOKED; NATURAL RIND; ARTISAN, FARMSTEAD, and COOPERATIVE
Appearance	Tiny 1- to 1½-ounce disks; thin rind is soft and dry and ranges in color from ivory to golden brown with white and blue molds and an indented crisscross pattern; interior ranges from white to ivory to yellow-brown, depending on age
Texture	Supple and creamy, becoming firm and hard as it RIPENS
Flavor	Sweet, milky, and nutty when young, becoming spicy and eventually very barnyardy in older versions

Rocamadour has been produced for at least 600 years, evidenced by written references mentioning it as a unit of payment. It's a member of the CABÉCOU family of goat cheeses made throughout southwest France, which is why this cheese is still sometimes referred to as **Cabécou de Rocamadour.** In the dialect used in southwestern France, *cabécou* means "kid" or "little goat." The kindred word *chabichou* comes from *chabi* (from the Arabic *chebli,* for "goat") and is tied to CHABICHOU DU POITOU, another French goat cheese. Rocamadour undergoes a minimum RIPENING period of 6 days but some are aged for up to 4 weeks. It's made from unpasteurized milk and is not aged long enough to currently be imported into the United States (*see* UNPASTEURIZED MILK/IMPORTED CHEESE DILEMMA). The FAT CONTENT is about 45 percent.

Roche Baron; Rochebaron [rohsh BEA-ruhn] *see* MONTBRIAC

Rofumo [roh-FOO-moh] *see* GRANQUESO

Rogue Creamery *see* ROGUE RIVER BLUE

Rogue River Blue

Origin	United States (Oregon)
Milk	Unpasteurized cow's
Type	SEMIHARD; MOLDED UNCOOKED; BLUE–VEINED; NATURAL RIND; FARMSTEAD
Appearance	5-pound wheels; exterior is wrapped in grape leaves; interior is ivory (darker toward the rind) with blue-green to blue-gray veins and a scattering of EYES
Texture	Dense, creamy, moist, and crumbly
Flavor	Creamy, salty, earthy, spicy, and tangy

The **Rogue Creamery** was originally established by Tom Vella of California's **Vella Cheese Company**, home of today's renowned Sonoma Dry Jack (*see* JACK). In 1935, Tom—with backing from the famous cheese mogul J. L. Kraft—bought a nonoperational cheese plant in southern Oregon's Central Point, near Ashland. The refurbished creamery wound up producing millions of pounds of cheese during World War II. In the 1950s Tom traveled to Roquefort, France, and learned the secrets of making blue cheese. Upon his return, he began producing Oregon Blue Vein, which immediately earned accolades. In 2002, Tom's son, Ignazio "Ig" Vella, who continues to run California's Vella Cheese Company, sold the Rogue Creamery to Cary Bryant and David Gremmels. Ig, who's listed as Rogue Creamery's master cheesemaker, continues his involvement as a mentor to the new owners. Since they took over, the creative team of Bryant and Gremmels has added several cheeses to the dairy's line,

R

including Rogue River Blue. This cheese has won many honors, including "Best Blue Cheese" at the annual World Cheese Awards, a first for an American cheese. Rogue River Blue is highly sought after—the creamery usually runs out by Christmastime, and the cheese isn't available until the following summer. It's RIPENED for at least 8 months, and when the wheels have aged for 3 to 4 months, the cheeses are wrapped in grape leaves that have been soaked in an Oregon pear brandy. This brandy-soaked wrap adds complexity to the creamy Rogue River Blue. Other award-winning cheeses from Rogue Creamery include **Crater Lake Blue** (the most robust of the Creamery's blues, made with a complex blend of molds), **Oregon Blue Vein** (with a minimum of 90 days of aging), **Oregonzola** (a GORGONZOLA-style blue aged for at least 120 days), and **Smokey Blue** (smoked overnight in hazelnut shells and winner of the coveted "Best New Product in the World" award at the 2005 New York National Association for the Specialty Food Trade [NASFT] Show). Rogue River also makes cheddars variously flavored with kalamata olives and garlic, pesto, and rosemary.

Romanian cheeses *see* Cheeses by Country of Origin, page 514

Romano [roh-MAH-noh]

Origin	Italy
Milk	Unpasteurized and pasteurized cow's, sheep's, and goat's
Type	HARD; PRESSED COOKED; NATURAL RIND; GRANA STYLE; ARTISAN and FACTORY
Appearance	Various shapes and sizes, including large wheels up to 73 pounds; rind is hard, smooth, and pale yellow; interior ranges from ivory to pale yellow

Texture	Finely grained, flaky, and brittle
Flavor	Salty, fruity, and piquant, intensifying as the cheese ages; sheep's and goat's milk versions are sharper and tangier

R

Romano, which takes its name from the city of Rome, shows up in a variety of forms around the world. It's generally a hard, salty cheese that's used primarily for grating. The best known of the Romanos is PECORINO ROMANO (PDO and DOC), which is made from sheep's milk. Pecorino Romano and the goat's-milk-based Caprino Romano are Italian originals and have been produced in Italy for over 2,000 years. Vacchino Romano, made from cow's milk, is another popular version. In the United States this cow's milk style (sometimes with the addition of sheep's and/or goat's milk) is produced on a very large scale. Cheese aficionados typically prefer the sheep's and goat's milk versions, which have sharper, tangier, more pronounced flavors than the milder cow's milk versions. Romano is RIPENED for at least 5 and often up to 12 months. It has a FAT CONTENT of 27 to 29 percent. BelGioioso Cheese of Denmark, Wisconsin, produces an award-winning Romano that took "Best of Show" in an American Cheese Society competition. In the United States containers of pregrated Romano are available.

Roncal (DO; PDO) [rohng-KAHL]

Origin	Spain (Roncal Valley, Navarre (Navarra)
Milk	Unpasteurized sheep's
Type	HARD; PRESSED, UNCOOKED; NATURAL RIND; FARMSTEAD and FACTORY
Appearance	4- to 7-pound wheels; rind color ranges from straw to reddish brown to dark gray—some have exterior mold, and some imports are

R

	lightly waxed; interior is beige to amber colored, darkening with age
Texture	Firm, moist, and smooth, with a scattering of small EYES
Flavor	Sweet, herbaceous, and nutty, becoming increasingly piquant with age

Produced in the historical region of Navarre at the foot of the Pyrénées, Roncal was the first of Spain's cheeses to be granted DENOMINACIÓN DE ORIGEN PROTEGIDA (DO) status. In the Middle Ages the seven villages of the Roncal Valley formed a cooperative of shepherds that still manages the region's natural resources, overseeing everything from TRANSHUMANCE to time-honored cheese production methods. Today there is farmstead as well as factory production, both forms using closely guarded traditions handed down from generation to generation. The DO regulations for this cheese require that it be produced in the Roncal Valley from the raw milk of Lacha and/or Rasa-Aragonesa sheep. Roncal undergoes brining (*see* SALTING) for 36 hours before beginning its minimum 4-month RIPENING period. It has a FAT CONTENT of 45 to 50 percent. This cheese is also called *Queso del Valle del Roncal.*

rond [RAWN] French for "round" and one of the many shapes into which CHÈVRE is formed.

Rondo [RON-doh] *see* NOCTURNE

Roomkaas [ROAM-kahss] *see* GOUDA

Roquefort (AOC; PDO) [rohk-FOR]

Origin	France (Aquitaine; Midi-Pyrénées; Languedoc-Roussillon; Provence-Alpes-Côte-d'Azur; Corsica)

R

Milk	Unpasteurized sheep's
Type	SEMISOFT; MOLDED UNCOOKED; BLUE–VEINED; NATURAL RIND; ARTISAN and FACTORY
Appearance	5½- to 6½-pound foil-wrapped wheels; rind is pale ivory and slightly moist; interior is ivory with blue-green to blue-gray veining and scattered EYES
Texture	Creamy, moist, and crumbly
Flavor	Buttery, salty, and tangy with a zesty spiciness that intensifies as it ripens

Cheese, presumably Roquefort or its kin, has been made in the region for at least 2,000 years—prehistoric cheesemaking relics attest to it, the Romans enjoyed it, Caesar was a fan, and in the eighth century Roquefort was a favorite of Charlemagne. Many refer to Roquefort as the "King of Cheeses," although France's BRIE DE MEAUX also holds this title, and several other countries have declared their own "King of Cheeses." The center of Roquefort cheesemaking is the village of Roquefort-sur-Soulzon, located in southern France's Aveyron *département*. In 1411, Charles VI signed a charter giving the area's cheesemakers the sole right to make Roquefort, a bond reaffirmed over the centuries. In 1961 it was ruled that the production of this cheese could be started in other regions of France (Aquitaine, Languedoc-Roussillon, Provence-Alpes-Côte-d'Azur, and Corsica). RIPENING, however, must take place near the village of Roquefort-sur-Soulzon in the famous Combalou caverns, which were transformed by man in the seventeenth century into today's elaborate architectural labyrinth. The key to Roquefort's success is the mold *Penicillium roqueforti,* found inside these natural limestone caves. For centuries the mold was cultivated by placing loaves of rye bread in the caves. The bread, which naturally attracted and developed ambient molds, was then dried and ground to a powder, which was then

R

used to seed new batches of cheese. Today laboratories replicate this mold, a relatively easy process that provides greater consistency. APPELLATION D'ORIGINE CONTRÔLÉE (AOC) regulations require that Roquefort be made from the raw milk of Lacaune sheep. The *P. roqueforti* is added to the milk in the initial stages of cheesemaking. When the cheese is ready, each wheel is pierced with thick needles to allow oxygen to get in and feed the bacteria that create the bluing. The cheeses then begin ripening in the Combalou caverns, where the wheels are placed on wooden shelves and evenly spaced to provide optimum air circulation. The shelving is covered with a layer of coarse salt, which keeps undesirable bacteria from infecting the cheese; the wood absorbs moisture and helps establish a balanced relative humidity. After a few weeks, a master cheesemaker determines when each cellar's cheese is ready to be wrapped in foil to continue a slower maturation. Roquefort is ripened for a minimum of 3 months, usually 4 months, and often for 9 months or more. The minimum FAT CONTENT for this cheese is 52 percent. Authentic Roquefort is identified by a red sheep on the wrapper's emblem.

Roth Käse USA, Ltd. [ROTH kayss] *see* BUTTERKÄSE; GRANQUESO; GRUYÈRE

Rouge et Noir [roozh ay NWAHR] The name under which the cheeses of the **Marin French Cheese Company** are labeled.

Royalp; Royalp Tilsiter *see* TILSIT; TILSITER

rubbery *see* Glossary of Cheese Descriptors, page 503

runny *see* Glossary of Cheese Descriptors, page 503

S

Saenkanter [SAY-en-kahn-ter] *see* GOUDA

saganaki [sah-gah-NAH-kee] A Greek specialty of fried cheese, typically KASSERI. The cheese is cut into ½-inch-thick slices, fried in olive oil or butter, and served hot sprinkled with lemon juice and sometimes fresh herbs.

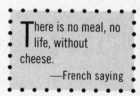

There is no meal, no life, without cheese.
—French saying

Sainte-Maure de Touraine (AOC; PDO) [sant-MOHR deuh too-RAYN]

Origin	France (Centre; Poitou-Charentes)
Milk	Unpasteurized goat's
Type	SEMISOFT to HARD; MOLDED UNCOOKED; rindless or NATURAL RIND; ARTISAN, FARMSTEAD, and COOPERATIVE
Appearance	5- to 8-inch logs weighing from 9 to 14 ounces with a long straw or stick running lengthwise through the center; rind is thin, moist, and white when young, developing blue mold as it ripens; long-ripened versions become hard and dark beige with dense blue mold; some are coated with powdered charcoal; interior is white to off-white

Texture	Young versions are soft and moist; older ones are firmer, becoming hard and dry with time
Flavor	Mild, piquant, and slightly nutty when young, becoming richer, more complex, and stronger with ripening

Touraine is a former province of France that covered an area in the Loire Valley now split between the Indre, Indre-et-Loire, and Loir-et-Cher *départements*, which are all part of the current Centre region. Goat's milk cheeses date back many centuries in this area. Sainte-Maure cheeses became known about the nineteenth century and achieved formal APPELLATION D'ORIGINE CONTRÔLÉE (AOC) status as Sainte-Maure de Touraine in 1990. For this cheese the CURDS are neither cooked or pressed, but placed in long log-shaped molds and allowed to drain. Once the cheese is removed from the mold, a long straw or thin dowel is inserted lengthwise to help hold the cheese together and allow it to aerate. Sainte-Maure de Touraine undergoes RIPENING for a minimum of 10 days, but more often for 3 to 6 weeks. Cheese made with raw milk meets AOC regulations and may be labeled *Sainte-Maure de Touraine* but cannot be exported to the United States at this writing (*see* UNPASTEUR-IZED MILK/IMPORTED CHEESE DILEMMA). Cheeses labeled simply *Sainte-Maure* are produced with the same techniques as Sainte-Maure de Touraine but with pasteurized goat's milk. They meet U.S. standards but are not AOC cheeses and are generally not as flavorful. The FAT CONTENT of these cheeses is at least 45 percent.

Saint-Marcellin [san mahr-sehl-LAN]

Origin	France (Rhône-Alpes)
Milk	Unpasteurized and pasteurized cow's or goat's

Type	SOFT; MOLDED UNCOOKED; NATURAL RIND; ARTISAN, FARMSTEAD, and FACTORY
Appearance	3- to 4-ounce wheels; thin rind is wrinkled, beige to light gold, and develops light blue and gray molds as it ripens; interior is beige
Texture	Firm when young, becoming soft, creamy, and runny with age
Flavor	Mild, lightly tangy, and savory with nutty traits; becomes more complex and yeasty with age

This cheese is named after the town of Saint-Marcellin, located near Grenoble in southeastern France's Rhône-Alpes region. It's made throughout this region, which is sometimes referred to as the *Dauphiné,* a former province that covered what are now parts of the Isère, Drôme, and Hautes-Alpes *départements.* According to legend, in the fifteenth century the governor of the Dauphiné (the future King Louis XI) became lost and was taken in by locals, who fed him bread and the local Saint-Marcellin cheese. Later, as king, he introduced it to the French court. Saint-Marcellin was originally produced primarily from goat's milk but has transitioned over time into chiefly a cow's milk cheese. It's similar to BANON, which is made farther south in Provence, except Banon is typically based on goat's milk. Saint-Marcellin is sometimes eaten fairly fresh, after only 2 weeks of RIPENING. Often, however, it's aged for 6 or more weeks, when it becomes rich and oozy. It has a FAT CONTENT of about 45 percent.

Saint-Nectaire (AOC; PDO) [sa*n* NEHK-tehr]

Origin	France (Auvergne)
Milk	Unpasteurized or pasteurized cow's

S

Type	SEMISOFT; PRESSED UNCOOKED; NATURAL RIND; ARTISAN, FARMSTEAD, and FACTORY
Appearance	3½- to 4-pound wheels; tough gray rind is covered with red, yellow, and white molds; interior is ivory to pale yellow with a scattering of small EYES
Texture	Soft, creamy, and supple
Flavor	Complex, earthy, mushroomy, nutty, grassy, and savory with a slight tanginess

Produced for centuries in central France's mountainous Auvergne region, this cheese became known as *Saint-Nectaire* in the seventeenth century. The cheese and the town of Saint-Nectaire, with which the cheese is associated, both took their name from a prominent local family headed by Henri de Sennecterre. He presented Louis XIV with the cheese, which became one of the king's favorites. APPELLATION D'ORIGINE CONTRÔLÉE (AOC) regulations require that milk for Saint-Nectaire cheese come from Salers cows. The best cheeses are available in the summer and fall, when the cattle can graze in high mountain pastures. Production includes molding and pressing the CURDS, which are then salted and pressed again. Saint-Nectaires are RIPENED for 3 to 8 weeks, during which time they're washed several times with BRINE and/or plain water. Most cheese lovers agree that raw-milk farmstead versions (identified by an oval green label imprinted with *fermier*) are the most flavorful. Unfortunately, these unpasteurized cheeses currently cannot be imported into the United States because they are not aged over 60 days (*see* UNPASTEURIZED MILK/IMPORTED CHEESE DILEMMA). Luckily, there are small producers that produce excellent pasteurized versions, though for the most part factory-produced pasteurized versions (identified with a square green label) are comparatively tasteless. The minimum FAT CONTENT for Saint-Nectaire is 45 percent.

sajt [SHOYT] Hungarian for "cheese."

Salers (AOC; PDO) [sah-LEHR]

Origin	France (Auvergne, Midi-Pyrénées, Limousin)
Milk	Unpasteurized cow's
Type	SEMIHARD; PRESSED UNCOOKED; NATURAL RIND; FARMSTEAD and MOUNTAIN
Appearance	Tall wheels that weigh from 77 to 121 pounds; rind is thick and rough with a dark brownish yellow color; interior is medium to dark yellow, depending on age
Texture	Firm and supple
Flavor	Complex, sweet, savory, meaty, and nutty

Salers takes its name from a small town positioned at an altitude of over 2,900 feet in the Cantal Mountains. It's also called *Fourme de Salers* or *Salers Haute Montagne*. Salers is considered an elite CANTAL, and like the latter it's been made in the same central-France region in a similar way for over 2,000 years. However, whereas much of Cantal is FACTORY produced with pasteurized milk, Salers is a MOUNTAIN cheese made only with raw milk. It's also France's single *wholly* FARMSTEAD-made *(fermier)* cheese. Salers is produced in stone huts called *burons* and is made only from May through October, when the local breed of Salers cows graze in high mountain pastures. During the other months the milk from these cows goes into making Cantal cheeses. Though Salers is considered a much more flavorful cheese than its factory-produced cousin, its production is less than 6 percent of Cantal's. Like Cantal, Salers goes through a double PRESSING, which is unique for French cheeses. Once the CURD is formed it's cut into ½-inch cubes, wrapped in cloth and pressed. It's then allowed to rest for about 8 hours. The curd is then put through a grinder to

S

break it into small pieces, salted (*see* SALTING), MOLDED, and then pressed a second time. For the next month the cheese is turned and frequently rubbed with salt. Salers is RIPENED longer than Cantal—a minimum of 3 months and sometimes for 18 months or more. FAT CONTENT is a minimum of 45 percent.

Salers Haute Montagne *see* SALERS

salting This vital cheesemaking step takes place after the WHEY is drained and before RIPENING begins. The salting process seasons, preserves, and helps reduce the moisture content of cheese. And, because salt is also a natural antibacterial agent, it helps retard bacterial growth, which slows the aging process so cheese can be held long enough to acquire the desired texture and flavor. Salt is added at various stages, depending on the type of cheese. There are four salting techniques: In some cases (as with CHEDDAR) salt is added directly to the CURDS. A second method is **brining,** where some cheeses (typically HARD and SEMIHARD, such as EMMENTAL and GOUDA) are immersed in brine—a solution of water and a great deal of salt. This brine bath produces the desired degree of saltiness and can also firm the rind. Depending on the style of cheese, this saltwater submersion can last anywhere from 15 minutes to months. **Dry-salting** (surface salting) is a third method whereby the surface of the cheese is rubbed with salt, which assists the development of a NATURAL RIND. This technique is used with cheeses like PARMIGIANO-REGGIANO and many English cheeses. Last, cheese can be salted by washing or brushing it with anything from brine to beer to cider (*see* WASHED-RIND CHEESES). These last two methods are often applied at regular intervals during ripening. The salt used in cheesemaking is generally noniodized and coarsely flaked.

Samsoe; Samsø [SAM-soh]

Origin	Denmark
Milk	Pasteurized cow's
Type	SEMIHARD; PRESSED COOKED; NATURAL RIND or rindless; FACTORY
Appearance	31-pound wheels or rectangles; rind is dry and yellow to golden or rindless and may be wax covered; interior is ivory to yellow with a few irregular-size EYES
Texture	Supple, elastic, and smooth
Flavor	Mild and buttery with hints of nuts when young, becoming stronger and more pungent with age

Samsoe (or *Samsø*) is named after a Danish island located 9 miles off the Jutland Peninsula. The cheese originated there in the nineteenth century when the Danish king brought in a Swiss cheesemaker to assist in diversifying Denmark's cheesemaking. The outcome was Samsoe, which became the forerunner of other, similar Danish cheeses. Although modeled after EMMENTAL, Samsoe is not as hard and has less complex flavors. It's brined (*see* SALT-ING) for about 3 days (rindless versions are not) before being RIPENED for at least 6 weeks but generally for 3 to 6 months or more. The minimum FAT CONTENT for standard Samsoe is 45 percent; the lower-fat version has at least 30 percent fat.

San Andreas

Origin	United States (California)
Milk	Unpasteurized sheep's
Type	SEMIHARD; MOLDED UNCOOKED; NATURAL RIND; FARMSTEAD

S

S

Appearance	3-pound wheels; rind is smooth and golden; interior is ivory colored with scattered EYES
Texture	Smooth and supple
Flavor	Creamy and mild with a slight tang

Bellwether Farms, California's first sheep dairy, was founded in 1986 by Cindy and Ed Callahan. Today their son Liam is Bellwether's cheesemaker, producing highly praised cheese from both sheep's milk (San Andreas and Pepato) and cow's milk (CARMODY, CARMODY RESERVE, and CRESCENZA). The word *bellwether* is Middle English for the lead sheep, which wears a bell around its neck to lead the flock. The name *San Andreas* comes from the renowned earthquake fault that runs through the Bellwether property. This cheese is aged for 3 to 4 months and has a FAT CONTENT of about 30 to 35 percent. It's an award winner in the farmstead sheep's milk category at the annual American Cheese Society Competition.

San Ignacio Blue [san eeg-NAH-syoh bloo]

Origin	Argentina (Santa Fe)
Milk	Pasteurized cow's
Type	SEMISOFT; MOLDED UNCOOKED; BLUE-VEINED; NATURAL RIND; ARTISAN
Appearance	10-pound foil-wrapped wheels; rind is pale ivory and slightly moist; interior is ivory with blue-green to blue-gray veining
Texture	Soft, creamy, and slightly crumbly
Flavor	Mild, buttery, somewhat tangy

San Ignacio Blue is made in the province of Santa Fe in the northern portion of Argentina. Monks, who were once the keepers of cheesemaking knowledge, were the first to bring recipes and techniques for making BLUE-VEINED CHEESES from Europe to Argentina. The practices for making San Ignacio Blue have been passed down over the centuries, and today cheesemakers rely on *Penicillium roqueforti* imported from France to inoculate the milk. This is the same mold used for producing the world-famous blues ROQUEFORT, GORGONZOLA, and STILTON. San Ignacio Blue may be aged for anywhere from 4 to 6 months.

San Joaquin Gold [SAN wah-KEEN]

Origin	United States (California)
Milk	Unpasteurized cow's
Type	SEMIHARD; PRESSED COOKED; NATURAL RIND; FARMSTEAD
Appearance	30- to 34-pound wheels; rind is thin, rigid, rough, and ranges in color from yellow-gold to reddish brown; interior can be pale to golden yellow and has a tiny number of small EYES
Texture	Firm and crumbly
Flavor	Mellow and buttery with hints of sweetness and nuts

San Joaquin Gold is produced by the **Fiscalini Cheese Company** of Modesto, California, which has its own herd of 1,400 Holstein cows. Fourth-generation dairyman John Fiscalini set out to produce a FONTINA-style cheese but wasn't happy with the results, though the public seemed to like it. When cheesemaker Jorge "Mariano" Gonzalez (who trained at England's Montgomery Farms) came on board, they continued to refine the process, ultimately ending up with today's acclaimed San Joaquin Gold. This cheese has won many awards, including medals from the American Cheese Society and London's

World Cheese Awards. The wheels are rubbed with oil and turned daily for several months. San Joaquin Gold has a total RIPENING time of 14 months and a FAT CONTENT of 45 to 50 percent. Fiscalini has also won awards for some of its other cheeses, including its **18- and 30-Month Bandage Wrapped Cheddars** (*see* CHEDDAR), **Purple Moon** (cheddar soaked in Cabernet Sauvignon), **Cheddar with Sage, Cheddar with Dill, and Cheddar with Tarragon.**

San Simón [SAN see-MOHN]

Origin	Spain (Galicia)
Milk	Unpasteurized and pasteurized cow's
Type	SEMIHARD; PRESSED UNCOOKED; NATURAL RIND; ARTISAN and FARMSTEAD; SMOKED
Appearance	2¼- to 4½-pound pear shapes; rind is glossy and amber to dark reddish brown; interior is pale yellow to amber
Texture	Firm, dense, and supple
Flavor	Smoky, creamy, slightly nutty, and tangy, becoming piquant with age

This smoked cheese hails from northwestern Spain's Galicia region, south of the Bay of Biscay. It's also known as *Queso de San Simón de la Cuesta*. Milk from the Rubia Gallega (Galician Blond) breed is used to make San Simón. One of the traditional ways of preserving cheese was to smoke it, and this ancient approach continues with San Simón. The gently pressed cheese is lightly smoked for about 2 weeks, and total RIPENING takes approximately 2 months. The FAT CONTENT is 40 to 45 percent. Some San Simón cheeses, particularly the smaller sizes, are called *bufones* ("dunce caps").

SAPSAGO; SAP SAGO 421

S

São Jorge *see* QUEIJO SÃO JORGE

sapid; sapidity [SAP-ihd; sa-PIHD-ih-tee] *see* Glossary of Cheese
Descriptors, page 503

Sapsago; Sap Sago [sap-SAY-goh]

Origin	Switzerland (Glarus)
Milk	Unpasteurized and pasteurized cow's
Type	HARD PRESSED COOKED; ARTISAN and COOPERATIVE
Appearance	3- to 7-ounce truncated cone wrapped in silver foil; rindless and pale grayish green in color; interior is pale grayish green
Texture	Very hard and granular
Flavor	Strong, savory, pungent, herbal, tangy, and spicy

Sapsago has been made since the 1500s in east-central Switzer-
land's mountainous canton of Glarus. In this German-speaking
area, it's also known as *Grünerkäse* ("green cheese"), *Glarnerkäse,*
Krauterkäse, and *Schabzieger.* Sapsago has a very low FAT CON-
TENT (from 3 to 9 percent) because it's made from nonfat milk,
WHEY, or buttermilk (or sometimes a combination of the three).
For production, the milk product is soured, then heated and
COAGULATED. The CURD is pressed, then RIPENED for 6 or more
weeks, until it is completely dried. It's then ground, salted, and
mixed with dried blue melilot, a special variety of clover, and/
or fenugreek, a plant known for its pleasantly bitter, slightly
sweet seeds. The mixture is then turned into truncated cone-
shaped molds, pressed, and ripened until very hard. Sapsago is
used as a grating cheese to flavor salad greens or cooked foods or
can be combined with butter to make a spread.

satiny *see* SMOOTH in the Glossary of Cheese Descriptors, page 504

savory *see* Glossary of Cheese Descriptors, page 503

Sbrinz (AOC) [ZBRIHNZ]

Origin	Switzerland
Milk	Unpasteurized cow's
Type	HARD; GRANA STYLE; PRESSED COOKED; NATURAL RIND; ARTISAN, FARMSTEAD, COOPERATIVE, and FACTORY
Appearance	Large 55- to 100-pound wheels; rind is dry, rigid, and smooth and ranges in color from gold to golden brown; interior can be from pale yellow to deep gold with occasional small EYES
Texture	Finely grained, becoming flaky and crumbly with age
Flavor	Mellow, fruity, nutty, spicy, with hints of toffee, intensifying as the cheese ages

Sbrinz is Switzerland's oldest cheese and thought to be the one that Roman scholar and naturalist Pliny the Elder referred to in the first century A.D. as *caseus helveticus* ("Swiss cheese"). It originated in Switzerland's central mountains and is named after the market town of Brienz in the canton of Bern. There's some speculation that the Italians modeled their hard cheeses GRANA PADANO and PARMIGIANO-REGGIANO after Sbrinz. Today fewer than three dozen cheesemakers produce this cheese. The cows, mostly Brown Swiss, are fed grass in the summer and hay in the winter—no silage is permitted. The milk is delivered to the dairies and quality tested before production begins. It takes over 156 gallons of milk to produce one 100-pound wheel. Sbrinz is brined (*see* SALTING) for about 18 days before undergoing RIPENING for at least 1½ years, but generally for 2 years and sometimes 4 years or more. It has a FAT CONTENT of at least 45 percent.

scalding *see* COOKING

Scamorza [skah-MOHRD-tsah]

Origin	Italy (primarily Abruzzi, Basilicata, and Molise)
Milk	Unpasteurized or pasteurized cow's, sheep's, and water buffalo's
Type	SEMISOFT to SEMIHARD; PRESSED UNCOOKED; PASTA FILATA; NATURAL RIND; FARMSTEAD, ARTISAN, and FACTORY; some SMOKED
Appearance	5 ounces to 2¼ pounds, depending on where it's made—various shapes, mostly pear- or gourdlike, often with a large knob at the top where the cheese has been tied; rind is very thin and smooth and varies in color from off-white to dark brown, depending on whether the cheese was smoked; the interior ranges from white to pale yellow
Texture	Smooth, elastic, and stringlike (drier than Italian MOZZARELLA)
Flavor	Mild, milky, and slightly sweet; also smoked versions

Scamorza was first made in southern Italy, where many of the CACIOCAVALLO cheesemakers produced it from excess milk. The Scamorza cheesemaking process is very similar to that of Caciocavallo—it's a PASTA FILATA cheese but aged for only 2 or 3 days. This shortened period gave cheesemakers a way of producing income while their Caciocavallo aged for 2 months to 2 years. The majority of today's Scamorza is made in large cheesemaking plants in northern Italy. Smoked Scamorzas (labeled *affumicato*) have become popular because they're more flavorful. Although cow's milk is commonly used, some Scamorzas are also made from sheep's milk as well as water buffalo's milk, the latter referred to as ***Scamorza di Bufala***. The FAT CONTENT of this cheese is approximately 25 percent.

Schabzieger [SHUB-tsee-ger] *see* SAPSAGO

Schloss; Schlosskäse; Schlosskaese [SHLOSS; SHLOSS-ki-zer (-kah-zeh)]

Origin	Austria
Milk	Pasteurized cow's
Type	SEMISOFT; PRESSED UNCOOKED; WASHED RIND; ARTISAN and FARMSTEAD
Appearance	Various-sized wheels and blocks; rind is thin and beige to reddish orange in color with white mold; interior is ivory to light gold with a small scattering of EYES
Texture	Smooth, creamy, and supple, becoming oozy as it ripens
Flavor	Creamy, savory, spicy, and nutty, becoming pungent with age

Schlosskäse or *Schlosskaese* ("castle cheese") originated in Austria and was inspired by the more famous LIMBURGER. It's also made in Germany and Switzerland, as well as the United States, where it's referred to simply as *Schloss*. *Schlosskäse* is not as odoriferous as Limburger and has a slightly milder yet strikingly complex flavor. It's RIPENED for 3 to 4 weeks, during which time the rind is washed with BRINE to encourage the growth of *BREVIBACTERIUM LINENS,* which ripens the cheese from the outside in. Schlosskäse is made from either whole or partially skimmed milk, which is why the FAT CONTENT can range from 35 to 55 percent. In the United States, California's **Marin French Cheese Company** has been producing Schloss since 1900. It's sold under the Rouge et Noir label. Cheesemaker Howard Bunce creates a version based on the American creation and much beloved **Liederkranz,** which disappeared from the cheese scene about 25 years ago due to a plant fire. Bunce's Schloss is made only from the whole milk of Jersey cows. It's cellar-aged for a minimum of 3 weeks but isn't sent out to retailers for at least 2 months. The Marin French Cheese Company also produces **Schlosskranz** and **Schlosskranz-Herz**— both are washed-rind cheeses made from the same recipe as Schloss. Schlosskranz comes in a 2-pound wreath-shaped wheel (*kranz* means "wreath") and is aged somewhat longer than the Schloss, which gives it a slightly stronger, more complex flavor profile. Schlosskranz-Herz comes in a 5-ounce wheel and is the center of the wreath (*herz* means "heart").

Scottish cheeses *see* Cheeses by Country of Origin, page 514

séchoir [say-SHWAHR] French for "dryer," which, in cheese-making terms, refers to a "drying room" used for RIPENING cheeses.

sell-by date *see* PRODUCT DATING

Selles-sur-Cher (AOC; PDO) [sehl-soor-SHEHR]

Origin	France (Centre)
Milk	Unpasteurized and pasteurized goat's
Type	SEMISOFT to SEMIHARD; MOLDED UNCOOKED; NATURAL RIND; FARMSTEAD, COOPERATIVE, and FACTORY

S

Appearance	5- to 7-ounce wheels; rind is thin and coated with black ASH, becoming wrinkled and developing pale-colored molds with age; interior is white
Texture	Soft and creamy, becoming drier and firmer with age
Flavor	Delicate, sweet, nutty, and slightly tangy when young, developing fuller, stronger, more savory flavors with age

This cheese takes its name from Selles-sur-Cher, a small town in the southern Loire Valley, which is in the center of this cheesemaking area. Originally developed for home consumption, Selles-sur-Cher began to be produced commercially during the nineteenth century. APPELLATION D'ORIGINE CONTRÔLÉE (AOC) and PROTECTED DESIGNATION OF ORIGIN (PDO) rules state that the curd must be hand-ladled into the molds. Once the cheese is set and the molds removed, the cheese is covered with a mixture of ash and salt, which helps drain the WHEY and assists in RIPENING. Selles-sur-Cher must be aged for a minimum of 10 days, though it's often ripened for 3 to 4 weeks. It has a FAT CONTENT of about 45 percent.

semicooked (semi-cooked) cheese *see* COOKING

semihard cheeses (semi-hard) *see* TEXTURE, CHEESE

semisoft cheeses (semi-soft) *see* TEXTURE, CHEESE

separator Used by many industrial cheese manufacturers, this centrifugal device separates the hot CURD from the WHEY in a matter of minutes, rather than the hours such a process typically takes. This allows the product (such as CREAM CHEESE) to be packaged while the curd is hot, which doubles the shelf life.

Serena; Serenita [seh-REE-nah; seh-reh-NEE-tah]

Origin	United States (California)
Milk	Unpasteurized cow's
Type	HARD (Serena) and SEMIHARD (Serenita); PRESSED COOKED (Serena); PRESSED UNCOOKED (Serenita); NATURAL RIND; FARMSTEAD
Appearance	18-pound wheels; rind is hard and pale yellow; interior is butter colored
Texture	Serena is smooth, tight, and dry—longer aging produces a GRANA-type quality; Serenita is firm, supple, and smooth
Flavor	Serena is sharp, acidic, faintly nutty, and piquant, taking on nuances of nuts and caramel with age; Serenita is savory-sweet, mildly tangy, and buttery with herbal notes and a caramellike finish

A relative overnight success story, young cheesemaker Marisa Hilarides Simoes (**Three Sisters Farmstead Cheese**) created two award-winning cheeses within about 5 years. She teams with her father Rob Hilarides, a third-generation dairyman with 2,400 acres and a herd of 6,000 Jersey cows. Simoes began making cheese at nineteen, and her first batch produced Serena (described as a cross between a GOUDA and a PARMESAN), which a few months later took honors in the farmstead cheese category at the American Cheese Society (ACS) Competition. To make Serena, the cut, drained CURDS are scooped into cheesecloth-lined molds and mechanically pressed over the next 24 hours—first in their molds, then unmolded, turned, stacked, and pressed to further extract WHEY and compress the curds. Serena then undergoes brining (*see* SALTING) for 24 hours before being set on racks for a 2-week drying period.

S

During this time, the wheels are rubbed with olive oil, which encourages the mold that flavors the cheese so provocatively. The wheels are then transferred to a cool and humid aging room to RIPEN for 6 to 12 months. Before the cheese is marketed, most of the mold is scrubbed off the rind with a mixture of vinegar and salt. Serena has a FAT CONTENT of about 32 percent. **Serenita**—the second creation of Simoes and Hilarides—outdid its older sibling by winning the prestigious blue ribbon in the American Originals category at an ACS competition. This cheese, which is often compared to BEAUFORT, was serendipitous in that it came about because the cheese vat's failing heating unit couldn't warm the curds above 100°F. Simoes and Hilarides knew that change would affect the cheese but were curious as to how, so they continued the process. Serenita is handmade in the manner of Serena, but aged for only 60 to 90 days. This cheese was originally named *Bella Sorella* (Italian for "beautiful sister"), but because of a trademark dispute it's now called Serenita. The FAT CONTENT for this cheese is about 35 percent.

Serena, Queso de la *see* QUESO DE LA SERENA

Serpa [SERR-pah] *see* QUEIJO SERPA

Serra da Estrela [SEHR-rah dah ish-TRAY-ler (ehs-TRAY-lah)] *see* QUEIJO SERRA DA ESTRELA

serum *see* MILK SERUM

Sfela (PDO) [SFEH-lah]

Origin	Greece
Milk	Sheep's and goat's

Type	SEMIHARD; MOLDED UNCOOKED; ARTISAN, FARM-STEAD, and FACTORY
Appearance	Bars about 6 inches long and 2 inches wide; rindless and white
Texture	Smooth, firm, and slightly crumbly
Flavor	Sharp, salty, and creamy

S

Hailing from the Messinia and Lakonia prefectures in the southern Peloponnese, Sfela—a FETA-style cheese cured in BRINE—has been produced for over a century. Its name comes from the Greek *sfelida,* which means "slice." Sfela is traditionally made from sheep's milk, goat's milk, or a mixture of the two. The CURD is lightly pressed, cut into strips, and then salted. Sfela is sometimes referred to as "Feta of the Fire" because the cut curd is scalded at 100°F to 104°F, not a normal step in the production of Feta-style cheeses. The cheese is placed in vessels and covered with brine for 1 month at room temperature and then for at least 3 months at about 40°F. The FAT CONTENT of Sfela is around 45 percent. Sfela is also referred to as *Feta Tis Fotias.*

sharp *see* Glossary of Cheese Descriptors, page 503

sheep's milk cheeses *see* Cheeses by Milk Type, page 524

Shelburne Farms *see* CHEDDAR

Shropshire Blue [SHRAHP-sher BLOO]

Origin	England (Nottinghamshire)
Milk	Pasteurized cow's
Type	SEMISOFT to SEMIHARD; MOLDED UNCOOKED; BLUE-VEINED; NATURAL RIND; ARTISAN and FARMSTEAD

Appearance	18-pound wheels; rind is rough, reddish brown (darkening with age), and covered with a variety of molds; interior is orange with bluish green veins
Texture	Moist and creamy when young; aged versions are firmer and crumbly
Flavor	Mild, creamy, and caramellike with a piquant touch; becomes fuller flavored and creamier with age

There are a number of stories regarding the origin of Shropshire Blue, but the most popular version relates to Scottish cheese-maker Andy Williamson, who learned the art of making STILTON in Nottinghamshire. When he returned to Inverness, Scotland, in the 1970s, Williamson began making blue cheese at the Castle Stuart Dairy. Locally this cheese was called *Invernessshire Blue* and *Blue Stuart,* but for marketing purposes the dairy renamed it Shropshire Blue. Unfortunately, the Castle Stuart Dairy was closed in 1980. After a few failed attempts to resurrect this cheese, Shropshire Blue production began a few years later in Notting-hamshire, not far from where Andy Williamson first learned to make Stilton. As with BLUE CHESHIRE, Shropshire Blue has a deep orange color that comes from the addition of ANNATTO. It's simi-lar to Stilton in flavor, although not quite as rich and complex. In fact, Shropshire Blue is produced very much like Stilton, and several manufacturers use the same forms as for Stilton. This milk is inoculated with *Penicillium roqueforti*, the same mold used for STILTON, GORGONZOLA, and ROQUEFORT. As with most blue cheeses, needles are used to pierce the cheese to create channels for air to feed the beneficial mold during RIPENING. Shropshire Blue is typically aged for 8 to 12 weeks (Stilton for 3 to 4 months) and has a FAT CONTENT of about 48 percent.

Sierra Nevada Cheese Company *see* CREAM CHEESE

S

silky *see* SMOOTH in the Glossary of Cheese Descriptors, page 504

Single Gloucester (PDO) [GLOSS-ter] *see* GLOUCESTER

sizes and shapes of cheeses *see* BARREL; BESACE; BICORNE; BLOCK; BONDON; BOUCHON; BOULE; BOUTON; BRIQUE; BROCHETTE; BÛCHE; CARRÉ; CERISE; CLOCHETTE; COEUR; CROTTIN; DAISY; FIGUE; FLAT (2); FLEUR; LINGOT; LOAF; LONGHORN; MAMMOTH; MÉDAILLON; MOON; PAVÉ; PYRAMIDE; QUATRE FEUILLE; ROND; TAUPINIÈRE; TRUCKLE; WHEEL

skim milk; skimmed milk; skimming Another term for fat-free milk (*see* MILK). Skimming simply refers to removing all or part of the cream from the milk's surface.

Slovakian cheeses *see* Cheeses by Country of Origin, page 514

smear ripened; smear-ripened cheeses *see* WASHED RIND

Smith's Country Cheese *see* GOUDA

smoked cheeses A style of cheese that has undergone a natural smoking process using wood chips, nut shells, or the like. Cheese is cold smoked, meaning that it's not placed directly over the source of smoke, and no cooking takes place. Some cheese producers take a shortcut by adding a liquid smoke product to the BRINE or WHEY in which a cheese is soaked. *See also* FLAVORED CHEESES.

Smokey Blue *see* ROGUE RIVER BLUE

smoky *see* Glossary of Cheese Descriptors, page 504

smooth *see* Glossary of Cheese Descriptors, page 504

S

soapy *see* RANCID in the Glossary of Cheese Descriptors, page 502

soft cheeses *see* TEXTURE, CHEESE

soft-ripened cheeses A type of cheese that ripens (*see* RIPENING) from the outside in. Surface ripening occurs when the cheese is exposed to MOLD naturally or when the surface is brushed or sprayed with a harmless bacteria (such as *Penicillium candidum*). Soft-ripened cheeses (also known as *surface-ripened, bacterial-ripened,* or *bloomy-rind cheeses*) typically have a distinctive flavor, an edible rind, and a soft or semisoft texture. Examples include BRIE, CAMEMBERT, and LIMBURGER. *See also* TYPE(S), CHEESE.

Solé GranQueso [SOH-lay grahn KAY-soh] *see* GRANQUESO

solids *see* DRY MATTER

Sonoma Jack *see* JACK

Sottocenere [SOHT-toh-CHAY-nay-ray]

Origin	Italy (Veneto)
Milk	Unpasteurized cow's
Type	SEMISOFT; MOLDED UNCOOKED; NATURAL RIND; ARTISAN
Appearance	12-pound wheels covered in a grayish brown ASH mixture; rind is thin and fragile; interior is cream colored with bits of black truffle scattered throughout
Texture	Smooth, semisoft, and creamy
Flavor	Mellow, savory, creamy, and dominated by the distinctive flavor of truffles

This unique cheese has surfaced only in the last decade. It has bits of black truffle blended into the interior, truffle oil rubbed into the exterior, and a coating of wood ash blended with cinnamon, cloves, coriander, fennel, licorice, and nutmeg. This ash coating ties into its name—*sotto* ("under") and *cenere* ("ash"). Even with all the spices in the ash coating, it's the flavor of truffles that dominates. Sottocenere is RIPENED for at least 3 months and has a FAT CONTENT of about 45 percent.

Soumaintrain [soo-man-TRAN]

Origin	France (Burgundy)
Milk	Unpasteurized and pasteurized cow's
Type	SEMISOFT; MOLDED UNCOOKED; WASHED RIND; ARTISAN, FARMSTEAD, and FACTORY
Appearance	12- to 20-ounce wheels; rind is wrinkled and orange to reddish brown; interior is off-white to yellow
Texture	Creamy and supple, becoming very soft with ripening
Flavor	Mild and tangy when young, developing with age into a complex mélange of strong, creamy, savory, and zesty flavors

Soumaintrain has been compared to a small ÉPOISSES DE BOURGOGNE and, as with époisses, it almost faded away after being produced for centuries. However, it was resurrected in the 1980s and has gained a steady following since then. Soumaintrain is now made in Burgundy's Côte d'Or and Yonne *départements*. The cheese is RIPENED for a minimum of 3 weeks, but more often for 6 to 8 weeks. During ripening, Soumaintrain is frequently brushed with BRINE or a mixture of water and MARC, a potent brandy distilled from skins and seeds left over from winemaking.

S

This washing helps spread desirable bacteria evenly over the cheese's surface. Fully ripened Soumaintrain is packaged in small wooden boxes to protect its soft contour. It has a FAT CONTENT of about 45 percent. Unlike Époisses, Soumaintrain does not have APPELLATION D'ORIGINE CONTRÔLÉE or PROTECTED DESIGNATION OF ORIGIN (PDO) accreditation, and legal guidelines are not in place regarding production methodology. That means that some cheeses called *Soumaintrain* have not been produced by traditional methods and do not resemble the original in flavor or texture. To get the real thing, look for a Burgundian version.

sour; sour milk *see* ACIDIC in the Glossary of Cheese Descriptors, page 493

Spanish cheeses *see* Cheeses by Country of Origin, page 515

specialty cheese A term used used subjectively, depending on the cheese manufacturer. Some use it to refer to ARTISAN or FARMSTEAD CHEESES—high-quality examples made in limited quantities. Others apply the term *specialty* to unusual styles of cheese, such as BLEU DE BRESSE and BLUE CASTELLO, which combine the qualities of BLUE CHEESE and BRIE.

Spenwood [SPEN-wood]

Origin	England (Berkshire)
Milk	Unpasteurized sheep's
Type	HARD PRESSED UNCOOKED; NATURAL RIND; ARTISAN
Appearance	4½- to 5-pound wheels; rind is hard, yellowish gray to brownish gray with white mold; interior is off-white to pale yellow with a scattering of tiny EYES

Texture	Dense and firm yet creamy on the palate
Flavor	Rich, complex, creamy, sweet, with toffee and nut flavors and a slight tang

Spenwood is produced by Ann and Andy Wigmore at their farm, The Village Maid, near Reading in Berkshire. The closest village is Spenwood; hence the name of the cheese. This award-winning cheese is made from unpasteurized sheep's milk and RIPENED for 6 to 7 months. Spenwood's FAT CONTENT is about 50 percent. The Wigmores also make two other cheeses, **Waterloo** and **Wigmore**.

spiced cheeses *see* FLAVORED CHEESES

spicy *see* Glossary of Cheese Descriptors, page 504

spiking *see* NEEDLING

Spressa delle Giudicarie (PDO) [SPRAY-sah DEH-lay joo-dee-KAH-ree]

Origin	Italy (Trentino–Alto Adige)
Milk	Unpasteurized cow's
Type	SEMIHARD to HARD; PRESSED COOKED; NATURAL RIND; ARTISAN
Appearance	15- to 22-pound wheels; rind is hard with blends of brown, orange, and yellow; interior is white to pale yellow with a scattering of irregular EYES
Texture	Firm and elastic to granular
Flavor	Mild, delicate, and sweet when young, becoming more savory with age

S

This cheese has been made in the mountains of Trentino–Alto Adige for centuries, and some references to it date as far back as the thirteenth century. The word *Spressa* comes from *spress*, referring to pressed CURD. Spressa delle Giudicarie, a DENOMINAZIONE DI ORIGINE CONTROLLATA (DOC) cheese, can be produced only in a contiguous area encompassing the alpine towns and villages in four valleys in the Trentino–Alto Adige region: Chiese, Giudicarie, Ledro, and Rendena. Milk from the following breeds must be used: Rendena, Bruna (Brown Mountain), Grigio Alpina (Grey Alpine), Frisona (Holstein-Friesian), and Pezzata Rossa (Italian Red Spotted). The milk is partially skimmed, a tradition dating back centuries, when the primary focus was butter, not cheese. RIPENING takes place for 3 months for *giovane* (young) cheeses and 6 months for *stagionati* (mature) cheeses. The FAT CONTENT for Spressa delle Giudicarie ranges from 29 to 39 percent.

springy *see* Glossary of Cheese Descriptors, page 504

spun curd *see* PASTA FILATA CHEESES

squeakers; cheddar squeakers; squeaky cheese Invented by Wisconsin cheesemakers, squeakers are freshly made cheddar CURDS that are packaged and sold on the day they're made. If sold the next day, they must be marked as "day old." The bite-sized, mild-flavored randomly shaped squeakers get their name from the fact that, because they're so fresh, they emit audible squeaks when eaten.

starter; starter culture Also known as a *bacterial culture* or *starter culture,* a starter typically consists of LACTIC ACID (sometimes from the previous day's milk or WHEY), ENZYMES or other microorganisms, bacterial or mold spores, and natural elements. Starters come in several forms—fresh liquid culture, freeze-dried, or as a frozen concentrate. Two types of cultures are used in cheesemaking: **mesophilic cultures** function at temperatures between 70°F and 100°F; **thermophilic cultures** work best at temperatures over 100°F. In the initial step of cheesemaking, the necessary acid level is achieved by combining a starter with warmed milk. Starters, which usually contain *Streptococci* and *Lactobacilli,* work by converting the milk's LACTOSE (milk sugar) into lactic acid. This balances the milk's acidity (pH level) so the CASEIN (milk protein) will more readily COAGULATE into a CURD when RENNET is added. Starters also contribute to a cheese's flavor, texture, and other characteristics, depending on the style of cheese. For example, *Propionibacter shermanii* is added to the starter for EMMENTAL to create its characteristic EYES, *Penicillium roqueforti* in a ROQUE-FORT starter produces this cheese's distinctive blue veins, and *Penicillium candidum* or *Penicillium camemberti* in the starter of BRIE and CAMEMBERT is what makes such cheeses ripen from the outside in, rather than vice versa.

St. George

Origin	United States (California)
Milk	Pasteurized cow's
Type	SEMIHARD; PRESSED UNCOOKED; NATURAL RIND; FARMSTEAD
Appearance	8- to 22-pound wheels; hard rind is yellow to tan with a light covering of white mold; interior is ivory to golden with numerous small EYES
Texture	Supple, smooth, and firm, becoming crumbly with age
Flavor	Buttery and creamy with grassy and earthy traits, becoming tangy with additional ripening

St. George is produced by the **Joe Matos Cheese Company** operated by Joe and Mary Matos and their daughter, Sylvia Tucker, on their northern California farm near Santa Rosa. Joe is from the Portuguese island of São Jorge in the Azores where QUEIJO SÃO JORGE is made. St. George is modeled after this Portuguese cheese and the name of the Matoses' cheese is an anglicized translation. Milk from the farm's small herd of Holsteins and Jerseys is gently heat treated (*see* PASTEURIZATION), and vegetarian RENNET is used for COAGULATION. The handcrafted St. George is made with traditional methods and RIPENED for at least 3 months and occasionally for as long as 7 to 9 months. St. George has a FAT CONTENT of approximately 50 percent.

Stilton (PDO) [STIHL-tn]

Origin	England (Nottinghamshire, Derbyshire, Leicestershire)
Milk	Pasteurized cow's
Type	SEMISOFT to SEMIHARD; MOLDED UNCOOKED; BLUE-VEINED; NATURAL RIND; FARMSTEAD
Appearance	18-pound cylinder, 8 inches in diameter, and 12 inches tall (5½-pound mini-drums are also sometimes produced); rind is rough, grayish brown, and covered with a variety of molds; the interior is ivory with bluish green veins—older versions are pale yellow
Texture	Moist, firm, and somewhat crumbly, becoming smoother and almost buttery with age
Flavor	Complex array of rich, creamy, and savory flavors, nuanced with spice, fruit, nuts, and syrup

England's "King of Cheeses," Stilton ranks as one of the top three blues in the world, along with GORGONZOLA and ROQUE-

FORT. But even though this cheese is named for Cambridgeshire's village of Stilton, no Stilton is made in Stilton. There never has been and now legally cannot be. It's believed that Stilton cheese dates back at least to the early eighteenth century, with its origin actually near Melton Mowbray, a town in Leicestershire. One thing historians agree on is that the identity of its creator cannot be established. What is clear is that the cheese's name and fame were generated by Cooper Thornhill. This East Midlands entrepreneur was the landlord of Stilton's famous Bell Inn, an important coach stop on the way to York, about 80 miles north of London. He bought the cheese from Frances Pawlett, a cheesemaker and farmer's wife from Wymondham, near Melton Mowbray. Thornhill sold it to coach passengers traveling to and from London, and it soon became known as "the cheese from Stilton." In 1910, cheesemakers established legal regulations for Stilton, defining geographic production zones, technical specifications, and the cheese's final attributes. Today over 1 million Stilton cheeses are made annually. Until recently, it was the only British cheese controlled in a fashion similar to the regulation of other countries, such as the APPELLATION D'ORIGINE CONTRÔLÉE (AOC) of France. Since the European Union's PDO (PROTECTED DESIGNATION OF ORIGIN (PDO) system was established, several other British cheeses have joined Stilton in obtaining name protection. Although **Blue Stilton** is by far the most famous, there's also a **White Stilton.** Both have PDO status, and to be called "Stilton" each cheese must be made in one of three counties (Nottinghamshire, Leicestershire, or Derbyshire) from pasteurized local milk (though milk from surrounding counties can be used during times of shortage), be made in the traditional cylindrical shape, be allowed to form its own rind, be unpressed, have delicate veining radiating from the center, and have a taste profile typical of Stilton. Only six dairies are licensed to make Stilton cheese. Blue Stilton has

S

Penicillium roqueforti (the same mold used for GORGONZOLA and ROQUEFORT) added to the milk during production. Once COAGU-LATED and drained, the CURD is milled, salted, and placed in tall, perforated molds. The molds are stacked on shelving and turned several times daily for 5 to 6 days to ensure natural, even WHEY drainage without pressing. The molds are then removed, and the surface of the cheese is smoothed and sealed by hand, a process that prevents air from entering the PASTE. The cheese cylinders are then placed in special RIPENING rooms, where they're turned frequently. At 6 to 8 weeks of age the cheeses are pierced with stainless-steel needles to create air channels that allow in the oxygen that promotes the growth of beneficial molds and creates the bluing. Blue Stilton is ripened for about 8 to 9 weeks before a master grader selects it for shipping. Cheeses that miss the mark of perfection are sold simply as "blue cheese." Cheese labeled *mature Stilton* is aged for 12 to 14 weeks and has a creamier texture. White Stilton is made in a similar fashion, except no *P. roqueforti* is used and the cheeses are ripened for only 3 to 4 weeks. It's very mild and has a slightly acidic milky taste. The FAT CONTENT for Stilton cheeses is approximately 48 percent.

Stokes Point Smoked Cheddar *see* CHEDDAR

St. Pat

Origin	United States (California)
Milk	Pasteurized cow's
Type	SEMISOFT; MOLDED UNCOOKED; BLOOMY RIND; ARTISAN
Appearance	12-ounce round; rind is wrapped in leaves with a velvety coating of white mold; interior is ivory colored with numerous small EYES

S

Texture	Soft, smooth, and silky
Flavor	Buttery, woodsy, and mildly tangy with a faintly smoky artichoke nuance

This seasonal springtime cheese hails from the renowned **Cowgirl Creamery,** located in Point Reyes Station, a nature lover's paradise just a little over an hour north of San Francisco. Unlike some cheeses, whose seasonality depends on the availability of the milk, St. Pat's availability is related to the stinging nettle leaves in which it's wrapped. The leaves' sting is removed by washing, freezing, and thawing them before they're wrapped around the cheese. This whole-milk cheese is aged for a minimum of 3 weeks and has a FAT CONTENT of about 48 percent. *See also* MT. TAM; RED HAWK.

stracchino [straht-CHEE-noh] A large family of cheeses favored throughout Italy's Lombardy region and made there since at least the tenth century. The term comes from the Italian word *stracch,* which is Lombardian dialect for "tired" or "exhausted," referring to the weary cows after their lengthy trek down from the alpine meadows to the valleys where they could be milked. That long journey concentrated the milk, making it more acidic and richer than that of cows that had grazed only on the plains. There are numerous cheeses that start or end their name with *stracchino* and others that fit into this category that don't. Well-known cheeses in this family include CRESCENZA, QUARTIROLO LOMBARDO, TALEGGIO, and Robiola Lombardia (*see* ROBIOLA). Stracchino cheeses are typically soft, square-shaped, and have a FAT CONTENT of about 50 percent. *See also* GORGONZOLA.

stretched-curd cheeses *see* PASTA FILATA CHEESES

S

string cheese A type of PASTA FILATA cheese (such as MOZZARELLA) that has been stretched into a long, thin strand, which is stacked in switchback fashion before being packaged. String cheese (also called *Syrian* or *Armenian string cheese*) is particularly popular with children, who love to pull off the strings and eat the mild, chewy cheese.

strong *see* Glossary of Cheese Descriptors, page 504

style *see* TYPE

substitute cheese A "cheese" derived from imitation milks or other nondairy components, such as soy milk, with vegetable oil replacing the butterfat. Such substitutes (also called *analog cheeses*) may be LACTOSE-free and reduced-fat, but they lack any resemblance to the flavor and texture of real cheese. Substitute cheeses are nutritionally equivalent to natural cheeses and PASTEURIZED PROCESS(ED) CHEESES, whereas IMITATION CHEESE is not.

Summertomme *see* VERMONT BREBIS

supple *see* Glossary of Cheese Descriptors, page 505

surface-ripened cheeses *see* SOFT-RIPENED CHEESES

Svecia (PDO); Sveciaost [SVEH-chah; SVEH-chah-oost]

Origin	Sweden
Milk	Pasteurized cow's
Type	SEMISOFT to SEMIHARD; PRESSED UNCOOKED; rindless; FACTORY

S

Appearance	26- to 33-pound wheels; rindless, covered with wax; interior is ivory to pale yellow with small irregular EYES
Texture	Smooth, creamy, and supple
Flavor	Full-bodied mellow, buttery, and slightly tangy

Although Svecia-style cheeses have been made in Sweden since the thirteenth century, the name *Svecia* didn't come into being until the early 1900s. It comes from the Latin *Suecia,* meaning "Sweden." Svecia has never been produced outside Sweden, and it now has PDO status from the European Union. *Ost* is Swedish for "cheese," and this cheese is sometimes referred to as *Sveciaost.* Svecia is RIPENED for at least 2 months. It has three categories of FAT CONTENT—30, 45, and 55 percent.

Swedish cheeses *see* Cheeses by Country of Origin, page 515

sweet *see* Glossary of Cheese Descriptors, page 505

Swiss cheese; Swiss-style cheese

Origin	Throughout the world
Milk	Pasteurized cow's
Type	SEMIHARD; PRESSED COOKED; NATURAL RIND; FACTORY
Appearance	185- to 210-pound wheels and 25- to 28-pound rectangular blocks; rind is thin, hard, and pale to dark yellow in color—some Swiss-style cheeses are rindless; interior is ivory to pale yellow with evenly distributed, abundant EYES
Texture	Pliable and smooth
Flavor	Mellow and nutlike

S

A generic name for cheeses that are patterned after Switzerland's world-famous EMMENTAL. Swiss cheeses are typified by large EYES, a pale yellow color, and a nutty, earthy, slightly sweet flavor. Swiss cheese is made around the world in countries including Argentina, Austria, Denmark, Finland, France, Germany, Italy, Russia, and the United States. Partially skimmed milk is used for this type of cheese. The cheese is brined (*see* SALTING) for about 3 days. The eyes for which Swiss-style cheeses are so famous form during a RIPENING period of about 30 days in warm rooms. It's there that heat-loving bacteria in the cheese begin to ferment and throw off carbon dioxide bubbles, which create holes that can range in size from that of a cherry to that of a walnut. Final ripening takes place in cool rooms and can take anywhere from 2 to 12 months, depending on the manufacturer. The minimum FAT CONTENT for most Swiss cheeses is 43 percent. **Baby Swiss** is a smaller (2- to 5-pound wheels) version of Swiss cheese. Most producers make it with whole milk rather than partially skimmed, as with regular Swiss cheese. Baby Swiss also isn't aged as long as the regular version. It has smaller and fewer eyes, a milder, sweeter flavor, and softer texture. Many producers make a smoked rendition of Baby Swiss.

Swiss harp *see* CHEESE HARP

Switzerland cheeses *see* Cheeses by Country of Origin, page 516

Syrian string cheese *see* STRING CHEESE

T

table cheeses A general term for multipurpose cheeses that are good for cooking as well as for sandwiches, snacks, and salads.

Taleggio (DOC; PDO) [tah–LAYD–jee-oh; tah–LED-joh]

Origin	Italy (Lombardy, Piedmont, Veneto)
Milk	Unpasteurized and pasteurized cow's
Type	SEMISOFT; PRESSED UNCOOKED; WASHED RIND; ARTISAN, FARMSTEAD, and FACTORY
Appearance	8- to 10-inch squares weighing 3¾ to 4¾ pounds; rind is thin, soft, and wrinkly with varied coloring of yellow, orange, and pink, often with blotches of brown and/or gray mold, which becomes darker with age; interior is pale yellow near the crust, becoming

> I have fed too many teenagers to have illusions. Given a choice between cheese, for example, they will skirt the Pont l'Éveque, the Reblochon, the Appenzeller and the triple crème, and head with unerring aim for the prepackaged process slices of the supermarket Swiss (which has the texture, but nowhere near the flavor, of rubber gloves).
> —Robert Farrar Capon

	lighter toward the middle and has a sprinkling of eyes
Texture	Creamy and supple, becoming softer as it ages
Flavor	Mild, sweet, nutty, and faintly tangy when young, becoming rich, full flavored, mushroomy, and tangier with age

Taleggio is another Italian cheese that dates back many centuries, almost certainly to the tenth century and possibly before. It's a style of cheese historically known as STRACCHINO. Its name comes from the Val Taleggio (Taleggio Valley) in the Bergamo province of Lombardy, where it's thought to have originated. Taleggio, a DENOMINAZIONE DI ORIGINE CONTROLLATA (DOC) cheese, has a defined production area that includes provinces in three regions: Lombardy (Bergamo, Brescia, Como, Cremona, Lecco, Lodi, Milan, and Pavia provinces), Piedmont (Novara province), and Veneto (Treviso province). Although most Taleggio is now made from pasteurized milk (particularly in factories), raw milk is still used in most parts of the Como, Bergamo, and Brescia provinces. The cheese may be dry salted (*see* SALTING) but is more typically dipped in BRINE (*see* SALTING). Taleggio is generally aged for 25 to 50 days (sometimes longer) and is stamped with the mark of the Consorzio Tutela Formaggio Taleggio. It has a fat content of about 48 percent.

tangy *see* Glossary of Cheese Descriptors, page 505

Tarentaise [tah-rahn-TEHZ]

Origin	United States (Vermont)
Milk	Unpasteurized cow's
Type	HARD; PRESSED COOKED; NATURAL RIND; FARMSTEAD

Appearance	15- to 20-pound (sometimes 12-pound) wheels with concave sides; rind is thin and butterscotch colored with an occasional dusting of mold; interior is golden yellow
Texture	Firm, dense, even, and smooth with infrequent EYES
Flavor	Buttery, grassy, fruity, and nutty, with caramel tones

This acclaimed cheese is the creation of John and Janine Putnam, owners of **Thistle Hill Farm** in North Pomfret, Vermont. In 1999, these inveterate cheese lovers toured the major cheesemaking regions of the French, Italian, and Swiss Alps. Their goal was to find a cheese they loved, made in a climate close to that of Vermont. They returned the following year to find a copper cheese vat and search out someone who would teach them how to make an alpine cheese in the tradition of BEAUFORT. The Putnams were successful on both counts and named their distinctive cheese after the Tarentaise Valley in the Savoie region of the French Alps. Thistle Hill Farm has been certified organic (*see* ORGANIC CHEESE) for over 15 years, and Tarentaise has been made since 2002. The milk comes from the Putnams' own herd of grass-fed Jerseys and the cheese is handmade by time-honored methods. The process for making Tarentaise begins in a custom-made copper cauldron, of which there are only a few in the United States. The Putnams say the copper vat is essential to creating the distinctive flavor of alpine-style cheese. Once the cheeses enter the RIPENING room, they're hand-rubbed twice a week with a culture indigenous to the Savoie—another step in creating the unique flavor of Tarentaise. This cheese is aged for a minimum of 6 months (sometimes for over a year) and has a minimum FAT CONTENT of 45 percent. Since its inception, Tarentaise has won many honors including a prestigious gold medal at an annual American Cheese Society competition.

taupinière [toh-pan-NYEHR] French for "molehill," this mound shape is one of the many contours into which CHÈVRE is formed.

Teleme [TEHL-uh-may]

Origin	United States (California)
Milk	Pasteurized cow's
Type	SOFT TO SEMISOFT; PRESSED UNCOOKED; NATURAL RIND; ARTISAN
Appearance	12-ounce, 1½- and 6-pound squares; rind is thin, ivory colored, and coated with rice flour, becoming spotted with flecks of green and black mold as it ages; interior is ivory with occasional EYES and creases, the hue of the paste becomes more bone colored with age
Texture	Soft, smooth, and creamy, becoming liquescent with age
Flavor	Delicate, mildly tangy, fruity, and yeasty, becoming earthy and more assertive as it ages

It was 1919 when the Peluso family began making artisan cheeses in Los Banos, California. The family isn't positive about how patriarch Giovanni Peluso began making this cheese but thinks it may have started with his efforts to replicate a cheese made by a Greek family in Pleasanton, California. Teleme has also been compared to Romania's Telemea, which further supports the Eastern Europe connection. There's also speculation that Giovanni Peluso was trying to produce a cheese in the style of Italy's large family of STRACCHINOS, which have soft textures and square shapes (think CRESCENZA). Whatever the origins, the senior Peluso produced a true American original with fans around the world. In 2005, third-generation cheese-maker Franklin Peluso, who had 25 years of family cheesemaking experience, sold Peluso Cheese, Inc., which by this time was producing primarily Hispanic cheeses. After a brief stint in Maine, Peluso returned to California, reestablishing the enterprise in San Luis Obispo as Franklin's Teleme, focusing on making Teleme. In fact, Peluso's company is the only one in the United States that produces this handcrafted cheese. It's formed into squares and dusted with rice flour, which helps to absorb excess dampness in this high-moisture cheese. Teleme is made from whole milk supplied by nearby farms. It's RIPENED for a minimum of 2 weeks and has a FAT CONTENT of about 50 percent. By the time it reaches markets at about 3 weeks of age, packaged securely in a cardboard box, the cheese is soft and relatively mild with a crème fraîche tang and yeasty fragrance. It's engaging at that stage, but some people like it aged longer, and at 2 months the texture becomes liquescent, the flavor appealingly earthy, woody, and nutty. Noted cheese expert and author Steve Jenkins suggests ripening Teleme in its box on the bottom shelf of the refrigerator for 2 months, "or 3 if you're particularly daring." Mind you, Jenkins is talking about the 6-pound format, which will age differently than the smaller cheeses. Check the long-aged cheese by poking it with your finger—it's ready if it quivers like jelly. To serve it, Jenkins suggests removing the top flaps and cutting a ½ inch down the sides of the box. Slice off the top of the rind (which by this time will be coated with greenish black mold) and scoop out the fondue-texture cheese. Any bits of rind that may fall into the cheese are completely harmless. At this writing Franklin Peluso has plans to produce a goat's milk Teleme, as well as a washed-rind TALEGGIO-style cheese.

T

terroir [teh-RWAHR] French for "soil." In the worlds of both wine and cheese, however, *terroir* refers to a sense of place— the contribution of environmental factors that affected how grapes were grown or what ruminants fed on. With cheese, for example, both pasturage and water are affected by the environment—milk from an animal that grazed in a salt-air climate will be different from that of a mountain-grazing animal. Likewise, cheeses ripened (*see* RIPENING) in a natural cave will have different nuances from those that have matured in man-made aging rooms. The word *terroir* is associated with FARMSTEAD CHEESES, rather than those produced by large manufacturers. *See also* Glossary of Cheese Descriptors, page 505.

Tête de Moine (AOC) [teht deuh MWAHN]

Origin	Switzerland (Bern)
Milk	Unpasteurized cow's
Type	SEMIHARD to HARD; PRESSED COOKED; NATURAL RIND; ARTISAN, FARMSTEAD, COOPERATIVE, and some MOUNTAIN
Appearance	1½- to 4½-pound drums typically wrapped in foil or plastic; rind is hard, slightly sticky, and light reddish tan to reddish brown; interior is ivory to pale yellow with occasional small EYES and tiny cracks
Texture	Very dense and compact yet supple
Flavor	Strong blend of savory, fruity, nutty, tangy, and earthy flavors

Tête de Moine was created by the monks at the Abbey of Belle-lay, founded in 1136 in the canton of Bern. This cheese was originally known as *Bellelay,* but the name was changed after the

French Revolution. Two different stories explain the name *Tête de Moine* ("monk's head"). The derivation of one refers to a fee or tax paid to the abbey by local farmers for permission to produce the cheese using the recipe the monks gave them. The annual levy for each farmer was one cheese for each monk (per monk's head). The other story refers to the way the cheese is traditionally served. The top of the rind is removed, and paper-thin "petals" are horizontally scraped or shaved off the top. After the top and some of the side rind is removed from the cheese, it resembles a monk's haircut (tonsure), with its darker sides and lighter crown. Tête de Moine is small and strongly flavored compared to other Swiss mountain cheeses such as GRUYÈRE and SBRINZ. It's made much like a Gruyère but because of its smaller format is RIPENED for 3 to 6 months versus up to 16 months for Gruyère and 4 years for Sbrinz. During ripening, Tête de Moine is regularly BRINE washed, which produces the slightly sticky, reddish brown rind. It has a FAT CONTENT of at least 51 percent. Tête de Moine owes much of today's success to the GIROLLE, a specially designed tool for shaving this cheese into thin layers.

Tetilla [tay-TEE-yah] *see* QUESO TETILLA

Tetilla de Vaca [tay-TEE-yah day BAH-kah] *see* QUESO TETILLA

texture, cheese One of the many ways cheeses are classified (*see* TYPES) is by texture. A cheese's moisture content directly affects its texture—in general, the more moisture, the softer the cheese. The primary textural styles are soft, semisoft, semihard, and hard, with ranges in most categories. **Soft cheeses** are uncooked cheeses that have not been pressed (*see* PRESSING), which gives them a high moisture content of around 80 percent. Most soft cheeses (such as BRIE, CRESCENZA, and REBLOCHON) undergo RIPENING for a relatively short period of time. **Semisoft**

T

cheeses** have a moisture content of between 50 and 75 percent. They may be pressed or not and cooked or not, depending on the cheese. Examples include FONTINA, HAVARTI, and TELEME. **Semihard cheeses** range between 40 and 50 percent moisture and have been pressed but may or may not have been cooked. Semihard cheeses include EDAM, EMMENTAL, and GOUDA. **Hard cheeses** are long-RIPENED cheeses that have a maximum moisture content ranging between 30 and 40 percent. GRUYÈRE is a hard cheese. **Very hard cheeses,** such as dry JACK and PARMESAN, have the lowest moisture (in the low 30 percentile) and are particularly good for grating. *See also* Glossary of Cheese Descriptors, page 505.

thermalization [ther-muhl-ih-ZAY-shuhn] *see* PASTEURIZATION

thermization; thermisation [ther-mih-ZAY-shuhn] *see* PASTEURI-ZATION

thermophilic culture [ther-muh-FIH-lihk] *see* STARTER

30-Month Bandage Wrapped Cheddar *see* CHEDDAR

Thistle Hill Farm *see* TARENTAISE

Three Sisters Farmstead Cheese *see* SERENA

Tilsit; Tilsiter [TIHL-ziht; TIHL-zih-ter]

Origin	Denmark, Germany, Switzerland, and various other countries
Milk	Unpasteurized and pasteurized cow's
Type	SEMISOFT to SEMIHARD; PRESSED COOKED; NATURAL RIND, WASHED RIND, and rindless;

	ARTISAN, FARMSTEAD, COOPERATIVE, and FACTORY
Appearance	6- to 10-pound wheels or blocks; rind is thin, reddish yellow to reddish brown, with some blocks rindless; interior is ivory to pale yellow with a scattering of irregular EYES
Texture	Supple and elastic
Flavor	Nutty, fruity, spicy, and tangy, developing stronger flavors with age

Tilsit was first made in the nineteenth century by Dutch cheese-makers who settled in East Prussia near the town of Tilsit (which is now part of Russia and known as Sovetsk). They intended to make a GOUDA-style cheese, but the milk wasn't quite the same, and environmental yeasts and bacteria were different, factors that produced a markedly different cheese, which they named after the nearby town. From those beginnings, various forms of this popular cheese are now made in Denmark, Germany, Switzerland, and other parts of Europe. To produce Tilsit, the pressed cheese is bathed in brine (SEE SALTING) for 24 to 40 hours. During RIPENING the rind is regularly washed and brushed with brine (rindless versions do not go through this process). In Switzerland this cheese was called *Royalp* or *Royalp Tilsiter* (the latter primarily for exported cheese), but today it's generally referred to as *Tilsiter* or *Tilsit*. The Swiss product is ripened for 3 to 5 months, has a minimum FAT CONTENT of 45 percent, and is made in 8- to 9-pound wheels. In Germany this cheese is known as *Tilsiter* or *Tollenser* and is produced in 6- to 10-pound wheels and blocks. German versions, which aren't quite as hard as those from Switzerland, are aged for up to 6 months and have a fat content that ranges from 30 to 50 percent (the lower range because partially skimmed milk is sometimes used). Denmark's rendition is also called *Havarti Tilsit*. It's similar to though slightly milder than Germany's version and more flavorful than Danish HAVARTI. Danish Tilsits are made in 6- to 10-pound blocks. Tilsit is also made in Belgium, Finland, Poland, and Lithuania. At this writing, there's only one producer in the United States (in Colorado). Tilsit is occasionally flavored with caraway seeds or peppercorns.

Tiroler Almkäse; Tiroler Alpkäse (PDO) [tih-ROH-ler AHLM-ki-zer; AHLP-ki-zer (-kah-zeh)]

Origin	Austria (Tyrol)
Milk	Unpasteurized cow's
Type	SEMIHARD; PRESSED COOKED; NATURAL and WASHED RIND; ARTISAN, FARMSTEAD, and COOPERATIVE; MOUNTAIN
Appearance	66- to 132-pound loaves; rind is dry, smooth, and yellow to brown in color, some versions having a reddish character from washing with a BREVIBACTERIUM LINENS mixture; interior is ivory to medium yellow with a small number of irregular EYES
Texture	Smooth and supple, becoming firmer with age
Flavor	Mild, delicate, and slightly sweet, becoming stronger, savory, tangy, and more aromatic with longer ripening—washed-rind versions are stronger and more pungent

This style of cheese dates back to the mid 1500s, and the terms *Almkäse* ("mountain cheese") and *Alpkäse* ("alpine cheese") have both been used for centuries. It's produced in both North Tyrol and East Tyrol, and cheese production in this region is a time-honored way of preserving the flavorful alpine milk collected during the brief 3- to 4-month grazing period. The official PROTECTED DESIGNATION OF ORIGIN (PDO) name is *Tiroler Almkäse/Tiroler Alpkäse,* which is often shortened to *Tiroler Almkäse/Alpkäse.* PDO regulations state that the milk for this cheese must come from cows who've fed on alpine pastures, some as high as 8,000 feet—milk from the valley floor cannot be used. Production begins with evening milk that's left to sit overnight, then skimmed the next morning and combined with the morning's milking. The cheese is immersed in a BRINE bath for 2 to 3 days to encourage rind formation, and the RIPENING period for Tiroler Almkäse/Alpkäse ranges from $4\frac{1}{2}$ to 6 months. During ripening the rind may be dry-salted (*see* SALTING) or washed with a mixture of brine and *BREVIBACTERIUM LINENS.* The second approach promotes bacteria that cause the washed-rind cheese to develop a more pungent flavor and aroma. The FAT CONTENT for these cheeses is at least 45 percent.

Tiroler Bergkäse (PDO) [tih-ROH-ler BEHRK-ki-zer (-kah-zeh)]

Origin	Austria (Tyrol)
Milk	Unpasteurized cow's
Type	HARD; PRESSED COOKED; NATURAL RIND; ARTISAN, FARMSTEAD, COOPERATIVE, and some MOUNTAIN
Appearance	Wheels of 26 pounds or more; rind is grainy and yellowish brown to brown; interior is ivory to pale yellow with a random scattering of small EYES
Texture	Firm, supple, and smooth
Flavor	Mellow, slightly sweet, spicy, fruity, and nutty when young, becoming more piquant with age

T

Tiroler Bergkäse dates back to at least the nineteenth century, when cheese production spread throughout Tyrol, a state located in western Austria and bordering on Bavaria, Italy, and Switzerland. It's made in both North Tyrol and East Tyrol. *Bergkäse* means "mountain cheese," referring to the area's Austrian Alps. Strict PROTECTED DESIGNATION OF ORIGIN (PDO) rules govern the making of Tiroler Bergkäse. Cows may graze only in alpine pastures or eat hay or grass grown in the area—no silage is allowed. The milk is brought directly to the dairy once a day and partially skimmed. After being brined (*see* SALTING), the cheese is RIPENED for a minimum of 14 weeks and typically for 6 months or more. During this aging period, cheeses are brushed with brine twice a week. The FAT CONTENT of Tiroler Bergkäse is a minimum of 45 percent.

Tiroler Graukäse (PDO) [tih-ROH-ler GROU-ki-zer (-kah-zeh)]

Origin	Austria (Tyrol)
Milk	Unpasteurized or pasteurized cow's
Type	SEMISOFT to SEMIHARD; MOLDED UNCOOKED; NATURAL RIND; ARTISAN, FARMSTEAD, COOPERATIVE, and FACTORY
Appearance	2- to 9-pound loaves or cylinders; rind is thin, covered with blue-gray mold, and laced with small surface cracks; interior color varies from white in the center (which yellows with age) to marbled gray-green and gray toward the rind
Texture	Dry near the rind but moist and supple at the center
Flavor	Tangy, sour, and spicy

Hailing from Tyrol, a state in western Austria, this cheese began as a by-product of buttermaking and is therefore made with very-low-fat milk. It's often called simply *Graukäse,* German for "gray cheese." No RENNET is used in the production of Tiroler Graukäse—the milk is COAGULATED by natural souring or by the addition of lactic acid bacteria. During RIPENING, this cheese is washed with *Penicillium roqueforti,* the same mold used for producing ROQUEFORT, GORGONZOLA, and STILTON. It ripens from the outside in, which causes color changes and marbling, both of which are heavier near the rind and sometimes nonexistent at the center. Tiroler Graukäse has a short ripening period of 2 weeks and a FAT CONTENT of about 2 percent.

Tobermory *see* CHEDDAR

Tollenser [TOHL-len-tzer] *see* TILSIT; TILSITER

toma [TOH-mah] *see* TOMA PIEMONTESE; TOMME

Toma Piemontese (DOC; PDO) [TOH-mah pyay-mawn-tay-say]

Origin	Italy (Piedmont)
Milk	Unpasteurized or pasteurized cow's
Type	SEMISOFT to SEMIHARD; PRESSED COOKED; NATURAL RIND; FARMSTEAD
Appearance	4- to 19-pound wheels; rind is thin, ranging from pale yellow to medium yellow to reddish brown, darkening and wrinkling as it ages; interior is ivory to golden yellow with faint to noticeable eyes
Texture	Supple and springy when young, becoming firmer with aging

T

T

Flavor	Young versions are mild and sweet with a slight tanginess; older versions are more intense, savory, and piquant

Toma cheeses have been produced in Italy's Piedmont and Lombardy regions for centuries, some think back to Roman times. The origin of the name *toma* is controversial. The most popular theory is that in the regional dialect the term *tomé* means "fall" (the French, *tomber,* also means "to fall"), referring to the process that occurs when milk proteins begin to bond and form CURDS, which fall to the bottom of the container. There are myriad toma cheeses, but Toma Piemontese is the only one with DENOMINAZIONE DI ORIGINE CONTROLLATA (DOC) status. It's produced in an area in Piedmont encompassing the provinces of Biella, Cuneo, Novara, Turin, and Vercelli, plus some neighboring villages in the Alessandria and Asti provinces. Although it's a PROTECTED DESIGNATION OF ORIGIN (PDO) cheese, the cheesemaking regulations are flexible, so finding consistency from one producer to another is unusual. Though there are two styles of Toma Piemontese—one made with whole milk and one with partially skimmed milk (called *semigrassa*)—they're made in the same way. RIPENING takes place for anywhere from 15 days to 5 months (smaller sizes are aged for less time). The FAT CONTENT for whole-milk cheeses ranges from 44 to 54 percent and for the partially skimmed milk cheese from 30 to 38 percent.

tome [TUHM] *see* TOMME

Tomino; *pl.* **Tomini** [toh-MEE-noh; toh-MEE-nee]

Origin	Italy (Piedmont)
Milk	Pasteurized cow's; sometimes goat's or a mixture of the two

Type	SOFT to SEMISOFT; FRESH; rindless; ARTISAN
Appearance	Stark white, small (2- to 4-ounce) rindless disks about 1 inch thick
Texture	Soft, smooth, and creamy
Flavor	Ranging from pleasantly mild and sweet to tangy and yeasty as it ages

Although Tomino hails predominantly from the Piedmont, it's also produced in other regions of northern Italy. This uncomplicated cheese is briefly brined (*see* SALTING), then typically packed in oil flavored with garlic, herbs, and/or hot pepper flakes. Olive oil is classically used, but sunflower or safflower oils are more often the choice for exported Tomini because they don't break down the delicate cheese as fast. Occasionally Tomini can be found wrapped in paper.

tomme; tome; tommette [TOM; to-MEHT] This French term is presumed to come from the Greek *tomos* (Latin *tomus*) for a cutting or section—a part of a whole. Over the centuries the term has evolved in cheese terminology to describe variously small cheeses made from partial milkings, those produced from small-yield winter milkings, and cheeses made from milk gathered from more than one herd. In general, these were cheeses produced when there wasn't enough milk to make large cheeses. They were more often than not nonfat cheeses, as the cream was used to make butter. Today the terms *tomme* and *tome* have broadened to refer to a range of small to medium-size (2- to 3-pound) rounded WHEEL-shaped cheeses that can be made from cow's, goat's, or sheep's milk or a mixture of milks. A *tommette* is the smallest version of these, typically weighing in at under a pound. In Italy such cheeses are referred to as *toma*.

T

Tomme à l'Ancienne [TUHM ah lah*n*-see-EHN] *see* BANON

Tomme d'Abondance [TUHM dah-bohn-DAHNC] *see* ABONDANCE

Tomme de Savoie (AOC; PGI) [TUHM deuh sah-VWAH]

Origin	France (Rhône-Alpes)
Milk	Unpasteurized or pasteurized cow's
Type	SEMISOFT to SEMIHARD; PRESSED UNCOOKED; NATURAL RIND; ARTISAN, FARMSTEAD, COOPERA-TIVE, and FACTORY
Appearance	3½- to 12-pound wheels; thick, brownish gray rind with patches of red and yellow mold; interior is white to pale yellow with a few small EYES
Texture	Soft and supple, becoming firmer with age
Flavor	Mild, delicate, milky, nutty, and savory

Tomme de Savoie cheeses are small to medium-sized (*see* TOMME) and made in the Savoie and Haute-Savoie *départments* in the mountains of eastern France. They're produced from milk that hasn't been used for BEAUFORT, one of the area's great cheeses that comes in 40- to 150-pound wheels. This origi-nally took place during winter, when cows returned from the mountain pastures and milk yields were low. Whole milk is sometimes used to make Tomme de Savoie, but many times the choice is partially skimmed milk. This produces cheese with a FAT CONTENT ranging from 20 to 40 percent instead of 45 percent or more. This cheese is RIPENED for 2 to 3 months. To ensure that you're buying an authentic Tomme de Savoie cheese, look for *fabriqué en Savoie* ("made in Savoie") on the label. Pretenders—cheeses made elsewhere and sometimes ripened in the APPELLATION D'ORIGINE CONTRÔLÉE (AOC) region—sometimes label their cheese *affiné en Savoie* ("finished in Savoie").

Tomme du Lévézou [TUHM doo lay-vay-ZOO]

Origin	France (Midi-Pyrénées)
Milk	Unpasteurized sheep's
Type	SEMIHARD; PRESSED UNCOOKED; NATURAL RIND; FARMSTEAD
Appearance	5- to 6-pound wheels; rind is thick and brownish gold with white mold; interior is pale ivory-yellow with a few tiny EYES
Texture	Firm yet supple
Flavor	Mellow, rich, savory, and nutty

Tomme du Lévézou is produced in the Aveyron *département,* part of the Midi-Pyrénées region in south-central France. The Lévézou is a lofty limestone plateau in an area that harbors more sheep than people. Production of Tomme du Lévézou is limited since it's made by only a small number of local farms from their own herds. Unpasteurized sheep's milk is taken from the evening milking and combined with that of the next morning's milking. Tomme du Lévézou is RIPENED for 60 to 120 days and has a FAT CONTENT of 45 to 50 percent.

tommette [tuhm-MEHT] *see* TOMME

topfen [TOP-fen] *see* QUARK

top stirring The cheesemaking process whereby the surface layer of nonhomongenized milk is stirred down to keep the cream from rising after the addition of RENNET.

T

Torta del Casar (DO; PDO) [TOHR-tah dehl kah-SAHR]

Origin	Spain (Extremadura)
Milk	Unpasteurized sheep's
Type	SOFT to SEMISOFT; PRESSED UNCOOKED; NATURAL RIND; FARMSTEAD, ARTISAN, and FACTORY
Appearance	3- to 4-pound flattened wheels with slightly bulging sides and top; rind is soft, delicate, waxy, and pale golden in color—it can have small cracks when mature; interior is ivory colored (turning pale golden with age) with a scattering of EYES
Texture	Creamy, supple, and spoonable when fully ripe
Flavor	Buttery rich, nutty, and tangy, with a pleasantly bitter undertaste

One of Spain's great cheeses, Torta del Casar is named for its place of origin, Casar de Cáceres, a small town about 6 miles outside the province capital Cáceres in west-central Spain's central and southern portions of the Extremadura region. The DENOMINACIÓN DE ORIGEN PROTEGIDA (DO) regulations for this cheese require that the milk come from Merino and/or Entrefina sheep, and it takes almost twenty sheep to produce enough milk for about 2 pounds of cheese. Torta del Casar, a cousin of QUESO DE LA SERENA is made year-round from two daily milkings. Eight family-run dairies produce it by traditional methods handed down through the ages. The milk is COAGULATED with an extract of dried cardoon thistle, which gives the cheese a pleasantly subtle bitter note. The rice-sized pieces of CURD are scooped into molds that traditionally are made of esparto grass, but today plastic look-alikes are typically used. Torta del Casar is RIPENED and turned daily for a minimum of 2 months. It has a FAT CONTENT of 45 to 50 percent.

Although younger versions of this cheese can be sliced when chilled, fully ripe cheese becomes spoonable at room temperature. The traditional way to eat it then is to slice off the rind's top and scoop out the PASTE.

Trade Lake Cedar

Origin	United States (Wisconsin)
Milk	Unpasteurized sheep's
Type	SEMIHARD; PRESSED COOKED; NATURAL RIND; FARMSTEAD
Appearance	8-pound wheels topped with a cedar bough; rind is beige to golden brown spotted with mold; interior is ivory to tan with irregular scattering of EYES and cracks
Texture	Very dense and compact yet supple when young, becoming harder and granular in older versions
Flavor	Complex, fruity, and nutty, with caramel and cedar traits

Trade Lake Cedar is named after one of the eight small lakes on the 200-acre sheep farm called **LoveTree Farmstead.** David and Mary Falk operate this farm in northern Wisconsin near Grantsburg, which is 60 miles northeast of Minneapolis. Dave proposed to Mary under a pair of trees that had twisted together, essentially becoming one. This tree has become the symbol of LoveTree Farmstead. Since the farm is next to a wilderness area full of predators, the sheep are protected by the LoveTree Livestock Guardian Dogs (which they breed and sell), some of which are Spanish Ranch mastiffs, which were initially brought from Spain specifically for this purpose. Trade Lake Cedar has won numerous awards over the years, including Best of Show at an

American Cheese Society competition. Some of the cheese's character comes from RIPENING it on top of cedar branches in a fresh-air cave, which allows access to the morning fog replete with woodland odors. Trade Lake Cedar is aged for a minimum of 2½ months.

Tradition du Berry [trah-dee-SHOH*N* deuh BEH-ree] *see* VALENÇAY

transhumance [trans-HYOO-muhnz] Common in many European countries, such as France, Italy, and Switzerland, transhumance is the seasonal migration of livestock from one grazing area to another. In the springtime the animals are gradually herded (sometimes transported in multideck trailers) out of the lowlands up to lush mountain pastures for spring and summer grazing. By mid-August, herds can reach an altitude of almost 10,000 feet, just below the snowline. The mountain pastures provide an abundant range of grasses, herbs, flowers, and fresh clear water. At the first sign of snow, the animals begin gradually eating their way back down to the sheltered valleys, where they spend fall and winter. This migration is managed by herders (also known as *bergers* or *alpagistes*), who also milk the animals twice a day and produce wonderful handmade MOUNTAIN CHEESES during the summer in small alpine chalets or huts. *See also* ALPAGE.

Trappist cheeses *see* MONASTERY CHEESES

triple-cream cheeses *see* DOUBLE-CREAM/TRIPLE-CREAM CHEESES

truckle A term used by cheesemakers, primarily in Britain and Australia, for a cylindrical or barrel-shaped cheese that is typically cloth bound and sometimes waxed. Truckles come in various sizes, the most common ranging from 4.4 to 13.2

pounds. The word *truckle* comes from the Latin *trochlea* and Middle English *trocle,* both words referring to pulleys. *See also* CHEESE SIZES AND SHAPES.

truffly *see* EARTHY in the Glossary of Cheese Descriptors, page 497

Tulare Cannonball [too-LEHR-ree] *see* EDAM

Tumalo Tomme [TOO-mah-loh TUHM]

Origin	United States (Oregon)
Milk	Unpasteurized goat's
Type	SEMISOFT to SEMIHARD; PRESSED UNCOOKED; WASHED RIND; FARMSTEAD
Appearance	4-pound wheels; rind is thin and beige with splotches of orange and a light coating of white mold; interior is the palest yellow with a few small EYES
Texture	Firm, creamy, and smooth
Flavor	Mild and sweet with hints of earth, mushrooms, and pine trees

Tumalo Tomme is produced by **Juniper Grove Farm** of Redmond, Oregon. Its owner-cheesemaker, Pierre Kolisch, is a former attorney who studied cheesemaking in Normandy for several years (apprenticing with mentor François Durand) prior to establishing his farm. Tumalo Tomme is patterned after the TOMME cheeses found in Europe, such as TOMME DE SAVOIE and TOMME D'ABONDANCE, though both of these cheeses are made with cow's instead of goat's milk. To produce Tumalo Tomme, Kolisch uses raw milk from his herd of about eighty goats. He employs traditional farmstead techniques, brining (*see* SALTING) the cheeses for a day, then repeatedly turning and washing

T

them during the RIPENING period. Ideally aging is 3 months for tommes produced from summer milk, 4 months plus for those made from autumn milk. Kolisch also makes eleven other goat cheeses, including **Pyramid,** a truncated pyramid-shaped raw goat's milk cheese featuring an ASH-covered BLOOMY RIND, a velvety smooth texture, and creamy, tangy flavor. The Juniper Grove Pyramid is aged for about 2 months. Kolisch also raises Red Duroc pigs on his farm, using WHEY from cheesemaking as part of their feed.

turophile [TOOR-uh-file] A person who loves cheese, taken from the Greek words for cheese (*turos*) and loving (*philos*).

type(s), cheese In the world of cheese, the word *type* refers to a cheese's classification according to common characteristics such as texture, rind, or the way it's processed. However, there's simply no single way to classify the type (or style) of cheese—it's too multifaceted a subject. For example, cheese may be grouped by its size, shape, or color. Or by the way it's processed (BLUE-VEINED CHEESES, DOUBLE-CREAM AND TRIPLE-CREAM CHEESES, FRESH CHEESES, GRANA CHEESES, PASTA FILATA CHEESES, PROCESS(ED) CHEESES, SOFT-RIPENED CHEESES) or by its rind (ARTIFICIAL RIND, BLOOMY RIND, NATURAL RIND, WASHED RIND) or by its texture (HARD CHEESES, SEMIHARD CHEESES, SEMISOFT CHEESES, SOFT CHEESES) or by whether or not it's RIPENED. Then again cheese may be classified by *how* it's made—by hand (ARTISAN CHEESES, FARMSTEAD CHEESES, and sometimes COOPERATIVE CHEESES) or industrially (FACTORY CHEESES). And it can certainly be categorized by MILK source (cow's, goat's, and so on) and whether that milk has undergone PASTEURIZATION or not (RAW-MILK CHEESES) or if it's whole, low-fat or nonfat; or it could be an ORGANIC CHEESE. Then there are WHEY CHEESES, produced with a by-product

from making other cheeses. And there's a whole family of
near-cheeses (IMITATION CHEESES, PROCESS(ED) CHEESES,
SUBSTITUTE CHEESES) and cheeses with add-ins (FLAVORED
CHEESES, PICKLED CHEESES, SMOKED CHEESES). Another
classification method is to group cheeses by country of origin.
Of course this can be problematic for some cheeses, such as
GRUYÈRE, which is made in at least five different countries
(Australia, France, Germany, Switzerland, and the United
States). And therein lies the conundrum, for there are myriad
cheeses that may be classified in several different ways. Take
CAMEMBERT, for example, which can be placed in any of several
categories including soft cheese, bloomy-rind cheese, soft-
ripened cheese, and aged cheese. And that's just for starters
because, you see, although traditional Camembert is from
France, it's now also being made in the United States and can be
made from raw or pasteurized milk, and although classically
produced from cow's milk, it's sometime made with goat's and
sheep's milk in the United States. So there you have it. It's
useless to try to categorize cheese . . . just sit back and enjoy it.
See also COLD PACK CHEESES; KOSHER CHEESES; MONASTERY
CHEESES; MOUNTAIN CHEESES; SWISS CHEESES; TABLE CHEESES.

U

umami [oo-MAH-mee] *see* Glossary of Cheese Descriptors, page 506

> I love cheese! It's a marvelous product, inscribed in that great trinity of the table, which it forms with bread and wine.
> —Joël Robuchon

uncooked molded cheeses *see* MOLDED UNCOOKED CHEESES

uncooked pressed cheeses *see* PRESSED UNCOOKED CHEESES

United Kingdom cheeses *see* Cheeses by Country of Origin—England, page 509; Ireland, page 512; Scotland, page 514; Wales, page 518

United States cheeses *see* Cheeses by Country of Origin, page 516

unpasteurized milk; unpasteurized-milk cheeses Milk that hasn't undergone PASTEURIZATION (or the cheese made from it); also called *raw milk* and *raw-milk cheeses*.

unpasteurized milk/imported cheese dilemma At this writing, the U.S. Food and Drug Administration (FDA) requires cheese made with unpasteurized milk to be ripened for 60 days or more. Therefore, cheeses with less aging cannot be legally imported into the United States. To add insult to injury, the FDA has banned all RAW-MILK "soft cheeses" (including SEMISOFT and SOFT-RIPENED) even if aged for more than 60 days. In response, many countries are creating pasteurized-milk versions of their raw-milk cheeses that age under 2 months. Unfortunately, most are using flash PASTEURIZATION (heating at 161°F for 15 seconds), which typically produces a telltale "cooked" flavor and slows down the RIPENING process of cheese, which affects its complexity, character, flavor, and texture. However, ARTISAN cheesemakers around the world (including those in the United States) are using a technique called *heat treatment pasteurization,* which gently warms the milk at 145°F for 30 minutes. This method produces a cheese with a more natural flavor that's closer to the versions made with raw milk. Still, for informed cheese lovers, the FDA's ban on raw-milk cheeses—all in the name of food safety—is maddening. After all, people around the world have been consuming raw-milk cheeses on a daily basis without dying. What's true is that most food-borne illness from cheese is caused by postproduction contamination, whether or not the cheese has been made with pasteurized milk.

unripened cheeses *see* FRESH CHEESES

Uplands Cheese Company *see* PLEASANT RIDGE RESERVE

Urgelia [oor-KHAY-lya] Brand name for QUESO DE L'ALT URGELL Y LA CERDANYA.

use-by date *see* PRODUCT DATING

V

vaca; vacca [*Sp.* BAH-kah, *Port.* VAH-ker; VAHK-kah] *Vaca* is both the Spanish and Portuguese word for "cow"; *vacca* is the Italian word. Seen on some labels for cow's milk cheeses from these countries.

> Cheese is the soul of the soil.
> —Pierre Androuët

vache [VAHSH] French for "cow," seen on some labels for cheese made of cow's milk.

Vacherin du Haut-Doubs (AOC; PDO); Mont d'Or (AOC; PDO) [vash-RAN doo oh-DOOB; mawn DOR]

Origin	France (Franche-Comté)
Milk	Unpasteurized cow's
Type	SEMISOFT; PRESSED UNCOOKED; WASHED RIND; ARTISAN and FACTORY
Appearance	Flat 1- to 2¼-pound or 4- to 6½-pound wheels encircled by a band of spruce wood; rind is wrinkled and light to dark gold in color with some white mold, reddish splotches, and cheesecloth marks; interior is ivory colored
Texture	Smooth, creamy, and satiny, becoming thickly molten as it ripens
Flavor	Earthy, mushroomy, and complex but mild with creamy, smoky, grassy, and woody traits

V

Vacherin du Haut-Doubs, also called *Mont d'Or*, is a French cheese with APPELLATION D'ORIGINE CONTRÔLÉE (AOC) accreditation. The names cause some confusion because the cheese known as VACHERIN MONT D'OR is actually produced by the Swiss. This style of cheese was made by both countries for several centuries on Mont d'Or, which lies in both France and Switzerland. Each country called its cheese *Vacherin Mont d'Or* until the Swiss gained lawful use of the name in 1973. When the French established their AOC designation in 1981, they determined the cheese could be called either *Vacherin du Haut-Doubs* or simply *Mont d'Or*. The French and Swiss cheeses are made almost identically except that the French versions are made only with unpasteurized cow's milk, whereas the Swiss renditions can use either raw or pasteurized milk. Vacherin du Haut-Doubs is made only from August 15 through March 31. During the rest of the year the milk is used to make COMTÉ. To produce Vacherin du Haut-Doubs, the CURD is placed in a mold and lightly pressed. After it's unmolded, the cheese is banded with an aromatic spruce strip and then set on spruce planks to RIPEN for at least 3 weeks, during which time it's frequently washed with BRINE. Vacherin du Haut-Doubs is packed in a wooden box to protect its soft contour. It has a minimum FAT CONTENT of 45 percent. When serving it, leave the spruce band in place to hold the cheese together, bring it to room temperature, cut into the top, and serve with a spoon. The AOC-designated French Vacherin du Haut-Doubs (Mont d'Or) cheeses cannot be exported into the United States at this writing (*see* UNPASTEURIZED MILK/IMPORTED CHEESE DILEMMA). There is, however, a French Vacherin du Haut-Doubs–style cheese made with milk that has undergone gentle PASTEURIZATION. Called *l'Édel de Cleron* or **Faux Vacherin,** this pasteurized-milk cheese is considered by many to be very good, though it cannot use the AOC designation.

V

It looks like a Vacherin (though the surface is more off-white than golden), complete with wood banding and wooden-box packaging. L'Edel de Cleron comes in two sizes—7 ounces and 4½ pounds. The PASTE, though not as oozy as true Vacherin, is still soft and spreadable. Swiss versions made with pasteurized milk can be exported to the United States but are not as highly regarded as those from France.

Vacherin Fribourgeois (AOC) [vash-RAN free-boor-ZHWAH]

Origin	Switzerland (Fribourg)
Milk	Unpasteurized cow's
Type	SEMIHARD; PRESSED UNCOOKED; NATURAL RIND; ARTISAN, FARMSTEAD, COOPERATIVE, FACTORY, and some MOUNTAIN
Appearance	15½- to 20-pound wheels; rind is rough and golden to reddish brown; interior is ivory to pale yellow with small, irregular EYES
Texture	Supple, smooth, and firm
Flavor	Blend of savory, nutty, spicy, and caramellike flavors

Vacherin Fribourgeois, sometimes simply called *Fribourgeois,* is one of Switzerland's oldest cheeses and dates back to at least the fifteenth century. It's made in western Switzerland's canton of Fribourg. This cheese shouldn't be confused with VACHERIN MONT D'OR, which is made in the canton of Vaud, adjacent to Fribourg. Although similar to a small GRUYÈRE, Vacherin Fribourgeois is moister because it's uncooked and only lightly pressed. It's available in several versions: *Bio*, which is RIPENED for 10 weeks; *Select*, aged for 12 weeks; and *Extra*, which has 17 weeks of ripening. *Alpage* is a designation set aside for cheeses made in alpine huts according to traditional methods from the milk of cows that graze only in mountain pastures. The FAT CONTENT of Vacherin Fribourgeois is a minimum of 48 percent.

Vacherin Mont d'Or (AOC) [vash-RAN mawn DOR]

Origin	Switzerland (Vaud)
Milk	Unpasteurized and pasteurized cow's
Type	SEMISOFT; PRESSED UNCOOKED; WASHED RIND; ARTISAN and FACTORY
Appearance	Flat 1- to 6½-pound wheels encircled by a band of pinewood; rind is wrinkled and light to dark gold in color with some white mold, reddish splotches, and cheesecloth marks; interior is ivory colored
Texture	Smooth, creamy and satiny, becoming thickly molten as it ripens
Flavor	Earthy, mushroomy, and complex but mild with creamy, smoky, grassy, and woody notes

Vacherin Mont d'Or is made in the canton of Vaud in southwestern Switzerland. The name causes confusion with cheeses that are produced across the border in France. This style cheese was made by both countries for several centuries on Mont d'Or, which straddles the boundary between France and Switzerland. Both countries called their cheese *Vacherin Mont d'Or* until 1973, when Switzerland acquired lawful use of that name. In 1981, the French obtained an APPELLATION D'ORIGINE CONTRÔLÉE (AOC) designation for its cheese and decided it would be called either *VACHERIN DU HAUT-DOUBS* or simply *Mont d'Or*. The recipes and techniques for producing Vacherin Mont d'Or and Vacherin du Haut-Doubs are almost identical except that the Swiss versions can be made with either raw or pasteurized milk, whereas the

V

French style must be produced from raw milk. Vacherin Mont d'Or is made only in the winter months when the cows are safely confined to their barns. During the rest of the year the milk is used to make GRUYÈRE. To produce Vacherin Mont d'Or, the CURD is placed in a mold and lightly pressed. After it's unmolded, the cheese is banded with an aromatic pine strip, known as a *sangle,* and then set on wooden planks to RIPEN for at least 3 weeks, during which time it's frequently washed with BRINE. Vacherin Mont d'Or is packed in a wooden box for protection. It has a minimum FAT CONTENT of 50 percent. To serve perfectly ripe room-temperature Vacherin, leave the pine band in place to hold the cheese together, cut off the top of the rind, and use a spoon to scoop out the cheese.

Valais [va-LAY] *see* RACLETTE

Valdeón [vahl-day-OHN] *see* QUESO DE VALDEÓN

Valençay (AOC; PDO) [vah-lahn-SAY]

Origin	France (Centre)
Milk	Unpasteurized goat's
Type	SEMISOFT to SEMIHARD; MOLDED UNCOOKED; NATURAL RIND; ARTISAN, FARMSTEAD, and FACTORY
Appearance	7- to 9-ounce, truncated pyramid 2½ to 3 inches tall; rind is beige and usually ash covered with blue, white, and gray mold; interior is white to ivory
Texture	Young versions are soft and moist, older ones becoming firm
Flavor	Mild, tangy, and slightly nutty when young, becoming stronger with age

This cheese takes its name from Valençay, a small town in the Loire Valley. There are several stories regarding the truncated pyramid shape. One is that Talleyrand, famous statesman and friend of Napoleon, had the cheese made for the emperor in the form of a pyramid (complete with peak) because of Napoleon's obsession with Egypt. Upon visiting Talleyrand after his return from the failed Egyptian campaign, Napoleon is said to have angrily whacked the top off the cheese. Another story indicates that the resourceful Talleyrand had the top cut off before Napoleon's visit so the emperor would not be upset. Valençay resembles POULIGNY-SAINT-PIERRE, another pyramid-shaped cheese from this area. The shape is obtained with special molds, perforated to allow WHEY drainage. The unmolded cheese is covered with salted charcoal ASH and RIPENS for 3 to 8 weeks. Valençay has a minimum FAT CONTENT of 45 percent. At this writing it cannot be imported into the United States (*see* UNPASTEURIZED MILK/IMPORTED CHEESE DILEMMA). **Tradition du Berry** is made exactly like Valençay but with pasteurized goat's milk so it can pass U.S. import restrictions.

Valle d'Aosta Fromadzo (DOC; PDO) [VAHL-lay dah-OH-stah froh-MAHD-zoh]

Origin	Italy (Valle d'Aosta)
Milk	Unpasteurized cow's (a small amount of goat's milk may be added)
Type	SEMIHARD; PRESSED COOKED; NATURAL RIND; ARTISAN; MOUNTAIN
Appearance	2- to 15-pound wheels; rind is firm and ranges in color from pale yellow to dark yellow mottled with brown, gray, and red; interior is light to dark yellow with irregular eyes
Texture	Firm and supple

V

Flavor	Mild, slightly sweet with a light tang, becoming stronger, saltier, and pungent with age

This cheese dates back to at least the fifteenth century and is the region's lower-fat alternative to FONTINA. Etymologists indicate that local inhabitants historically used the word *fromadzo* when referring to partially skimmed milk cheeses and *fontina* for whole-milk cheeses. The production area for this DENOMINAZI-ONE DI ORIGINE CONTROLLATA (DOC) cheese is the whole region of Valle d'Aosta, northern Italy's mountainous area near the French and Swiss borders. There are two Valle d'Aosta Fromadzo versions, one containing less fat than the other, which is achieved by letting the milk stand for from 12 to 36 hours before the cream is skimmed off. Up to 10 percent goat's milk can be added to the cow's milk for this cheese. Fragrant herbs or seeds may also be used. Valle d'Aosta Fromadzo is aged for 3 to 12 months. Its FAT CONTENT ranges between 20 and 35 percent for the higher-fat version and under 20 percent for the lower-fat style.

Valtellina Casera (DOC; PDO) [vahl-tehl-LEE-nah kah-ZEH-rah]

Origin	Italy (Lombardy)
Milk	Unpasteurized cow's
Type	SEMISOFT TO SEMIHARD; PRESSED COOKED; NATURAL RIND; COOPERATIVE
Appearance	15- to 27-pound wheels; rinds are thin and range from straw colored when young to brownish gray as they age; interiors are compact with tiny EYES and range from off-white to golden yellow, deepening in color with age

Texture	Ranges from smooth and supple to almost granular, depending on age
Flavor	Younger cheeses are mild, delicate, and slightly sweet, and aged cheeses are stronger, savory, tangy, and more aromatic

Valtellina Casera is a variant of BITTO, another Lombardian DE-NOMINAZIONE DI ORIGINE CONTROLLATA (DOC) cheese. However, Bitto can be made only at an altitude of at least 4,900 feet from June through September, when cows graze in alpine pastures. Valtellina Casera can be made throughout Lombardy's Sondrio province and is produced year-round from the milk of cows that graze at lower altitudes near the valley floor. The name of this cheese comes from the Valtellina, a specific area in the Sondrio province; *casera* refers to the cellars used for aging. Once the cheese is formed in round molds it's dry-salted or brined (*see* SALTING). Valtellina Casera must be aged for a minimum of 70 days and has a FAT CONTENT of approximately 45 percent.

Varé; Queso de Varé [vah-RAY; kay-soh day vah-RAY]

Origin	Spain (Asturias)
Milk	Pasteurized goat's
Type	SEMIHARD; PRESSED COOKED; NATURAL RIND; FARMSTEAD
Appearance	4-inch, 1-pound cylinders; rind is pale golden, mottled with white and gray mold; interior is ivory with occasional small EYES
Texture	Smooth, compact, and supple
Flavor	Clean, mellow, herbaceous, and fruity

Eponymously named for the tiny village from which it hails, Varé is a relative newcomer on the cheese scene. Husband and

V

wife team Valentin Forcelledo and Anita Gonzalez have been producing this aged goat cheese for a little over a decade. The milk comes from Murciana goats, a breed renowned for superior production. It should be noted that the goats outnumber humans in the village by about four to one. Varé is brine-soaked (*see* SALTING) for 12 to 24 hours, then RIPENED for up to 50 days. It has a minimum FAT CONTENT of 45 percent.

vegetable-based rennet *see* RENNET

vegetal [VEHJ-ih-tl] *see* Glossary of Cheese Descriptors, page 506

vegetarian cheeses Cheeses made using nonanimal coagulants (*see* RENNET). Look for label descriptions such as "suitable for vegetarians" to find such cheeses. The terms *microbial enzyme* and *vegetable rennet* describe animal-free production and may appear on the contents. As with other cheeses, vegetarian cheeses can range in texture from soft to hard. They are widely available at natural foods stores and supermarkets.

Vella Cheese Company *see* JACK CHEESE; ROGUE RIVER BLUE

Velveeta cheese *see* PROCESS(ED) CHEESES

velvety *see* Glossary of Cheese Descriptors, page 507

Vermont Brebis [breuh-BEE]

Origin	United States (Vermont)
Milk	Pasteurized sheep's
Type	SOFT; MOLDED UNCOOKED; BLOOMY RIND; FARMSTEAD

Appearance	6-ounce wheels; rind is thin with a velvety coating of white mold that shows light patches of beige, orange, and red as it ripens; interior is off-white to ivory
Texture	Soft, smooth, and creamy, becoming oozy with age
Flavor	Rich, sweet, and slightly herbaceous, gaining earthy and wild mushroom traits as it ripens

Willow Smart and David Phinney produce Vermont Brebis at their **Willow Hill Farm** near Milton, Vermont. They raise sheep (East Friesian and Icelandic Friesian crosses) and cows (Dutch Belted and Brown Swiss) in a certified organic (*see* ORGANIC CHEESE) environment in Vermont's Green Mountains. Their Vermont Brebis is modeled after CAMEMBERT, but rather than being made from cow's milk it's made from sheep's milk (*brebis* is French for "ewe"). Available from May through October, Vermont Brebis undergoes RIPENING in the farm's underground cave. This cheese has won awards at both the American Cheese Society competition and the World Cheese Awards in London. In addition to Vermont Brebis, Willow Hill Farm produces other national and international award-winning cheeses including **Alderbrook** (a soft sheep's milk cheese resembling VALENÇAY), **Autumn Oak** (a SEMIHARD cave-aged sheep's milk cheese with nuances of wild mushrooms), **Cobble Hill** (a buttery, creamy sheep's milk cheese resembling BRIE), **Fernwood** (a cow's milk cheese similar to a French REBLOCHON), **La Fleurie** (made with cow's milk and reminiscent of a small Camembert), **Mountain Tomme** (produced with a blend of cow's and sheep's milk in a GRUYÈRE style), and **Summertomme** (an herb coated sheep's milk cheese somewhat similar to a Corsican BRIN D'AMOUR).

V

Vermont Butter & Cheese Company *see* BONNE BOUCHE; FROMAGE
  BLANC; MASCARPONE; QUARK

Vermont Fromage Blanc *see* FROMAGE BLANC

Vermont Quark *see* QUARK

Vermont Shepherd

Origin	United States (Vermont)
Milk	Unpasteurized sheep's
Type	SEMIHARD; PRESSED UNCOOKED; NATURAL RIND; FARMSTEAD
Appearance	Rounded 6- to 8-pound wheels; rind is golden brown; interior is golden with a small number of irregular EYES
Texture	Supple and creamy yet firm
Flavor	Rich, sweet, and earthy with nutty, slightly herbal nuances

After an initial false start with their cheesemaking endeavors,
Cindy and David Major made an extended visit to France's
Basque region to learn how to make aged sheep's milk cheese—
their focus was on OSSAU-IRATY. In 1993, on their farm in Put-
ney, Vermont, the Majors began producing what many consider
to be one of today's premier American farmstead cheeses.
These sheep's milk cheese pioneers have won numerous
awards for Vermont Shepherd, including Best of Show in an
American Cheese Society competition, Best of Class in a United
States Championship Cheese Contest, and a medal at the World
Cheese Awards in London. This handmade cheese is produced
using traditional farmstead methods with raw milk from the
farm's herd of 180 sheep. It's RIPENED for 2 to 6 months on the

property's cool, humid, manmade cave 4 feet underground. This seasonal cheese is available from August through April. In the late 1980s, the Majors began a search for simple, durable stanchions to hold sheep during milking. They found the Cascade Yoking System in England and acquired the rights to manufacture it in the United States as Major Farms Cascade Yoking Systems. Today many producers of sheep's and goat's milk use this yoking system to make milking easy and foolproof. The Majors are also well known for mentoring aspiring cheesemakers, and a number of successful American producers credit Vermont Shepherd as their training ground.

Vieux Lille [vyeuhr LEEL] *see* MIMOLETTE

Vorarlberger Alpkäse (PDO) [foh-RAHRL-behrk-gehr AHLP-ki-zer (-kah-zeh)]

Origin	Austria (Vorarlberg)
Milk	Unpasteurized cow's
Type	SEMIHARD; PRESSED COOKED; NATURAL RIND; ARTISAN, FARMSTEAD, and COOPERATIVE; MOUNTAIN
Appearance	Up to 77-pound wheels; rind is dry, grainy, and golden yellow to brown in color; interior is ivory to pale yellow with a small number of EYES
Texture	Smooth and supple
Flavor	Mild, delicate, and slightly sweet, becoming stronger, piquant, and more aromatic with additional ripening

Historical evidence tells us that cheese of this style was made at least as early as the Thirty Years' War (1618 to 1648) and that the designation *Vorarlberger Alpkäse* was being used by the eighteenth century. *Alpkäse* means "alpine cheese," and Vorarlberg is Austria's westernmost state, bordering Germany, Switzerland, and Liechtenstein. Vorarlberger Alpkäse is made only from milk collected during a 3- to 4-month period when cows can graze in local alpine pastures (at elevations of 3,200 to 6,000 feet). Milk from cows grazing on the valley floor cannot be used. For this cheese, milk from the evening milking is left to sit overnight before being skimmed the next day and combined with the morning's milking. The cheese is soaked in brine (*see* SALTING) for 2 to 3 days until the rind forms. Vorarlberger Alpkäse is RIPENED from 3 to 6 months and has a FAT CONTENT of at least 45 percent.

Vorarlberger Bergkäse (PDO) [foh-RAHRL-behrk-gehr BEHRK-ki-zer (-kah-zeh)]

Origin	Austria (Vorarlberg)
Milk	Unpasteurized cow's
Type	HARD PRESSED COOKED; NATURAL RIND; ARTISAN, FARMSTEAD, COOPERATIVE, and some MOUNTAIN
Appearance	17- to 77-pound wheels; rind is grainy and yellowish brown to brown in color; interior is ivory to pale yellow with a random scattering of small EYES
Texture	Firm, supple, and smooth
Flavor	Mellow, slightly sweet, spicy, fruity, and nutty when young, becoming more piquant with age

Vorarlberger Bergkäse dates back to at least the nineteenth century, when records show that it was being sold to Italy.

Some historians believe it harks back much further—to the fourteenth or fifteenth century. This cheese is produced in Austria's westernmost state of Vorarlberg, which borders Germany, Switzerland, and Liechtenstein. This area is high in the Austrian Alps—*Bergkäse* means "mountain cheese." The production of this PROTECTED DESIGNATION OF ORIGIN (PDO) cheese is governed by stringent regulations. Cows may graze only in alpine pastures or eat hay grown in the area—no silage is allowed. Milk is brought directly to the dairy once a day. After being brined (*see* SALTING) for 2 to 3 days, the Vorarlberger Bergkäse is ready for RIPENING, which lasts for at least 3 months but usually for 6 or more. The FAT CONTENT of this cheese is about 50 percent.

Wabash Cannonball

Origin	United States (Indiana)
Milk	Pasteurized goat's
Type	SEMISOFT; MOLDED UNCOOKED; FARM-STEAD
Appearance	3- to 4-ounce spheres; rind is somewhat wrinkly and covered with

> This place certainly reeks of hospitality and good cheer, or maybe it's this cheese.
>
> —Jean Harlow, actress, in *Red Dust*

W

	dark gray ASH mottled with a soft white mold; interior is white
Texture	Smooth, dense, and chalky, becoming slightly creamy under the rind as it ages
Flavor	Mellow and slightly acidic

Made by master cheesemaker Judy Schad of the acclaimed **Capriole** Farm, Wabash Cannonball took the Best of Show prize in 1995 at the American Cheese Society competition and has been gathering fans and winning awards ever since. Schad makes several notable cheeses (including CROCODILE TEAR, MONT ST. FRANCIS, and O'BANON) from the milk of her blended herd of about 400 Alpine, Sannen, and Nubian goats. Wabash Cannonball is typically ripened for 8 to 10 days and sometimes for up to 3 weeks.

washed curd A cheesemaking practice whereby the CURDS are drained of WHEY before they're thoroughly bathed with water while being continually stirred. This process rinses off all traces of LACTOSE that natural bacteria might convert to acid. Washed-curd cheeses, such as COTTAGE CHEESE, are typically tender, pliable, and mild.

washed rind; washed-rind cheeses A technique whereby the rinds of certain cheeses are periodically washed (brushed, rubbed) with a liquid to keep the surface moist and supple. Although brine (*see* SALTING) is most often used for this RIPENING technique, other liquids employed include beer, brandy, cider, MORGE, oil, WHEY, and wine. This "bathing" process can be done by hand or by machine. Keeping the rind moist stimulates the growth of *BREVIBACTERIUM LINENS,* a friendly BACTERIUM that ripens the cheese from the outside in (*see* SOFT-RIPENED CHEESES) and turns the rind various shades of pink, orange, or red. The finished product typically has a moist rind with a uniquely earthy, mushroomy flavor. Notable washed-rind cheeses include ÉPOISSES, PONT-L'ÉVÊQUE, and TALEGGIO. The terms *red smear* and *smear-ripened* are sometimes used synonymously for washed rind. *See also* BRUSHED-RIND CHEESES; RIND.

W

water buffalo's milk cheeses *see* Cheeses by Milk Type, page 525

wax; waxed Some cheeses—EDAM, for example—are coated with a soft, supple, airtight layer of wax for protection. This wax (also called *paraffin, paraffin wax,* or *cheese wax*) may be clear or variously colored black, red, or yellow. When buying such cheese, make sure the wax is free of slits, which would allow air in and deteriorate the cheese.

waxy *see* Glossary of Cheese Descriptors, page 507

weedy *see* Glossary of Cheese Descriptors, page 507

weeping *see* Glossary of Cheese Descriptors, page 507

Weisskäse; Weißkäse [VIGHSS-ki-zer (-kah-zeh)] *see* QUARK

Weisslacker [VIGHSS-lah-ker] *see* BIERKÄSE

Welsh cheeses *see* Cheeses by Country of Origin, page 518

Welsh rarebit; Welsh rabbit A traditional British creation that consists of toast topped with a thick, smooth melted cheese mixture that can include beer, cream, and seasonings such as Worcestershire, mustard, salt, and pepper. Welsh rarebit is often accompanied by sliced tomatoes and usually served as a main dish. A shortcut snack version consists of toast topped by cheese slices, broiled until browned, then quickly spread with mustard or sprinkled with paprika or cayenne. In short, an open-faced grilled cheese sandwich.

W

Wensleydale [WENS-lee-dale]

Origin	England (Yorkshire)
Milk	Pasteurized cow's and sheep's
Type	SEMISOFT to SEMIHARD; PRESSED COOKED; some BLUE-VEINED; NATURAL RIND; ARTISAN and FACTORY
Appearance	Wide range of sizes from 7-ounce mini-wheels to 46-pound drums; rind is thin, dry, beige to reddish brown with patches of white mold, and covered with cloth or WAX; interior is white to ivory; blue version has veining throughout
Texture	Firm, tight, and creamy yet slightly crumbly
Flavor	White version is mild, nutty, citrusy, and has a honeyed aftertaste—it becomes richer and more piquant with age; blue version is mellow, creamy, and spicy

In the mid-1100s, Cistercian monks from southern France (the land of ROQUEFORT) settled in the Wensleydale area, which is in England's North Yorkshire County. There they began producing a sheep's milk blue cheese. In the 1300s, cows outnumbered sheep, and their milk became the basis for cheesemaking. The 1500s saw the departure of the monks, and local farmers took over cheesemaking chores, a practice that continued until World War II. Throughout this entire time, Wensleydale was essentially a blue cheese. However, the classic blue Wensleydale essentially disappeared during the war, and afterward only one creamery was producing it. That creamery was closed in 1992, but former managers bought it and began producing

Wensleydale again within 6 months. Since then several other creameries and individual farms have begun producing this cheese. Today, though most Wensleydale is made from cow's milk, some cheesemakers are taking the traditional route and using sheep's milk. One of those artisanal producers is Hawes Dairy, whose Wensleydale is slightly tangy, fresh, and milky. There are now blue and white (non-blue-veined) Wensleydales, as well as smoked versions, and some with added flavorings such as onions and chives or fruit (apricots, blueberries, or cranberries). **Blue Wensleydale** is produced in large drum shapes, lightly pressed for 24 hours, then wrapped in muslin. It's pierced with stainless-steel needles to facilitate the growth of the beneficial molds that are fed by oxygen. Blues are ripened for at least 6 to 9 weeks and often for 6 months. **White Wensleydale** cheeses are shaped like flattened disks and are well pressed, which produces a fine, dense PASTE. They're typically aged for 3 to 4 weeks. The FAT CONTENT of Wensleydale cheese is about 45 percent.

West Country Farmhouse Cheddar (PDO) *see* CHEDDAR

wheel A cheese shape that's cylindrical and relatively flat. A wheel typically has a diameter about three to four times its height. This shape is also called *cylinder* and *millstone*. *See also* CHEESE SIZES AND SHAPES.

whey [HWAY] The high-protein, watery liquid that separates from the solid mass (CURD) during cheesemaking. Whey is comprised of water, LACTOSE (milk sugar), albuminous proteins, and minerals. It can be processed further into WHEY CHEESE, whey drinks, and foods such as crackers. Primarily, however, whey is used as livestock feed. Whey is also referred to as *milk serum*.

W

whey cheeses Cheeses made from WHEY (the liquid remaining from making other cheeses) rather than from MILK. The whey is cooked (typically with RENNET) to create a secondary cheese. Whey cheeses run the gamut in style from fresh and mild to RIPENED and sharp. Whey cheeses include GJETOST, MANOURI, and MIZITHRA; RICOTTA can also be made from whey. *See also* TYPE.

white mold *see* MOLD (2)

White Stilton *see* STILTON

White Wensleydale *see* WENSLEYDALE

whole milk *see* MILK

Widmer's Cheese Cellars *see* COLBY

Willow Hill Farm *see* VERMONT BREBIS

Winchester Cheese Company *see* GOUDA

Windsor Blue

Origin	New Zealand (Otago)
Milk	Pasteurized cow's
Type	SEMISOFT; MOLDED UNCOOKED; BLUE-VEINED; ARTISAN
Appearance	4-pound wheels; rind is thin and golden in color with patches of white, gray, green, and blue molds; interior is ivory to pale gold with blue-green veining
Texture	Moist, smooth, and creamy

Flavor   Sweet, rich, creamy, and slightly spicy,
intensifying with age

Windsor Blue by Whitestone Cheese Company is New Zealand's most award-winning cheese. It took a gold medal at the inaugural Brisbane International Cheese Awards and has repeatedly won top honors at the New Zealand Cheese Awards competitions, including the Cuisine Champion of Champions award. Cheesemaker Jason Tarrant has also been named Champion Cheesemaker. Whitestone Cheese Company is located near Oamaru, in the South Island's North Otago region. It's certified organic (*see* ORGANIC CHEESE) and uses only natural fertilizers, such as rock phosphates and seaweed products, in its pastures. The organic label also means that cows don't receive any growth hormones, antibiotics, or other chemicals and that natural products must be used for RENNETS and STARTERS. The handmade Windsor Blue, named after a town in North Otago, is turned twice a week during its 60-day RIPENING period. Whitestone Cheese Company also produces four sheep's milk cheeses and ten other cow's milk cheeses—all handcrafted. One of those in the latter category is **Livingstone Gold,** which has also won several awards. This full-flavored, SEMIHARD cheese is colored with ANNATTO, which gives it a brilliant golden hue—a shade that relates to the historic Livingstone gold fields of North Otago. Another multiple award winner is **Airedale,** a semihard cow's milk cheese with a pale golden interior and a coating of red wax. Younger Airedales are fruity and tangy; more aging makes them more savory, piquant, and full flavored.

X

Xinomizithra; Xynomizithra; Xynomyzithra Kritis (PDO) *see* MIZITHRA

> **B**lessed are the cheesemakers, for they are pure of heart.
> —Monty Python, *Life of Brian*

Y

yeasty *see* Glossary of Cheese Descriptors, page 507

> **S**ome cultures are defined by their relationship to cheese.
> —Mary Stuart Masterson, actress, in *Benny & Joon*

young *see* Glossary of Cheese Descriptors, page 507

Z

Zamorano [thah- moh–RAH–noh; sah–moh–RAH–noh]
see QUESO ZAMORANO

Ziegenkäse [TSEE–gern–ki–zer (–kah–zeh)] German for "goat cheese."

> Beware of young women who love neither wine nor truffles nor cheese nor music.
>
> —Colette

GLOSSARY OF CHEESE DESCRIPTORS

No doubt about it, taste is intensely subjective, whether relating to wine, cheese, or other food or drink. But some cheese-tasting terms are used by pros and TURO-PHILES alike to help describe the characteristics of cheese, both positive and negative. What follows is a basic list of cheese vocabulary terms for your edification. Are such terms necessary? Certainly not. Your enjoyment and interpretation of cheese is all that really matters.

How to use this glossary: Throughout the main A-to-Z section of *The Cheese Lover's Companion,* SMALL CAPS are used to indicate cross-references to other terms in the body of the book (see "How to Use This Book," page xxiii). But there are exceptions to every rule. So, in this Glossary of Cheese Descriptors:

- Terms in SMALL CAPS still point you to the main A-to-Z portion of the book.

- Underlined <u>SMALL CAPS</u> tell you to look within this cheese-descriptor glossary.

- The phrase *See also main listing* points you to the main A-to-Z definition whenever a cheese-tasting term has a tangential or expanded meaning.

A

acidic; acid A good acid balance in cheese is exhibited by a pleasantly TANGY flavor. Excessive acid produces a harsh, BITTER flavor, sometimes referred to as *sour* or *sour milk,* and is considered a fault. The words *acidic* and ACIDITY are sometimes used synonymously.

acidity A cheese with good acidity has an agreeably TANGY flavor. One with too much acidity can taste harsh or BITTER. Acidity and ACIDIC are sometimes used as synonyms. *See also main listing.*

acrid A detrimental descriptor for cheese with a biting or BITTER smell or flavor.

ammoniated; ammoniacal [uh-MOH-nee-ay-ted; uh-MOH-nee-uh-kal] Cheese that has the smell and/or flavor of ammonia, typically the result of its being OVERRIPE or having been mishandled (such as being stored at too warm a temperature). SOFT-RIPENED CHEESES like BRIE and CAMEMBERT are most likely to become ammoniated. As with most things, a hint of this characteristic is permissible—more than that is distasteful and considered a fault. On the other hand, ammoniated cheeses are safe to eat if you can get past the smell.

A

à point [ah PWAN] In the cheese world, this French phrase describes a cheese that's at its peak—perfectly RIPE and ready to eat.

aroma A broad term describing a cheese's smell, which is most pronounced when the cheese is first cut. The aroma may range from lightly fragrant to overwhelming, although the smell may not necessarily telegraph the strength or mildness of flavor.

aromatic A term describing cheese with a definitive AROMA.

assertive A cheese with a definitive AROMA or flavor.

astringent As with wine that's too tannic, an astringent cheese exhibits a harsh, puckery MOUTHFEEL.

barnyardy; barny Descriptor for cheese with an AROMA (and, sometimes, flavor) reminiscent of, well, a barnyard. Unless overpowering, this EARTHY, MUSTY characteristic is generally considered a positive quality. It can be found in some aged goat and sheep's milk cheeses. Also called *cowy*.

bitter A bitingly unpleasant aftertaste akin to that of coffee that's been sitting over heat for an hour or more.

B

blind A description sometimes used for SWISS-STYLE CHEESES that have very few or no EYES.

body The textural characteristics of cheese—by touch, when cut, and by MOUTHFEEL. For the most part, body depends on moisture content—the more there is, the softer the cheese. By the mouth, body can range from CREAMY to GRAINY; to the touch it can vary from soft to CRUMBLY. Other descriptions for body include *elastic, firm, flaky, hard, resilient,* RUBBERY, *semisoft,* SUPPLE, and WAXY.

butterscotch A BUTTERY, caramelized flavor characteristic of some aged cheeses, such as the Dutch Saenkanter (*see* GOUDA).

buttery This descriptor is applicable to both flavor and TEXTURE. Flavorwise, buttery refers to a RICH, creamlike essence. Texturally, it describes a high-fat cheese with a CREAMY, full-bodied MOUTHFEEL.

chalky An adjective that can be both desirable and undesirable. The clean white color and fine TEXTURE of an older CHÈVRE is said to be chalky. On the palate, chalkiness describes a GRAINY, almost powdery sensation that leaves an unpleasant coating on the tongue.

C

citrusy A lively, tart flavor found in YOUNG CHÈVRES and other high-acid cheeses.

clean A fresh, wholesome flavor. A clean FINISH refers to cheese with no lingering aftertaste.

close; closed Describing cheese with a tight, SMOOTH TEXTURE without EYES or mars of any kind. A good example of a cheese with a close texture is CHEDDAR. *See also* OPEN.

cooked Cheese that has a flavor or AROMA of overheated milk, a characteristic of overPASTEURIZED milk.

cowy *see* BARNYARDY

creamy An adjective that can describe a cheese's TEXTURE, flavor, and/or color. Cheeses with a creamy consistency are soft, SMOOTH, and sometimes oozingly RUNNY—prime examples include RIPE BRIE or ÉPOISSES. When used to describe flavor, *creamy* suggests a RICH, BUTTERY quality, such as those found in TRIPLE-CREAM CHEESES.

crumbly A descriptor for cheese that crumbles when cut. Examples are BLUE-VEINED CHEESES and well-aged FETA.

current *see* YOUNG

delicate When describing cheese, *delicate* refers to a soft, mellow (sometimes bordering bland) flavor and/or AROMA. Such delicate attributes can be found in cheeses like a YOUNG JACK or TELEME.

earthy Cheese with a flavor and/or AROMA reminiscent of freshly turned soil or the wholesome yet somewhat MUSTY nuance of a forest floor or a lush pasture. The term *truffly* is sometimes used synonymously with *earthy*. This hearty, rustic characteristic is considered a positive trait. CHÈVRES and MONASTERY CHEESES are often described as earthy.

farmlike Cheese that has a fresh, GRASSY or haylike flavor that is definitively milky.

feed A characteristic of cheese that displays the flavor and AROMA traits of what the animal ate just before being milked. It can be a positive or negative trait, depending on what the animal consumed.

finish The final aftertaste, which can be variously described as *natural*, CLEAN, EARTHY, BITTER, and so on. *See also main listing.*

flat An essentially insipid cheese with no sign of character in either AROMA or flavor. *See also main listing.*

floral A fresh, fragrant quality.

F

friability [fry-uh-BIH-lih-tee] A cheese that crumbles readily is said to have good friability.

fruity A sweet, fragrant AROMA and/or flavor evocative of fresh fruit. The fruity quality may be general, as with American-made MUNSTER, or specific, as with the applelike nuance of GRUYÈRE.

furry Describing the downy white coating on BLOOMY-RIND cheeses, such as BRIE. *Furry* can also be used negatively to describe undesirable MOLD on other cheeses.

gamy; gamey The STRONG, EARTHY characteristics of the animal from which the cheese came (goat, cow, and so on). *Gamy* can be used positively or negatively, depending on the cheese. Such attributes should not be evident in YOUNG cheeses, whereas they might be favorable in an aged cheese.

garlic; garlicky When used in reference to cheese, this term describes an undesirable flavor that's typically the result of what the animal ate just before milking.

goaty Usually a positive descriptor for the distinctively TANGY flavor of goat's milk cheeses. Conversely, older aged goat cheeses can take on an assertively goaty flavor that some find offputting.

grainy A descriptor for cheeses like PARMESAN and ROMANO, which have a coarse, granular TEXTURE. *See also* GRANA-STYLE CHEESES.

grassy; grassiness Describing cheese with a flavor and, sometimes, AROMA analogous to grass. This characteristic is generally attributable to what the animal has consumed before being milked. Grassiness, which is typically perceived as fresh and slightly tart, is usually considered a favorable trait and can be found in fresh GOAT CHEESES.

gummy A negative descriptor for cheese with a sticky, chewy TEXTURE, which is typically caused by excessive moisture.

herbaceous Cheese with a flavor and/or AROMA reminiscent of herbs, a quality usually attributable to what the animal ate before being milked. An herbaceous trait is often found in aged cheeses made from sheep's or goat's milk. Of course herbal flavors and aromas may also come from herbs being added to the cheese during processing or used during RIPENING.

intense An "intense" cheese has ASSERTIVE, concentrated AROMAs and flavors.

L

lactic The word itself is an adjective for things relating to or derived from milk. In cheese-tasting parlance, it describes a cheese with the pleasantly TANGY flavor and AROMA characteristic of sour milk. It can also describe a SMOOTH, CREAMY TEXTURE.

lipase [LIP-ays] *see* RANCID

liquescent [lih-KWEHS-uhnt] A descriptor for cheese that is decidedly oozy or thickly liquid. Also used for cheese that seems to melt in the mouth.

metallic A negative descriptor for a cheese that tastes tinny.

mild A light, almost soft flavor, a common trait in many YOUNG cheeses.

mottled Cheese with a blotchy color variation—both on the rind and in the PASTE—is described as mottled. Such cheeses are typically made from two different batches of CURDS.

mushroomy The CLEAN, EARTHY AROMA and flavor reminiscent of mushrooms and found in some SOFT-RIPENED CHEESES such as BRIE and CAMEMBERT.

musty A negative descriptor for a dank earth AROMA and/or flavor, typically caused by mold growth.

N

nerveux [nehr-VUR] French for "nervous," sometimes used to describe a slightly ACIDIC or tart flavor.

nutty A flavor and aromatic characteristic reminiscent of toasted nuts. SWISS-STYLE CHEESES, such as GRUYÈRE, are often described as nutty.

oniony A generally negative flavor characteristic that's usually the result of the pasturage on which the animal fed.

oozy Synonymous with RUNNY.

open A textural description for cheese with EYES, which can range from pinpoints to the size of walnuts. *See also* CLOSE.

overripe A negative term describing cheese past its prime, which can manifest in a RANCID or AMMONIATED flavor and/or AROMA.

pasty A textural descriptor for an undesirable stickiness.

peppery A SPICY flavor trait with a nice bite. A peppery quality can sometimes be found in well-aged CHEDDARS as well as in some BLUE-VEINED CHEESES.

P

perfumy A descriptor for the almost SWEET, NUTTY, FLORAL AROMA found in some cheeses, such as aged GOUDAS and GRUYÈRES.

piquant A positive flavor characteristic that can range from TANGY to SHARP. Cheeses with this trait include some aged CHEDDARS and ASIAGOS, as well as some YOUNG goat's milk cheeses.

pungent An assertively penetrating AROMA and/or flavor found in many SOFT-RIPENED CHEESES, such as LIMBURGER and BRICK.

rancid; rancidity A rancid flavor or odor is caused by the decomposition of fat as lipase ENZYMES release fatty acids. This flavor can exemplify as a stale, somewhat BITTER and spoiled quality. Oddly enough, a slightly rancid quality lends a few cheeses, such as ROMANO, some of their distinctive flavor characteristics. On the whole, however, rancidity is decidedly a fault. In relation to cheese, the term *rancid* is also called *lipase* or *soapy*.

rich A cheese described as rich is typically high in BUTTERFAT and produces a full-bodied (*see* BODY), complex flavor impression on the palate.

ripe A cheese is ripe and ready to be consumed when it reaches its optimum flavor after being aged (*see* RIPEN-

ING). Depending on the cheese, aging can take any-where from a few days to several weeks to over a year or more for a cheese such as PARMIGIANO-REGGIANO.

robust Describes an assertively complex and full-bodied mouth sensation—a "pop" of flavor that lingers pleas-antly on the palate.

rubbery A negative textural term for cheese with a bouncy, elastic quality that is overly chewy. A rubbery TEXTURE is a characteristic found in many bulk-manufactured reduced fat MOZZARELLAS.

runny Describes the interior of a cheese that, when cut, gently oozes from its rind rather than retaining its shape. Such a characteristic may either be positive, as with a perfectly RIPE ÉPOISSES, or negative, as with a cheese that's been stored improperly at too warm a tempera-ture.

sapid; sapidity [SAP-ihd; sa-PIHD-ih-tee] Cheese that exhibits a pleasantly full-flavored, mouth-filling sensa-tion.

savory A deep, RICH, almost meaty flavor and/or AROMA. See also UMAMI.

sharp In cheese-tasting parlance, the word *sharp* is syn-onymous with *pronounced*. Therefore, a cheese may

S

have a sharp flavor or AROMA, or be sharply salty, BITTER, and so on. Such cheeses are typically fully developed and assertively flavored.

smoky An evocative flavor and/or AROMA descriptor that can describe cheese that has been smoked (*see* SMOKED CHEESE) or an earthy, ashy characteristic.

smooth Synonymous with *silky* or *satiny,* this term describes a spreadable cheese with a TEXTURE that's smooth and RICH. The MOUTHFEEL is CREAMY and luscious.

soapy *see* RANCID

sour *see* ACIDIC

spicy When used to describe AROMA, *spicy* refers to a PIQUANT or PUNGENT characteristic. Flavor-wise, *spicy* describes cheeses with a kick of heat, as through the addition of jalapeños, black pepper, and the like.

springy A cheese (such as one that's SOFT-RIPENED and ready to eat) that, when gently pressed on the surface, rebounds to its original shape.

strong A somewhat ambiguous cheese-tasting term for a pronounced, incisive flavor and/or AROMA.

S

supple A textural term describing a cheese that's firm yet pliable and yielding to the touch. A good example of supple cheese is FONTINA.

sweet When describing cheese, this term relates not to sugar but rather to a flavor that exhibits a reduced level of acid or sodium or both. It can also describe a fruity quality. The end result is a sweet essence on the palate.

tangy Describes the SHARP, distinctive flavor of higher-acid cheeses such as those made of goat's milk, such as CHÈVRE.

terroir [teh-RWAAR] When used as a cheese descriptor, *terroir* refers to characteristics reflective of the area from which the cheese came. For example, a cheese from a heartland producer might have a distinct GRASSY characteristic, while one from an oceanside producer is more likely to have the tang a salt-air environment contributes. The terroir is distinctive in each location, and the cheese is unique to the terroir. *See also main listing.*

texture The general feel of a cheese, whether by hand or by mouth. Texture may be described in numerous ways—firm, soft, GRAINY, SUPPLE, WAXY, CRUMBLY, and so on. When referring to EYES or lack thereof, the textural terms used are OPEN (eyes) and CLOSED

U

(without holes). For the most part, texture is a result of the cheese's moisture content (soft cheeses have more moisture than hard ones), but also its processing, as in the case of PASTA FILATA CHEESES.

umami [oo-MAH-mee] It's long been accepted in the Western world that there are four elements of taste—sweet, salty, sour, and bitter. In 1908, Tokyo Imperial University researcher Kikunae Ikeda identified a fifth taste that he called *umami,* a word that has no exact English translation but may be loosely interpreted as "delicious" or "savory"—the essence of flavor, another dimension. Ikeda determined that glutamic acid (glutamate) was the ingredient that produced this unique fifth taste and developed the seasoning monosodium glutamate (MSG) to provide the umami flavor. Ikeda concluded that, of the five tastes, umami and sweetness were the only two the palate perceives as singularly pleasant. Compared to the other four tastes, umami is exceedingly subtle, resonating more as an overall distinctive palate sensation than a taste. Cheeses described as exhibiting an umami character are those that are long aged, such as aged CHEDDAR and PARMIGIANO-REGGIANO.

vegetal [VEHJ-ih-tl] The flavor and AROMA characteristic of fresh or cooked vegetables. A natural degree of plant character can be attributed to what the animal ate before being milked. However, a dominant vegetal quality is considered a fault.

velvety The downy rind of some SOFT-RIPENED CHEESES (BRIE, for example) can be described as velvety. Some depict the MOUTHFEEL of such a cheese as velvety, though the more apt description would be SMOOTH.

waxy A term describing the firm waxlike TEXTURE of cheeses like EDAM and EMMENTAL.

weedy Refers to a flavor in a cheese that is overly VEGETAL and/or GRASSY and/or EARTHY.

weeping Description for SWISS-STYLE CHEESES that have EYES beaded with minuscule droplets of moisture, the natural result of the dissolution of proteins during RIPENING. In such cheeses, weeping signals peak ripeness and flavor. On the other hand, a cheese may weep if stored improperly at a warm temperature—not a positive signal.

yeasty An AROMA and flavor associated with fermenting yeast—think freshly baked bread just from the oven or a bottle of just-opened beer.

young A term applied to cheeses that have undergone a RIPENING period of only 14 to 30 days. The short aging time produces MILD-flavored cheeses. Young cheeses are also called *current*.

CHEESES BY COUNTRY OF ORIGIN

AMERICA *see* UNITED STATES

ARAB COUNTRIES
Ackawi
Akawi
Damiati
Damietta
Domiati
Gibbneh Beda
naboulsi
nabulsi
nabulsieh
nabulsiyye

ARGENTINA
Reggianito
San Ignacio Blue

AUSTRALIA
Black Label Black Waxed
    Cheddar
Black Label Cloth-Matured
    Cheddar
C²
Endeavor Blue
Parmesan
Roaring Forties Blue
Stokes Point Smoked
    Cheddar

AUSTRIA
Gailtaler Almkäse
Gailtaler Alpkäse
Graukäse
Schloss
Schlosskaese
Schlosskäse
Tiroler Almkäse
Tiroler Alpkäse
Tiroler Bergkäse
Tiroler Graukäse
topfen
Vorarlberger Alpkäse
Vorarlberger Bergkäse

BELGIUM
Chimay
Chimay Grand Classic
Chimay Grand Cru
Chimay Trappiste with Beer
Chimay Vieux
Fromage de Herve

Herve
Limburger
Passendale Classic
Plateau de Herve

CANADA
Chèvre Noir, Le
Oka
Oka Classique
Oka Léger

DENMARK
Bla Castello
Blue Castello
Christian
Christian IX
Danablu
Danbo
Danish Blue
Danish (Dutch) Port Salut
Esrom
Havarti
Havarti Tilsit
Kosher Cheeses
Marmora
Münster
Samsø
Samsoe
Tilsit
Tilsiter

ENGLAND
Beacon Fell Traditional
    Lancashire
Beenleigh Blue
Berkswell

Blue Cheshire
Blue Fade
Blue Stilton
Blue Wensleydale
cheddar
Cheshire
Cheshire-Stilton
Chester
Cornish Wild Garlic Yarg
Cornish Yarg
Cotswald
Derby
Double Gloucester
Gloucester
Green Fade
Kosher Cheeses
Lancashire
Leicester
Lincolnshire Poacher
Montgomery's Cheddar
pub cheese
Red Leicester
Sage Derby
Shropshire Blue
Single Gloucester
Spenwood
Stilton
Wensleydale
West Country Farmhouse
    Cheddar
White Stilton
White Wensleydale

FRANCE
Abbaye de Belloc
Abondance

Affidelice
Aisy Cendré
Ardi-Gasna
Banon
Beaufort
Bleu d'Auvergne
Bleu d'Aveyron
Bleu de Bresse
Bleu de Gex
Bleu des Causses
Bleu de Septmoncel
Bleu du Haut-Jura
Bleu du Vercors-Sassenage
Boule de Lille
Boursault
Boursin
Brie
Brie de Coulommiers
Brie de Meaux
Brie de Melun
Brie de Montereau
Brie de Nangis
Brie de Provins
Brillat-Savarin
Brin d'Amour
Brindamour
Broccio
Brocciu Corse
Brucciu
cabécou
Cabécou de Rocamadour
Camembert
Camembert de Normandie
Cantal
Cendré d'Aisy
Chabichou

Chabichou du Poitou
chabis
Chaource
Chavignol
Chevrotin des Aravis
Comté
Coulommiers
Crottin de Champcol
Crottin de Chavignol
Édel de Cleron, l'
Emmental de Savoie
Emmental Français est-Central
Époisses de Bourgogne
Etorki
Explorateur
Faux Vacherin
Fleur du Maquis
Fourme d'Ambert
Fourme de Cantal
Fourme de Montbrison
Fourme de Salers
fromage blanc
Fromage de Savoie
Fromager d'Affinois
Gaperon
Géromé
Gratte-Paille
Gruyère de Comté
Iraty
Kosher Cheeses
Laguiole
Langres
Livarot
Maroilles
Marolles
Mimolette

Mimolette Française
Montbriac
Mont Briac
Mont d'Or
Morbier
Munster
Munster-Géromé
Neufchâtel
Ossau-Iraty
Ossau-Iraty Brebis Pyrénées
Pavé d'Auge
Pavé de Moyaux
Pavé du Plessis
Pélardon
Pérail
Pérail de Brebis
Petit Brie
Petit Cantal
Petit-Suisse
Picodon de l'Ardèche
Picodon de la Drôme
Pierre Robert
Pont-l'Évêque
Port Salut
Pouligny-Saint-Pierre
Reblochon
Reblochon de Savoie
Rocamadour
Roche Baron
Rochebaron
Roquefort
Sainte-Maure de Touraine
Saint-Marcellin
Saint-Nectaire
Salers
Salers Haute Montagne

Selles-sur-Cher
Soumaintrain
Tomme à l'Ancienne
Tomme d'Abondance
Tomme de Savoie
Tomme du Lévézou
Tradition du Berry
Vacherin du Haut-Doubs
Valençay
Vieux Lille

GERMANY

Allgäuer Bergkäse
Allgäuer Emmenthaler
Altenburger Ziegenkäse
Beer Kaese
Beer Käse
Bierkaese
Bierkäse
Bruder Basil
Butterkäse
Cambozola
Damenkäse
Münster
quark
Rauchkäse
Royalp
Tilsit
Tilsiter
Tollenser
Weisskäse
Weisslacker

GREECE

Anthotiro
Batzos
Feta

Feta Tis Fotias
Formaella Arachovas Parnassou
Formaella of Parnassos
Graviera
Halloumi
Hallumi
Haloumi
Kaseri
Kasseri
Kefalograviera
Kefalotiri
Kefalotyri
Ladotyri Mytilinis
Manouri
Metsovone
Mitzithra
Mizithra
Mytzithra
Myzithra
Sfela
Xinomizithra
Xynomyzithra Kritis

HOLLAND *see* NETHERLANDS

HUNGARY
Liptauer

INDIA
Chenna
Paneer
Panir

IRAN
Chenna
Paneer
Panir

IRELAND
Ardrahan
Boilie
Cashel Blue
Cashel Irish Blue
Coolea
Crozier Blue
Durrus
Gubbeen
Irish Cashel Blue

ISRAEL
Kosher Cheeses

ITALY
Asiago
Bel Paese
Bitto
Bra
Burielli
Burrata
Burri
Burrini
Burrino
Butirro
Caciocavallo
Caciocavallo Silano
Caciotta
Canestrato Pugliese
Casciotta d'Urbino
Castelmagno
Crescenza
Fiore Sardo
Fontina
Fontina Valle d'Aosta
Formai de Mut dell'Alta Valle
    Brembana

Gorgonzola
Grana Padano
La Tur
Manteca
mascarpone
Montasio
Monte Veronese
mozzarella
Mozzarella di Bufala Campana
Murazzano
Parmesan
Parmigiano-Reggiano
Pecorino Romano
Pecorino Sardo
Pecorino Siciliano
Pecorino Toscano
Piave
Piticelle
Provole
Provolone
Provolone Valpadana
Quartirolo Lombardo
Ragusano
Raschera
ricotta
Robiola
Robiola di Roccaverano
Romano
Scamorza
Sottocenere
Spressa delle Giudicarie
Taleggio
Toma Piemontese
Tomino
Valle d'Aosta Fromadzo
Valtellina Casera

LATIN AMERICA

añejo enchilado
asadero
Chihuahua
Cotija
enchilado
Menonita
Oaxaca
panela
quesillo
queso añejado
queso añejo
queso blanco
queso blanco fresco
queso cotija
queso de bagaces
queso de canasta
queso de crema
queso de la tierra
queso del pais
queso de prensa
queso enchilado
queso estera
queso fresco
queso Oaxaca
queso para freír

NETHERLANDS

Beemster
Boerenkaas
Boeren-Leidse met
    Sleutels
Edam
Frieskaas
Gouda
Kanterkaas

Kanterkomijnekaas
Kanternagelkaas
Leiden
Leidenkaas
Leyden
Noord-Hollandse Edammer
Noord-Hollandse Gouda
Prima Donna
Rembrandt
Roomkaas
Saenkanter

New Zealand
Airedale
Livingstone Gold
Windsor Blue

Norway
brunost
clove cheese
Ekte Geitost
Geitost
Gjetost
Gudbrandsdalsost
Jarlsberg
Kuminost
mysost
Nökkelost
prim
primost
Ridder

Pakistan
Chenna
Paneer
Panir

Portugal
Amarelo da Beira Baixa
Azeitão
Castelo Branco
Évora
Mondegueiro
Nisa
Picante da Beira Baixa
Queijo Amarelo da Beira
    Baixa
Queijo de Azeitão
Queijo de Castelo Branco
Queijo de Évora
Queijo de Nisa
Queijo Picante da Beira Baixa
Queijo São Jorge
Queijos da Beira Baixa
Queijo Serpa
Queijo Serra da Estrela
São Jorge
Serpa
Serra da Estrela

Romania
Brinza
Bryndza

Scotland
Bishop Kennedy
Isle of Mull Cheddar
Reade's Isle of Mull Cheddar
Tobermory

Slovakia
Brinza
Bryndza

Spain

Afuega'l Pitu
Ahumado de Áliva
Áliva
Alt Urgell, l'
Arzúa Ulloa
Cabrales
Cantabria
de Murcia al Vino
Gamonedo
Gamoneú
Garrotxa
Ibérico
Ibores
Idiazábal
La Peral
Mahón
Mahón-Menorca
Majorero
Manchego
Monte Enebro
Murcia al Vino
Nata de Cantabria
Nevat
Palmero
Pau
Peral
Picón
Picón Bejes-Tresviso
Picos de España Pau
Picos de Europa
Queso Azul Asturiano
Queso de Cantabria
Queso de la Garrotxa
Queso de l'Alt Urgell y la
    Cerdanya
Queso de la Palma
Queso de la Peral
Queso de la Serena
Queso de los Ibores
Queso del Valle del
    Roncal
Queso de Murcia
Queso de Murcia al Vino
Queso de Perilla
Queso de Valdeón
Queso de Varé
Queso Gallego
Queso Gallego de Teta
Queso Gamonedo
Queso Gamoneú
Queso Ibérico
Queso Ibores
Queso Majorero
Queso Manchego
Queso Palmero
Queso Tetilla
Queso Zamorano
Quesucos de Liébana
Roncal
San Simón
Serena
Tetilla
Tetilla de Vaca
Torta del Casar
Valdeón
Varé
Zamorano

Sweden

Gräddost
Präst

Prästost
Svecia
Sveciaost

SWITZERLAND
Appenzeller
Bellelay
Emmental
Emmentaler
Emmenthal
Étivaz, l'
Fribourgeois
Fromage à Raclette
Glarnerkäse
Grünerkäse
Gruyère
Hock Ybrig
Krauterkäse
l'Étivaz
Prattigauer
Prättigauer
Raclette
Sap Sago
Sapsago
Sbrinz
Schabzieger
Tête de Moine
Tilsit
Tilsiter
Vacherin Fribourgeois
Vacherin Mont d'Or
Valais

UNITED KINGDOM *see* ENGLAND; IRELAND; SCOTLAND; WALES

UNITED STATES
Acapella
Adagio
Alderbrook
Andante
Asiago
Aspenhurst
Autumn Oak
Bayley Hazen Blue
beer cheese
Bella Sorella
Bel Paese
Bermuda Triangle
Big Holmes
Bijou
Blanca Bianca
Bleu de Bresse
Block's Landing
Blü
Bonne Bouche
Braukäse
Bresse Bleu
brick
Brie
Bucheret
Burrata
Butterkäse
cabécou
Cabot Clothbound Cheddar
Cadenza
Camellia
Camembert
Capricious
Capriella
Carmody

Carmody Reserve
Cheddar
chèvre
Cobble Hill
Colby
ColoRouge
Coupole
Constant Bliss
cottage cheese
Crater Lake Blue
cream cheese
Creole cream cheese
Crescenza
Crocodile Tear
Crowley
Deep Ellum Blue
Desperado
dry Jack
Drunken Hooligan
Drunk Monk
Dutch Farmstead
Edam
Ewe-F-O
Evangeline
Fernwood
Feta
Figaro
Fleur-de-Lis
Fleur-de-Teche
fromage blanc
Gabrielson Lake
Gouda
GranQueso
Great Hill Blue
Gruyère

Harvest Cheese
Havarti
Haystack Peak
Hilltown Wheel
Hoja Santa
Hooligan
Hudson Valley Camembert
Humboldt Fog
Jack cheese
Kosher Cheeses
Lace Käse
La Fleurie
Lamb Chopper
Largo
Liederkranz
Limburger
mascarpone
Maytag Blue
Merry Goat Round
Metronome
Midnight Moon
Minuet
Montasio Festivo
Monterey Jack
Mont St. Francis
mozzarella
Mozzarella di Bufala Campana
Mountain Tomme
Mountain Top Bleu
Mt. Tam
Muenster
Nocturne
O'Banon
Oregon Blue Vein
Oregonzola

Paniña
Parmesan
Pepato
Pepper Jack
Pianoforte
Picolo
Piedmont
Pleasant Ridge Reserve
Plymouth
Point Reyes Original Blue
pot cheese
Pride of Bacchus
Prima Käse
Provolone
Pyramid
quark
Queso de Mano
Red Hawk
ricotta
Rofumo
Rogue River Blue
Romano
Rondo
San Andreas
San Joaquin Gold
Schloss

Schlosskäse
Schlosskaese
Serena
Serenita
Smokey Blue
Solé GranQueso
Sonoma Jack
St. George
St. Pat
Summertomme
Tarentaise
Teleme
30-Month Bandage Wrapped
    Cheddar
Trade Lake Cedar
Tulare Cannonball
Tumalo Tomme
Vermont Brebis
Vermont Shepherd
Wabash Cannonball

WALES

Caerphilly
Llangloffan

CHEESES BY MILK TYPE

NOTE Some cheeses may be listed under more than one milk type because, though most are made from a single milk (such as goat's), some are produced from a mixture of milks, while others can be made from one milk or another (depending on the region), and yet others may be made, for example, with cow's milk and—at the producer's discretion—up to 10 percent of another kind of milk.

COW'S MILK

Abondance
Afuega'l Pitu
Airedale
Aisy Cendré
Akawi
Allgäuer Bergkäse
Altenburger Ziegenkäse
Appenzeller
Ardrahan
Arzúa Ulloa
asadero
Asiago
Banon
Bayley Hazen Blue
Beaufort
Bel Paese
Bierkäse
Bishop Kennedy
Bitto
Blanca Bianca
Bleu d'Auvergne
Bleu de Bresse
Bleu des Causses
Bleu du Haut-Jura
Bleu du Vercors-Sassenage
Blue Castello
Boeren-Leidse met Sleutels
Boilie
Boursault
Boursin
Bra
Braukäse
brick
Brie
Brie de Meaux
Brie de Melun
Brillat-Savarin
Bruder Basil
Bryndza
Burrata
Burrino
Butterkäse
C^2

Cabrales
Caciocavallo
Cadenza
Caerphilly
Cambozola
Camembert
Camembert de Normandie
Canestrato
Cantal
Capriella
Carmody
Casciotta d'Urbino
Cashel Blue
Castelmagno
Chaource
cheddar
Cheshire
Chihuahua
Chimay
Colby
ColoRouge
Comté
Constant Bliss
Coolea
Cornish Yarg
Cotija
cottage cheese
Coulommiers
cream cheese
Creole cream cheese
Crescenza
Danablu
Danbo
Danish (Dutch) Port Salut
Deep Ellum Blue
Derby

Domiati
Durrus
Dutch Farmstead
Edam
Emmental
enchilado
Époisses de Bourgogne
Esrom
Étivaz, l'
Explorateur
Fernwood
Feta
Fleur-de-Lis
Fleur-de-Teche
Fontina
Formai de Mut Dell'Alta Valle
    Brembana
Fourme d'Ambert
fromage blanc
Fromage de Herve
Fromage de Meaux
Fromager d'Affinois
Gabrielson Lake
Gailtaler Almkäse
Gaperon
Gjetost
Gloucester
Gorgonzola
Gouda
Gräddost
Grana Padano
GranQueso
Gratte-Paille
Graviera
Great Hill Blue
Gruyère

Gubbeen
Halloumi
Havarti
Hock Ybrig
Hooligan
Hudson Valley Camembert
Ibérico
Jack cheese
Jarlsberg
Kanterkaas
Kanterkomijnekaas
Kanternagelkaas
Kasseri
Lace Käse
La Fleurie
Laguiole
Lancashire
Langres
La Tur
Leicester
Limburger
Lincolnshire Poacher
Liptauer
Livarot
Livingstone Gold
Llangloffan
Mahón
Maroilles
mascarpone
Maytag Blue
Metronome
Metsovone
Mimolette
Montasio
Montbriac
Monte Veronese

Morbier
Mountain Tomme
mozzarella
Mt. Tam
Munster
Murazzano
Neufchâtel
Nocturne
Nökkelost
Oka
Oka Classique
Oka Léger
paneer
Parmesan
Parmigiano-Reggiano
Passendale Classic
Pavé d'Auge
Petit-Suisse
Pianoforte
Piave
Picodon (non-AOC)
Picón Bejes-Tresviso
Pierre Robert
Pleasant Ridge Reserve
Plymouth
Point Reyes Original Blue
Pont-l'Évêque
Port Salut
Prästost
Prättigauer
Prima Donna
Provolone
quark
Quartirolo Lombardo
Queijo São Jorge
queso blanco

Queso de Cantabria
Queso de l'Alt Urgell y la
   Cerdanya
Queso de la Peral
Queso de Valdeón
Queso Gamonedo
queso Oaxaca
Queso Tetilla
Quesucos de Liébana
Raclette
Ragusano
Raschera
Reblochon
Red Hawk
ricotta
Ridder
Roaring Forties Blue
Robiola
Robiola di Roccaverano
Rofumo
Rogue River Blue
Romano
Rondo
Saint-Marcellin
Saint-Nectaire
Salers
Samsoe
San Ignacio Blue
San Joaquin Gold
San Simón
Sapsago
Sbrinz
Scamorza
Schloss
Schlosskaese
Schlosskäse

Serena
Serenita
Shropshire Blue
Sottocenere
Soumaintrain
Spressa delle Giudicarie
St. George
Stilton
St. Pat
Svecia
Swiss cheese
Taleggio
Tarentaise
Teleme
Tête de Moine
Tilsit
Tiroler Almkäse
Tiroler Bergkäse
Tiroler Graukäse
Toma Piemontese
Tomino
Tomme de Savoie
Vacherin du Haut-Doubs
Vacherin Fribourgeois
Vacherin Mont d'Or
Valle d'Aosta Fromadzo
Valtellina Casera
Vorarlberger Alpkäse
Vorarlberger Bergkäse
Wensleydale
Windsor Blue

GOAT'S MILK
Acapella
Adagio
Altenburger Ziegenkäse

Banon
Batzos
Bermuda Triangle
Bijou
Bitto
Boilie
Bonne Bouche
Bra
Brin d'Amour
Brocciu Corse
Bryndza
Bucheret
Cabrales
Camellia
Canestrato
Capricious
Capriella
Castelmagno
Chabichou du Poitou
Chèvre Noir, Le
Chevrotin des Aravis
Cotija
Coupole
Crocodile Tear
Crottin de Chavignol
Doeling Dairy Goat Farm
   Gouda
Domiati
Ekte Geitost
enchilado
Evangeline
Feta
Figaro
Formaella Arachovas Parnassou
fromage blanc
Gailtaler Almkäse

Garrotxa
Gjetost
Graviera
Halloumi
Haystack Peak
Hilltown Wheel
Hoja Santa
Humboldt Fog
Ibérico
Kasseri
Kefalograviera
Kefalotyri
Ladotyri Mytilinis
La Tur
Merry Goat Round
Metronome
Metsovone
Midnight Moon
Mizithra
Montasio Festivo
Monte Enebro
Mont St. Francis
Mountain Top Bleu
Nevat
O'Banon
Pau
Pélardon
Picodon de l'Ardèche
Picodon de la Drôme
Picón Bejes-Tresviso
Pouligny-Saint-Pierre
Pyramid
Queijo Amarelo da Beira Baixa
Queijo de Castelo Branco
Queijo Picante da Beira Baixa
queso blanco

Queso de Mano
Queso de Murcia
Queso de Valdeón
Queso Gamonedo
Queso Ibores
Queso Majorero
Queso Palmero
Quesucos de Liébana
Raschera
ricotta
Robiola
Robiola di Roccaverano
Rocamadour
Romano
Rondo
Sainte-Maure de Touraine
Saint-Marcellin
Selles-sur-Cher
Sfela
Tomino
Tumalo Tomme
Valençay
Valle d'Aosta Fromadzo
Varé
Wabash Cannonball

SHEEP'S MILK

Abbaye de Belloc
Alderbrook
Ardi-Gasna
Autumn Oak
Banon
Batzos
Beenleigh Blue
Berkswell
Big Holmes

Bra
Brin d'Amour
Brocciu Corse
Bryndza
Cabrales
Canestrato Pugliese
Casciotta d'Urbino
Castelmagno
Cobble Hill
Crozier Blue
Etorki
Ewe-F-O
Feta
Fiore Sardo
Formaella Arachovas Parnassou
fromage blanc
Fromager d'Affinois
Graviera
Halloumi
Hudson Valley Camembert
Ibérico
Idiazábal
Kasseri
Kefalograviera
Kefalotyri
Ladotyri Mytilinis
La Tur
Lamb Chopper
Liptauer
Little Holmes
Mahón
Metsovone
Mizithra
Mountain Tomme
Murazzano
Ossau-Iraty

Pecorino Romano
Pecorino Sardo
Pecorino Siciliano
Pecorino Toscano
Pepato
Pérail
Picón Bejes-Tresviso
Piedmont
Pride of Bacchus
Queijo Amarelo da Beira Baixa
Queijo de Azeitão
Queijo de Castelo Branco
Queijo de Évora
Queijo de Nisa
Queijo Picante da Beira Baixa
Queijo Serpa
Queijo Serra da Estrela
queso blanco
Queso de la Peral
Queso de la Serena
Queso Gamonedo
Queso Majorero
Queso Manchego
Queso Zamorano
Quesucos de Liébana
Raschera
ricotta
Robiola
Robiola di Roccaverano
Romano
Roncal
Roquefort
San Andreas
Scamorza
Sfela
Spenwood

Summertomme
Tomme du Lévézou
Torta del Casar
Trade Lake Cedar
Vermont Brebis
Vermont Shepherd
Wensleydale

WATER BUFFALO'S MILK
Burrata
Domiati
Mozzarella di Bufala
  Campana
paneer
ricotta
Scamorza

COMBINATION OF MILKS
Altenburger Ziegenkäse (cow's
  and goat's)
Banon (cow's, goat's, and/or
  sheep's)
Batzos (sheep's and/or goat's)
Bitto (cow's, plus 10 percent or
  less goat's)
Boilie (cow's and goat's)
Bra (cow's and goat's or sheep's)
Brin d'Amour (goat's and
  sheep's)
Brocciu Corse (sheep's and/or
  goat's)
Bryndza (sheep's or sometimes
  cow's or goat's or a mixture)
Cabrales (traditionally cow's,
  sheep's, and goat's; today
  mostly cow)

Canestrato (non–DOC cheeses) (cow's and goat's)

Capriella (half goat's and half cow's)

Casciotta d'Urbino (sheep's and cow's)

Castelmagno (cow's, goat's, and/or sheep's)

Domiati (cow's, goat's, and water buffalo's)

Feta (sheep's, cow's, and goat's)

fromage blanc (cow's, goat's, or sheep's)

Gailtaler Almkäse (cow's and goat's)

Gjetost (cow's and goat's)

Graviera (cow's, sheep's, and/or goat's)

Halloumi (sheep's and goat's, sometimes cow's)

Hudson Valley Camembert (cow's and sheep's)

Ibérico (cow's, goat's, and sheep's)

Kasseri (cow's, sheep's, and goat's)

Kefalograviera (sheep's and goat's)

Kefalotyri (sheep's and goat's)

Ladotyri Mytilinis (sheep's and/or goat's)

La Tur (cow's, sheep's, and goat's)

Liptauer (sheep's, sometimes with cow's)

Mahón (primarily cow's with up to 5 percent sheep's)

Metronome (goat's and cow's)

Metsovone (cow's and some sheep's or goat's)

Mizithra (sheep's and goat's)

Mountain Tomme (cow's and sheep's)

Murazzano (cow's and sheep's)

Picón Bejes-Tresviso (cow's, sheep's, and goat's)

Queijo Amarelo da Beira Baixa (sheep's and goat's)

Queijo de Castelo Branco (sheep's and goat's)

Queijo Picante da Beira Baixa (sheep's and/or goat's)

queso blanco (cow's, sheep's, and goat's)

Queso de la Peral (primarily cow's, though some sheep's may be added)

Queso de Valdeón (primarily cow's, though some goat's may be added)

Queso Gamonedo (traditionally a mix of unpasteurized cow's, sheep's, and goat's; now primarily cow's)

Queso Majorero (primarily goat's with up to 15 percent sheep's)

Quesucos de Liébana (primarily cow's, although a mix of cow's, goat's, and sheep's may be used)

Raschera (cow's but may have sheep's or goat's added)

ricotta (cow's and/or sheep's and/or goat's and sometimes water buffalo's)

Robiola (cow's, goat's, and/or sheep's)

Robiola di Roccaverano (cow's, goat's, and/or sheep's)

Romano (cow's, sheep's, and goat's)

Rondo (goat's and cow's)

Saint-Marcellin (cow's or goat's)

Scamorza (cow's, sheep's, and water buffalo's)

Sfela (sheep's and goat's)

Tomino (cow's or goat's, or a mixture of the two)

Valle d'Aosta Fromadzo (cow's, but a small amount of goat's may be added)

Wensleydale (cow's and sheep's)

CHEESES BY TYPE

NOTE This section is sorted by types of cheese in the following order: FRESH, SOFT, SEMISOFT, SEMIHARD, HARD, BLUE, DOUBLE-CREAM, TRIPLE-CREAM, and PASTA FILATA. Some cheeses appear in multiple categories. For example, if a cheese is listed as "semisoft to semihard" (either because it can be made in different styles or because it hardens with age), it will be listed in both groups. The same applies to a cheese that is both semisoft and blue and so on.

FRESH CHEESES
Boilie
Brocciu Corse
cottage cheese
fromage blanc
Liptauer
Mizithra
paneer
quark
Robiola
Robiola di Roccaverano

SOFT CHEESES
Afuega'l Pitu
Akawi
Altenburger Ziegenkäse
Banon
Blanca Bianca
Bleu de Bresse
Boilie
Boursin
Bresse Bleu
Brie

Brie de Meaux
Brie de Melun
Brocciu Corse
Bryndza
Burrata
Burrino
Camembert
Camembert de Normandie
Chaource
ColoRouge
Coulommiers
cream cheese
Creole cream cheese
Crescenza
Deep Ellum Blue
Evangeline
Fleur-de-Lis
Fleur-de-Teche
fromage blanc
Fromager d'Affinois
Haystack Peak
Hoja Santa
Humboldt Fog

mascarpone
Mizithra
mozzarella
Murazzano
Neufchâtel
Nevat
Nocturne
O'Banon
Pecorino Sardo
Pecorino Toscano
Pélardon
Pérail
Petit-Suisse
Picodon de la Drôme
Picodon de l'Ardèche
quark
Queijo Serpa
Queijo Serra da Estrela
Queso de La Serena
queso Oaxaca
ricotta
Robiola
Robiola di Roccaverano
Saint-Marcellin
Teleme
Tomino
Torta del Casar
Vermont Brebis

SEMISOFT CHEESES
Afuega'l Pitu
Aisy Cendré
Akawi
Ardrahan
Arzúa Ulloa
asadero

Asiago
Banon
Beenleigh Blue
Bel Paese
Bermuda Triangle
Bierkäse
Big Holmes
Bishop Kennedy
Bitto
Blanca Bianca
Bleu des Causses
Bleu du Haut-Jura
Bleu du Vercors-Sassenage
Blue Castello
Bonne Bouche
Boursault
Bra
Braukäse
Brillat-Savarin
Brin d'Amour
Brocciu Corse
Bruder Basil
Butterkäse
Cabrales
Caciocavallo
Caerphilly
Cambozola
Camellia
Casciotta d'Urbino
Cashel Blue
Chabichou du Poitou
Chevrotin des Aravis
Chihuahua
Chimay
Constant Bliss
Cotija

Crocodile Tear
Crottin de Chavignol
Crozier Blue
Deep Ellum Blue
Despearado
Domiati
Drunken Hooligan
Drunk Monk
Durrus
Edam
Époisses de Bourgogne
Explorateur
Feta
Fontina
Formaella Arachovas Parnassou
Formai de Mut Dell'Alta Valle
     Brembana
Fourme d'Ambert
Fourme de Montbrison
Fromage de Herve
Gaperon
Garrotxa
Gjetost
Gorgonzola
Gräddost
Gratte-Paille
Great Hill Blue
Gubbeen
Halloumi
Havarti
Haystack Peak
Hooligan
Humboldt Fog
Jack
Kasseri
Langres

La Tur
Limburger
Little Holmes
Livarot
Maroilles
Maytag Blue
Mizithra
Montasio
Montbriac
Monte Enebro
Monte Veronese
Morbier
Mountain Top Bleu
mozzarella
Mt. Tam
Munster
Nevat
O'Banon
Oka
paneer
Paniña
Passendale Classic
Pau
Pavé d'Auge
Pecorino Sardo
Pecorino Toscano
Pélardon
Piave
Picodon de la Drôme
Picodon de l'Ardèche
Picón Bejes-Tresviso
Pierre Robert
Plateau de Herve
Point Reyes Original Blue
Pont-l'Évêque
Pouligny-Saint-Pierre

Quartirolo Lombardo
Queijo Amarelo da Beira Baixa
Queijo de Azeitão
Queijo de Castelo Branco
Queijo Serpa
Queijo Serra da Estrela
queso blanco
Queso de Cantabria
Queso de l'Alt Urgell y la
   Cerdanya
Queso de La Serena
Queso Ibores
queso Oaxaca
Queso Palmero
Queso Tetilla
Raschera
Reblochon
Red Hawk
ricotta
Ridder
Roaring Forties Blue
Rocamadour
Rofumo
Roquefort
Sainte-Maure de Touraine
Saint-Nectaire
San Ignacio Blue
Scamorza
Schloss
Schlosskaese
Schlosskäse
Selles-sur-Cher
Shropshire Blue
Sottocenere
Soumaintrain
St. Pat

Stilton
Svecia
Taleggio
Teleme
Tilsit
Tiroler Graukäse
Toma Piemontese
Tomino
Tomme de Savoie
Torta del Casar
Tumalo Tomme
Vacherin du Haut-Doubs
Vacherin Mont d'Or
Valençay
Valtellina Casera
Wabash Cannonball
Wensleydale
Windsor Blue

SEMIHARD CHEESES

Abbaye de Belloc
Abondance
Airedale
Appenzeller
Ardi-Gasna
Arzúa Ulloa
Asiago
Batzos
Bayley Hazen Blue
Bel Paese
Bierkäse
Big Holmes
Bitto
Bleu d'Auvergne
Boeren-Leidse met Sleutels
Bra

brick
Brin d'Amour
Caciocavallo
Caerphilly
Canestrato Pugliese
Cantal
Capricious
Carmody
cheddar
Cheshire
Chèvre Noir, Le
Chihuahua
Chimay
Coolea
Cornish Yarg
Cotija
Crottin de Chavignol
Danablu
Danbo
Derby
Domiati
Dutch Farmstead
Edam
Emmental
enchilado
Esrom
Étorki
Feta
Fiore Sardo
Fontina
Formaella Arachovas Parnassou
Formai de Mut Dell'Alta Valle
    Brembana
Fourme d'Ambert
Fourme de Montbrison
Gailtaler Almkäse

Gaperon
Gjetost
Gloucester
Gorgonzola
Gouda
Grana Padano
GranQueso
Graviera
Gruyère
Havarti
Hilltown Wheel
Hock Ybrig
Idiazábal
Jack
Jarlsberg
Kanterkaas
Kanterkomijnekaas
Kanternagelkaas
Kasseri
Laguiole
Lamb Chopper
Lancashire
Leicester
Limburger
Little Holmes
Livingstone Gold
Llangloffan
Mahón
Metsovone
Midnight Moon
Mimolette
Mizithra
Montasio
Monte Veronese
Mont St. Francis
Nökkelost

Ossau-Iraty
Pecorino Sardo
Pecorino Toscano
Piave
Piedmont
Plymouth
Pouligny-Saint-Pierre
Prästost
Prättigauer
Prima Donna
Provolone
Queijo Amarelo da Beira Baixa
Queijo de Castelo Branco
Queijo de Évora
Queijo de Nisa
Queijo Picante da Beira Baixa
Queijo São Jorge
queso blanco
Queso de la Peral
Queso de Mano
Queso de Murcia
Queso de Valdeón
Queso Gamonedo
Queso Ibores
Queso Majorero
Queso Manchego
Queso Palmero
Quesucos de Liébana
Raclette
Ragusano
ricotta
Rocamadour
Rogue River Blue
Sainte-Maure de Touraine
Salers
Samsoe

San Andreas
San Joaquin Gold
San Simón
Scamorza
Selles-sur-Cher
Serenita
Sfela
Shropshire Blue
Spressa delle Giudicarie
St. George
Stilton
Svecia
Swiss cheese
Tête de Moine
Tilsit
Tiroler Almkäse
Tiroler Graukäse
Toma Piemontese
Tomme de Savoie
Tomme du Lévézou
Trade Lake Cedar
Tumalo Tomme
Vacherin Fribourgeois
Valençay
Valle d'Aosta Fromadzo
Valtellina Casera
Varé
Vermont Shepherd
Vorarlberger Alpkäse
Wensleydale

HARD CHEESES

Allgäuer Bergkäse
Appenzeller
Ardi-Gasna
Asiago

Batzos
Beaufort
Berkswell
Boeren-Leidse met Sleutels
Brin d'Amour
Canestrato Pugliese
Capricious
cheddar
Cheshire
Chèvre Noir, Le
Colby
Comté
Coolea
Cotija
Edam
enchilado
Étivaz, l'
Fiore Sardo
Formaella Arachovas Parnassou
Gouda
Grana Padano
Graviera
Gruyère
Hilltown Wheel
Ibérico
Jack
Kanterkaas
Kanterkomijnekaas
Kanternagelkaas
Kefalograviera
Kefalotyri
Ladotyri Mytilinis
Lancashire
Leicester
Lincolnshire Poacher
Mahón

Metsovone
Mimolette
Mizithra
Montasio
Montasio Festivo
Parmesan
Parmigiano-Reggiano
Pecorino Romano
Pecorino Sardo
Pecorino Siciliano
Piave
Pleasant Ridge Reserve
Plymouth
Prättigauer
Queijo de Évora
Queijo de Nisa
Queijo Picante da
    Beira Baixa
Queijo São Jorge
queso blanco
Queso Manchego
Queso Zamorano
Ragusano
ricotta
Romano
Roncal
Sainte-Maure de Touraine
Sapsago
Sbrinz
Serena
Spenwood
Spressa delle Giudicarie
Tarentaise
Tête de Moine
Tiroler Bergkäse
Vorarlberger Bergkäse

Blue

Bayley Hazen Blue
Beenleigh Blue
Bleu d'Auvergne
Bleu de Bresse
Bleu des Causses
Bleu du Haut-Jura
Bleu du Vercors-Sassenage
Blue Castello
Blue Cheshire
Bresse Bleu
Cabrales
Cambozola
Cashel Blue
Castelmagno
Crozier Blue
Danablu
Deep Ellum Blue
Fourme d'Ambert
Fourme de Montbrison
Gorgonzola
Great Hill Blue
Maytag Blue
Montbriac
Mountain Top Bleu
Picón Bejes-Tresviso
Point Reyes Original Blue
Queso de la Peral
Queso de Valdeón
Queso Gamonedo
Roaring Forties Blue
Rogue River Blue
Roquefort
San Ignacio Blue
Shropshire Blue
Stilton

Wensleydale
Windsor Blue

Double-Cream

Gratte-Paille
mascarpone
Petit-Suisse

Triple-Cream

Boursault
Boursin
Brillat-Savarin
Evangeline
Explorateur
Fleur-de-Lis
Fleur-de-Teche
Largo
mascarpone
Mt. Tam
Pierre Robert
Red Hawk

Pasta Filata

asadero
Burrata
Burrino
Caciocavallo
Halloumi
Kasseri
Metsovone
mozzarella
Provolone
queso Oaxaca
Ragusano
Scamorza

BIBLIOGRAPHY

NOTE Hundreds of cheese-producer Web sites were consulted while researching this book. However, they have not been listed because such Web site addresses change so frequently.

Agricultural Research Service, U.S. Department of Agriculture. *Cheese Varieties and Descriptions*. Honolulu: University Press of the Pacific, 2005.

Androuët, Pierre. *Guide du Fromage: The Complete Encyclopedia of French Cheese*. New York: Harper & Row, 1973.

Anifantakis, Emmanuel. *Greek Cheeses: A Tradition for Centuries*. Athens: National Dairy Committee of Greece, 1991.

Baboin-Jaubert, Alix. *Cheese, Selecting, Tasting, and Serving the World's Finest*. San Diego, CA: Laurel Glen Publishing, 2002.

Barthélemy, Roland, and Arnaud Sperat-Czar. *Guide to Cheeses of the World*. Longdon: Hachette Illustrated UK, 2005.

Battistotti, Bruno, et al. *Cheese: A Guide to the World of Cheese and Cheesemaking*. New York: Facts on File, 1983.

Carr, Sandy. *Simon & Schuster Pocket Guide to Cheese*. New York: Simon & Schuster, 1981.

Cheese Facts. Washington, DC: National Cheese Institute, 1998.

Devi, Yamuna. *The Art of Indian Vegetarian Cooking.* New York: E. P. Dutton, 1987.

Edelman, Edward, and Susan Grodnick. *The Ideal Cheese Book.* New York: Harper & Row Publishers, 1986.

Ensrud, Barbara. *The Pocket Guide to Cheese.* New York: Perigee Books, 1981.

Freeman, Sarah. *The Real Cheese Companion.* London: Little, Brown and Company, 1998.

Ganugi, Gabriella. *Cheese, An Italian Pantry.* South San Francisco, CA: The Wine Appreciation Guild, 2004.

Gayler, Paul. *A Passion for Cheese.* New York: St. Martin's Press, 1997.

Harbutt, Juliet. *The World Encyclopedia of Cheese.* New York: Lorenz Press, 2002.

Herbst, Ron, and Sharon Tyler Herbst. *New Wine Lover's Companion.* 2nd ed. Hauppauge, NY: Barron's, 2003.

Herbst, Sharon Tyler. *Never Eat More Than You Can Lift, and Other Food Quotes and Quips.* New York: Broadway Books, 1997.

Herbst, Sharon Tyler. *New Food Lover's Companion*. 3rd ed. Hauppauge, NY: Barron's, 2001.

Herbst, Sharon Tyler, and Ron Herbst. *The Ultimate A-to-Z Bar Guide*. New York: Broadway Books, 1998.

Hickman, Trevor. *The History of Stilton Cheese*. Gloucestershire, England: Alan Sutton Publishing Limited, 1995

Jackson, Michael. *Ultimate Beer*. New York: DK Publishing, 1998.

Jenkins, Steven. *Cheese Primer*. New York: Workman Publishing, 1996.

Jones, Evan. *The World of Cheese*. New York: Alfred A. Knopf, 1984.

Lambert, Paula. *The Cheese Lover's Cookbook and Guide*. New York: Simon & Schuster, 2000.

McCalman, Max, and David Gibbons. *The Cheese Plate*. New York: Clarkson Potter, 2002.

Masui, Kazuka, and Tomoko Yamada. *French Cheeses*. New York: DK Publishing, 2000.

Nantet, Bernard. *Cheeses of the World*. New York: Rizzoli International Publications, 1992.

Rance, Patrick. *The Great British Cheese Book*. London: Macmillan, 1982.

Ridgway, Judy. *The Cheese Companion*. Philadelphia: Running Press, 1999.

Robinson, R. K., and R. A. Wilbey. *Cheesemaking Practice*. 3rd ed. Gaithersburg, MD: Aspen Publishers, 1998.

Slow Food Foundation. *Italian Cheese, A Guide to Its Discovery and Appreciation*. 2nd ed. Milan, Italy: Slow Food Editore, 2005.

Teubner, Christian. *The Cheese Bible*. New York: Penguin Studio, 1998.

Tewksbury, Henry. *The Cheeses of Vermont*. Woodstock, Vermont: The Countryman Press, 2002.

Timperley, Carol, and Cecilia Norman. *A Gourmet's Guide to Cheese*. Los Angeles: HP Books, 1989.

Werlin, Laura. *The New American Cheese*. New York: Stewart, Tabori & Chang, 2000.

Widcome, Richard. *The Cheese Book*. Secaucus, NJ: Chartwell Books, 1978.

Wisconsin Cheesecyclopedia: Cheese at Foodservice. Madison: Wisconsin Milk Marketing Board, 1995.

ABOUT THE
AUTHORS

Sharon Tyler Herbst, award-winning author of seventeen books, has been dubbed the foremost writer of user-friendly food and drink reference works. Her reputation as a culinary powerhouse was established with the first edition of *The Food Lover's Companion* (broadly hailed as "A must for every cook's library"), and the fourth edition of the *Companion* has just been released. Many Internet sites (including Condé Nast's Epicurious.com, FoodNetwork.com, and Answers. com) feature *The Food Lover's Companion* as their on-line dictionary. Sharon's other books include *The New Food Lover's Tiptionary, The Ultimate Guide to Pitcher Drinks,* and *The Ultimate Liquor-Free Drink Guide.* She's also a food and travel journalist, spokesperson, consultant, and media personality.

Ron Herbst, long a passionate and dedicated oenophile, is a wine and travel journalist and consultant. His bestselling *Wine Lover's Companion* received rave reviews and is now the wine dictionary on several Internet sites, including Condé Nast's Epicurious.com. Ron is the co-author (with Sharon Tyler Herbst) of *The Ultimate A-to-Z Bar Guide* (which has sold over 100,000 copies), as well as the fourth edition of *The New Food Lover's Companion* (which has sold over 1 million copies), and has contributed to many other of his wife's books on food and drink. He and Sharon have been tagged as "the dynamic duo of food and drink."